Where Are They Now?

**Andy Pringle
& Neil Fissler**

D0277338

First published in 1996 by
Two Heads Publishing
9 Whitehall Park
London N19 3TS

ISBN 1 897850 92 1

Cover and book design by Lance Bellers

Cover photographs:
Steve Archibald, Gary Bailey, Colin Bell, Clyde Best,
Stan Bowles, Gordon McQueen, Bobby Moncur – Football Archive
Alan Brazil, Charlie George – Allsport

Printed and bound in Great Britain by Biddles Limited

ACKNOWLEDGEMENTS

This book would not have been published without the assistance and patience of a great number of people to whom we offer our sincere thanks.

Richard Arnwell; Mike Blackstone; Tony Bugby; Peter Creed; Mike Davage; Tom Finney OBE; Terry Frost; Dave Goody; Johnny Haynes; Duncan Holly; Graham Hughes; Mike Jones; Peter Jones; Tony Matthews; Craig Monk; Peter Osgood; Richard Owen; Andy Porter; Dave Powter; Mr & Mrs Poynter; Richard Sharp; Roger Wash; Sid Woodhead; Steve Whitney; the staff at all the League and Non-League clubs who helped with information; the many newspapers and photographers who supplied information and pictures; the staff at Shooters Bar & Diner in Windsor.

And finally, special thanks to all the former players who co-operated to make this book possible.

AAS, Einer
Notts Forest 1980-81
Bought to replace Larry Lloyd and went on to play 20 games for Forest after joining them from Bayern Munich. Now lives in his native Norway where he works in a bank.
Norwegian International.

ADAMS, Chris
Tottenham, Norwich, Watford, 1948-1955
Ex-Spurs outside left who played non-league football with Dartford for eight years. Now a painter & decorator in Essex.
Scored on his league debut against Derby County March 1952.

ADAMS, Micky
Gillingham, Coventry, Leeds, Southampton, Fulham, 1979-1996
Experienced former Leeds United and Southampton full back who seems to have found the knack of scoring goals whilst combining his playing role with that of managing his current club, Fulham.
Became Football League's youngest manager when he took over from Ian Branfoot in early 1996.

ADDISON, Colin
York, Notts Forest, Arsenal, Sheff Utd, Hereford, 1957-1973
Joined West Brom as assistant to Ron Atkinson, then followed him to Atletico Madrid in 1988. Has also held posts at Hereford Utd twice; Durban City South Africa; Notts County; Newport Co twice; Derby County; Celta Spain. In October 1994 Colin became Merthyr Tydfil's fourth manager in 15 months. His stay was brief, ending in the following February. Lives in Hereford and was apppointed Merthyr boss again in July 1996.
Manager of Hereford when they were elected to the Football League.

AHERNE, Thomas
Luton 1948-1956
Full back who played both for Northern Ireland and the Republic. Settled in Luton after playing 267 League games for the Hatters and worked locally for Vauxhall for many years until his retirement.
Played four times for Northern Ireland and 16 times for the Republic.

AITKEN, Charles
Aston V 1960-1975
Aitken was one of Aston Villa's all time greats. He spent 17 years at Villa Park playing a total of 561 games. He quit in 1976, moving to New York Cosmos before returning to start a jewellery and antiques business in Birmingham.
Holds record for most number of League Appearances for the club.

AIZLEWOOD, Mark
Newport, Luton, Charlton, Leeds, Bradford C, Bristol C, Cardiff, 1975-1995
Well travelled Welsh international who was player/coach at Cardiff. Now with Newport.
Played 39 times for Wales.

AIZLEWOOD, Steve
Newport, Swindon, Portsmouth, 1968-1983
Strong full back, has returned to his home town of Newport in Gwent where he now practices as a Chartered Surveyor.
Played over 400 league games.

AKERS, Vic
Cambridge, Watford, 1971-1976
Made his name in non-league football where he helped Dartford win the Southern League Cup. Works on the admin staff at Arsenal and manages their women's side.
Helped Cambridge to their ever Football League promotion in 1974.

ALBISTON, Arthur
Manchester United, WBA, Dundee, Chesterfield, Chester, 1974-1993
Played 464 games for United in his 15 years with the club, won 14 international caps and is now manager of Droylesden in the North West Counties League.
Won a record three FA Cup winners medals.

ALCOCK, Terry
Port V, Blackpool, Bury, Blackburn, Port V,

Halifax, 1963-1977
A central defender who was restricted through injury. Now licensee at the Bull public house in Burscough.

ALDRIDGE, John
Newport Co, Oxford, Liverpool, Tranmere, 1979-1996
A true goal machine with nearly 400 to his credit and a regular for the Republic of Ireland for a number of years. Has been Tranmere boss since March 1996.
Honours include a Welsh Cup, Division One and Two Championships, League Cup and FA Cup medals.

ALEKSIC, Milija
Plymouth, Luton, Tottenham, 1973-1981
Goalkeeper who returned to South Africa on his retirement in 1982. Now works as a sales representative selling photocopiers and fax machines, having previously spent ten years selling golf equipment.
Played for Spurs in the 1981 FA Cup final.

ALEXANDER, Ian
Rotherham, Motherwell, Morton, Bristol Rovers, 1983-1994
Played nearly 300 league games for the Pirates and is now manager of Doc Martens League Yate Town.
Sent off three times against local rivals Bristol City.

ALEXANDER, John
Millwall, Reading, Northampton, 1977-1981
After retiring in 1981, John is Secretary of Watford Football Club.

ALEXANDER, Keith
Grimsby, Stockport, Lincoln, 1988-1994
Lanky forward who joined the professional game at a relatively late age, but has now progressed into track-suited roles: firstly at Lincoln City as manager, and then as a coach at Mansfield. Is now manager of non-league Ilkeston Town.

ALEXANDER, Phil
Norwich 1981

Played only one league game for Norwich. Made his name in American Football as a kicker for the London Monarch's having had trials with Philadelphia Eagles and the Chicago Bears. Had a long spell in non-league football and was recently Swindon's marketing man, moving to a similiar post at Crystal Palace.
Despite playing only 19 minutes of league football made the New Zealand national squad for a game against Russia.

ALLARDYCE, Sam
Bolton, Sunderland, Millwall, Coventry, Huddersfield, Bolton, Preston, WBA, 1973-1989
Played for eight clubs as a reliable defender and had a spell in America with Tampa of Florida before moving into management. Occupied the Blackpool hot seat but was sacked just hours after Vicky Oyston took over at the club.
Played over 500 league matches.

ALLCHURCH, Len
Swansea, Sheff Utd, Stockport, Swansea, 1950-1969

For some years was a hotelier, but now runs a successful leather goods business, the 'Len Allchurch Shoe, Leather, and Sheepskin Centre' in Swansea. Enjoys his golf which he plays off an eight handicap and still occasionally turns out for charity soccer matches.
Capped 11 times by Wales.

A

ALLCHURCH, Ivor
Swansea, Newcastle, Cardiff, Swansea, 1947-1965
Brother of Len. Awarded the MBE in 1966 for his contribution to soccer. Lives in Swansea and is now retired having been a van driver for several years, prior to which he had worked as a coach for a local Leisure Centre.
Played 68 times for Wales and holds the Swansea City goal scoring record with 166.

ALLCOCK, Terry
Bolton, Norwich, 1952-1958
Played 334 games in 11 years at Norwich, scoring 84 goals. Managed City's youth side, was chief coach had a coaching role at Manchester City before being appointed assistant manger. Now a partner in a Yarmouth garage.
First man to score a hat trick in the FA Cup and League Cup in the same season.

ALLDER, Doug
Millwall, Orient, Watford, Brentford, 1969-1979
A tricky and fast outside left, Allder made well over 300 League appearances for his four clubs, including 215 for Millwall where he scored 13 goals. He now works as a security guard at Heathrow airport.
The first League player to have a drugs test when he played for Brentford v Swindon.

ALLEN, Clive
QPR, Crystal Palace, QPR, Spurs, Manchester City, Chelsea, West Ham, Millwall, 1978-1994
A former Footballer of the Year who was sold for over £1m four times. Is now out of the game but can be seen on Sky Sports football programmes.
Played for The Football League against The Rest of The World in 1988.

ALLEN, Dennis
Charlton, Reading, Bournemouth, 1956-1970
An inside forward who was the brother of Les and father of Portsmouth star Martin until. Died in July 1995.

ALLEN, Jimmy
Portsmouth, Aston Villa, 1932-1944
The British transfer record was smashed in 1933 by Jimmy's move from Portsmouth to Aston Villa, for a fee of £10,750! He ran a pub for many years and died at home in Southsea in February 1995.
Played for Pompey in the 1934 FA Cup final.

ALLEN, Keith
Portsmouth, Grimsby, Stockport, Luton, Plymouth, 1962-1970
Still lives in Plymouth where he works as a car salesman.

ALLEN, Les
Chelsea, Tottenham, QPR, 1956-1968
Former England Under-23 striker. Now lives in Hornchurch and is a professional model maker. Father of Clive and Bradley.
Scored 27 goals in Spur's double-winning year.

ALLEN, Peter
Leyton Orient, Millwall, 1965-1978
One of Orient's all time great players appearing in over 400 league games. Was born in Hove and still lives in Brighton where he practices as a solicitor.

ALLEN, Ronnie
Port Vale, WBA, Crystal Palace, 1946-1961
Won 5 England caps and scored over 200 goals in his 400-plus games for West Brom. He then managed Wolves, Atletico Bilbao, Sporting Lisbon, Walsall, WBA, Panathinaikos in addition to a spell coaching in Saudi Arabia. Most recently back at the Hawthorns as coach.
Averaged a goal every other game for the Baggies.

ALLEN, Tony
Stoke, Bury, 1957-1971.
England international left back, winning three caps, who was a regular for Stoke for over a decade. Still lives in Stoke where he is now a licensee.
Played over 400 league games and was capped by England before his 20th birthday.

ALLINSON, Ian
Colchester, Arsenal, Stoke, Luton,
Colchester, 1974-1989
Winger who rose to fame with Arsenal, but
begun and ended his league career at
Colchester United. Appointed player/manag-
er at Baldock Town and now manages
Stotfold in the United Counties League.
Played over 300 league games for Colchester.

ALLISON, Malcolm
Charlton, West Ham, 1949-1957

Flamboyant manager who achieved incredible success with Manchester City, as well as
bringing colour to a number of other clubs.
Lives near Middlesbrough and his last
league post was manager of Bristol Rovers in
1993– the year he celebrated 50 years in the
game. In 1995 embarked on a nation-wide
tour with Tommy Docherty.
Founded the West Ham 'football academy'.

ALSOP, Gilbert
Coventry, Walsall, WBA, Ipswich, Walsall,
1929-1938
Prolific goal scorer for Walsall who went on
to work on the ground staff for twenty years.
Died in 1992, and had a stand in the new
Bescot Stadium named in his honour.
*Scored 40 goals in a season for Walsall two
years running which is still a club record.*

ANDERSON, Peter
Luton, Sheff Utd, Millwall, 1971-1982
Midfielder who served three English clubs
interspersed with spells in America with
Tampa of Florida. Now back home working
as a Sportswear representative based in
Newcastle.

ANDERSON, Terry
Arsenal, Norwich, Colchester, Scunthorpe,
Crewe, Colchester, 1961-1975
England Youth international who played
over 200 games for Norwich. Ran a pub in
Caister but died in 1980 at the age of 36,
drowning after taking a training run.
*Scored Norwich's first ever away goal in the
First Division.*

ANDERSON, Tommy
Queen of the South, Watford, Bournemouth,
QPR, Torquay, Stockport, Doncaster,
Wrexham, Barrow, Watford, St Mirren,
Leyton Orient, 1955-1967
In a well-travelled career Tommy had two
spells in Australia with Hellas where he now
lives in Sydney working as a journalist.

ANDERSON, Trevor
Man U, Swindon, Peterborough, 1972-1978
Now working as Manager of Linfield, who
swept the board – winning the League, Irish
Cup, League Cup and Budweiser Cup – in
Ireland in 1993/4.
Capped 22 times for Northern Ireland.

ANDERSON, Viv
Notts For, Arsenal, Man U, Sheff Wed,
Barnsley, 1974-1993
Joined Nottingham Forest as an apprentice
having briefly worked as a printer before
deciding to pursue a footballing career.
Established himself as one of the best in the
country which prompted big money moves
to Arsenal, and then Manchester United. He
also made 30 full international appearances.
Also played for Sheffield Wednesday and
was player/manager at Barnsley, before joining his old United pal, Bryan Robson, at
Middlesbrough FC.
The first black footballer to play for England.

ANDERSON, Willie
Man U, Aston Villa, Cardiff, 1963-1976
Played over 300 League games, 229 of them for Aston Villa. Now works as an executive with a radio station in Oregon, USA.
Played for Villa in the 1971 League Cup Final.

ANDREWS, Jimmy
Dundee, West Ham, Leyton O, 1951-1961
The Hammers paid £4,750 to bring Jimmy south of the border – a lot of money in the '50s. A former Cardiff boss who now scouts for Southampton.

ANSELL, William
Northampton 1947-1951
Northampton's goalie for several post war years. Now retired and living in Bletchley.

ARCHIBALD, Steve
Clyde, Aberdeen, Tottenham, Blackburn, Reading, 1974-1991
Scottish international striker who joined Tottenham from Aberdeen in 1980. His 58 goals from 128 games in Spurs colours led to his move to Barcelona. Later he had two brief spells back in the English League, firstly with Blackburn 1987, then with Reading 1991. Steve returned to Scotland where he was manager of Manager of East Fife until September 1996. Now works on Sky TV.
Cost Spurs a then record £800,000 fee between English and Scottish clubs.

ARDILES, Osvaldo
Tottenham, Blackburn, QPR, Swindon, 1978-1989
Appointed Manager of Swindon Town in August 1989. Later managed Spurs but fell short of the success he achieved there as a player. In March 1995 became an advisor to a London Law firm specialising in sports contracts, before setting off to coach in Mexico and latterly in Japan's J-League.
1978 World Cup winner with Argentina.

ARMFIELD, Jimmy
Blackpool 1954-1970
An eye-catching defender who played for Blackpool between 1954 and 1970. After a brilliant display in the 1962 World Cup finals in Chile, was voted 'best right-back in the world'. Capped 43 times by England – 37 of them in consecutive appearances. After playing almost 600 games for Blackpool, went on to manage Bolton, then Leeds. He still lives in Blackpool, works as a journalist and can often be heard on radio sports programmes.
Record number of games for Blackpool – 568 between 1952-1971.

ARMSTRONG, David
Middlesbrough, Southampton, Bournemouth, 1971-1987
A full England international and former under-23 player. Made over 350 appearances for Middlesbrough before his transfer to Southampton in 1981. Finished his career at Bournemouth but still lives just outside Southampton. Joined Waterlooville FC as General Manager in March 1995 having previously spent a number of years as an officer for Football in the Community, latterly at Reading.
A record 356 consecutive appearances.

ARMSTRONG, Gerry
Spurs, Watford, WBA, Chesterfield, Brighton, Millwall, 1975-1986

Won 63 Northern Ireland caps. Managed Worthing & Crawley in the Beazer Homes League. Appointed assistant manager of

Northern Ireland in 1994 before becoming a coach to the Sussex FA.
A Northern Ireland 1982 World Cup hero.

ARMSTRONG, George
Arsenal, Leicester, Stockport, 1961-1978
A left winger who signed for Arsenal in 1961, Armstrong went on to give the Gunners sterling service for over 500 league games, before joining Leicester City in 1977. Gained experience at Aston Villa coach; Fulham coach; Enderby Town manager; Middlesbrough coach; Narvik Norway, coach; Kuwait coach before becoming reserve team coach at Highbury.
Member of the Gunners double-winning side of 1971.

ARMSTRONG, Ken
Chelsea 1947-1956
Joined Chelsea from Bradford Rovers in 1946, played 362 league games and won one England cap in 1955. Emigrated to New Zealand where he became National Coach. Died in 1984 and his ashes were scattered at Stamford Bridge.
His record number of appearances for Chelsea is only surpassed by Peter Bonetti.

ARNOLD, Jim
Blackburn, Everton, Preston, Port Vale, 1979-1986
Was England semi-pro keeper with Stafford Rangers, prior to joining Blackburn Rovers. Now lives back in Stafford where he works as a Recreation Officer for the Police Force.

ASHCROFT, Billy
Wrexham, Middlesboro, Tranmere, 1970-1985
Played over 300 league games for his three clubs. Had a spell in Holland but now runs the 'George' pub in Southport.

ASHMAN, Alan
Notts Forest, Carlisle, 1948-1957
Very experienced manager, who prior to his retirement held posts both home and abroad. Probably best remembered for the period in charge of Carlisle and for his four years with West Bromwich Albion when they were in the first division. Now works as a part time scout from his home in Walsall.

ASHMAN, Ron
Norwich 1946-1962
A one club man eventually becoming manager for three years between 1963 and 1966. Also had a spell as Grimsby boss either side of a double stint at Scunthorpe. Now a grandfather of three, Alan runs the transport side of a Scunthorpe travel agency.
Record 662 appearances for Norwich.

ASKEW, Billy
Middlesbrough, Hull, Newcastle, Shrewsbury, 1979-1994
Made his name with Hull and has since played for a number of non-league clubs. Now youth team coach at Darlington.

ASTLE, Jeff
Notts Co, WBA, 1959-1973
Started his career at Notts County scoring 32 goals in 103 games, which persuaded West Brom to buy him in 1964. At the Hawthorns he became a popular and deadly goal scorer, especially good in the air. Played five games for England without scoring however his record of 137 league goals more than made up for this. Won a League Cup winners medal, followed by scoring the deciding goal in the 1968 F.A. Cup final against Everton. Now lives in Ashby-de-la-Zouch and runs his own industrial cleaning business. Has also been resident singer on BBC TV's 'Fantasy Football'.
First Division's leading scorer 1969/70.

ASTON, John
Manchester United 1946-1955
A full back who won 17 full England Caps playing 253 league games. Father of John jnr and held a number of posts in the Old Trafford back room set up.
Played in United's 1948 Cup winning and 1952 League championship winning sides.

ASTON, John
Man U, Luton, Mansfield, Blackburn, 1964-1981

Played 346 league games, won Championship and European Cup winners medals with Manchester United. His father also played for the Reds. Retired from football in 1981 and now runs his own pet shop, Pet World, in Stalybridge.
England Under-23 international.

ATKINS, Ian

Shrewsbury, Sunderland, Everton, Ipswich, Birmingham, Camb U, 1974-1993
Appointed manager of Northampton Town in January 1995, having previously held posts at Cambridge, Birmingham, and Doncaster Rovers.
Won First Division Championship and Cup Winners Cup with Everon.

ATKINSON, Ron

Aston Villa, Oxford, 1956-1971
Born in Liverpool but brought up in Birmingham, Ron has become one of the big names in soccer, but started his illustrious career in the Birmingham Works League, for B.S.A. Tools. His first managerial post was with Kettering in 1971, after making 383 League games for Oxford United.
Managerial stints at Cambridge United, West Brom, Manchester United, Atletico Madrid and Sheffield Wednesday followed before he returned to Villa Park where he had previously played as a youngster. Despite a poor run of results, it was still a surprise to most people, Ron included, when he was dismissed in November 1994. However, it was not long before he was back, with Coventry City - where he immediately won the Manager of the Month award, in record time, only 44 days!
Played in Oxford's first ever football league game in 1962.

ATYEO, John

Portsmouth, Bristol City, 1950-1965
315 goals in 597 games earned international recognition by way of six England caps. He retired in May 1966, qualified as a teacher and taught in Warminster, before suffering a fatal heart attack at his Wiltshire home in 1993, aged 61.

Holds Bristol City record for appearances and goals scored.

AULD, Bertie

Celtic, Dunbarton,Birmingham, Celtic, Hibs, 1955-1971
Illustrious career with Celtic which included the famous 1967 European Cup win. Played for Birmingham City between 1961 and 1964 then after his playing days managed Partick, but after 18 months left the game. He returned briefly to manage Dumbarton but is now a licensee in Glasgow.
A member of Celtic's European Cup winning side.

AUSTIN, Terry

C.Palace, Ipswich, Plymouth, Walsall, Mansfield, Huddersfeld, Doncaster, Northampton, 1974-1983
His career covered seven clubs and over 300 league appearances. Now works as an Insurance Broker in the Mansfield area.

AYRE, Billy

Hartlepool, Halifax, Mansfield, Halifax, 1977-1985
Experienced central defender who went on

to manage Blackpool, then Scarborough Town until December 1994. Took over as manager of Vauxhall Conference side Southport in April 1995 and is now assistant manger of Swansea City.

BACON, Ron
Norwich, Gillingham,1955-1961
Started at Norwich after leaving the army
and moved to Gillingham, playing alongside
Ron Saunders. He drifted into non-league
football, playing for King's Lynn for seven
years where he now works as a painter and
decorator.

BACUZZI, David
Arsenal, Man C, Reading, 1960-1969
Despite being a qualified printer, this former
England youth international now works as
a travel agent in Dublin.
*His father, Joe, was also a player for Fulham
and England.*

BACUZZI, Jo
Fulham 1936-1955
Fulham full back who played 283 League
games during his time at Craven Cottage.
Died in February 1995 at the age of 79.

BADGER, Len
Sheff U, Chesterfield, 1962-1977
Long-serving Sheffield United defender and
England under-23 cap, Len is now licensee
of the Fox & Goose in Old Brampton.
Played 457 league games for The Blades.

BAILY, Eddie
Spurs, Port Vale, Notts Forest, 1946-1955
After serving his country in the Second
World War, Eddie returned to White Hart
Lane playing over 300 league games before
leaving for Port Vale. A full England inter-
national, with nine caps, he returned to
Spurs as assistant manager to Bill
Nicholson. Later became Chief Scout at
West Ham.

BAILEY, Gary
Man U 1978-1986
Born in Ipswich, son of Roy (Crystal Palace
& Ipswich), this England International goal-
keeper has spent much of his life in
Johannesburg where he now lives and
works as an anchorman for South African
TV's version of Match of The Day.
Played in three FA Cup finals.

BAILEY, John
Blackburn, Everton, Newcastle, Bristol C,
1975-1990
Made his name with Blackburn Rovers
before joining Everton for £300,000 in 1979.
Was youth coach at Everton until 1993.
Now assistant manager at Sheffield Utd.
FA Cup winner with Everton in 1984.

BAILEY, Mike
Charlton, Wolves, Hereford, 1959-1978
Won two England caps and made over 500
League appearances for his three clubs.
Managed Hereford United, Charlton
Athletic and had a spell as player-coach to
Minnesota Kicks in the USA. Sacked as
reserve team coach at Portsmouth in
February 1995 he now manages non-league
Leatherhead.
*Skipper of Wolves in the 1974 League Cup
final.*

BAILEY, Ray
Gillingham, Northampton, 1966-1971
Wing half who also played cricket for
Northants, where he is groundsman.

BAILEY, Roy
C Palace, Ipswich, 1949-1965
Father of former Manchester United goal-
keeper Gary, Roy won a First Division
Championship medal in 1962 having won a
Second Division medal 12 months earlier
with Ipswich under Alf Ramsey. Emigrated
to South Africa and died in Johannesburg in
April 1993 at the age of 61.

BAINES, Steve
Notts Forest, Huddersfield, Bradford,
Walsall, Bury, Scunthorpe, Chesterfield,
1972-1986
After 400 games in a long career he now
works for Swindon Insurance and was
appointed to the Football League Referee's
panel in 1995.

BAIRD, Henry
Man U, Huddersfield, Ipswich, 1936-1951
This Northern Ireland international wing
half was a Man Utd player before the war

then made 200 appearances for Ipswich. He died in 1973, aged 60.
Won one cap for Northern Ireland, against England in 1939.

BAKER, Alan

Aston V, Walsall, 1960-1970
Went into the leather trade but now lives in Walsall where he works as a Castings Inspector.

BAKER, Graham

Soton, Man C, Soton, Aldershot, Fulham, 1976-1991
Southampton-born Graham started at his home town club. Three moves later, including a return to the Dell, he hung up his boots to set up a driving school near his home in Surrey.
Won two England under-21 caps.

BAKER, Joe

Hibs, Arsenal, Notts F, Sunderland, Hibs, Raith, 1956-1974
A brilliant centre forward who scored an incredible 93 goals in 144 games for Arsenal. Won three full England caps, although he had played for Scotland schoolboys as a youngster. Ended his playing career at Raith Rovers before taking over as manager in 1974. He later ran a pub in Craigneeuk and worked in the building trade. He suffered a heart attack suffered a couple of years ago and now spends his time doing after dinner speaking and some coaching in the Motherwell area for the SFA.
Played for AS Torino in Italy for 12 months proir to joining Arsenal.

BAKER, Peter

Tottenham 1952-1964
A right back seen by many as one of the most under-rated members of the double winning side. He emigrated to South Africa where he runs a sports centre after previously starting an office furniture and stationery business.
Played a total of 400 games for Spurs.

BALCOMBE, Steve

Leeds Utd 1979-1982
A Welsh under-23 international who played for Home Farm, Dundalk, Shamrock Rovers and Oaklands before returning to Yorkshire where he now runs the Crown Inn in Great Ouseburn, nr York.

BALDERSTONE, Chris

Huddersfield, Carlisle, Doncaster, 1959-1975
Chris was an inside forward who made over 500 League appearances. He also played cricket for Leicestershire and Yorkshire and on one occasion batted until close of play and was then driven away to play soccer for Doncaster Rovers an hour later, returning the next day to complete a century. He is still involved with cricket, but these days dons the white coat of a first-class umpire.
Played 369 league games for Carlisle.

BALDWIN, Tommy

Arsenal, Chelsea, Millwall, Manchester U, Brentford, 1964-1977

England under-23 international who was a part of the Chelsea 'glory years' team of the seventies. Now lives in Fulham and enjoys playing lots of of golf.
Won F.A.Cup and European Cup Winners Cup medals.

BALL, Alan
Blackpool, Everton, Arsenal, Soton,
Blackpool, Soton, Bristol R, 1962-1982
Tenacious midfielder Alan made no less
than 72 appearances for England. He
became player-manager at Blackpool and
also tried his luck with Vancouver
Whitecaps. His varied life as a coach has
also included service with Bristol Rovers,
Portsmouth, Stoke City, and Exeter City.
Appointed team manager at Southampton in
1994 but after only one season accepted an
offer from his old friend Frannie Lee to take
over at Manchester City – he lost his job 13
months later.
1966 World Cup winner.

BALL, Keith
Walsall, Port V, Walsall, 1958-1972
Port Vale's first choice goalie between 1968-
1971, who also had three spells with his
home town club, Walsall. He still lives there
and works for the Local Authority.
Played over 700 games in his career.

BAMBRIDGE, Keith
Rotherham, Darlington, Halifax, 1955-1965
Now a draughtsman living and working in
Rotherham.

BAMFORD, Harry
Bristol R 1946-1958
A full back, who once caused a stir when it
was discovered that he practised ball control
by dribbling around the racing pigeons that
he owned. Died 1958 aged only 38.
Almost 500 league appearances for Rovers.

BANJO, Tanji
Leyton Orient 1977-1981
One of the forerunners of today's League
contingent from Africa. Tanji only played 20
league games but was a full Nigerian
International. Last seen working as a bus
driver in north London.

BANKS, Frank
Southend, Hull, Southend, 1962-1977
A full back who was born in Hull but started
and ended his career on the Essex coast.

Played over 300 games for The Tigers. Now
community officer at Southend.

BANKS, Gordon
Chesterfield, Leicester, Stoke, 1958-1972

Acknowledged as one of the world's greatest
ever keepers, whose playing career was
ended prematurely following a car accident
in 1972. Spent two years in America, where
despite having lost one eye, was voted best
goalkeeper. After a spell managing Telford
he became self-employed in the sports promotion business when the corporate entertainment company he worked for folded.
*His save from Pele in the 1970 World Cup
was one of the greatest ever.*

BANNISTER, Bruce
Bradford, Bristol R, Plymouth, Hull, 1965-1979
Played over 500 league games and runs a
Bradford sports shop, Sportshoes Unlimited.
*Played 202 league games for Rovers scoring
80 goals.*

BANNISTER Gary
Coventry, Sheff Weds, QPR, Coventry, WBA,
Oxford, Notts Forest, Stoke, Lincoln,
Darlington, 1978-1996
A long career was ended by injury in 1996.
Gary now lives in Cornwall where he has
interests in two guest houses.

BARKER, Richie
Derby, Notts Co, Peterborough, 1967-1971

Has had spells as assistant manager at Wolves and also manager of Shrewsbury and Stoke City. Most recently assistant manager to Trevor Francis at Sheffield Weds and is now development manager at the club.

BARLOW, Colin
Man C, Oldham, Doncaster, 1957-1964
Had five years as a player at Maine Road, then went on to become a successful businessman running his own import/export company which has offices in Milan and Prague. His love of the club encouraged him to become a key figure in the consortium which took control in 1994 and he is now City's Chief Executive.
Scored 78 goals in 179 games with City.

BARNARD, Mike
Portsmouth 1953-1958
Inside forward who played 116 games for Portsmouth between 1953 and 1958. Also played cricket for Hampshire. Can be heard on BBC Radio Solent's sports programmes.

BARNES, Ken
Man C, Wrexham, 1951-1964
Wing half who played over 250 games for Man City and won representative honours with the Football League XI. Father of Peter, he now scouts for Man City.
Played in both 1955 and 1956 FA Cup finals.

BARNES, Peter
Man C, WBA, Leeds, Coventry, Man U, Man C, Bolton, Port V, Hull, Bolton, Sunderland, 1974-1988
A full England international winger who made his name with Manchester City. After joining City as an apprentice he moved to West Bromwich Albion in 1979 and went on to play for a number of league clubs before ending his playing career with a spell in America. Returned to Maine Road in 1991 to work in the Social Club but now helps coach youngsters at the club's Platt Lane complex. Had a short spell as manager of non-league Runcorn and coached in Norway in 1996. Also works on Picadilly Radio.
Capped 22 times by England.

BARNES, Ron
Blackpool, Rochdale, Wrexham, Norwich, Peterborough, Torquay, 1954-1968
A well travelled outside right who started his career as understudy to Stanley Matthews at Blackpool. Played his best football at Torquay and later emigrated to South Africa where he has spent the last 20 years in the printing trade.
Scored a hat trick for Wrexham in their club record 10-1 win over Hartlepool in 1962.

BARNETT, Geoff
Everton, Arsenal, 1965-1975
A former England schoolboy and youth international goalkeeper who after living in America for a number of years returned to run a pub in Cheshire.
Played in the 1972 Cup Final against Leeds.

BARNWELL, John
Arsenal, Notts F, Sheff U, 1956-1970
John served Peterborough as coach before taking over the managerial reins in 1977. He resigned in November 1978 to take the helm at Wolverhampton Wanderers and was then manager of Northampton Town until December 1994. Is now Chief Executive with the League Managers' Association and controls team affairs at Grantham Town.

BARRETT, Les
Fulham, Millwall, 1965-1977

Won England under-23 honours whilst with Fulham – for whom he made over 400 league appearances. Then spent eleven years as a

British Telecom engineer and now runs a garden centre with his wife in Earlsfield, south-west London.
In Fulham's losing 1975 FA Cup final side.

BARRON, Paul
Plymouth, Arsenal, C Palace, WBA, Stoke, QPR, Reading, 1976-1986
Goalkeeper whose seven-club career spanned ten years. Paul now lives in Egbaston, West Midlands and is working in sports management. He also acts as a fitness consultant to Aston Villa.
Won promotion with Palace in 1981.

BARRON, William
Charlton, Northampton, 1937-1950
Now retired and living in Northampton where he played most of his career.
Played County cricket for Lancashire and Northampton.

BARROW, Graham
Wigan, Chester., 1981-1994
Experienced midfielder who was appointed manager at Wigan Athletic in 1994, having taken Chester City to promotion the previous season. Is now Rochdale boss.

BARTLEY, Tony
Bury, Oldham, Chesterfield, 1958-1966
Now lives in his home town of Stalybridge where he works as a Sports Centre manager and is a fully trained sports coach.

BARTON, John
Everton, Derby, 1978-1983
Now lives in Derby and works as a PT instructor at Burton College. Managed Nuneaton Borough from May 1993 until March 1994 when he was appointed boss at BHL League side Burton Albion.

BARTON, Tony
Fulham, Notts F, Portsmouth, 1953-1966
A former England youth winger, Tony gained experience as coach at Portsmouth before becoming manager at Aston Villa. His coaching skills also took him to Southampton, Portsmouth and Northampton. He suffered a heart attack during his time at Northampton and died at his Southampton home in August 1993.
Won the European Cup with Villa.

BARTRAM, Sam
Charlton 1934-1955
The greatest goalkeeper never to be capped for England. In his younger days he was an outfield player but took up keeping while working in the pits. He went on to keep goal for Charlton for over 20 years. Opened a sports shop near The Valley after his playing days were over. Died 1981.
Played in two Cup Finals, 1946 and 1947, winning one and losing the other.

BASON, Brian
Chelsea, Plymouth, C Palace, Portsmouth, Reading, 1972-1982
Former Chelsea apprentice who played most of his league soccer for Plymouth. He still lives in the West Country, currently managing an hotel in Truro.
An England schoolboy international.

BASSETT, Dave
Wimbledon 1977
Dave was a distinguished non-league player, winning ten caps for England as a semi-pro, before becoming professional. Ran a highly successful insurance business prior to being appointed assistant manager, then manager at Wimbledon. In six very colourful years he guided them from the fourth to first division. He left for Watford and spent eight years at Sheffield United before returning to Crystal Palace in early 1996 where he previously had a short spell.
Missed the Dons first ever League game through suspension.

BASTIN, Cliff
Exeter, Arsenal, 1927-1947
Played 350 games for Arsenal between 1929 and 1946, during which time he won 21 England caps. By the age of 21 had won a League Championship, FA Cup winners medals and a full England cap. During his stay in the capital he established himself as

one of The Gunners all time greats. Became a licensee in his native Devon and died aged 79 in an Exeter hospital after a short illness in 1991.
Holds the Gunners league goals record.

BATER, Phil
Bristol R, Wrexham, Bristol R, Brentford, Cardiff, 1973-1987
A former Welsh under-21 international who has settled in the Bristol area where he works as a landscape gardener.
Played over 300 games for Rovers.

BATES, Chic
Shrewsbury, Swindon, Bristol Rovers, Shrewsbury, 1974-1985
Played most of his 274 games with The Shrews. Since hanging up his boots Chic has been involved with the management of Shrewsbury, Swindon, Brimingham, Celtic and is currently is his second spell with Stoke, this time as assistant manager.

BATES Don
Brighton 1957
Don played County cricket for Sussex as well as soccer for Brighton. Still lives in the town and teaches at a local school.

BATES, Mick
Leeds, Walsall, Bradford, Doncaster, 1966-1980
A midfield player who was a squad member during the Leeds United glory years. Now lives near Doncaster and works as a steward at a Working Mens Club.
Scored for Leeds in the first leg of the 1971 Inter Cities Cup final against Juventus.

BATSON, Brendon
Arsenal, Camb U, WBA, 1971-1982
Born in the West Indian island of Grenada, England 'B' cap Brendon became deputy secretary of the PFA and is now PFA chairman.

BAXTER, Billy
Ipswich, Hull, Watford, Northampton, 1960-1972

Long serving centre half and veteran of over 400 games for Ipswich Town who now lives in Dunfermline, Scotland. Has been a British Telecom engineer for over 20 years.

BAXTER, Jim
Raith, Rangers, Sunderland, Notts F, Rangers, 1957-1970

Played for Scotland at under 23-level and 43 times for the full national team. Started his career at Raith Rovers then moved to Rangers. Moved south to Sunderland in 1965 for £85,000 and then on to Nottingham Forest in 1967 before finishing his career back at Rangers. Retired in 1970 and became a publican in his native Glasgow. Has suffered from poor health recently.
Completed the double and treble with Rangers in successive years, 1963 and 1964.

BAXTER, Mick
Preston, Middlesboro, Portsmouth, 1974-1984
Mick made his name in 200-plus games for Preston before going on to play a further 100 games for Middlesbrough. Tragically died of a heart attack in 1989 aged only 32.

BAXTER, Stuart

Preston, Stockport, 1972-1976
Although not as well known as a player, Stuart achieved incredible success as a manager in Japan, guiding Sanfrecce Hiroshima to the Suntory championship title in 1993. Is now coach of J-League side Kobe.
Played in the same Preston side as his brother Mick.

BEAL, Phil

Tottenham, Brighton, Crewe, 1963-1979
Defender who progressed through the youth ranks at Tottenham and went on to play 330 league games for them. Now splits his time between his home in Devon and Surrey, where he runs a car hire business in West Drayton.
Won the UEFA Cup in 1971 with Spurs.

BEAMISH, Kenny

Tranmere, Brighton, Blackburn, Port V, Bury, Tranmere, Swindon, 1965-1981
In a sixteen-year professional career Kenny played for seven clubs and has now returned to one of them, Blackburn Rovers, where he is commercial manager.

BEARDSLEY, Don

Hull, Doncaster, Grimsby, 1966-1974
Became a partner in an estate agency before leaving to set up on his own.

BEATTIE, Kevin

Ipswich, Colchester, Middlesbrough, 1972-1982
England international defender whose career was dogged by injuries. After almost a decade with Ipswich went on to play in Sweden, then became player/coach to Kongsberg in Norway before returning to England to run a pub. Illness has prevented Kevin working since 1991 but he is keen to find a coaching job.
Played in Ipswich's record win (7-0) against WBA in 1976.

BECK, John

QPR, Coventry, Fulham, Bournemouth, Cambridge, 1972-1989
Experience gained from over 400 league games with five clubs enabled John to move into management with Cambridge. Also managed Preston until December 1994. During a spell out the game worked as a van driver delivering parcels. Is now manager of Lincoln City.
Manager of the Year in 1991.

BEDFORD, Brian

Reading, Southampton, Bournemouth, QPR, Scunthorpe, Brentford, 1954-1966
Had a terrific goal scoring rate throughout a career that took in six clubs. Upon retiring from the game took up tennis and became a registered professional, qualifying as a LTA coach in 1972. He was the tennis pro at Richmond Lawn Tennis Club from 1980-1985 but a knee injury forced him to give up in 1986. He became Stadium Manager at Loftus Road until he was made redundant in 1992.
Scored 163 league goals for QPR.

BEECH, Cyril

Swansea, Newport, 1949-1956
Cyril has been scouting for Luton Town for over fourteen years and was responsible for discovering players such as Mark Pembridge, Ceri Hughes and John Hartson among others.

BEGLIN Jim

Liverpool, Leeds, Plymouth, Blackburn Rovers, 1983-1992
Forced to quit after a short comeback following a serious leg break, Jim has carved himself a career as a football pundit in the media, working for Radio Five, Granada and Sky among others.
A 1986 double-winner with Liverpool.

BELFIT, Rod

Leeds, Ipswich, Everton, Sunderland, Fulham, Huddersfield, 1963-1975
Moved to clubs on almost a yearly basis after leaving Leeds. Now working as a draughtsman, his orginal profession before he turned pro with Leeds.
Netted a hat trick in the 1967 Inter Cities

Fairs Cup semi final against Kilmarnock.

BELL, Colin
Bury, Man C, 1963-1978
Started at Bury before being transferred to Manchester City for a then record fee of £45,000. In a particularly successful four year period he was a key member of the City team that won the Football league, European Cup winners cup, and League Cup. Played over 400 games before having to retire early due to injury. Ran his own restaurant in Manchester until 1989 but is now back at Maine Road as Youth Development Officer.
Manchester City's most capped international player (48).

BELL, Graham
Oldham, Preston, Huddersfield, 1974-1986
Well travelled midfielder who saw active service with six northern clubs is currently working in the insurance industry.
Played 446 League games.

BELL, Harold
Tranmere 1946-1959
Played a total of 595 matches before retiring in 1959. Lived in Sefton and worked as a club steward before his death in 1994, co-incidentally on the same day as the great Bobby Moore.
Made a record 401 consecutive league appearances, over nine years.

BELL, Willie
Queens Park, Leeds, Leicester, Brighton, 1957-1970
His Elland Road career ended when Don Revie signed Terry Copper. When his playing days ended he had spells in managment with Birmingham and Lincoln then moved to the USA where he joined Campus Crusade for Christ. Now works as a College Coach at the Liberty Baptist College in Virginia.

BELLAMY, Arthur.
Burnley, Chesterfield, 1962-1975
Started as a junior with Burnley, signing pro terms at the age of 19. Now back at Turf Moor, where he is the club's groundsman.
Won promotion to the Division 1 with Burnley in 1971.

BELLAMY, Gary
Chesterfield, Wolves, Cardiff, Leyton O, 1980-1996
A very experienced centre half who after being handed a free moved to non-league Chelmsford City where he combines playing with being commercial manager.
Won two Division Four Championship winners medals, a Division Three medal and also Welsh Cup honours.

BENNETT, Albert
Rotherham, Newcastle, Norwich, 1961-1971
Forced to quit at the age of 26. After taking a number of jobs including working in the prison service, in hotel catering and a position in a Lowestoft joke shop he took on the Bricklayers Arms pub in Norwich which he still runs.

BENNETT, David
Machester City, Norwich, 1976-1984
Never played a game for City prior to his move to East Anglia. Knee inuries forced him to quit at the age of 25 and his insurance payout helped start a bar in Spain called *Confusion*.

BENNETT, Dave
Man C, Cardiff, Coventry, Sheff W, Swindon, 1977-1991
Was forced to retire from the full-time game through injury. Made a comeback with Nuneaton Borough in 1994/5.
A member of Coventry's FA Cup winning side.

BENNETT, Peter
West Ham, Leyton O, 1963-1978
Midfielder who played almost 200 league games for Orient, now works as a carpenter. Recent interesting contracts have included a five month stint in Moscow. His son is a talented golfer who was the top amateur in the 1994 British Open Golf Championship.

A member of the Orient side which reached an FA Cup semi final in 1978.

BENNION, Stan
Wrexham, Chester, 1959-1963
Now senior payments officer at Cheshire County Council. Lives near Chester.
Scored in Wrexham's record 10-1 victory over Hartlepool 1962.

BENSON, John
Man C, Torquay, Bournemouth, Exeter, Norwich, Bournemouth, 1961-1978
Full back who played most of his league football for Torquay. Managed Bournemouth from 1975-1979 and is now a member of the backroom staff at another of his former clubs, Norwich.
Played 468 league games.

BENTLEY, Bill
Stoke, Blackpool, Port Vale, 1965-1979
Spent eight years at Blackpool in the seventies and is now self employed, living in Stoke on Trent.
Won promotion to Division One with Blackpool in 1971.

BENTLEY, Dave
Rotherham, Mansfield, Chesterfield, Doncaster, 1966-1979
Made almost 250 League appearances for Rotherham then became assistant manager at Leeds. Now a Football in the Community officer based at Mansfield Town.

BERNARD, Mike
Stoke, Everton, Oldham, 1965-1978
Took a pub in the Dee Valley after he was forced to quit the game due to a knee injury in 1979. Lives near Swindon and now makes his living by mending lawnmowers and gardening.

BERRY, George
Wolves, Stoke, Doncaster, Peterborough, Preston, 1976-1991
Only the second black player to appear for Wales – he made his debut for them against West Germany, ironically enough the coun-
try where he was born! At one time had his own programme on the local radio station. Was commercial manager and player for Stafford Rangers but now works for the PFA.
Won five international caps.

BERTSCHIN, Keith
Ipswich, Birmingham, Norwich, Stoke, Sunderland, Walsall, Chester, 1975-1990
Well travelled forward who is still knocking in the goals, currently for Stafford Rangers. Now works as a financial advisor in the West Midlands.
England Under-23 international.

BERTOLINI, Jack
Stirling, Workington, Brighton, 1952-1965
Moved down from Stirling to join Workington in 1953, then progressed further south to Brighton five years later. Now runs a pub in nearby Shoreham.
Played 439 league games.

BEST, Clyde
West Ham 1969-1975
Former Hammers favourite who made his debut against Arsenal in 1969. Clyde had become a Bermudan international by the time he left Upton Park to play in America, firstly for Tampa Bay Rowdies and then Portland Timbers. After a spell in Holland with Feyenoord, Clyde ended up back in Portland, Oregon where he owns a succesful dry cleaning business.

BEST, David
Bournemouth, Oldham, Ipswich, Portsmouth, Bournemouth, 1960-1975
The only time that goalkeeper David played in the First Division was with Ipswich. Managed Dorchester Town for a spell and now lives in Wareham where he is manager of Wareham Rangers in the Dorset Combination.

BEST, George
Man U, Stockport, Fulham, Bournemouth, 1963-1982
One of the greatest ever individual players of all time. Made his debut for Manchester

United at the age of seventeen, and played his first game for Ireland before his eighteenth birthday. In 1968 became both British and European footballer of the year. After brief spells with Fulham and Bournemouth he played in the American League, before ending his competitive playing days far too early. Now makes his living though public and media appearances, both home and abroad. Recently toured the country with Rodney Marsh in a popular stage double act. *Won two League Championship medals and a European Cup winners medal.*

BICKLES, Dave
West Ham, Crystal Palace, Colchester United, 1961-1969
Former England youth international who works as a PE Teacher at Brampton Manor School which is just half a mile from Upton Park. Runs the Hammers under-16 side.

BIGGS, Alfie
Bristol Rovers, Preston, Bristol Rovers, Walsall, Swansea, 1953-1970
A local lad who still lives in the area. Since hanging his boots up has been a car salesman, postman. baker, maintenance man at Eastville and latterly a parcel delivery man. *Played over 400 leagues games for Rovers in two spells, scoring 178 goals.*

BILEY, Alan
Camb U, Derby, Everton, Stoke, Portsmouth, Brighton, Camb U, 1975-1986

Much travelled, Alan is now back in the Cambridge area, after a career scoring goals for a number of clubs and several big money moves. Spells in Ireland and Greece preceded his return to manage Ely in the Jewson League. However, business commitments which include running his own gym and health club, 'Bileys' in Biggleswade, forced him to relinquish this role, although he has been known to turn out for local league side Potton United. *His 74 goals between 1975-1980 is still a Cambridge record.*

BINGHAM, Billy
Sunderland, Luton, Everton, Port Vale, 1950-1964
Found fame with Sunderland before a broken leg ended Billy's playing career. Went into management in Greece and later was manager of Everton in the seventies. Became manager of the Northern Ireland side, until 1993, and was awarded the MBE for services to football. Now a Director of Blackpool FC. *Won 56 caps for Northern Ireland.*

BIRD, John
Doncaster, Preston, Newcastle, Hartlepool, 1967-1984
Solid central defender who remained in the game as manager of Hartlepool, then York City, before taking over at Halifax Town. *Promoted to Division Two with Preston in 1974.*

BIRTLES, Gary
Notts F, Man U, Notts F, Notts C, Grimsby, 1976-1993
Lives in Nottingham and sells fish from Grimsby! Does occasional promotional work and radio commentaries on Radio Nottingham. Signed for Ilkeston Town before Grestly Rovers appointed him assistant to Paul Futcher. *Cost Manchester United £1.25m in 1980.*

BLACK, Alan
Sunderland, Norwich Dumbarton, 1964-1975
Moved south to join Sunderland but made

more of an impression during six years at Norwich. Eventually returned to Scotland and held various positions within the licensing trade. Is now a partner in a Dumbarton taxi firm.

BIRCHENALL, Alan
Sheff U, Chelsea, C Palace, Leicester, Notts Co, Blackburn, Luton, Hereford, 1964-1979

Played for eight clubs during a sixteen-year career. After a two and half year stint as manager of Trowbridge, became press officer at Leicester, a post he has now held for fifteen years. Alan's commercial interests include owning a village pub and running a ladies foootwear import business. He also helps local charities with his annual end-of - season run around Filbert Street.
England Under 23 international.

BLACKLAW, Adam
Burnley, Blackburn, Blackpool, 1956-1970
Scotland international who guarded the goal for Burnley for over a decade. Still lives in Lancashire and is a publican.
A member of Burnley's 1960 Championship winning squad.

BLACKLEY, John
Hibs, Newcastle, Preston, Hamilton, 1977-1981

Moved from Hibs to Newcastle in 1977 for £100,000. Then had a period at Preston before returning to Scotland to play for Hamilton Academical. Became their player/manager for a few months before being appointed assistant manager at Hibernian in 1983, then manager until his resignation in November 1986. Currently on the staff at St Johnstone.
Cup final winner once in four appearances with Hibs.

BLACKWELL, Kevin
Scarborough, Notts C, Torquay, Huddersfield, Plymouth, 1987-1996
Goalie who gained league experience late in his career after many years in non-league soccer. Made his football comeback for Plymouth Argyle in the 1995-96 season where he is now youth developement officer.

BLAIR, Andy
Coventry, Aston Villa, Wolves, Sheff W, Aston Villa, Barnsley, Northampton, 1977-1988
After an eleven year league career he continued playing for Kidderminster. Now extremely busy building up a variety of business interests including selling sportswear and owning a playschool. Can be heard on local radio in the Midlands covering Aston Villa matches.
Five Under-21 caps for Scotland.

BLAIR, James
Hibs, St Mirren, Norwich City, 1964-1972
Never hit the mark after moving south. Made his name in Belgium where he still lives today working for the Belgian Aviation Authority and coaching club side Haact.
Played for Norwich in a League Cup final.

BLAIR, Ronnie
Oldham, Rochdale, Oldham, Blackpool, Rochdale, 1966-1982
A defender who played the bulk of his 450 plus league games for Oldham Althletic. Now runs a printing firm in nearby Shaw.
Capped five times by Northern Ireland.

BLANCHFLOWER, Danny

Barnsley, Aston Villa, Tottenham, 1948-1963
Barnsley paid Glentoran £6,500 in 1949 to
bring Danny across the water – the first step
in a glittering career. He won the Player of
the Year award twice, 1957 and 1961 and
retired in 1963/4 for a new career in journalism, which he maintained until his death in
Chobham, Surrey in December 1993.
Skippered Spurs through their glory years,
winning many honours including the famous
double in 1960/1.

BLANCHFLOWER, Jackie

Manchester United 1950-1959
Career was cut short at Munich. Now lives
in Stalybridge near Manchester and is a
popular after dinner speaker.
Brother of Danny, capped 12 times by
Northern Ireland.

BLISSETT, Luther

Watford, AC Milan, Bournemouth, Watford,
1975-1994
Powerful centre forward who was one of
Watford's star's in their exciting 'Elton John/
Graham Taylor' years. Played non-league
football for Fakenham Town whilst working
in the commericial office at Watford. When
Taylor returned to the club in 1996 he was
appointed to the coaching staff and is now
assistant manager.
AC Milan paid £1m for him in 1983.

BLOCKLEY, Jeff

Coventry, Arsenal, Leicester, Notts Co, 1967-
1979
Steady performances in defence for Coventry
prompted a £200,000 move to Arsenal in
1972. Spent two years at Highbury before
moving to Leicester and finally Notts
County. He still lives in the East Midlands
where he runs a successful engineering
business.
Won one England cap, against Yugoslavia in
1973.

BLOOMFIELD, Jimmy

Brentford, Arsenal, Birmingham, Brentford,
West Ham, Plymouth, Leyton O, 1952-1968
Although remembered as a successful manager at Leicester and Orient, Jimmy was a
player for sixteen years and served seven
clubs. Died in 1983 at the age of only 49. His
son David is head of sponsorship at the FA.
Played in Two Inter City Fairs Cup finals.

BLOOR, Alan

Stoke, Port Vale, 1961-1978
Although he ended his playing days at Port
Vale it was at nearby Stoke City that Alan
played for over fifteen years. Still lives in the
Potteries where he runs a newsagents in his
home town of Stoke.
A member of Stoke 's 1972 League Cup win-
ning side.

BLY, Terry

Norwich, Peterboro, Coventry, Notts Co,
1956-1964
One of the most prolific goalscorers in the
lower divisions, Terry started at Norwich
then moved on to Peterborough. Now owns a
sports shop in Grantham, Lincolnshire.
Set a post war scoring record by netting 52
goals in the 1960-61 season.

BLYTH, Jim

Preston, Coventry, Hereford, Birmingham,
1971-1982
Capped twice by Scotland and is now goalkeeping coach at Coventry City.
A member of Scotland's 1978 World Cup
squad.

BLYTH, Mel

Scunthorpe, C Palace, Soton, C Palace,
Millwall, 1967-1980
Strong central defender who made his name
at Crystal Palace. Although an electrician by
trade, Mel became a driving instructor
before setting up his own building company
in south London.
FA Cup winner in 1976 with Southampton.

BOAM, Stuart

Mansfield, Middlesboro, Newcastle,
Mansfield, Hartlepool, 1966-1982
After a career of over 500 league appear-
ances, including 320 games for
Middlesbrough, he briefly went into man-

agement at Mansfield, but now lives in Kirkby-in-Ashfield and works for Kodak Photographic Co.
Won promotion to the Division One in 1974.

BOERSMA, Phil
Liverpool, Wrexham, Middlesboro, Luton, Swansea, 1969-1978
Started his career with Liverpool as a junior before moving on to Middlesbrough for £72,500 in 1975. Retired in 1981 while at Swansea to become physiotherapist at Rangers in Scotland. Then returned to Merseyside to rejoin Liverpool and is now at Southampton.

BOLDER, Bob
Sheff W, Liverpool, Sunderland, Charlton, 1977-1994
Joined Sheffield Wednesday in 1977 from non-league Dover Town and retired from the pro game seventeen years later when a back injury ended his career. Is now back with The Addicks as community coach.
Played at Wembley with Charlton in the 1987 Full Members Cup Final.

BOLLAND, Gordon
Chelsea, Leyton O, Norwich, Charlton, Millwall, 1961-1974
Was born in Boston, Lincs but played his League football for five southern clubs. Gordon has now returned to his roots, living in Boston and working as a Sales Rep for a tyre company. On the Board of Boston Utd.
Played 239 games for Millwall.

BOLTON, Joe
Sunderland, Middlesboro, Sheff U, 1971-1985
Left back who was a Sunderland regular for eight years before moving to Middlesbrough in 1981. Now works as a lorry driver for a haulage firm in Sheffield.
Promoted to Division One with Sunderland in 1977.

BOND, John
West Ham, Torquay, 1951-1968
Colchester born John played for the West Ham side of the sixties which produced so many future managers. After thirteen years and 381 League appearances for the Hammers he started his travels, firstly as a player with Torquay, followed by a nomadic coaching trail. His management career started at Gillingham as a coach and he subsequently held appointments at Bournemouth, Norwich City, Manchester City, and latterly Shrewsbury Town where he worked from 1991 until May 1993.
FA Cup winner with West Ham in 1964.

BOND, Kevin
Norwich, Man C, Southampton, Bournemouth, Exeter, 1975-1994
Full back son of John who lived near Southampton and owned a cafe in the area, until returning to Maine Road in August 1996 as reserve team boss.
Capped twice by England at B level.

BOND, Len
Bristol, Exeter, Torquay, Scunthorpe, Colchester, Brentford, Exeter, 1970-1983 .
Ran a newsagents in Exeter but now works coaching the keepers at Exeter and Torquay.
Helped Exeter to an FA Cup quarter final appearance.

BONDS, Billy
Charlton, West Ham, 1964-1987
An extremely competitive half back and captain. Joined West Ham from Charlton in May 1967 for a bargain £50,000. He collected two FA Cup winners medals and was instrumental in helping the Hammers back to the first division, with a runaway title victory in 1980/1. After over 25 years service at Upton Park, as player, coach, then as manager, Billy resigned in August 1994. Worked for QPR as their youth team manager until September 1996.
His 663 League appearances is a Hammers record.

BONE, Jim
Partick, Norwich, Sheff U, Celtic, Arbroath, St Mirren, Hearts, Arbroath, 1968-1985
A bustling forward whose long career was spread over a wide selection of clubs. An

electrician by trade, Bone became player/manager at Arbroath before joining St Mirren as their manager but left in August 1996. Now manager of Alloa.
Helped Norwich to the Division Two title in 1972.

BONETTI, Peter
Chelsea 1959-1978
Nicknamed 'The Cat', son of a Swiss-born restaurateur, Peter was unfortunate to be in the shadow of the great Gordon Banks and consequently collected only seven England caps. With Chelsea he made 600 League appearances before taking his family off to the Isle of Mull, where he worked as a postman and occasionally turned out for Scottish league sides. He now lives in Birmingham and coaches goalies for several league clubs as well as helping out with the current England squad.
Played for England in the 1970 World Cup quarter final against Germany.

BONNYMAN, Phil
Hamilton, Carlisle, Chesterfield, Grimsby, Stoke, Darlington, 1975-1988
Lives in his home town of Glasgow and works at Hamilton, his first club, as an officer for Football in the Community.

BOOK, Tony
Plymouth, Man C, 1964-1966

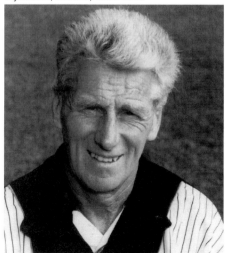

Was plucked from relative obscurity with Bath City when working as a bricklayer at the age of 29 to become a great success at full back with Plymouth Argyle. Malcolm Allison and Joe Mercer took him to Man City in July 1966 where he won many honours.
Manager of City's 1977 League Cup winning side.

BOOKER, Bob
Brentford, Sheff U, Brentford, 1978-1994
Currently youth team coach at Brentford, where he played most of his professional career.
Won promotion to the First Division with Brentford in 1993.

BOOTH, Dennis
Charlton, Blackpool, Southend, Lincoln, Watford, Hull, 1966-1984
Eighteen years as a player preceded Dennis's progression into management. Currently working with Huddersfield as assistant manager after holding a similar post with Bristol Rovers.

BOOTH, Tommy
Man C, Preston, 1968-1984
Earned four caps at under-23 level with England during his thirteen years at Manchester City. He spent eighteen months as manager of Preston North End and now lives near Manchester where he works for locally based television rental firm, Granada TV.
Scored the winning goal in the 1968 FA Cup final against Everton.

BOROTA, Peter
Chelsea 1978-1981
Joined Chelsea from Partizan Belgrade in March 1987. Returned to Yugoslavia where he ran a duty free shop and was implicated in a stolen picture racket resulting in a major court case.
Chelsea Player of the Year in 1980 and 1981.

BOTHAM, Ian
Scunthorpe 1979-1984
Although now internationally known as a

cricketer/television celebrity and charity fund-raiser, Ian was also a talented footballer. He signed for Scunthorpe as a non-contract player in March 1980, played seven league games and another four as sub, staying until 1984. He also played non-league football for Yeovil. Recently signed as one of several big names to work as a commentator on Sky TV.

BOULTON, Colin

Derby, Soton, Lincoln, 1964-1980

Colin established himself as Derby's regular keeper for twelve years following his move from Cheltenham Town in 1964. Played for three years in America but a leg injury forced him to quit and he returned home to become a policeman. Still lives in Derby, but now sells sports equipment for Huddersfield based sports firm, Mitre.

Ever present in Derby's two Championship winning sides.

BOVINGTON, Edward

West Ham 1959-1967

Former West Ham wing half now runs his own women's clothes store, Jays Fashion Discount Market at Archway, London. He has also run the London marathon.

A member of West Ham's 1964 FA Cup winning side.

BOWEN, Dave

Northampton, Arsenal, Northampton, 1947-1959

Retired from soccer in 1986 and decided to activate the bookmakers license that he had held since 1966 but could not use due to League regulations. Was also a football reporter for the Sunday People. Died in September 1996 in Northampton.

Took Northampton from the Fourth to First Division in the 1960s.

BOWEN, Keith

Northampton, Brentford, Colchester, 1976-1985

Son of Dave, Keith followed in his father's footsteps by playing for Northampton Town. Now works as an accountant and still lives

in the town. Also acts as assistant manager for United Counties side, Northampton Spencer.

A Welsh Schoolboy international.

BOWKER, Keith

Birmingham, Exeter, Cambridge, Northampton, Exeter, Torquay, 1970-1981

Served his apprenticeship with Birmingham City but made his biggest impression in his two spells at Exeter City. The area clearly suited him as Keith has lived there ever since and now works as a postman.

Scored 56 goals in over 200 games for Exeter.

BOWLES, Stan

Man C, Bury, Crewe, Carlisle, QPR, Notts F, Leyton O, Brentford, 1967-1980

One of the game's most colourful characters who never fully realised his potential. Although a real entertainer and fans' favourite, Stan's love of gambling has taken its toll and he was unemployed for a long spell before being invited by David Webb to help out with some coaching at former club, Brentford.

Won five England caps.

BOWYER, Ian

Man C, Leyton O, Notts F, Sunderland, Notts F, Hereford, 1968-1989

Born in Ellesmere Port and started his career with Manchester City. Appointed assistant manager to Peter Shilton at Plymouth Argyle in 1994 and then moved to Rotherham until September 1996. Now coaches at Birmingham.

Won a European Cup winners medal with Forest.

BOYCE, Ronnie

West Ham 1960-1972

A one-club man, who signed professional terms in 1960 having come through the ranks at West Ham. Ronnie then went on to play 275 League games for them over the next twelve years. Appointed chief scout at Upton Park in October 1992. Was axed as part of cost cutting measures in 1996 and was briefly a scout for QPR.

Scored an injury time winner in the 1964 Cup Final.

BOYER, Phil
Derby, York, Bournemouth, Norwich, Southampton, Man C, 1966-1982
Formed a deadly partnership with Ted MacDougall firstly at York, then later at Norwich and Southampton. Won one England cap against Wales in 1976. Phil was assistant manager at Grantham FC from December 1985 until February 1987, but now works as a bank courier as well as acting as a scout for a number of clubs.
Played in a League Cup final for Norwich.

BOYLE, Terry
Tottenham, C Palace, Wimbledon, Bristol C, Newport, Cardiff, Swansea, 1975-1989
Captained both the Welsh schools and youth international teams. Moved into non-league soccer in a £5,000 transfer from Swansea to Merthyr, whom he he rejoined after a spell as player/manager at Barry Town. Is now with Cinderford Town in the Doc Martens League.
Capped twice by Wales in 1981.

BOYLEN, David
Grimsby 1966-1977
Still lives in Grimsby, working as a sales repsentitive for Caxios E & I Ltd. and still plays with a number of other ex-professionals for the 'Tartan Forties' in the Grimsby local league.

BRABROOK, Peter
Chelsea, West Ham, Leyton O, 1954-1970
Full England international who won three caps during his Chelsea days. Ran a butchers shop but now lives in Hornchurch and works for paper tycoon, Neville Ovendon.
A 1964 FA Cup winner.

BRADD, Les
Rotherham, Notts Co, Stockport, Wigan, Bristol R, 1967-1982
After twelve years as promotions manager at Meadow Lane has now crossed the Trent to take up a similar role for Nottingham Forest.

Scored 125 goals in 381 league games for Notts County.

BRADY, Liam
Arsenal, West Ham, 1973-1989
One of the few players to have succeeded abroad, Liam had successful spells with Juventus, Ascoli and Sampadoria in addition to a distinguished career in this country, particularly with Arsenal. Joined Brighton as manager in 1993 having cut his teeth with the mighty Celtic. Left the Goldstone and was later was appointed youth developement officer at Arsenal in August 1996.
Midfield maestro for Ireland.

BRADFORD, Geoff
Bristol R 1949-1963
Bristol Rovers' only full England international, who scored on his one appearance against Denmark in 1955. Played 523 games for Rovers and worked for a company at Avonmouth Oil refinery after his playing days. Died in December 1994, aged 67.
Scored 260 goals for Rovers, a club record.

BRADLEY, Don
WBA, Mansfield, 1943-1961
Now works as an engineer and still lives in Mansfield.

BRADLEY, Warren
Manchester United, Bury, 1958-1963
Joined United shortly after Munich and won a total of three England caps in his short career. Became the headmaster of a Manchester Comprehensive school and is now chairman of the United Former Players Association.
Won the FA Amatuer Cup twice.

BRADSHAW, Paul
Blackburn, Wolves, WBA, Bristol R, Newport Co, WBA, Peterboro, 1973-1990
Goalkeeper who saw action with seven league clubs and won four under-23 caps with England. Currently working as a Security Supervisor and living back in Wolverhampton.
Won the League Cup with Wolves.

BRANFOOT, Ian
Sheff Wed, Doncaster, Lincoln, 1965-1977
Solid right back and veteran of over 300
league games. Joined Sheffield Wednesday
from Gateshead in 1965. Was in charge at
both Reading (1984-1989) and Southampton
(1991-1994) before being offered the vacant
manager's chair at Fulham, moving upstairs
in February 1996.

BRANSTON, Terry
Northampton, Luton, Lincoln, 1960-1972
Centre half who now lives in Rugby where
he runs his own Driving School.
*Played more than 400 league games for three
clubs.*

BRAY, John
Blackburn, Bury, 1954-1965
Blackburn's first team regular full back for
several years in the early sixties. Lives in the
town but has had to retire from work due to
ill health.
*Played in the 1960 FA Cup final for
Blackburn Rovers.*

BRAZIER, Colin
Wolves, Birmingham, Lincoln, Walsall, 1975-
1986
Lives in Tamworth, Staffs and joined
Midland Division side Tamworth in 1995
after three years rest from the game.

BRAZIL, Alan
Ipswich, Tottenham, Man U, Coventry, QPR,
1977-1986
Started at Celtic Boys Club in Glasgow
before moving south to become an apprentice at Ipswich, turning professional in 1977.
Moved to Tottenham for £400,000 in 1983,
then on to Manchester United for £700,000
in June 1984. Won a total of 13 Scotland
caps. Was player/manager at Witham Town,
and then Dartford. Was host at the Black
Adder Inn, Ipswich until he went out of
busines. Now a match summariser on Radio
Five Live.
Won a UEFA Cup winners medal in 1981.

BRECKIN, John
Rotherham, Darlington, Bury, Doncaster,
1971-1983
Played over 400 games for Rotherham in
twelve years from 1971. After spells with
three other clubs, John then returned to
Millmoor as assistant manager.
*Played in The Millers' record FA Cup win
against Spennymoor in December 1977.*

BREMNER, Des
Hibs, Aston V, Birmingham, Fulham, Walsall,
1979-1989
Best known as a member of the successful
Villa side of the early eighties. Retired in
1991 after a spell with Stafford Rangers and
now a working as a financial advisor with
the PFA based in their Birmingham offices.
*Won the League and the European Cup with
Villa.*

BREMNER, Billy
Leeds, Hull, Doncaster, 1959-1981

Made his debut for Leeds United as a seventeen year old alongside Don Revie in 1960,
eventually becoming a key player in the
clubs great successes under his former partner. Appeared for Scotland 54 times and was
voted Player of the Year in 1970. Managed
Leeds from October 1985 until October 1988
and had two spells as boss at Doncaster
Rovers. Now lives in the Doncaster area and
is in regular demand for public appearances.
Captained Leeds to two League

Championships, an FA Cup and two Inter Cities Fairs Cup titles.

BRENNAN, Robert

Luton, Birmingham, Fulham, Norwich, 1947-1959

Inside forward who played five times for Northern Ireland. Now lives in retirement in Norwich, his adopted home since moving to the City from Fulham in 1953.

BRENNAN, Shay

Man U 1957-1969

Republic of Ireland international who played 19 times for his country. Spent fourteen years at Old Trafford after signing professionally in 1955 at the age of 17. Now lives in Tremore, near Waterford, from where he runs his own parcel courier company. Shay has recovered from triple heart bypass surgery, and is the father of five children.
Won two League Championships and was a European Cup winner.

BRIDGES, Barry

Chelsea, Birmingham, QPR, Millwall, Brighton, 1958-1973

A sprint champion who joined Chelsea after winning international honours at school. He was the centre of a controversy which resulting in him being sold to Birmingham City after the 'Doc' dropped him to allow the young Peter Osgood to play regularly – by then he had already won four England caps. Played in South Africa, then managed St Patricks Athletic and Sligo Rovers in Ireland before returning to Norfolk where he took on a milk round and managed a couple of local non-league sides.
Won the league Cup with Chelsea in 1965.

BRIGGS, Max

Norwich, Oxford, 1968-1977

Lives in Norwich, where he has run his own conservatory and double glazing firm since 1990, having been employed in the business since 1978 when he has forced to quit the game with cartilage and ligament trouble.
Won promotion to Division One with Norwich, for the first time, in 1972.

BRIGGS, Tommy

Plymouth, Grimsby, Coventry, Birmingham, Blackburn, Grimsby, 1946-1958

England 'B' international goalscorer who netted 256 times from 392 League appearances. Died on 10th February 1984 at the age of 61 in Grimsby where he had become a butcher.
Netted seven goals in a single game for Blackburn (against Bristol Rovers in 1955) but ironically failed to score in their 9-0 record league win.

BRIGNULL, Phil

West Ham, Bournemouth, Wrexham, Cardiff, Newport Co, 1978-1987

Former West Ham apprentice. Now lives in the Cardiff area and works in the insurance business for Allied Dunbar.

BRILEY, Les

Chelsea, Hereford, Wimbledon, Aldershot, Millwall, Brighton, 1974-1994

Started at Chelsea, but is remembered for his six years as a bustling midfielder with Millwall. Was player/manager of Slough Town until May 1994 and now works for a building business.
Promotted to the First Division with Millwall in 1990.

BRINDLEY, John

Notts For, Notts Co, Gillingham, 1965-1976

Is now a sales manager for a cleaning company and used to manage Ilkeston Town.
A fomer England youth and schoolboy international.

BRISLEY, Terry

Leyton O, Southend, Millwall, Charlton, Portsmouth, 1967-1980

Now lives in Brentwood, Essex and works in the City of London as a Foreign Exchange Broker.

BROADBENT, Peter

Brentford, Wolves, Shrewsbury, Aston V, Stockport, 1950-1969

Was one of Wolves' key players during the fifties and sixties, He also played for the

England under-23 and 'B' sides before winning seven full caps. Now a publican in Codsall, Staffordshire.
League Championship winner three times and FA Cup winner in 1960.

BROADHURST, Kevin
Birmingham, Walsall, 1976-1983
Now on the coaching staff at Birmingham City where he served his apprenticeship and played most of his League football.

BROADIS, Ivor
Carlisle, Sunderland, Man C, Newcastle, Carlisle, 1946-1958
Won 14 England Caps as a goalscoring inside forward. After over 400 League games he became a journalist, but is now retired, living in Carlisle, Cumbria.
Played for Newcastle in the 1955 Cup Final.

BROCK, Kevin
Oxford, QPR, Newcastle, 1979-1994
An England under-21 international who was hailed as a great prospect during his days at Oxford. Big money moves to QPR (£260,000) in 1987 and Newcastle (£300,000) in 1988 followed before dropping into non-league football, initially with Stevenage and then with team-mate Graham Roberts to Yeovil Town. Still registered to Rushden but unable to play because of injuries.
League Cup winner with Oxford in 1986.

BRODIE, Chic
Man C, Gillingham, Aldershot, Wolves, Northampton, Brentford, 1954-1970
Now a taxi driver based in West London.
Scottish Schoolboy International.

BROGAN, James
Celtic, Coventry, Ayr, 1963-1978
A no nonsense tackling full back who was a member of the all conquering Celtic side of the late 60s and early 70s but only won a handful of Scottish caps. Still lives in Glasgow where he runs Wintergill's Bar.
Won an astonishing seven Scottish League Championship medals with Celtic between 1964-1974.

BROMLEY, Brian
Bolton, Portsmouth, Brighton, Reading, Darlington, 1962-1974
Born in Burnley and spent six years with Bolton Wanderers before moving South to play for Portsmouth. Settled in the area and now runs the White Hart public house in nearby Porchester, Hampshire.

BROOKES, Eric
Barnsley, Northampton, Peterborough, 1960-1972
Ended his League days at Peterborough, where he now lives and has a job working at the Cummings Diesel factory.
Played 324 games for Barnsley.

BROOKING, Trevor
West Ham 1967-1983

Trevor spent his 16 year career in professional football with West Ham, making over 500 appearances, scoring nearly 100 goals and gaining FA Cup winners medals in 1975 and 1980. He represented England at all levels, winning his first full international cap in 1974 and making a total of 47 England appearances before retiring after the 1982 World Cup. Trevor is now a regular contributor to Match of the Day and is part of the

commentary team for BBC Radio. In 1989 he was appointed to the Sports Council as the representative of regional chairmen. He runs Colbrook Plastics Ltd, a plastic binding company based in the East End of London and was awarded the MBE for services to football in 1981.
Netted the winner in the 1980 FA Cup final against Arsenal.

BROOME, Frank
Aston V, Derby, Notts Co, Brentford, Crewe, 1934-1954
England international forward who won seven caps. Finished playing in 1954 and went on to manage Notts County, Exeter and Southend as well as coaching in Ireland, Australia and the Middle East. Died in 1994.
Division Two Championship medal in 1938.

BROTHERSTON, Noel
Spurs, Blackburn, Bury, Scarborough, 1972-1989
A Northern Ireland international who became a painter and decorator when his career ended. Died suddenly of a heart attack in May 1995.
Won 27 caps for Northern Ireland.

BROWN, Alistair
Leicester, WBA, C Palace, Walsall, Port V, 1968-1986
Played over 250 games for the 'Baggies'. Became a publican at The Beech Tree Public House, Aldridge, but is now landlord of the Throstles Club in West Bromwich.
Leading scorer in Leicester's 1971 Second Division Championship winning side.

BROWN, Allan
Blackpool, Luton, Portsmouth, 1950-1962
Joined Blackpool form East Fife and won fourteen full Scottish caps. Went on to manage Wigan, Torquay, Bury, Notts Forest, Southport and had a stint in Qatar before returning to his first club, Blackpool. Remained in the area, living in retirement in nearby Lytham St Anne's, until he died in March 1996.

BROWN, Bill
Dundee, Tottenham, Northampton, 1949-1967
Probably Scotland's greatest post-war goalkeeper. Ended his career in Canada, moved back to England briefly but soon returned. Retired last year from a job in the land department of the Ontario Government.
A Spurs double-winner.

BROWN, John
Plymouth Argyle, Bristol Rovers, 1960-1968
An inside forward who had an unsuccessful trial with Arsenal but went on to play over 150 games for Rovers. Now lives and works on a farm near Bodmin, Cornwall.
Played in front of a crowd of 56,000 fans at an FA Cup tie at Old Trafford.

BROWN, Tony
WBA, Torquay, 1963-1982
A lethal finisher, Tony scored 217 goals for West Brom before a spell in the USA and finally Torquay. Won one full England cap. In a 17 year career he became the proud possessor of West Brom's appearance and goal scoring records. Returned to the Hawthorns as coach (1984-6) and held the same post at Birmingham (1987-9). He has had hip replacement operations and still keeps in touch with the game by attending all of West Brom's home games.
An FA Cup winner in 1968 with WBA.

BROWN, David
Middlesboro, Plymouth, Oxford, Bury, Preston, Scunthorpe, Halifax, 1977-1990
Well travelled goalkeeper. Now works at Manchester airport.

BROWN, Eddie
Preston, Southampton, Coventry, Birmingham, Leyton O, 1948-1960
Brown, one of the great clowns of the game, caused havoc to many opposing defences with roving tactics. He will probably be best remembered for shaking hands with the corner flag after scoring. After his playing days he became a schoolteacher and during his ten years as games master at Preston

Catholic School discovered Mark Lawrenson. Now describes himself as 'sublimely' retired and enjoying golf twice a week.
Played in the 1955 FA Cup final when Birmingham lost to Manchester City.

BROWN, Jim

Chesterfield, Sheff U, Cardiff, Chesterfield, 1972-1988
Played four times for Scotland at under-23 level and won one full cap. Enjoyed several spells playing in the North American League, where in 1981, with Washington Diplomats, he became the first keeper to score a goal. Now commercial manager at Chesterfield.

BROWN, Laurie

Darlington, Northampton, Arsenal, Tottenham, Norwich, Bradford, 1958-1969
Became a manager in non-league soccer with Kings Lynn and then Altrincham, before becoming a publican. Now lives in Shildon where he is working in a milk business.
Capped 14 times as an England Amateur International.

BROWN, Ken

West Ham, Torquay, 1952-1968
Went on to manage Plymouth but is now director of a Norwich Sports Centre. Son Kenny plays for his old club, West Ham, and daughter Amanda was a professional tennis player.
Played in FA Cup and Cup Winners Cup victories for he Hammers.

BROWN, Roger

Bournemouth, Norwich, Fulham, Bournemouth, 1977-1986
Made a name for himself in non-league football before moving into the League as a powerful central defender. Went on to manage Colchester.

BROWN, Sandy

Everton, Shrewsbury, Southport, 1963-1972
This popular Scottish defender went on to run a boarding house in Blackpool and was still enjoying his football with Blackpool Rangers in the West Lancs league after his 40th birthday. Now works in the Peak Frean factory and still lives on the Fylde.

BROWN Steve

Millwall 1970-74
A wing man who found first-team chances hard to come by. Drifted out of the game and now works in a flower market.

BROWN, Willie

Burnley, Carlisle, Barrow, Newport, Hereford, Brentford, Torquay, 1968-1977
Scottish born striker who started with Burnley then moved steadily further south, ending up at Torquay. Willie is now manager of a newsagents business in Minehead, Somerset.
Played 350 League games.

BROWNLIE, John

Hibs Newcastle, Middlesboro, Hartlepool, Berwick Rangers, 1978-1984
Defender who won seven Scottish caps during his playing days is now back in Scotland and was on the coaching staff at Clyde until September 1995.
Scottish League Cup winner in 1973 with Hibs.

BROWNSWORD, Jack

Hull, Scunthorpe, 1946-1964
Played a full 15 seasons for Scunthorpe Utd and was described by Bill Shankly as the best full-back never to play for England. Now retired in the area after many years as a representative for Solaglas, Glass & Glazing.
Club record of 600 appearances for Scunthorpe.

BRUCK, Dietmar

Coventry, Charlton, Northampton, 1960-1973
German full back who made his home in Britain and still lives in Coventry - where he started as an eighteen-year-old and played for the greater part of his career. Held non-league management positions at Weymouth and then Redditch and has been a financial

consultant for an insurance company for the past seventeen years.
Won promotion to Division One with Coventry.

BRUSH, Paul
West Ham, C Palace, Southend, 1977-1989
Former West Ham apprentice who ended his career at Southend United. Was a teacher until former West Ham team-mate Pat Holland offered him the chance to become Director of Coaching at Leyton Orient.
Substitute in the 1980 FA Cup final.

BRYCELAND, Tommy
St Mirren, Norwich, Oldham, St Mirren, 1956-1974
Joined Norwich City from St Mirren in 1962 and went on to play over 250 games for the Canaries, becoming one of the all time greats in the club's history. Has now returned to Scotland where he runs the Craiglea Hotel in Ayrshire.
Scottish Cup winner with St Mirren.

BUCHAN, Charles
Sunderland, Arsenal, 1909-1928
England international who was considered to be one of the best players of his time. Went into journalism upon retirement from the game and in 1951 was appointed editor of the newly launched 'Football Monthly' which still carried his name long after his death in 1960.
Won a League Championship medal and FA Cup runners-up medal in the same season.

BUCHAN, Martin
Aberdean, Man Utd, Oldham, 1971-1984
Born and bred in Aberdeen, captained his local side at the age of 20 to victory in the Scottish Cup final of 1970. When he was transferred to Manchester United in March 1972 he cost a then club record fee of £125,000. He then led United back into Division One in 1974-5 after their dramatic drop into the second and three F.A. Cup finals in four years, gaining a winners medal in 1977. Moved to Oldham in August 1983 but was forced to retired through injury in

October 1984, briefly becoming manager at Burnley. Now lives in Sale, Cheshire and works as a promotions manager for Puma.
Became the first Captain to lift the Scottish and English Cups.

BUCHANAN, John
Northampton, Cardiff, Northampton, 1970-1982
A former forward who now manges Ross County in Scotland.
Made 400 League appearances.

BUCK, Tony
Oxford, Newport, Rochdale, Bradford C, Northampton, 1962-1973
A centre forward who still lives in Northampton where he is a factory worker.

BUCKINGHAM, Vic
Tottenham 1935-1948
Joined Spurs in 1935 and played for them either side of the war, making over 200 league appearances. Managed Bradford Park Avenue, then led WBA to FA Cup and Division One runners up in his first season. Died January 1995.

BUCKLEY, Alan
Notts F, Walsall, Birmingham, Walsall, 1971-1984
Became manager of Walsall and also had a spell as the helm of Kettering Town before returning to management with Grimsby Town. He then took over at West Bromwich Albion in November 1994.
Took Grimsby out of the Fourth and Third Division in successive seasons.

BUCKLEY, Steve
Luton, Derby, Lincoln, 1974-1986
Luton Town lifted Steve from non-league football in 1974 but it was during his time at Derby County that he really made his name following a £165,000 move in 1978. Now lives in Long Eaton and scouts for his brother, Alan.

BULLESS, Brian
Hull 1952-1963

Lives in Hull, close to Boothferry Park, where he starred for thirteen years in the fifties. Works for a local building firm.
Played 327 games for Hull.

BULLIVANT, Terry
Fulham, Aston V Charlton, Brentford, 1974-1985
Lambeth born midfielder who played most of his football in the capital. Was briefly caretaker manager of Barnet in October 1996 where he still coaches.

BULLOCK, Norman
Chester 1952-1959
Was a regular for Chester City in the fifties. Lives and works in Chester – as a builder.
Played 190 games scoring 41 goals.

BUMPSTEAD, David
Luton, Millwall, Bristol Rovers, 1956-1966
A former England amatuer international who manged a couple of sides in Essex before taking over an off-license in Romford.
Played for Millwall when they were Fourth Division Champions in 1962.

BUNN, Frankie
Luton, Hull, Oldham, 1980-1989
Forced to quit through injury whilst playing for Oldham. Now community officer at Wigan Athletic. Plays for Radcliffe Borough in the Unibond League.
Set a record when he scored six goals against Scarborough for Oldham in the League Cup.

BURGESS, Ron
Tottenham, Swansea, 1938-1955
Signed by Tottenham just before the war and was an automatic choice for both club and country. Played for Great Britain against the Rest of Europe in 1947. Ron returned home to Swansea in 1954, becoming player-manager, returning to the London area to become Watford boss and then working as a stock controller and then a warehouseman. Now retired to Worthing, his birthplace.
Captained the great Spurs side which won Division One & Two titles in the early 1950s.

BURKETT, Jack
West Ham, Charlton, 1961-1969
Was assistant manager at Fulham and now lives in Southend where he organises educational programmes for youth training scheme clubs.
A member of West Ham's FA Cup and Cup Winners Cup sides.

BURGIN, Ted
Sheff U, Doncaster, Leeds, Rochdale, 1949-1965
England 'B' international goalie who played over 500 league games between 1949 and 1965. Was employed by Rochdale Council but has now retired and lives on the Fylde.
Played in the 1962 League Cup final for Rochdale.

BURKINSHAW, Keith
Liverpool, Workington, Scunthorpe, 1953-1967
Keith joined Liverpool from non-league Denaby United in 1953. However, after only one game he moved to Workington where he became a first team regular notching up almost 300 appearances. High profile coaching and management roles since have included six years at Tottenham and more recently a spell at West Brom.
Managed Spurs to two FA Cup finals.

BURLEY, George
Ipswich, Sunderland, Gillingham, 1973-1988
A Scottish under-23 international who made a memorable league debut when, at the age of seventeen, he marked George Best at Old Trafford. Joined Sunderland after twelve successful years at Portman Road and appointed manager of Colchester in May 1994, having had spells as manager of Ayr and coach at Motherwell. In January 1995 his career completed full circle when he returned to Ipswich as manager.
FA Cup winner with Ipswich in 1978.

BURNETT, Dennis
West Ham, Millwall, Hull, Millwall, Brighton, 1965-1976 .
After spending four successful years with

Ilauger in Norway, during which time the club achieved promotion twice, won the Cup and qualified for Europe, Dennis returned home and has run a building/decorating business in Brighton for the past fourteen years.
A League Cup runner up with West Ham in 1966.

BURNS, Michael
Newcastle, Preston, Ipswich, 1927-1951
Had a twenty-four year career as a keeper either side of the war. Died in 1982.

BURNS, Micky
Blackpool, Newcastle, Cardiff, Middlesboro, 1969-1980
An England amateur international while with Skelmersdale, Micky signed for Blackpool in 1969 and went on to play professionally for eleven years. Now works for the Professional Footballers Association.
Scored 116 goals during his 379 league game career.

BURNS, Francis
Man Utd, Southampton Preston, 1967-1980
Spent seven years at Manchester United before a £50,000 move in 1972 took him to Southampton. Now lives in Perth, where he runs his own cleaning business, having emigrated to Australia in 1987.
Picked up one cap for Scotland, against Austria in 1969.

BURNS, Kenny
Birmingham, Notts F, Leeds, Derby, Notts C, Barnsley, 1971-1985

A Scottish international who hails from Glasgow but came to England to join Birmingham as a youngster. Developed through their apprentice ranks and made 170 league appearances for the St Andrews club before moving to Notts Forest in July 1977. Voted Footballer of the Year by the Football Writers' Association at the end of 1977/8 season. Won 20 Scotland caps. Now licensee of a pub in Stoke on Trent.
League Championship winner followed by two European Cup winners medals.

BURNSIDE, Dave
WBA, Southampton, C Palace, Wolves, Plymouth, Bristol C, Colchester, 1957-1971
Now lives in Bristol and works as Regional Director for the FA programme of excellence. Had two spells as manager of the England youth team in 1983/4 and from 1989 to 1993.
Played once at under-23 level for England.

BURROWS, Adrian
Mansfield, Northampton, Plymouth, 1979-1992
Central defender who was the mainstay of many a Plymouth defence. Played for Great Mills Western League side Elmore before joining Taunton Town in 1995/6 season.

BURROWS, Frank
Raith, Scunthorpe, Swindon, Mansfield, 1965-1973
Scunthorpe brought Frank into the league from Raith in 1965 but he made his name at Swindon. Progressed into management with Cardiff, then achieved promotion in the first of his two spells at Portsmouth. Returned to Wales in 1991 to take over at Swansea but was sacked in early 1996. Was soon back in business as reserve team boss at West Ham.
A League Cup winner with Swindon in 1969.

BURTENSHAW, Steve
Brighton 1952-1966
A wing half who spent fourteen years at Brighton as a player. Managed QPR then worked for Arsenal as Chief Scout until he was sacked in August 1996. Now back at Loftus Road as Chief Scout.

Played 237 League games for Brighton.

BURTON, Alwyn Ollie

Newport, Norwich, Newcastle, 1958-1971
Won nine Welsh caps. After retiring in 1972
due to a knee injury, he was employed as a
brewery representative then set up a sandwich bar he now runs in Diss, Norfolk.
*Won League Cup and Fairs Cup winners
medals.*

BURVILL, Glen

Aldershot, Reading, Fulham, Aldershot,
1983-1990
Former West Ham apprentice who had two
separate spells at Aldershot and is now playing for Newhaven FC in the Sussex League.
*Played for Aldershot in their last ever League
game.*

BUSBY, Martin

QPR, Portsmouth, Notts Co, QPR, Burnley,
1970-1979
Brother of Viv, had a spell as manager of
Beaconsfield, ran a pub and is now joint
manager of non league Maidenhead.
Former England Youth International.

BUSBY, Sir Matt

Manchester City, Liverpool, 1928-1939
Died on 20th January 1994, just eight
months after his beloved Manchester United
won their first League title in 25 years.
Started his career with Manchester City in
1928 before moving on to Liverpool in 1936
for £8,000. Became Manchester United manager in 1945 and over the next 24 years won
five league titles, the F.A. Cup twice. Later
became a Director and Club President, having survived the Munich air crash which
wiped out much of his team that stood on
the verge of greatness. Looked upon as a
father figure at Old Trafford, and 'Sir Matt
Busby Way' at the ground is a permanent
tribute to his memory. One of football's true
greats.
*Managed Manchester United when they
won the Champions Cup in 1968 and was
Knighted in the same year.*

BUSBY, Viv

Luton, Newcastle, Fulham, Norwich, Stoke,
Sheff U, Blackburn, York, 1969-1983
After thirteen years and numerous clubs,
including two terms with Tulsa in America,
Viv became assistant manager at
Sunderland, then manager at Hartlepool in
February 1993. Since then worked for Metro
Radio in Newcastle, summarising on
Sunderland matches. Did some scouting for
West Bromwich Albion and Southampton,
until appointed to the Sheffield United
coaching staff.
*FA Cup runners up medal with Fulham in
1975.*

BUTCHER, Terry

Ipswich, Coventry, 1977-1990
After spells as manager at Coventry and
then Sunderland, former England international defender (77 caps) Terry decided to
change direction and now runs an eighteenth century hotel, 'The Old Manor Hotel',
in Bridge of Allen, near Stirling in Scotland.
He still has many football connections
including his weekly column in the Scottish
Daily Express, and his regular commentaries
on Radio Clyde and Sky Television's sports
channel.
UEFA Cup winner with Ipswich in 1981.

BUTLER, Ernie

Portsmouth 1946-1952
Pompey's goalkeeper during some of their
great years in the late forties. Ran a fruit &
vegetable shop, then was licensee of the
George & Dragon pub in the city for 18 years
before his retirement.
Won two League Championship medals.

BUTLER, Geoff

Middlesboro, Chelsea, Sunderland, Norwich,
Bournemouth, Peterborough, 1965-1981
Experienced full back, now manager of both
team affairs and the commercial department
at Salisbury City in the Beazer Homes
League.
*Won a Second Division Championship medal
and played in the 1973 League Cup final.*

BUTLER, Joe

Newcastle, Swindon, Aldershot, 1963-1977
Loyal servant to Swindon, for whom he
turned out on over 350 occasions. Now runs
a taxi firm in the same Wiltshire town.
*Played for Swindon in the 1969 League Cup
final.*

BUXTON, Mick

Burnley, Halifax, 1962-1970
Became player/coach at Halifax town before
holding coaching positions at Southend,
Sunderland, and Wimbledon. Moved into
management with Huddersfield and
Scunthorpe united before taking over at at
Sunderland in November 1993. He retained
this post until March 1995 but is now
manager of Scunthorpe
*Division One Championship with Burnley in
1960.*

BYRNE, Gerry

Liverpool 1957-1968
England international left back who played
273 League matches for his only club,
Liverpool. Worked as an odd-job-man at
Pontins, Prestatyn, but had to give up work
due to bad knees. Lives in Aintree.
*Played in two Championship winning sides
and broke his collar bone in the opening
minutes of the 1965 Cup final.*

BYRNE, Johnny

C Palace, West Ham, C Palace, Fulham,
1956-1968
Known as 'Budgie', Byrne, was capped by
England when playing third division soccer
for Crystal Palace, being transferred soon
after to West Ham in March 1962 for £58,000
plus a player, a then record between British
clubs. Played 11 times for England. Moved
to South Africa to manage Hellenic and has
lived there ever since.
*Part of West Ham's 1964 FA Cup winning
side.*

BYRNE, Roger

Man Utd, 1951-1957
Byrne joined United at the age of 20 and

went on to captain the Busby Babes. He won
33 England caps before he and his team
mates were struck down in the Munich air
disaster of 1958.
*Won three Football League Championship
medals.*

BYRNE, Tony

Millwall, Southampton, Hereford, Newport,
1963-1978
Finished his playing career at Hereford
United and went on to become foreman of a
golf course in the area.
*Republic of Ireland defender who won four-
teen caps for his country.*

CALLAGHAN, Ian

Liverpool, Swansea, Crewe, 1959-1981

Callaghan featured in the great Liverpool
sides of the 1960s and 1970s during which
time he won five Championship medals as
well as two FA Cup, two European Cup,
UEFA Cup and Super Cup winners medals.
Ian played four times for England and was
voted 'Football Writers Player of the Year' in
1974. He lives in Ormskirk and runs the
'Hesketh' public house in Rufford, that he
owns with his friend and old Liverpool team-
mate, Geoff Strong. In between this and his
part-time role on the Littlewoods Pools
Panel, he manages to play the occasional
round of golf with Roger Hunt and Ron
Yeats.
*Holder of the Liverpool club appearance
record of 640 games.*

CALLAGHAN, Fred
Fulham 1963-1973
Ex-Fulham full back and Brentford manager. Now a London taxi driver and manages ICIS League Carshalton after spending many years at Wealdstone.
Played 291 League games for Fulham.

CALLAGHAN, Nigel
Watford, Derby, Aston V, Derby, Watford, Huddersfield, 1980-1991
Spent six months running a disco on the island of Corfu after a spell in South Africa as player/manager of Hellenic FC. Now returned to the UK and passed his FA preliminary coaching badge.
Helped England win the 1984 UEFA Cup under-21 tournament.

CAMPBELL, Bobby
Liverpool, Portsmouth, Aldershot, 1958-1966
Started as a player with Liverpool but made his name as a manager at Portsmouth (1982-4) and then Chelsea (1988-91). Bobby is now coaching in Saudi Arabia.
Lead Portsmouth to the Division Three Championship in 1983.

CAMPBELL, Dave
Wrexham 1964-1966
Played 41 games for Wrexham in a one-club spell. Now works as a process worker for a fibreglass company and still lives in the Wrexham area.

CAMPBELL, Jock
Charlton 1946-1957
Full back who played 255 games for Charlton Athletic. Died in 1983.
Played in the Addicks record League and Cup wins.

CANNELL, Paul
Newcastle, Mansfield, 1973-1982
A Geordie born forward who now runs his own Tyneside Printing Company.

CANNON, Jim
C Palace 1972-1987
Went on to manage Dulwich Hamlet in the Diadora League. Now concentrates on running his own roofing business in Howley, Surrey.
Holds the Eagles record for most number of games played (572).

CANNOVILLE, Paul
Chelsea, Reading, 1981-1987
Played non-league football with Northwood and Egham after quitting the professional game because of injury. Attracted media attention when he was involved in a court case for a drugs problem but is now back playing for Erich.

CANTELLO, Len
WBA, Bolton, Hereford, Bury, 1968-1986
Played in over 360 games for West Brom and retired in 1986. He then became assistant manager at Stockport, managed Radcliffe Borough, then scouted for Peterborough.
Eight England caps at under-23 level.

CANTWELL, Noel
West Ham, Man U, 1952-1966
Full back who was capped 36 times by the Republic of Ireland. After managing Peterborough he remained in the area and runs the New Inn public house.
Skippered Manchester United to the 1963 FA Cup.

CARBERRY, Robert
Norwich, Gillingham, Port Vale, Exeter, 1949-1958
A retired Engineer who lives in Jersey. His son plays for Jersey Scottish.
Waited almost five years to make his debut, against Leyton Orient in 1953.

CAREY, Johnny
Manchester Utd 1936-1953
Held management jobs with a number of clubs – Blackburn (twice), Everton, Leyton Orient and Notts Forest. Played over 300 games for United and was capped by Northern Ireland and the Republic. Scouted for the club he loved until his retirement in 1985 when he was working for the Borough Treasurer's office in Sale, Cheshire. Died in

August 1995 aged 76.
In a four year period from 1948 skippered United to FA Cup success, a League title and voted Footballer of the Year.

CARLIN, Willie
Liverpool, Halifax, Carlisle, Sheff U, Derby, Leicester, Notts Co, Cardiff, 1959-1973
Moved to the island of Majorca where he runs a bar/restaurant in Cala Bona.

CARLING, Terry
Leeds, Lincoln, Walsall, Chester, 1956-1970
Found opportunities few and far between at Leeds. Ended his career with Chester and continued to live in the town working as a milkman.

CARR, Graham
Northampton, York, Bradford PA, 1962-1969
Managed Northampton then took over at Kettering in 1992. Relinquished this role in May 1995 to take over at BHL side Weymouth before moving to Dagenham & Redbridge for a largely unsuccessful spell when he was replaced just before the end of the 1995-96 season.
Took Northampton to the Fourth Division title 1987.

CARR, Willie
Coventry, Wolves, Millwall, 1967-1982
A Scottish international (6 caps) who ended his career at Millwall before joining non-league Worcester City. Now lives near Wolverhampton and has been a salesman selling nuts & bolts for the same company for the past fourteen years.
Won Second Division Championship (Coventry) and League Cup winners medal (Wolves).

CARRODUS, Frank
Man C, Aston V, Wrexham, Birmingham, Bury, 1969-1983
Had three knee operations in his fourteen year career. Now lives in Altrincham, Cheshire, where he runs his own company organising corporate hospitality and is still involved with the former-Manchester City

players charity team.
Won two League Cup winners medals during his time with Aston Villa.

CARTER, Raich
Sunderland, Derby, Hull, 1932-1951
One of England's greatest inside forwards, he played for England for 14 years in the 1930s and 1940s. Raich also excelled at other sports, playing Cricket for Derbyshire and Durham. He suffered a stroke in 1987 and died at home aged 80, in October 1994.
Captained Sunderland when they won the FA Cup in 1937.

CARTWRIGHT, John
West Ham, C Palace, 1959-1962
Played only a handful of League games, but has become a most accomplished youth coach who worked with Charlton Athletic before leaving for the Middle East. He is now back from his third stint coaching Sporting Club Kuwait.
Managed the England Youth team.

CARTWRIGHT, Les
Coventry, Wrexham, Camb U, Southend, 1973-1983
Played in midfield or on the wing. Retired in 1985 to take a sub post office in Wolvey, Leics but remains connected to the game by helping out at Coventry with the under-14s.
Capped seven times by Wales between 1974 and 1979.

CASE, Jimmy
Liverpool, Brighton, Southampton, Bournemouth, Halifax, Wrexham, Darlington, Brighton, 1973-1995
A midfield star with a thumping shot who played his best football at Liverpool. Appointed manager of Brighton in November 1995.
Won four League Championships, three European Cups and a UEFA Cup.

CASHLEY, Ray
Bristol City, Hereford, Bristol Rovers, Chester, Bristol City, 1970-1987
Started at City as a left back but moved to

goalkeeper for part of a game due to injury, staying in that position for 14 years. Now lotteries manager for Weston-Super-Mare. *Won promotion to the First Division with Bristol City in 1976.*

CASPER, Frank

Rotherham, Burnley, 1962-1975
Manager at his former club, Burnley, from January 1989 until his resignation in 1992. Now owns a retail clothing business in the area.
Promotion to the First Division with Burnley in 1971.

CASSIDY, Nigel

Norwich, Scunthorpe Oxford, Cambridge, 1967-1975
Lives in Oxfordshire where he is still involved in non-league football coaching Thame.

CASSIDY, Tommy

Newcastle, Burnley, 1970-1982
A Northern Ireland international midfield player who won 24 caps and had a spell managing a side in Cyprus. He returned in June 1994 to manage Irish side Glentoran.
Played for Newcastle in two Wembley defeats.

CATON, Tommy

Man C, Arsenal, Oxford, Charlton, 1979-1990
Made his league debut for Man City, aged 16, and was later sold to Arsenal for £500,000. Collapsed and died at his home near Oxford in April 1993, aged 30, whilst a Charlton player.
Played for Manchester City in the 1981 FA Cup Final.

CATTERICK, Harry

Everton, Crewe, 1946-1952
A distinguished career for Everton, as manager and player. Died in the Main Stand at Goodison Park while watching an FA Cup tie in March 1985.
Took Everton to League Championship titles in 1963 and 1970.

CATTLIN, Chris

Huddersfield, Coventry, Brighton, 1964-1978
Has been out of football since leaving Brighton in 1986 after two years as manager. He now owns property in Brighton, including an hotel, flats and some shops on the seafront. During his managerial days he once signed Dean Saunders for the price of his train ticket, which cost £18!

CAVENER, Phil

Burnley, Bradford C, Gillingham, Northampton, Peterboro, 1979-1985
Now a health centre manager, living in Sandy, Beds. Assistant manager at Arseley Town.

CAWSTON, Mervyn

Norwich, Southend, Newport, Gillingham, Southend, Stoke, Southend, 1970-1984
Had three separate spells at Southend playing over 200 games. Marvyn now plays for Southend Manor in the Essex Senior League and works as an Independent Financial Adviser.
Kept 25 clean sheets in the 1980/1 season.

CEGIELSKI, Wayne

Northampton, Wrexham, Port V, Hereford, 1973-1986
Started his career at Tottenham and also played for Stuttgart in Germany, Tacoma Tides in USA and Umes in Sweden. Now lives in the Potteries where he is employed as a sales rep.

CHADWICK, David

Southampton, Middlesboro, Halifax, Bournemouth, Torquay, Gillingham, 1961-1974
A Southampton junior who went on to play League soccer for six clubs. Now coaching in the United States.

CHAMBERS, Brian

Sunderland, Arsenal, Luton, Millwall, Bournemouth, Halifax, 1970-1980
Well travelled midfielder who is currently Manager of BHL League outfit, Poole Town.

C

CHANNON, Mick
Southampton, Man C, Southampton, Newcastle, Bristol R, Norwich, Portsmouth, 1965-1985

Made his debut in 1966 and formed a deadly partnership with Ron Davies. Mick played nearly 500 games for the Saints during two spells, scoring close to 200 goals and gaining 46 England caps. Now known as a very successful racehorse trainer based at his stables in Berkshire.
Won an FA Cup winners medal in 1976 against Man United.

CHAPMAN, Bob 'Sammy'
Notts F, Notts Co, Shrewsbury, 1963-1979
Played almost 350 games while at the City Ground. Now licensee of a pub in East Leake, Leics.
Promoted with Notts Forest to the First Division in 1972.

CHAPMAN, Lee
Stoke, Plymouth, Arsenal, Sunderland, Sheffield Wednesday, Notts Forest, Leeds, Portsmouth, West Ham Southend, Ipswich, Leeds, Swansea, 1978-1996.
A well travelled striker who won one cap for England at under-21 and 'B' level. Quit the game to run a wine bar in Chelsea and does media work as well. Married to 'Men Behaving Badly' star Leslie Ash.
Won a League Championship medal with Leeds in 1992.

CHAPMAN, Les
Oldham, Huddersfield, Oldham, Stockport, Bradford C, Rochdale, Stockport, Preston, 1966-1987
A playing career which spanned twenty years and eight clubs. Was reserve team boss at Man City until the summer of 1996.
Played over 700 League games.

CHAPMAN, Roy
Aston V, Lincoln, Mansfield, Lincoln, Port V, Chester, 1953-1969
Father of Lee who played in all four divisions over 20 years. Died in 1983.
On average scored a goal (200 in total) every other game.

CHAPPELL, Les
Rotherham, Blackburn, Reading, Doncaster, Swansea, 1965-1977
Now in industrial cleaning and living in Torquay.
Played for Swansea in their record league win at Hartlepool in 1978.

CHARLES, Clive
West Ham, Cardiff, 1971-1976
The younger brother of star player John. Now lives in America where he coaches in Oregon.

CHARLES, Jeremy
Swansea, QPR, Oxford, 1976-1986
Welsh international winger who played 224 games for Swansea before moving on to QPR and then Oxford. Son of Mel, Jeremy is now working as an insurance salesman.

CHARLES, John
West Ham 1962-1969
Retired aged 26 and set up a fruit and vegetable business. Unfortunately his health failed when the business collapsed but he is now on the mend.

CHARLES, John
Leeds, Cardiff, 1948-1965

'Gentle Giant', John's regular goal scoring earned him 38 Welsh caps, the first just after his 18th birthday. Had two spells in Italy, joining Juventus for a world record £65,000 but finished his career in his native Wales, at Cardiff. In 1973 he became youth coach at Swansea but left three years later to take on a pub in Leeds. He now looks after the toy department of the children's shop which he runs with his wife.
Won three Championship medals and was voted Italy's Footballer of the year.

CHARLES, Mel
Swansea, Arsenal, Cardiff, Port V, 1952-1966

Signed for Swansea City in 1952 and ended his playing days at Port Vale fourteen years later, having won 31 Welsh caps along the way. Upon retirement Mel ran a wholesale food business back in Swansea then later became involved in Swansea Council's Sport for the Unemployed scheme.
Played for Wales in the 1958 World Cup finals.

CHARLTON, Jack
Leeds 1952-1972
Jack retired at the age of 37 after winning FA Cup, League Championship, League Cup and Fairs Cup medals – not to mention being a World Cuip winner in 1966. He moved into management with Middlesbrough, Newcastle and Sheffield Wednesday before becoming the most successful Republic of Ireland manger in their history. In 1994, in recognition of his success in the World Cup of that year, Jack was granted the freedom of the city of Dublin – the first Englishman to be awarded such an honour this century. He quit after the Republic failed to qualify for Euro '96 to release time to follow his other interests – most notably fishing.
Leeds club record of 629 games.

CHARLTON, Bobby CBE
Man Utd, Preston NE, 1956-1974
A survivor of the Munich air crash, Bobby went on to win honours galore and become a national institution: two League Championship medals, an FA Cup winners medal, footballer of the year. He joined Manchester United in 1953 and scored twice on his debut in October 1956 – also scoring on his international debut two years later. He was awarded the CBE for services to football and was knighted in 1994. His playing career ended at Preston where he was player/manager. He is still involved with soccer as a director of Manchester United and runs his own highly successful sports school which started with football but now runs courses in 35 different sports !
Played 106 times for England, including the 1966 World Cup final.

CHARLTON, Stanley

Leyton O, Arsenal, Leyton O, 1952-1964
Was secretary/manager at Weymouth
between 1965 and 1972 but now works as a
district manager for a major pools company.
*Played for Great Britain in the 1952 Olympic
Games.*

CHARNELY, Ray

Blackpool, Preston, Wrexham, Bradford PA,
1957-1969
Prolific goal scorer, netting 193 times in 363
games for Blackpool. Now in business as a
painter and decorator.
Capped once by England, v France in 1963.

CHATHAM, Ray

Wolves, Notts C, 1946-1958
Although retired from a career as a mechani-
cal engineer, Ray is now President of
Sanderstead Cricket Club, having previously
held the posts of Captain and Club
Chairman.

CHATTERLEY, Lew

Aston V, Doncaster, Northampton, Grimsby,
Southampton, Torquay, 1962-1976
Formally assistant manager at Southampton
who he left in 1996.

CHEADLE, Tom

Port V, Crewe, 1946-1958
Joined Port Vale from the North Staffordshire
regiment. Now retired, living in Newcastle
under Lyme.
Played 332 games for Port Vale.

CHEESEBROUGH, Albert

Burnley, Leicester City, Port Vale, Mansfield,
1952-1965
After retiring from the game he had a spell
as Lancashire scout for Plymouth Argyle. Is
now a Southport businessman. Daughter
Susan became an international gymnast.
*Played in the 1961 FA Cup final but ended
on the losing side.*

CHEESLEY, Paul

Norwich, Bristol City, 1970-1977

Stayed in the west country when his career
ended, living in Whitchurch where he is a
salesman for a building company.
Promoted to Division One with York City.

CHERRY, Trevor

Huddersfield, Leeds, Bradford C, 1966-1984

Trevor missed less than 40 matches in nine
years at Leeds and won 27 England caps.
Became player/manger at Bradford City and
guided them to promotion into the second
division in 1985. Now runs a sports promotion company, SLP Consultancy, in
Huddersfield.
Won a League Championship medal in 1973.

CHIEDOZIE, John

Leyton O, Notts C, Tottenham, Derby, Notts
C, Chesterfield, 1976-1989
Started as an apprentice with Orient but big
money moves took him to Notts County
(£450,000) and Spurs (£375,000). Now runs a
company supplying bouncy castles, based in
the New Forest.
A Nigerian international.

CHILTON, Allenby

Man U, Grimsby, 1946-1956
England international centre half who
played 352 league games for Man United

before leaving to take over as player/manager of Grimsby Town. Now lives in retirement in Sunderland.
FA Cup winner in 1948.

CHILTON, Chris
Hull, Coventry, 1960-1971
Played 441 games for Hull City even though his career was ended prematurely by injury. Now works as a signwriter in Hull.
195 League goals scored is a Hull record.

CHIVERS, Martin
Southampton, Tottenham, Norwich, Brighton, 1962-1979
Martin scored over 200 league goals in his career – consistency which earned him 24 England caps. Now mine host at the Brookmans Park Hotel in Hertfordshire. Can also be regularly heard on Radio 5 Live and organises the ex-Spurs Charity XI.
Scored both goals in the 1971 League Cup final against Aston Villa.

CHRISTIE, Derrick
Northampton, Camb U, Reading, Cardiff, Peterboro, 1973-1986
Now a government clerk, living in Deeping St James.

CHRISTIE, Trevor
Leicester, Notts C, Notts F, Derby, Man C, Walsall, Mansfield, 1977-1990
Now a salesman in Mansfield and still playing non-league soccer, currently for Arnold Town.

CHUNG, Sammy
Reading, Norwich, Watford, 1953-1964
Played 220 League games for Watford before developing into a widely respected coach. Had a spell as boss at Wolves and then coach at Stoke, then managed Doncaster Rovers until August 1996.
Manager when Wolves were Second Division champions in 1977.

CHURCH, John
Norwich, Colchester, 1936-1950
Career spanned either side of the last war.

Lived in Lowestoft after spending 30 years as the UK representative for a London gold and silver company.

CLAESEN, Nico
Tottenham 1986-1988
Two years at Spurs between 1986-1988 making 50 appearances. Belgian international who joined FC Oostende from Royal Antwerp in the 1994/5 season.
Played in the 1987 FA Cup final.

CLAMP, Eddie
Wolves, Arsenal, Stoke, Peterborough, 1953-1964
Died in December 1995 after spending his last years living in Wednesfield, Wolverhampton working as a self employed builder and decorator.
Two League championships with Wolves.

CLAPTON, Daniel
Arsenal, Luton, 1954-1962
Became a publican in Hackney but had suffered with his health since retiring from soccer and died in June 1986 at the age of 52.

CLARK, Brian
Bristol C, Huddersfield, Cardiff, Bournemouth, Millwall, Cardiff, Newport, 1960-1978
Scored the first ever League goal on a Sunday while playing for Millwall. On the way to the match, his car broke down and was given a lift to the ground by Fulham fans, who then had to watch their side lose with Brian scoring the only goal of the game! He now lives in Cardiff working as a sales representative selling protective clothing to industry but he is still involved in the game running the Wales Boys Club under-14s.
Played 586 League games scoring 216 goals.

CLARK, Frank
Newcastle, Notts F, 1963-1978
His move into management came with his appointment as assistant manager at Sunderland, followed by a similar post at Leyton Orient, where he went on to become

Manager. He took over from Brian Clough at Forest and led them to promotion back into the Premiership in his first season.
Played in Newcastle's 1969 Fairs Cup success.

CLARK, John
Celtic, Morton, 1968-1973
Picked up no less than 11 winners medals during his time at Parkhead. Had a spell as Billy McNeill's assistant and worked for the Strathclyde Fire Department.

CLARKE, Allan
Walsall, Fulham, Leicester, Leeds U, Barnsley, 1963-1979
One of five brothers who all played League soccer, Allan won a championship medal in 1973/4. An outstanding forward who played 19 times for England, he went on to manage Barnsley, his old club Leeds and had a spell at Lincoln. He now lives in Scunthorpe and works as a travelling salesman for a firm that makes ventilating extractors for industry.
Scored the winning goal against Arsenal in the 1972 FA Cup final.

CLARKE, Bobby
Queen's Park, Aberdeen, Clyde, 1962-1982
Capped by his country at three levels and went on to manage the New Zealand national coach until mid 1996. Has also had a spell as a teacher in America.
Won a Championship medal in 1980, with Aberdeen.

CLARKE, Colin
Ipswich, Peterboro, Gillingham, Tranmere, Bournemouth, Southampton, QPR, Portsmouth, 1980-1992
Injury forced the blond striker to hang up his boots in 1992 and carve out a career in catering. He is now running a pub/restaurant in a village near Newbury.
Capped 38 times by Northern Ireland scoring 13 goals.

CLARKE, Colin
Arsenal, Oxford, 1965-1977

Played for 12 years at Oxford United making 443 appearances. Managed Kettering Town and Stafford Rangers prior to being youth boss at Charlton and Villa.

CLARKE, Dennis
WBA, Huddersfield, Birmingham C, 1966-1974
Career ended at Birmingham, then tried a number of business ventures from Ice Cream to fabrics – before finally becoming a partner in a property company.
The first substitute in FA Cup final history when he came on for West Brom when they beat Everton 1-0.

CLARKE, Derek
Walsall, Wolves, Oxford, Leyton O, Carlisle, 1967-1978
Played for five clubs but made most of his League appearances for Oxford United in the seventies. Ran his own builders merchants business in London for five years between 1979 until 1984 before returning to the West Midlands to live in Walsall, where he has worked as a machine operator ever since. A member of the famous Clarke footballing family.
Played for Orient in a 1978 FA Cup semi final.

CLARKE, Harry
Tottenham 1948-1956
Made 295 appearances for Spurs during which time he played once for England. Managed Romford for many years and still lives in the area where he worked for a security transit company.
Won a Fourth Division Championship medal with Mansfield.

CLARKE, Jeff
Man C, Sunderland, Newcastle, Brighton, 1974-1984
Yorkshire born Jeff is currently reserve team coach at Newcastle United, for whom he made more than 100 appearances during his ten year playing career.
Promoted to the First Division with Sunderland in 1977.

CLARKE, John
Northampton 1966-1974
Played 228 League games and is now a factory worker living in Northampton.

CLARKE, Paul
Southend, Brighton, Reading, Southend, Gillingham, 1976-1984
A midfield man who played over 300 League games for Southend where he had a spell as manager between 1987 and 1988.

CLARKE, Roy
Cardiff, Man C, Stockport, 1946-1958
Welsh international winger who found fame with Manchester City. Went on to run the Social Club at Maine Road until his retirement in 1988 and now runs the City Former Players Association.
FA Cup winners medal in 1956.

CLARKE, Wayne
Wolves, Birmingham, Everton, Leicester City, Manchester City, Shrewsbury, Stoke City, Wolves, Walsall, Shrewsbury, 1977-1994
Brother of Allan and Derek. Was appointed manager of Telford when he dropped out of League football.
Won a league Championship with Everton in 1987.

CLAYTON, Ronnie
Blackburn 1950-1968

Made nearly 600 appearances for Blackburn before leaving to become manager at Morecambe in 1969. Took early retirement from tyre company ATS after working for them for twelve years as a representative. Still attends all home games at Ewood Park and most away, plays a lot of squash and golf as well as turning out in charity games.
Captained England for five games at the end of his International career.

CLEMENCE, Ray
Scunthorpe Liverpool, Tottenham, 1965-1987
Retired at the age of 39. Won 61 England caps but may have achieved more had he not been around at the same time as a certain Peter Shilton. Had spells in management with Spurs and then Barnet is now England's full time goalkeeping coach.

CLEMENT, Dave
QPR, Bolton, Fulham, Wimbledon, 1966-1981.
England International full back who made 402 league appearances for Queens Park Rangers. Died in 1982 aged 34.
Played in the Ranger's side which won promotion the First Division in 1969.

CLEMENTS, Dave
Wolves, Coventry, Sheff Wed, Everton, 1963-1975
Played for Ireland at schoolboy, youth and amateur levels before playing 48 times for the full side. After leaving Everton in 1976, was still being capped while playing for New York Cosmos. He is still in the US running an Irish goods store in Georgetown, Colorado.
Promoted to Division One with Coventry.

CLEMENTS, Kenny
Man C, Oldham, Man C, Bury, Shrewsbury, 1975-1990
Kenny stayed in the game initially as manager of Limerick in Ireland, then as commercial manager at Huddersfield before achieving his life long ambition of driving heavy goods vehicles. Now runs his successful 'Kenny Clements School of Motoring' from

his home near Oldham. Retired from Curzon Ashton FC at end of 1994/5 season. He captained and won the player of the year award at all of his clubs.
Played in Manchester City's 1976 League Cup winning side.

CLIFTON, Brian

Southampton, Grimsby, 1957-1965
Now lives in Holton-Le-Clay near Grimsby and has taken early retirement from his job as a drawing house manager of a freezer company at the age of 61. His enthusiasm for sport allowed him to continue playing soccer until he was fifty - and cricket until he was sixty.
Played over 200 League games.

CLINTON, Tommy

Everton, Blackburn, Tranmere, 1948-1956
Played for Everton for five years then after spells with Blackburn and Tranmere played for Runcorn and ran a newsagents. Has since worked in the insurance business for a number of years.
Capped three times by the Republic of Ireland.

CLISH, Colin

Newcastle, Rotherham, Doncaster, 1961-1971
Newcastle born left back is now a British transport police officer in Doncaster.

CLOSE, Brian

Leeds, Arsenal, Bradford C, 1949-1952
Never played a league game for his first two clubs, Leeds and Arsenal, signed for Bradford City in 1952 but played only six games scoring two goals. Later went on to make his name in cricket, captaining Yorkshire, Somerset and England.

CLOSE, Shaun

Tottenham, Bournemouth, Swindon, Barnet, 1984-1994
Was at St Albans City after a previous spell with Bishop Stortford.

CLOUGH, Brian

Middlesbrough, Sunderland, 1955-1964
Although best remembered for his brilliant managerial ability, Brian scored an incredible 251 goals in 274 games, a post war ratio that is unlikely to be unbeaten. After spells in charge of Hartlepool, Derby, Brighton and Leeds, he took over at Notts Forest in 1975. Bowed out of management following the club's relegation from the top flight in 1993. In his 18 years at the City Ground they won the League; two European Cups; four League Cups and in 1978 he was voted Manager of The Year. Only the FA Cup eluded him.
Capped twice by England in 1962.

COATES, Ralph

Burnley, Tottenham, Leyton O, 1964-1980
Played four times for England and made 214 appearances for Burnley before moving on to White Hart Lane in 1971. Now runs a catering business in Hertfordshire and still occasionally turns out for charity soccer matches.
Scored the winning goal in the 1973 League Cup final.

COCHRANE, Jim

Middlesboro, Darlington, Torquay, 1973-1980
Now a Solicitor in Stockton-on-Tees.

COCHRANE, Terry

Burnley, Middlesboro, Gillingham, Millwall, Hartlepool, 1976-1986
Northern Ireland international is now a fully qualified soccer coach and trains the youngsters at Middlesbrough's school of excellence. Living in nearby Normanby, he can regularly be heard on local radio assisting match commentaries.
Played in Boro's First Division promotion side of 1982.

COCKBURN, Henry

Man U, Bury, 1946-1955
Full England international with thirteen caps to his name who played the best years of his career at Manchester United. After working as coach at Oldham Athletic, then Huddersfield Town, he joined Mitre Sports where he worked until retiring to Ashton-

Under-Lyne, the town of his birth.
Left Manchester United after losing his place to Duncan Edwards.

COCKER, Les
Stockport, Accrington S, 1946-1957
A strong centre forward who scored 91 goals during his 295 game career. Les qualified as an FA Coach and became Don Revie's right hand man at Leeds as well as working for many years as trainer with the England squad. Considered to be one of Britain's leading coaches, the world of football mourned his death in 1979.

COCKERILL, Ron
Huddersfield, Grimsby, 1955-1967
Now a lorry driver, living in Cleethorpes. Father of Glenn, who currently plays for Fulham and John, see below.

COCKERILL, John
Grimsby, 1988-1993
Joined Grimsby from non-league footbal, went on to become community officer and is now youth coach.

COCKRAM, Allan
Tottenham, Bristol R, Brentford, Reading, 1981-1991
Former Tottenham apprentice was player/manager at Diadora League premier division side St Albans City and now does the same job at Chertsey Town.

COCKROFT, Joe
Rotherham, West Ham, Sheff Wed, Sheff U, 1930-1948
Wing half whose career spanned either side of the second world war played over 250 games for the Hammers is now retired and living in Sheffield.
Played in the war time League Cup final win at Wembley for West Ham.

COHEN, George
Fulham 1956-1968
Even though he retired early, in 1968, Cohen played over 400 matches for Fulham and earned 37 England caps. George won a five-year battle with cancer and combines his interests in building and property development with raising money for cancer charities.
1966 World Cup winner.

COLDWELL, Cecil
Sheff U 1951-1966
Defender who played over 400 League games for the Blades and now runs a newsagents in the city.

COLEMAN, Keith
Sunderland, West Ham, Darlington, 1971-1979
Found first team chances were limited at Upton Park so he spent three years playing in Belgium for Mechelen. Now works at a Sports Centre in Brentwood, Essex.
Cup Winners Cup runners-up medal with West Ham in 1976.

COLEMAN, Tony
Tranmere, Preston, Doncaster, Man C, Sheff Wed, Blackpool, Southport, Stockport, 1962-1975
Now lives in Australia and works for the State Railways as a driver.
Won a League Championship and FA Cup winners medal with City.

COLLARD, Ian
WBA, Ipswich, Portsmouth, 1964-1975

Played more than 300 League games in a career spanning 14 years. A hip injury forced him to retire from soccer in 1976 but he has been involved with sport ever since. From his home near Bristol, Ian has travelled extensively and is currently employed in Australia as manager of Sunshine George Cross.
Won an FA Cup winners medal with WBA in 1968.

COLLETT, Ernie
Arsenal 1937-1946
Joined the backroom staff at Arsenal as a coach and later became chief scout. Died in London in 1980 after being knocked down by a fire engine.

COLLINS, Bobby
Celtic, Everton, Leeds, Bury, Morton, Oldham, 1958-1972
Went to Australia in 1971 as player/coach to Ringwood City, Melbourne followed by a spell coaching for Hakoah FC in Sydney. Returned to England in 1972 and held a number of coaching and management posts before leaving the game to spend eight years working in the wholesale fashion business. Now retired after two years working at Leeds University as a driver. Still plays in the occasional charity match and keeps fit by playing golf.
Captained Leeds into the First Division in 1963.

COLLINS, Peter
Tottenham 1968-1972
Now a physical education teacher in the Chelmsford and was part time manager of Braintree Town until late 1995. Other off-the-field activites have included being a record dealer and market trader.

COLQUOUN, Eddie
Bury, WBA, Sheff U, 1963-1977
Won nine full international caps for Scotland and played a total of 360 League games. Now runs a Post Office in South Yorkshire.
Also capped at Youth and under 23 level.

COLQUHOUN, John
Oldham, Scunthorpe, Oldham, 1961-1969
Now works as a driver for White Arrow, having previously been a salesman for various companies selling products as diverse as sweets and meat.

COMFORT, Alan
QPR, Camb U, Leyton O, Middlesbrough, 1982-1989
Injury ended Alan's career at the age of 24 in 1990. He became a Curate to St Chads, Chadwell Heath, Essex in September 1994, and also acts as Chaplain to Orient FC.

COMPTON, Denis CBE
Arsenal 1936-1949
As well as winning a League Championship medal in 1947/8 with Arsenal, Denis was also a brilliant cricketer for Middlesex and England. After his playing days he became a TV commentator and sports reporter for the Sunday Express.
Won League Championship and FA Cup winners medals as well as being an England cricketer.

COMPTON, Leslie
Arsenal 1931-1951
Elder brother of Denis, Leslie became coach and scout at Arsenal – his only League Club. Later took on a pub in north London but suffered with arthritis which resulted in him having a foot amputated in 1982. Died in Essex in December 1984 aged 72.
Won League Championship and FA Cup winners medals.

COMPTON, Paul
Bournemouth, Aldershot, Torquay, Newport, Torquay, 1980-1994
Well travelled central defender, formerly first, reserve and youth team manager at Torquay United.

CONEY, Dean
Fulham, QPR, Norwich, 1980-1989
A promising striker whose league career was cut short by injury. Now with Farnborough in

the Vauxhall Conference.
England under-21 international capped four times.

CONLON, Bryan
Newcastle, Darlington, Millwall, Norwich, Blackburn, Crewe, Cambridge, Hartlepool, 1964-1973
A powerful striker in his day who returned to live in his home town of Shilton, County Durham. Coached his works side for a time.

CONN, Alfie
Rangers, Tottenham, Celtic, Hearts, Blackpool, Motherwell, 1968-1983
Son of a Scotland international and a stylish striker who was capped twice by Scotland. Was a cult figure during his two spells in England with Spurs and Blackpool. Works at the Captains Rest pub in Glasgow.
Won Two Scottish Championships at Celtic.

CONNELLY, John
Burnley, Man U, Blackburn, Bury, 1956-1972
Started his career with St Helen's Town and went on to win 20 England caps as a winger. Now the owner of a fish and chip shop near Nelson.
Helped Burnley win the League in 1960 and won another championship medal in his first season at Man United in 1964.

CONNELLY John
St Johnstone, Everton, Birmingham, Newcastle, Hibs, 1968-1982
Won his only Scottish cap whilst at Goodison Park and managed several non-league clubs in the north east before returning to Scotland where he now lives in Ayr, working as an advertising sales manager for Golf Monthly magazine.
Scottish League Division One champions with Hibs.

CONNOR, Terry
Leeds, Brighton, Portsmouth, Swansea, Bristol C, 1979-1994
Bustling forward. Worked as a football in the community officer at Bristol Rovers then was appointed reserve team boss.

Capped by England at under-21 and Youth level.

CONROY, Terry
Stoke, Crewe, 1967-1980
Dublin born striker who won 26 Irish Republic caps. Spent eleven years at Stoke City following his move from Glentoran in 1967. Now runs his own insurance business in Ashton-Under-Lyne.
Scored Stoke's first goal in the 1972 League Cup final.

CONSTANTINE, David
Bury 1978-1981
Works as a fireman in Greater Manchester.
A former England semi professional international.

CONWAY, James
Fulham, Man C, 1966-1976
Played over 300 games for Fulham before ending his career with a brief spell at Manchester City. Won 19 full caps as well as amateur honours for the Republic of Ireland. Coaching at Oregon State University in America and lives in Portland. His son, Paul, now plays for Carlisle United.
Played for Fulham in the 1975 FA Cup final.

CONWAY, Jimmy
Celtic, Norwich, Southend, Partick, 1958-1966
Coached and scouted for Bolton and hoped to stay in the game as a physiotherapist. Still lives in the town.

COOK, Michael
Colchester 1969-1983
Now community office at his one and only club.
His 613 games is a club record.

COOKE, Charlie
Aberdeen, Dundee, Chelsea, C. Palace, Chelsea, 1959-1977
Played in Scotland before moving to Chelsea in April 1966 for £72,000. Stints with Memphis Rogues and later California Surf gave Charlie the taste of American life that

tempted him to stay. Now lives in Cincinnati and runs a successful soccer school.
FA Cup winner in 1970 with Chelsea.

COOKE, Robbie

Mansfield Peterboro, Camb U, Brentford, Millwall, 1976-1987
Works in Peterborough for a well known travel agents and is manager of Warboys Town in the Jewson League.

COOP, Mick

Coventry, York, Derby, 1966-1981
Dynamic full-back who turned professional in 1966. Is now back at Coventry on the coaching staff after a spell at Derby.
Played over 400 games for Coventry.

COOPER, Ian

Bradford 1965-1976
A left back who was a regular for almost a decade. Now works a joinery business.
Played over 500 games in his career.

COOPER, Leigh

Plymouth, Aldershot, 1979-1990
Reading born full back who joined Plymouth as an apprentice and played for the Pilgrims for the next ten years. Now manager of Truro in the South Western League.
Skippered Plymouth when they played in an FA Cup semi final in 1984.

COOPER, Paul

Birmingham, Ipswich, Leicester, Man C, Stockport, 1971-1990
Long serving goalkeeper who played over 400 League games for Ipswich Town in his thirteen year stay at Portman Road. Now lives in the Liverpool area where he works for a firm selling nuts and bolts.
Won a UEFA Cup medal with Ipswich in 1981.

COOPER, Terry

Leeds, Middlesboro, Bristol C, Bristol R, Doncaster, Bristol C, 1963-1984
Battling England international full back with 20 caps to his name. Became the country's first player/director at Bristol City who he

also managed until early 1988. Most recently had a second term of office at Exeter City after a brief interlude at Birmingham. He returned to St James's Park in January 1994 but resigned due to ill health in June 1995. Spent a year living in Tenerife before joined the Southampton coaching staff.
Scored the winner in the 1968 League Cup final.

COPPELL, Steve

Tranmere, Man U, 1973-1982
Signed for Tranmere while at Liverpool University. Manchester United spotted his promise and took him to Old Trafford in February 1975 for £60,000. Before injury cruelly took him out of the game, Steve had played for his country 42 times and made over 300 appearances for the Reds. Went into management at Crystal Palace and was tipped to be a future England manager. However, he chose to resign in 1993 and became Chief Executive of the Football League Managers Association, a post that he held until March 1995. Returned to Selhurst Park as technical director then enticed into becoming manager at Manchester City October 1996.
Played in three FA Cup finals, winning once.

CORK, Alan

Derby, Lincoln, Wimbledon, Sheffield United, Fulham, 1977-1995
Is now first team coach at Fulham after having previously been in charge of the youth team. Scored over 150 goals, had three moves, but never cost a penny having three free transfers.
1988 FA Cup winner with Wimbledon.

CORMACK, Peter

Hibs, Notts F, Liverpool, Bristol C, Hibs, 1962-1980
Retired when appointed Partick Thistle manager, a post he held until May 1984. Subsequently became manager of Anartosi FC, Cyprus; Botswana's national coach in 1986; assistant manager at Hibernian. Peter then invested in kareoke equipment and can now be found touring the pubs and clubs of

Edinburgh. Also runs a successful painting and decorating company.
Won League Championship and FA Cup winners medals.

CORRIGAN, Joe
Man C, Brighton, Norwich, Stoke, 1968-1984
A brilliant 6ft 4in goalkeeper, Joe proved himself outstanding in the losing FA Cup final side of 1981, where he collected the man of the match award. Now lives in Cheshire and has coached keepers at Celtic, Middlesbrough, Tranmere and Barnsley before being offered a post at Anfield as Liverpool's first full time goalkeeping coach.
Won two League Cup medals and an FA Cup runners up medal.

COURT, David
Arsenal, Luton, Brentford, 1962-1972
Retired in 1975 when he became a retail foodshop owner for ten years. Now employed by DBS Financial Management as a Compliance Official and is the current captain of the Arsenal ex-professional & celebrity XI.
Appeared at Wembley in the 1969 League Cup final.

COX, Freddie
Tottenham, Arsenal, WBA, 1938-1953
Became assistant manager at West Brom, before managing Bournemouth, Portsmouth and Gillingham. Eventually returned to Bournemouth to run a newsagents. Died in 1973.
Took Gillingham to the Fourth Division title in 1964.

COX, Geoff
Birmingham, Torquay, 1952-1966
Played most of his football in Devon having joined from Birmingham in 1957. Works for a local estate agents and still lives in the town.

COXON, William
Derby, Norwich, Lincoln, Bournemouth, 1950-1965
Now lives in Bournemouth, the home of his last club, where he runs a taxi firm and owns a guest house.
Scored Norwich's 2,000th League goal.

COYLE, Tony
Albion Rovers, Stockport, Chesterfield, Stockport, Exeter, 1979-1989
Still lives within a mile of Edgeley Park and works as a civil servant for the Benefits Agency within the DSS.

COZENS, John
Notts C, Peterboro, Camb U, 1970-1979
Londoner who joined Notts County from Hillingdon Borough. Works in Peterborough for Peterborough Automatics.

CRAGGS, John
Newcastle, Middlesboro, Newcastle, Darlington, 1966-1984

Spent his playing days in the north east. Runs a sports shop in Teeside Park which was once owned by Willie Maddren.
Won a Division Two Championship medal in 1974.

CRAIG Derek
Newcastle, Darlington, York City, 1969-1981
Despite six years at Newcastle he never played first team football. Made his name at Darlington and now works at a Newcastle Insurance Brokers.

CRAIG, David
Newcastle 1963-1977

Played 347 games during his fourteen years at St James Park. Became player/assistant-manager at Carlisle in July 1983 and player/coach at Hibernian in October 1984. Ran a newsagents in Dunston but now owns a milk business back in Newcastle.
Played in the 1969 Fairs Cup final for Newcastle.

CRAIG, Jim
Celtic, Sheffield Wednesday, 1963-1973
A tall right back who rarely wasted a ball has had many jobs since leaving the game. He has worked as a journalist but is now a dentist at a Glasgow health centre.
A member of Celtic's 1967 European Cup winning side.

CRAIG, Tommy
Aberdeen, Sheff Wed, Newcastle, Aston V, Swansea, Carlisle, Hibs, 1966-1985 .
Was chief scout at Celtic until October 1994. Tommy was appointed Aberdeen's assistant manager in May 1995 and is coach to the Scotland under-21 side. He was the first Scot to be transfered to an English club for a six figure fee.
Welsh Cup winner with Swansea in 1981.

CRAVEN, John
Blackpool, C Palace, Coventry, Plymouth, 1965-1977
Moved to Canada to play for Vancouver Whitecaps and still lives there.
Division Two runner up with Blackpool in 1970.

CRAWFORD, Ray
Portsmouth Ipswich, Wolves, WBA, Ipswich, Charlton, Colchester, 1957-1970
Great goalscorer who won only two England caps. Now lives in the Portsmouth area and works as a representative and merchandiser in large stores.
His 203 goals for Ipswich is a club record.

CRERAND, Pat
Celtic, Man Utd, 1958-1971
Joined the coaching staff at Man United when he hung up his boots in August 1981, later becoming their assistant manager until 1975. Managed Northampton Town from July 1976 until January 1977. On leaving football be became a public relations officer for a Manchester engineering company and is now pub landlord at the Park Hotel, Altrincham.
Played for United in the 1968 European Cup final.

CRIBLEY, Alex
Liverpool, Wigan, 1978-1987
Coaching at Wigan Athletic where he played over 250 league games in the 1980s.
Played in Wigan's record win 7-0 against Scunthorpe in 1982.

CRICKMORE, Charlie
Hull, Bournemouth, Gillingham, Rotherham, Norwich, Notts C, 1959-1971
A speedy winger and accomplished penalty taker, Charlie has now retired from his job as a fireman and lives in Hull.

CRIPPS, Harry
West Ham, Millwall, Charlton, 1958-1975
Played over 400 games for Millwall. Worked as an Insurance broker for the Royal London

Assurance company and lived in Essex where he coached East ham United in the Essex Senior League in his spare time. Died in December 1995 after suffering a heart attack whilst in hospital recovering from a stroke.

CRISP, Ron

Watford, Brentford, Leyton O, 1961-1969
Had two spells in America and after a brief spell back in England settled in South Africa where his is the managing director of a company supplying office machinery.
American player of the year in 1967.

CROKER, Ted

Charlton 1950
A former Secretary of the Football Association when he succeeded Denis Fellows in 1973, a position that he held until his retirement in 1989. He played only seven games for Charlton. Outside football, he owned a successful concrete business that made him his fortune. Died in his Cheltenham home on Christmas Day 1992, after a long battle against cancer.
Became the first professional footballer to become Secretary of the Football Association.

CROMBIE, Dean

Lincoln, Grimsby, Reading, Bolton, Lincoln, 1976-1990
Was assistant manager at Lincoln and is now youth coach at Bolton.

CROOKS, Garth

Stoke, Tottenham, Man U, WBA, Charlton, 1975-1990
Former England under-21 international who joined Tottenham from Stoke City in 1980 for £600,000. Garth is carving out a career in the media, appearing on BBC TV and co-hosting GLR Radio's 'Saturday Sport'. As well as being Chairman of the Institute of Professional Sport, he is Chairman and founder of SCAR – a charity for Sickle Cell Anaemia Relief.
Played for Spurs in the 1981 and 1982 FA Cup finals.

CROPLEY, Alex

Hibs Arsenal, Aston V, Newcastle, Portsmouth, 1968-1981
Scottish international who won three caps was lured to London by Arsenal in a £150,000 transfer from Hibernian in 1974. Retired in 1983 to run a pub in Edinburgh.
Played in League Cup finals on both sides of the border.

CROSBY, Malcolm

Aldershot, York, Wrexham, 1979-1991
Played most of his League soccer for Aldershot but moved into coaching at his last club, York City. He struck up a partnership with Dennis Smith which continued at Sunderland and now at Oxford, where he is assistant manager.
Managed Sunderland to the 1992 Cup Final.

CROSS, David

Rochdale, Norwich, Coventry, WBA, West Ham, Man C, Oldham, WBA, Bolton, Bury, 1969-1985
Has worked as a financial advisor for Allied Dunbar in Manchester since 1988. Scouts for Oldham and runs their under-15 side.
League Cup finalist with West Ham United.

CROSS, Graham

Leicester, Chesterfield, Brighton, Preston, Lincoln, 1960-1978
Graham was also an all-rounder at cricket with Leicestershire. Was jailed in February 1993 after using Post Office funds to pay off serious gambling debts.
Played in two losing FA Cup finals.

CROSS, Roger

West Ham, Leyton O, Brentford, Fulham, Brentford, Millwall, 1968-1978
Former West Ham striker who left QPR in November 1994 to follow Gerry Francis to White Hart Lane as assistant manager.

CROSS, Steve

Shrewsbury, Derby, Bristol R, 1976-1994
Enjoyed nine years at Shrewsbury were he played 240 league games. Was assistant manager at Bristol Rovers until the end of

the 1995/6 season. Now turns out for Mangotsfield United in the Western League.

CROWE, Matt
Partick Thistle, Bradford P.A.,Partick Thistle, Norwich, Brentford, 1952-1963
Had two spells in the league, playing for Partick Thistle in the interim. Matt now lives in Cape Province in South Africa where he works as a sales manager.
Fourth Division Championship medal with Brentford in 1964.

CROWE, Vic
Aston V, Peterboro, 1954-1966
Served Aston Villa as player, coach and manager. Vic played over 300 league games and skippered both his club and country (Wales). Left Villa in 1974 and had a second spell in the NASL with Portland Timbers. Now acts as an advisor to Doc Martens League side Bilston Town.

CROWN, David
Brentford, Portsmouth, Exeter, Reading, Camb U, Southend, Gillingham, 1980-1992
David moved into non-league soccer with Dagenham & Redbridge, then Purfleet. Is now running his own accountancy practice and turns out for Billericay Town.
Scored 165 League goals with his seven clubs.

CRUICKSHANK, Jim
Queens Park, Hearts, Dumbarton, 1960-1978
Played six times for Scotland over a period of 12 years and now works for the Loathian Health Board in Edinburgh.
On the losing side in three Cup Finals.

CRUDGINGTON, Geoff
Aston V, Bradford C, Crewe, Swansea, Plymouth, 1970-1987
Works for former Plymouth Argyle sponsors, Beacon Electrical, and still coaches regularly in the Plymouth area.

CUFF, Pat
Middlesboro, Grimsby, Millwall, Darlington, 1973-1982

Middlesbrough born former England school-boy international keeper now runs a chain of betting shops on Teeside.

CULLIS, Stan
Wolves 1934-1946
Became Wolves' manager two years after he had stopped playing due to bouts of concussion. They missed the League and Cup double in 1960 by one point but he was sensationally sacked in 1964. Joined an advertising agency and was appointed to the Midlands Sports Council in 1972, before retiring.
Took Wolves to three League titles.

CULPIN, Paul
Leicester, Coventry, Northampton, Peterborough, Hereford, 1981-19919
Former England semi-professional striker, moved to New Zealand in April 1995 to join Christchurch Utd.

CUMBES, Jim
Tranmere, WBA, Aston V, Southport, 1966-1977

During his Albion days he teamed up with John Osborne, a fellow keeper, and opened a sports shop in Bilston. He also played cricket for four counties. Now commercial manager at Lancashire CCC and lives in Altrincham.
Division Three and League Cup winners medals.

CUMMING, Bobby
Grimsby, Lincoln, 1974-1989
Full back who played 338 league games for Grimsby. Emigrated to the States in 1989.

CUMMINGS, George
Aston V 1935-1948
A Scottish international full back who was a regular for Aston Villa either side of the War. Retired in 1949 and had brief spells as coach at Villa Park and then as manager of Hednesford Town. Became a scout for Wolves while working for the Dunlop Rubber Company. Died in April 1987.
Division Two and a war time League Cup winner.

CUMMINGS, Tommy
Burnley, Mansfield, 1948-1963
Appeared in 432 first division games for Burnley as a solid centre-half. Following a spell out of football, he went on to coach abroad and has since scouted for several clubs including Burnley and Sunderland.
Managed Mansfield to Promotion from the Fourth Division in 1963.

CUNNINGHAM, Laurie
Leyton O, WBA, Man U, Leicester, Wimbledon, 1974-1987
Sadly died in 1989 aged only 33, while a player for Rayo Vallencano, Spain. He won six England caps and in 1979 moved from West Brom to Real Madrid, for the then staggering sum of one million pounds. He stayed at Real for five years, then played for five more clubs before moving to Rayo.
Played for Wimbledon in the 1988 FA Cup final.

CUNNINGHAM, Tommy
Chelsea, QPR, Wimbledon, Leyton O, 1973-1986
Played most of his football at Orient and is now back at Brisbane Road as assistant manager.
Pormoted to the Second Division with Orient in 1982.

CURBISHLEY, Alan
West Ham, Birmingham, Aston V, Charlton, Brighton, Charlton, 1974-1993 .
Former England schoolboy, youth, and under-21 international who started at West Ham. Was appointed joint manager at Charlton in July 1991 and was given full control four years later.

CURRAN, Hugh
Third Lanark, Millwall, Norwich, Wolves, Oxford, Bolton, Oxford, 1962-1978
Former Manchester United apprentice who went on to win five Scottish caps whilst with Wolves. Retired through injury in March 1979 and returned to his native Scotland. Lives in Carstairs where he is a publican after jobs as a hotelier and owning hairdressers and a grocery shops.
Fairs Cup Finalist with Wolves in 1972.

CURRAN, Terry
Doncaster, Notts F, Bury, Derby, Soton, Sheff Wed, Sheff U, Everton, Huddersfield, Hull, Sunderland, Grimsby, Chesterfield, 1973-1987
Have boots - will travel! Terry played for thirteen clubs over fourteen years before retiring in 1987. Now works as a salesman in Yorkshire. Managed Goole Town for a brief spell.
Played nearly 400 League games.

CURTIS, Alan
Swansea, Leeds, Swansea, Southampton, Stoke, Cardiff, Swansea, 1971-1989
Won 35 full Welsh international caps during a career which started and ended at Swansea City, the club where he worked firstly as football in the community officer and then as youth team coach.
Played for Swansea in their rise from the Fourth Division in the late 1970s.

CURTIS, George
Coventry, Aston V, 1955-19719
'Iron Man' played over 500 games in five divisions during his time at Coventry, starting in the old Third Division South, winning

medals in the Third and Second en route to the First Division for the first time in the Sky Blues' history. Retired in 1994, having previously been MD at Highfield Road. Still helps with Pools & Lotteries.

Along with John Sillett lead the Sky Blues to FA Cup success in 1987.

CURRIE, Tony

Watford, Sheff U, Leeds, QPR, Torquay, 1967-1984

One of the classiest players of his time, Tony won only 17 caps but was widely acclaimed as a true star. Now an officer for football in the community based at Sheffield United.

Played for QPR in the 1982 FA Cup Final.

CUSACK, Dave

Sheff Wed, Southend, Millwall, Doncaster, Rotherham, 1975-1989

Central defender who graduated from the junior ranks at Sheffield Wednesday. Appointed manager of Dagenham & Redbridge FC in 1994, replaced 12 months later to turn out in the Essex Senior League

for Ford United.

Amassed a career total of almost 500 league appearances.

CUTBUSH, John

Tottenham, Fulham, Sheffield U, 1966-1980

Born in Malta, John was an apprentice at Tottenham before playing over 250 games for his next two clubs. Has since worked in the insurance industry and in the car trade.

Played for Fulham in the 1975 FA Cup final.

DAINES, Barry

Tottenham, Mansfield, 1971-1983

Ex-Spurs keeper who is now running a shop in Chelmsford, Essex which specialises in the sale of a variety of continental ice creams.

Won promotion with Spurs in 1978 to the First Division.

DALEY, Steve

Wolves, Man C, Burnley, Walsall, 1971-1985

England 'B' international who was valued at over £1 million in 1979 when he moved from Wolverhampton Wanderers to Manchester City. After a couple of spells in America, Steve returned to play non-league football with Kettering but now turns out in the Birmingham Amateur Football Alliance and off the pitch he is a publican.

Won UEFA Cup, League Cup and Second Division Championships with Wolves.

DALGLISH, Kenny

Celtic, Liverpool, 1967-1989

When Kevin Keegan left Liverpool in the Summer of 1977 Kenny was purchased from Celtic complete with a goal-a-game strike rate. He has won almost every honour possible in Scotland, England and Europe. His move into management at Anfield was equally as successful, picking up three Championship titles and two FA Cup wins before deciding to quit the game for a less stressful existence. After taking Blackburn to the League Championship he resigned in August 1996.

Capped 102 times by Scotland and has scored 30 goal – both are records.

DALTON, George
Newcastle, Brighton, 1960-1967
After as league career as a full back, George studied to become a physiotherapist and currently works as club physio at Coventry City.

DALY, Gerry
Man U, Derby, Coventry, Leicester, Birmingham, Shrewsbury, Stoke, Doncaster, 1973-1988

Dublin born Gerry won 46 caps for his country during a career which spanned eight league clubs. Unfortunately he is now unable to work because of a back problem. His last job was as manager of Telford United, a post that he held from 1989 until 1994.
Helped Manchester United to the Second Division title in 1975.

DANIEL, Peter
Hull, Wolves, Sunderland, Lincoln, Burnley, 1974-1988
Manager of North Ferriby town in the North East Counties league for four years until the end of 1994. Now holds the same post at nearby Winterton Rangers FC.
Helped Wolves to League Cup win and Pormotion to the First Division.

DANIEL, Ray
Arsenal, Sunderland, Cardiff, Swansea, 1948-1959

Won 21 Welsh caps. Became a publican then area manager for Courvoisier Brandy. Now postmaster at Cockett Post office.
League Championship medal in 1953.

DARE, Billy
Brentford, West Ham, 1948-1958
Was the first soccer player to be transferred on television - signing for West Ham in front of the cameras in 1955. Died May 1994 aged 67.
Played in West Ham's Second Division Championship in 1958.

DARKE, Peter
Plymouth, Exeter, Torquay, 1971-1978
Exeter born defender who still lives in the city where he now works as a salesman.

DARRACOTT, Terry
Everton, Wrexham, 1967-1979
Following a twelve year league career Terry had a stint in America with Tulsa Roughnecks before progressing into coaching. Was assistant manager at Everton and is now on the coaching staff at Blackburn Rovers.
League Cup final runner up with Everton in 1977.

DAVENPORT, Peter
Notts Forest, Man Utd, Middlesboro, Sunderland, Airdrie, 1982-1994
Capped once by England but after a promising start never really fulfilled his true potential. Now player manager of Southport.
Played for Sunderland in the 1992 FA Cup final.

DAVEY, Steve
Plymouth, Hereford, Portsmouth, Exeter, 1966-1981
A former England youth international who played 214 games for Argyle and 415 in his career total. Now owns a residential rest home for the elderly in Plymouth.

DAVIDSON, Andy
Hull C 1952-1967
A consistently reliable defender who played

over 500 games for Hull despite suffering three broken legs. Now has a fish round in his adopted home.
Played a record 570 times for Hull and lead them to a Third Division Championship in 1966.

DAVIES, Alan
Man U, Newcastle, Swansea, Bradford C, Swansea, 1981-1991
A Welsh international winger who was found dead in his car near his home on the Gower Coast. He was thought to have been suffering from depression.

DAVIES, Cyril
Swansea, Carlisle, Charlton, 1966-1972
A promising inside forward who was forced to retire at the age of 25 due to a knee injury. Now works for the school playing fields department of a London Council.
Capped once against Romania for Wales in 1962.

DAVIES, Dai
Swansea, Everton, Swansea, Wrexham, Swansea, Tranmere, 1969-1983
Was involved in a Welsh book & craft shop in Mold and football commentating on Welsh TV. Although a qualified teacher he now runs a natural healing centre in Llangollen, North Wales.
Capped 52 times for Wales between between 1975 and 1983.

DAVIES, Reginald
Southend, Newcastle, Swansea, Carlisle, 1949-1963
Emigrated to Australia in 1971 after a spell in non-league football. Down under he achieved great success as a coach, winning the Cup with Bayswater, then the League title with Ascot. He also represented Western Australia against New Zealand at the age of 47, and finally hung up his boots at the age of 50! Now retired, living in Perth.
Capped six times by wales between 1953 and 1958.

DAVIES, Fred
Wolves, Cardiff, Bournemouth, 1961-1973
Liverpool born keeper Fred moved into coaching after 12 years minding the posts and has been manager at Shrewsbury since 1993.
Lifted the Third Division Championship as Shrews boss in 1994.

DAVIES, Gordon
Fulham, Chelsea, Man C, Fulham, Wrexham, 1977- 1993
Welsh international striker who made his biggest impact during two spells at Fulham, where he made 350-plus league appearances. Now lives in Leighton Buzzard, Bedfordshire and works as a pest control officer for Rentokil.
Scored 159 goals at Fulham which is an record.

DAVIES, Roger
Derby, Preston, Leicester, Derby, Darlington, 1971-1983
Goal-scoring England under-21 international who was plucked from non-league soccer by Derby County in 1971. The following twelve years included spells in Belgium and America. Roger now works as a manager for Rolls Royce and is still an active member of Derby County's Ex-Rams team.
Completed a League and Cup double with Brugge in Belgium.

DAVIES, Ron
Chester, Luton, Norwich, Southampton, Portsmouth, Man Utd, Millwall, 1959-1975
One of the all time great goalscorers and the holder of 29 full Welsh caps. Became a demolition worker for a while after retiring in 1975 and also proved that he had talent with his hands as well as his feet by selling art sketches - including portraits of players. Moved over to the States in 1988 where he still lives, in a luxury house within an acre of secluded woodland outside Orlando. Still involved with soccer, coaching local semi-pro side - Orlando Lions.
Scored 275 League Goals in a 16 year career.

DAVIES, Wyn
Wrexham, Bolton, Newcastle, Man C, Man U, Blackpool, C Palace, Stockport, Crewe, 1960-1977

Know affectionately as 'Wyn the Leap' because of his ball-winning skills in the air. Played for nine league clubs and won 32 full Welsh caps. He became a baker in Bolton but although happy in the area, he still holds on to the dream of owning a smallholding in his native Caernarfon.

A member of Newcastle's 1969 Fairs Cup winning side.

DAVIS, Gareth
Wrexham 1967-1983

Played for Wrexham for over 16 years during which time he made three appearances for the full Welsh side. On retirement moved into hotel management and now owns a hotel in Wrexham.

Third Division Championship medal in 1978.

D'AVRAY, Mich
Ipswich, Leicester 1979-1986

Although born in Johannesburg, Mich won two England under-21 caps during his ten years at Portman Road. Ended at Leicester and went on to manange South Africa's Olympic Soccer team.

DAWKINS, Derek
Leicester, Mansfield, Bournemouth, Torquay, 1977-1988

Started at Leicester but played most of his league soccer for Torquay, where he is now a community officer.

DAWTRY, Kevin
Soton, Bournmth, Reading, 1976-1982

Lives near Southampton and works as a Distribution Supervisor for Exxon Chemicals. Manager of Hampshire League, Esso Fawley.

DAY, Billy
Middlesboro, Newcastle, Peterboro, 1955-1963

Nippy winger who ended his days at Peterborough, but has now returned to Teeside, where he currently works as a book-maker.

Played in Boro's record 9-0 win over Brighton in 1958.

DAY, Eric
Southampton 1946-1956

Goalscoring outside right who played 398 games for Southampton. Worked as a handyman on a Country Estate in Wiltshire until his retirement.

Played nearly 400 games for Saints.

DAY, Mervyn
West Ham, Leyton O, Aston Villa, Leeds, Luton, Sheff U, Carlisle, 1973-1994.

Former England under-23 keeper, Mervyn played over 600 games for the Hammers, Leeds and Villa. ended his playing days at Carlisle, where he is now manager.

Won a Second Divsion Championship with Leeds in 1990.

DEACY, Eamonn
Aston Villa, Derby Co, 1979-1983

Republic of Ireland international (4 caps) who had a four year stay in England before returning to his home town of Galway where he now works in the family's fruit and veg business.

Wrote 20 letters to get a trial with Villa.

DEACY, Nick

Hereford, Workington, Hull City, Bury, 1974-1983

Born in Cardiff and had two spells in Holland with PSV Eindhoven and Beringen. Now works as a computer analyst with British Aerospace in Bristol.

Played twelve times for Wales between 1977 and 1979.

DEAKIN, Alan

Aston Villa, Walsall, 1959-1971

An England under-23 international and Villa skipper who now works as a fitter/welder for an engineering firm in Aldridge, West Midlands.

Won a League Cup Winners tankard with Aston Villa in 1962.

DEAN, Dixie

Tranmere, Everton, Notts County, 1923-1939

Died at Goodison Park, Everton in 1980 aged 73. One of the games greatest ever players known for his prolific goal scoring feats. Took a pub, 'The Dublin Packet', in 1946, which he gave up 15 years later. Went on to work for John Moores's pools empire as a security man. Finally retiring to Babington in 1971.

Scored 60 league goals, another 19 in representative matches and three in the FA Cup, making an incredible haul of 82 in 1927-28.

DEANS, Dixie

Motherwell Celtic, Luton, Carlisle, Partick Thistle, 1965-1980

A great character and very popular in Scotland, Dixie spent three years in Australia, playing for Adelaide City, then returned to Scotland via Shelbourne in Ireland and soccer in the States. He now lives in Baillieston near Glasgow where he runs a public house.

Scored a hat trick in the 1972 Scottish FA Cup against Hibs.

DEAR, Brian

West Ham, Brighton, Fulham, Millwall, West Ham, 1962-1970

Had few opportunities during his time at

West Ham due to the Peters/Hurst duet, but still managed to score a goal every other game during his six year stay at Upton Park. Now works as assistant club steward at the Freemasons hall in Southend.

Once scored five goals in a 20 minutes against WBA in 1965.

DEARDEN, Bill

Oldham, Crewe, Chester, Sheff U, Chester, Chesterfield, 1964-1978

Played for five clubs and played almost 400 League games. Now works as assistant manager at Port Vale.

DEEHAN, John

Aston Villa WBA, Norwich, Ipswich, Man C, Barnsley, 1975-1990

Capped seven times by England and became player/coach at Man City in July 1988. Switched to Barnsley in the same role in 1990 and returned to his old club, Norwich, to succeed Mike Walker in January 1994. He left the following year after a string of poor results and is now manager of Wigan.

Won a League Cup and Division Two Championship with Norwich.

DELAPENHA, Lloyd

Portsmouth, Middlesboro, Mansfield, 1948-1960

After 380 league games for his three clubs, Lloyd returned to Jamaica and became a popular face as a sports reporter on local television.

Promoted to Division One with Middlesbrough in 1954.

DEMPSEY, John

Fulham, Chelsea, 1964-1975

Republic of Ireland international (19 caps) who played 310 games in his career. John joined Chelsea from Fulham in 1969 for £70,000 then left Stamford Bridge for Philadelphia Furies six years later. Now works at a special school for handicapped children in north London.

Won FA Cup and Cup Winners Cup medals during his stay at the Bridge.

DENNIS, Mark
Birmingham, Soton, QPR, C. Palace, 1978-1990
A stormy career was wrecked by brushes with authority – he was cautioned 60 times and appeared before the FA on disrepute charges more than once. Undoubtedly a talented player who should have achieved more, Mark now works as a signwriter in Spain.
Capped three times by England at under-23 level.

DENNISON, Bob
Newcastle, Notts F, Fulham, Northampton, 1932-1947
Centre half whose four-club career spanned fifteen years either side of the war. Now retired living in Kent.

DENYER, Peter
Portsmouth, Northampton, 1975-1982
Played over 250 league games before moving to Australia to Coach Blacktown FC.
Promoted to Division Two with Pompey in 1976.

DEPLIDGE, Bill
Bradford PA 1946-1955
Inside forward who spent nine years with Bradford. Went on to manage in non-league football. Now retired, living in South Australia.
Scored 62 goals from 274 league games.

DERRETT, Steve
Cardiff, Carlisle, Aldershot, Rotherham, Newport, 1966-1977
A full back who played over 200 league games. Now a representative for a protective clothing firm in Cardiff.
Capped four times by Wales between 1969 and 1971.

DEVINE, John
Arsenal, Norwich, Stoke, 1977-1985
A badly broken leg terminated his career whilst playing for Stoke. He recovered sufficiently to play in non-league soccer and had a spell at Chelmsford before venturing east to play for East Bengal in India. Now closer to home as manager of Shelbourne in Ireland and married a former Miss Universe runner-up who later co-presented the 1988 Eurovision song contest.
FA Cup Finalist with Arsenal in 1980.

DEVONSHIRE, Alan
West Ham, Watford, 1976-1992
Was bought by the Hammers from non-league Southall, and he went on to play for England. His career was all but ended by a serious Achilles tendon injury. Now co-boss at ICIS League Maidenhead United.
FA Cup winner with West Ham in 1980.

DeVRIES, Roger
Hull, Blackburn, Scunthorpe, 1970-1981
Started as a left back but switched to the right to keep his place in the side. Still works in the Hull area today as a teacher in a local primary school.
Played 362 games for the Tigers.

DICK, John
West Ham, Brentford, 1953-1964
Fourth in the Hammers all-time list of leading scorers with 153 league goals. Has worked as a games teacher at a number of schools around the capital prior to retiring.
Scored four goals in the Hammers record 8-0 home win against Rotherham in 1958.

DICKENS, Alan
West Ham, Chelsea, Brentford, Colchester, 1982-1994
Former West Ham apprentice who won one England under-21 cap. Played non-league football with Chesham United, Hayes, Collier Row and currently Billericay Town, whilst training to become a taxi driver.

DICKIE, Alan
West Ham, Coventry, Aldershot, 1962-1968
Joined the Police force when his career ended and now works in the Coroners Office at St Mary's Hospital in Sidcup, Kent.

DICKINSON, Jimmy MBE
Portsmouth 1946-1964

A Pompey all time great who won 48 England caps as a dependable wing half. Jimmy continued to serve at Fratton Park as Scout; press officer; and briefly manager, having set a record of 764 appearances for one club, which stood until 1980 when John Trollope played six games more for Swindon Town. Suffered three heart attacks, and sadly died in 1982 at the age of 57.
Played in 764 League games – a club record.

DICKSON, Will
Notts Co, Chelsea, Arsenal, Mansfield T, 1946-1956
His stayed at Highbury was marred by a number of injuries. He returned to live and work as scout for Arsenal in Northern Ireland. Now works in the joinery trade.
Won 12 caps for Northern Ireland between 1951 and 1955.

DILLON, Kevin
Birmingham, Portsmouth, Newcastle, Reading, 1977-1994
Joined Stevenage after being released by Reading in September 1994, then followed team-mate Graham Roberts to Yeovil Town, as his assistant manager – a position he later resigned before returning to live in Newcastle.
Promoted to Division Two with Pompey in 1988.

DITCHBURN, Ted
Tottenham 1946-1958
He played well over 400 games for his only club, Tottenham, including a spell of 247 consecutive appearances. Played six times for England and now lives in retirement in Romford, Essex, where he built successful business interest's including a Sports Shop (which still bears his name), a toy and games shop and a printing business.
Won successive Second and First Division winners medals with Spurs.

DIXON, Johnny
Aston Villa 1946-1960
An inside forward who scored 131 goals in 292 appearances for Aston Villa. Coached the youngsters at Villa Park for six years before running an ironmongery business in Erdington. Now retired, in Sutton Coldfield.
Captain of the Villa side that won 1957 FA Cup.

DIXON, Kerry
Reading, Chelsea, Southampton, Luton, Millwall, Watford, Doncaster, 1980-1996
Failed to make the grade as an apprentice at spurs and drifted into non-league football with Dunstable. Made his name with Chelsea and developed into an England striker. Appointed player/manager of Doncaster in September 1996.
Won two Second Division Championship medals in 1984 and 1989.

DIXON, Will
Arsenal, Reading, Colchester, Swindon, Aldershot, 1968-1977
After serving his apprenticeship at Highbury, despite never establishing himself in the Arsenal first team, Will went on to make over 400 League appearances. Now on the coaching staff at Watford.
Won promotion to Division Two with Swindon in 1974.

DOBING, Peter
Blackburn, Man C, Stoke, 1955-1972
Peter's seventeen year career took in 564 league starts and saw him win England under-23 and Football League honours. Now running a business in the Potteries area selling crockery to hotels and restaurants.
League Cup winner with Stoke City in 1972.

DOBSON, Martin
Bolton, Burnley, Everton, 1966-1985
Midfielder who played five times for England. Became manager at Bury (1984/9) and Bristol Rovers (1991/2) before taking up a post in Malta. Coached youngsters back in Lancashire prior to his appointment as manager of Unibond League Chorley Town in 1995.
Division Two Championship medal with Burnley in 1973.

DOCHERTY, John
Brentford, Sheff U, Brentford, Reading,
Brentford, 1960-1973
Had three playing stints with Brentford and
went on to manage Millwall and Slough
Town, who he left in 1993.

DOCHERTY, Mick
Burnley, Man C, Sunderland, 1968-1978
Coached at Preston, then became assistant
manager at Rochdale in September 1991 and
was promoted to manager in January 1995.
Son of Tommy 'The Doc' Docherty.

DOCHERTY, Tommy
Celtic, Preston., Arsenal, Chelsea, 1948-1961
As a player 'The Doc' won 25 Scottish caps
and played over 400 league games following
his £4,000 move to Preston from Celtic in
1949. Became player/coach at Chelsea in
1961 and their manager in 1962. A full and
colourful management career then took in
stops at: Rotherham; QPR (twice); Aston
Villa; FC Oporto, Portugal; Hull; Scotland
national side; Man Utd; Derby; Sydney
Olympic, Australia (twice); Preston; South
Melbourne FC, Australia; Wolves. Now uses
all this experience to entertain as an after
dinner speaker.
*Division Two Championship medal with
Preston in 1951.*

DOCHERTY, Peter
Blackpool, Man C, Derby, Huddersfield,
Doncaster, 1933-1952
Northern Ireland international with 16 caps.
In 1949 at the age of 36 became player/man-
ager to Doncaster Rovers, winning promo-
tion that season from the Third Division
North. Lived at Poulton-le-Fylde, outside
Blackpool, until his death in 1990.
*Won a League Championship medal with
Man City in 1937 and a cup winners medal
in 1946 with Derby.*

DODSON, David
Arsenal, Swansea, Portsmouth, Aldershot,
1957-1966
England youth winger who ended his career
at the age of 26 in 1966. Now owns his own

plumbing business in Fleet.

DOHERTY, John
Fulham, Aldershot, 1956-1965
Centre forward who set off to Australia in
1965 to play for South Coast United FC.
John is now employed as an insurance con-
sultant.

DOIG, Russell
St Mirren, East Stirlingshire, Leeds,
Peterborough, Hartlepool, 1981-1990
Failed to hold down a first team place at
Elland Road after making 109 appearances
for East Stirling. Still lives in the Leeds area
where he works as a taxi driver.

DOLAN, Eamon
West Ham, Bristol City, Birmingham, Exeter,
1985-1993
Was forced to quit playing because of seri-
ous illness. Now community officer at
Exeter.
Republic of Ireland Under-21 international..

DOLAN, Terry
Bradford PA, Huddersfield, Bradford,
Rochdale, 1968-1981
Bradford born Terry played for both of his
hometown clubs and played over 350 league
games before moving into management. Has
since been manager at Hull City since April
1991.
*Won Promotion to Division Two with
Bradford in 1988.*

DONACHIE, Willie
Man C, Norwich, Burnley, Oldham, 1969-
1990
Glasgow born Scottish international (35
caps) who started at Celtic before moving
south to join Manchester City in 1968. Had
two spells in America with Portland Timbers
before ending his playing days at Burnley.
Then moved to Oldham where he became
assistant manager/coach. Moved to Everton
in the same capacity with Joe Royle in early
1995.
League Cup winners medal in 1976.

DONALD, Ian

Manchester United, Partick Thistle,
Arbroath, 1969-1975

The current chairman of Aberdeen having
taken over from his father in 1994 who appointed Alex Ferguson as Dons boss.
Former Scottish schoolboy international.

DONOVAN, Donal

Everton, Grimsby, 1951-1963

After five years with Grimsby Town went on
to manage Boston United, before taking a
job with a shipping company on the east
coast. Now working for the Volvo import terminal at Grimsby.
*Capped five times by the Republic of Ireland
between 1955 and 1957.*

DONOVAN, Terry

Grimsby, Aston Villa, Oxford, Burnley,
Rotherham, Blackpool, 1976-1984

Former Republic of Ireland international for-
ward who is now working as an insurance
broker living in picturesque Tetney,
Gloucestershire.
*Won his only international cap against the
Czech Republic.*

DOOLEY, Derek

Lincoln, Sheff Wed, 1946-1952

Scored 62 goals in 61 games for the Owls
before injury forced him to quit at the age of
23. Formerly a director at neighbouring
Sheffield United.
*Scored a Wednesday record of 46 goals in
the 1951/2 season.*

DORNEY, Alan

Millwall 1968-1976

A central defender who progressed through
Millwall's junior ranks to become a first
team regular, making almost 250 League
appearances. Now lives in Bexleyheath and
works as a general builder.

DOUGAN, Derek

Portsmouth, Blackburn, Aston Villa,
Peterborough, Leicester, Wolves, 1957-1974

Retired from playing in 1975 after playing
532 League games scoring 219 goals together with 43 Northern Ireland caps. Dougan
was Chairman of the PFA and later returned
to Molineux in August 1982 as Chairman
and Chief Executive. He still lives in the
Wolverhampton area where he now works as
a marketing and PR consultant.

DOUGLAS, Bryan

Blackburn 1954-1968

A one-club man who was a loyal servant to
his local side, Blackburn Rovers. He made
over 400 League appearances in their
colours. After 19 years at Ewood Park he
became northern area sales representative
for a paper manufacturing company until the
firm was taken over in 1992. Bryan then
accepted voluntary redundancy.
Won 36 England caps between 1958-1963.

DOWD, Henry W 'Harry'

Man City, Oldham, Stoke, 1961-1973

Guarded the goal at Manchester City for
eight years before finally ending his playing
days at Stoke City. Harry has worked in the
brewery trade since retiring from soccer and
is currently employed as an area manager
by the JW Lees Brewery, based in
Middleton.
*Won League Championship and FA Cup
winners medals with Man City.*

DOWMAN, Steve
Colchester, Wrexham, Charlton, Newport, Camb U, 1976-1986
Experienced defender who played over 350 league games, Steve is now manager at Wivenhoe Town.

DOWNES, Bobby
WBA, Peterborough, Rochdale, Watford, Barnsley, Blackpool, 1966-1983
Tricky winger who used the experience gained in over 450 league games to assist Graham Taylor at Wolverhampton Wanderers. Is now Director of Football at Watford.
Played on the wing for The Hornets under Graham Taylor in two successive promotions.

DOWNES, Wally
Wimbledon, Newport C, Sheff U, 1978-1994
Wally played almost 200 league games for the Dons before following his boss, Dave Bassett, to Sheffield United where he now works on the coachnig staff.
Played in the Dons 6-0 record League win over Newport in 1983.

DOWNS, Greg
Norwich, Torquay, Coventry, Birmingham, Hereford, 1977-1994
Left back who joined Hereford United in June 1991 as player/manager, a post he held until his dismissal in November 1994. Her then played for a succession of non-league sides, including Merthyr Tydfil and Forest Green Rovers, all in the following season. Now works as a salesmen after an unsuccesful spell in non-league management with Bridgenorth Town.
Played for Coventry in their 1987 FA Cup success.

DOWNSBOROUGH, Peter
Halifax, Swindon, Brighton, Bradford, 1959-1978
Veteran goalie who played over 650 League games and now lives in Elland near Huddersfield and works at a power station.
Played in Swindon Town's 1969 League Cup victory.

DOYLE, Bobby
Barnsley, Peterboro, Blackpool, Portsmouth, Hull, 1972-1986
Injuries forced Bobbie to quit after only 43 games for his last club, Hull City. However he remained in the area and set up a successful haulage business.
Played 537 League games in a long career.

DOYLE, Mike
Man C, Stoke, Bolton, Rochdale, 1964-1983
Defender who won five England caps. Lives in Ashton-under-Lyne and has been a sales manager for Slazenger for ten years. Commentates regularly on local radio.
League Championship and Cup Winners Cup medals.

DRAKE, Ray
Stockport Co 1956-1957
There aren't many footballers who have had to endure what Ray Drake did as a youngster, however, his courage and determination helped him play for the side he supported as a boy after meningitis suffered at the age of three seriouslu affected his hearing. Although predominantly a reserve team player, Ray had an incredible goal scoring record – when he left Edgeley Park he had scored a 234 goals from 201 games, including 19 in 23 first team appearances. After many years working for bookmaking firm, he retired in February 1992 but still lives a stones throw away from the club and remains a season ticket holder.

DRAKE, Ted
Southampton, Arsenal, Reading, 1931-1945
Scored seven goals in one game for Arsenal against Aston Villa on December 14th 1935 – the first six goals coming from his first six shots! That feat still stands as a record for goals scored by one player in an away match. Died in south London the age of 82 in June 1995.
The last Chelsea manager to land a Division One title.

DRINKELL, Kevin
Grimsby, Norwich, Coventry, Rangers,

Birmingham, 1976-1993
Grimsby born striker who caught the eye whilst playing for his hometown club. Moves to Norwich City and then to Rangers, north of the border, followed before Coventry paid £800,000 for his services in 1989. Kevin is currently back in Scotland, where he is manager at Stirling Albion.
Won a League Championship medal with Rangers.

DROY, Mickey
Chelsea, Luton, C Palace, Brentford, 1970-1986
Tower of strength upon which many a Chelsea defence was structured. Lives in south London and is a director of an Electrical Wholesalers. For many years was involved with Kingstonian FC, as player, coach, then briefly manager until 1994.
Promotion to Division One with Chelsea in 1975.

DUGDALE, Jimmy
WBA, Aston Villa, QPR, 1952-1962
For 25 years was a licensee, working in Perry Barr, Aston at the Villa Lions Club, Hall Green, Moseley Rugby Club and the Hasbury Conservative club. He had to have a leg amputated in 1990, forcing him to retire.
Two FA Cup winners medals, with WBA and Villa.

DUNCAN, John
Tottenham, Derby, Scunthorpe, 1974-1982
Scottish forward who scored 53 goals in just over 100 games for Spurs. Managed Ipswich, and now in his second spell as boss at Chesterfield, the first being 1983/7.
Lead Chesterfield to a Fourth Division Championship in 1985.

DUNGWORTH, John
Huddersfield, Barnsley, Oldham, Rochdale, Aldershot, Shrewsbury, Hereford, Mansfield, Rotherham, 1972-1987
A forward who played over 450 League games in a long career. Formerly youth coach at Sheffield United.

DUNMORE, Dave
York, Tottenham, West Ham, Orient, York, 1952-1966
A regular goalscorer who played most of his games at Orient. Ended his career with York and still lives in the town working as sheet metal worker.
Helped Leyton Orient to promotion to the First Division in 1962.

DUNN, Jimmy
Leeds, Darlington, 1947-1959
Still lives in Leeds, Jimmy's adopted home since he signed pro terms at Elland Road in 1947. Appeared in 443 first team games before working for the post office until his retirement in 1987.

DUNNE, Jimmy
Millwall, Torquay, Fulham, Torquay, 1966-1978
Coaching 'Combined 89' in the South Devon League and works as a maintenance man for the Churchill Hotel in Torquay which is owned by Gerald Rowell, whose wife was killed by Michael Rose, one of the inmates who caused a major alert by escaping from Parkhurst jail on the Isle of Wight.
Capped once by the Republic of Ireland against Austria in 1971.

DUNNE, Tony
Man Utd, Bolton, 1960-1978
Republic of Ireland full back who earned 32 full caps. Played over 400 League games for the Reds before moving to Bolton in 1973. Now runs a golf driving range in Altrincham, which he opened upon leaving the game. Lives in nearby Sale.
Won European Cup, Two League Championships and an FA Cup winners medal.

DUQUEMIN, Len
Tottenham 1947-1956
Guernsey born forward who scored 114 goals in 274 games for his only club. Ran a newagents in Northumberland Park and was later mine host at the 'Haunch of Venison' pub in Cheshunt until his retirement.

Scored the goal which sealed the 1951 League Championship.

DUNPHY, Eammon

Man U, York, Millwall, Charlton, Reading, 1962-1976

Back in Dublin working as a writer and broadcaster. He writes a regular column for an Irish Sunday newspaper, the Sunday Independent and frequently appears on Irish television. Played in England for 17 years, inclusind five with Manchester United. He is the author of the classic soccer book 'Only a Game' and also wrote the international best seller 'Unforgettable Fire - the Story of U2'. *Capped 23 times by the Republic of Ireland.*

DWIGHT, Roy

Fulham, Notts F, Coventry, Millwall, 1954-1964

Broke his leg in the 1959 Cup final. Uncle of Elton John and became a teacher. Now Racing manager of the Crayford Greyhound stadium and living in Bexleyheath.

DWYER, Alan

Wrexham, Stockport Co, 1974-1981

Played 169 games for Wrexham where he still lives and works as a lorry driver. *Promotion to Division Three in 1978.*

DWYER, Phil

Cardiff, Rochdale, 1972-1984.

After spending twelve years with Cardiff, Dwyer ended his playing days at Rochdale before joining the South Wales Police Force, based at Barry. *Played 471games for Cardiff which is a club record.*

DYSON, Barry

Tranmere, C Palace, Watford, Leyton O, Colchester, 1960-1974

Scored 99 goals in 174 games for Tranmere. Lived in Colchester and run his own road haulage business until his death in February 1995. *Won a Third Division title with Leyton Orient in 1970.*

DYSON, Paul

Coventry, Stoke, WBA, Darlington, Crewe, 1977-1989

England under-21 international defender. Went on to play non-league for Telford and Solihull Borough.

DYSON Terry

Tottenham, Fulham, Colchester, 1955-1968

Spent the early part of his time at White Hart lane as understudy to George Robb and Terry Medwin. After his playing career ended he managed several non-league clubs before teaching at a Hampstead School and later opening his own sports shop. *Scored two goals in the 1963 Cup Winners Cup final.*

EARLE, Steve

Fulham, Leicester, Peterboro, 1963-1977

Steve made his mark with Fulham and Leicester before jetting off to America. Lives in Tulsa, where he is an insurance salesman. *Scored 98 League goals.*

EARLS, Mick

Southampton, Aldershot, 1973-1978

A brief playing career for this central defender who is now out of the game and working as a social worker managing a home for children in care in Gosport, Hampshire.

EARLES, Pat
Southampton, Reading, 1974-1982
Started at Southampton but moved to
Reading after only a few games and went on
to play for the Royals for six years. Lives
near Portsmouth and works as a probation
officer.

EASTHAM, George OBE
Newcastle, Arsenal, Stoke, 1956-1973
Created history when he took his club,
Newcastle, to court in 1961 when they
refused to let him leave - thus the freedom of
contract clause was introduced. Became
manager at Stoke City. Awarded the OBE in
1975. Now lives in Johannesburg, where he
runs his own sportswear business and acts
as Vice President of the Arsenal Supporters
Club in South Africa.
League Cup winners medal in 1972.

ECCLES, Terry
Blackburn, Mansfield, Huddersfield, York,
1969-1980
Went over to Greece to play for Ethnikos as
well as knocking in the goals for four
English clubs. Now a publican at the 'White
Horse', Upper Poppleton, York.
Played over 250 League games.

EDDY, Keith
Barrow, Watford, Sheff Utd, 1962-1975
Midfielder remembered by fans of Watford
and Sheffield United. Ended his career in
1975 and now coaches soccer in Tulsa, USA
where he is also a successful businessman.
*Skippered Watford to promotion to the
Second Division.*

EDMUNDS, Paul
Leicester, Bournemouth, 1979-1982
Only played a handful of league games but
helped Bournemouth out of the Fourth
Division in 1982. A qualified school teacher
who runs Doncaster Belles womens football
team, for whom his wife is a squad member.

EDWARDS, Bryan
Bolton W 1950-1964
Wing half who played over 500 games in a

long career. Now retired and living in Lancs.
Won an FA Cup medal in 1958.

EDWARDS, Duncan
Manchester U 1952-1957
Potentially one of the best players that the
world may have ever seen. Duncan was
killed in the Munich air disaster, dying in his
sleep in February 1958. He was only aged 21
but had already won three FA Youth Cup
winners medals, two League Championship
medals, a FA Cup runners up medal and two
charity shield trophies. Two stained glass
windows are dedicated in his memory at St
Francis Church in his home town of Dudley.
Capped 18 times by England.

EDWARDS, Ian
WBA, Chester, Wrexham, C Palace, 1973-
1982
Retired injured in 1983 aged 28. Owned two
milk rounds in Wrexham for five years and
selling these made it possible to purchase
an old country house in Criccieth Gwnedd,
which he has converted into an hotel and
runs today.
*Scored four goals for Wales in an internation-
al against Malta.*

EDWARDS, Keith
Sheff U, Hull, Leeds, Hull, Stockport,
Huddersfield Plymouth, 1975-1990
Slightly built goal-scoring forward whose
consistent strike rate made him a popular
player at all his clubs. Now works as a lorry
driver in Sheffield.

EDWARDS, Paul
Manchester United, Oldham, Stockport,
1965-1980
A former England under-23 international
who never really lived up to his full potential. Still lives in Manchester and works in
the parts department of a motor company.
*Won a Third Division Championship medal
with Oldham in 1974.*

EGLINGTON, Tommy
Everton, Tranmere R, 1946-1960
Earned 24 caps for his native Eire, to where

he returned after playing over 500 games for Everton and Tranmere. Returned to Dublin in 1961 to become a successful butcher but was forced to retire due to a serious illness in 1992.
Promoted to the First Division with Everton in 1954.

ELLAM, Roy
Bradford C, Huddersfield, Leeds, Huddersfield, 1961-1974
Played all of his league football for Yorkshire sides, including two spells at Huddersfield Town which were separated by a brief stay at Leeds United. Now landlord of the 'Nelson Inn', Thornton Lees.
Division Two Championship medal with Huddersfield in 1970.

ELLIOTT, Billy
Bradford PA, Burnley, Sunderland, 1946-1958
Capped by England five times and went on to become a much travelled coach and manager. As well as posts in Norway, Belgium, and Germany (where he trained an American side), he also coached the Libyan National Team! At home he managed Darlington until his retirement.
Was on the staff at Sunderland when they reached the FA Cup final in 1973.

ELLIOTT, Paul
Charlton, Luton, Aston Villa, Celtic, Chelsea, 1981-1994
In 1992, aged 28, Paul was Chelsea's Player of the Year when his career was ended as a result of a tackle which has since been the subject of media publicity, a court case and much discussion. Now works as a TV pundit and helps in the sponsorship office at Chelsea.
England under-21 international.

ELLIOTT, Shaun
Sunderland, Norwich, Blackpool, 1976-1989
Former England 'B' International defender who played for Whitley Bay and now turns out for Durham City.
Helped Sunderland to promotion in 1980.

ELLIS, Benjamin
Died in 1966 but his memory lives on as probably one of very few footballers to have a road named after him – Ellis Way in Motherwell, Scotland.

ELLIS, Sam
Sheff Wed, Mansfield, Lincoln, Watford, 1965-1978
Former 'Owls' defender who managed Blackpool and was number two at Man City, before becoming Lincoln City's eighth managerial appointment in nine years when he took on a two year contract at Sincil Bank in 1994. On leaving Lincoln he returned to Bury as assistant manager.
Captained both Lincoln and Watford to Fourth Division titles under Graham Taylor.

ELSTRUP, Lars
Luton T 1989-1990
Danish international forward who joined Luton Town from Odense for a 50-game stay in 1990. Returned to Denmark, where he was most recently reported to have joined a religious cult.

ELWISS, Mike
Doncaster, Preston, C Palace, Preston, 1971-1979
Liked Preston so much he married the daughter of the Preston Chairman! Mike played a total of 201 league games for the Lancashire club in two spells. He now runs a dairy just outside the town.

EMSON Paul
Derby, Grimsby, Wrexham, Darlington, 1978-1991
Played over 100 games for Derby. Now a postman in Richmond.

ENDERSBY, Scott
Tranmere, Swindon, Carlisle, York, Cardiff, 1979-1987
Goalie who had an eight year career. Now working as a chef for a bistro/restaurant in York.
Became the youngest player to play in the FA Cup as a 16 year old for Kettering.

ENGLAND, Mike

Blackburn, Tottenham, Cardiff, 1959-1975

After a long and successful career which saw him win 44 Welsh caps and star as a dominant feature in the Spurs side, England became manager of the Welsh national side in 1980. He held this post for eight years, during which time he was awarded the MBE for services to football. He is now a businessman and owns residential homes in Rhyl and Colwyn Bay.

Won the UEFA Cup in 1972 and scored in the final two years later.

ENTWISTLE, Wayne

Bury, Sunderland, Leeds, Blackpool, Crewe, Wimbledon, Bury, Carlisle, Bolton, Burnley, Stockport, Wigan, Hartlepool, 1976-1990

A former England youth international who turned into a well travelled striker. Had the best spell of his career at Bury second time around and now lives in the town and works as a meat wholesaler.

EUSTACE, Peter

Sheff Wed, West Ham, Rotherham, Sheff Wed, Peterborough, 1962-1975

Manager of Sheffield Wednesday in 1989 but has been out of the game since being sacked as Leyton Orient boss in four years later. Now back in his native Yorkshire, running a pub in Sheffield.

FA Cup runner-up against Everton in 1966.

EVANS, Allan

Aston Villa, Leicester, Darlington, 1977-1990

Enjoyed a successful career at Villa Park and won four full England Caps. Evans was eventually released by Aston Villa in 1990, and after a spell in Australia he returned to England in May 1991 to become assistant manager/coach of Leicester City. Then, in 1994, he followed his manager Brian Little to Aston Villa.

A member of Aston Villa's 1982 European Cup winning team.

EVANS, Alun

Wolves, Liverpool, Aston Villa, Walsall, 1967-1977

Son of the former West Brom left-half of the same name, Alun became Britain's first £100,000 teenage footballer when he was sold by Wolves to Liverpool in 1968. Also played for Aston Villa and Walsall before trying his luck in America and then Australia, eventually quitting soccer in 1980. Now lives near Melbourne in Australia where he has worked as a used car salesman and a delivery driver at a fish market, but is currently trying his hand at painting and decorating.

Played for Liverpool in the 1971 FA Cup final.

EVANS, Brian

Swansea, Hereford, 1963-1974

A winger who played over 350 games for Swansea after joining them from Abergavenny in 1963. Now runs a successful painting and decorating business in Swansea.

Played seven times for Wales between 1972 and 1974.

EVANS, David

Once on the professional books of Aston Villa and also a cricketer who played with Gloucestershire and Warwickshire. He founded an office cleaning business in 1980 and became a director of Luton Town. He took over as Chairman seven years later and was behind the controversial move to ban away fans from Kenilworth road in 1987 to save on Policing costs. He remained in charge until 1989, two years after being elected as Conservative Member of Parliament for Welwyn Hatfield.

EVANS, Dennis
Arsenal 1951-1959
Became assistant manager at Arsenal in 1963 where he had played for eight years. Was coach at Luton Town before becoming a private hire driver.

EVANS, Doug
Norwich, Cambridge, 1974-1981
A former Welsh youth international who spent most of his career playing abroad. Is now a supervisor with Norwich City Council and plays golf off a 12 handicap.
Capped by Wales at youth level.

EVANS, George
Wrexham, Chester, 1957-1968
Wing half with over 275 games of League experience. Now lives in Hightown, Wrexham and works at the nearby Bersham Colliery.

EVANS, Ian
QPR, C Palace, Barnsley, Exeter, Cambridge U, 1970-1983
Ended his league career at Cambridge United in 1983. Worked as first team coach at Millwall before following Mick McCarthy to the Republic of Ireland in 1996.
Welsh international capped 13 times.

EVANS, Maurice
Reading 1955-1966
Played all of his career at Reading and became their manager. Took over at Oxford until March 1988 when he was appointed General Manager.
Played over 400 league games.

EVANS, Mickey
Wolves, Wrexham, 1964-1978
Served Wrexham for 16 years, eventually leaving in 1982 as assistant manager. He then returned to his home village of Caersws

and took up work as a sales manager for a petroleum company.
Capped twice by Wales at under-23 level.

EVANS, Ray
Tottenham, Millwall, Fulham, Stoke, 1968-1981
Former England youth player who ended his career at Stoke in 1981. Now living near Seattle in America, where he coaches youngsters.

EVANS, Roy
Liverpool 1969-1973
Joined Liverpool straight from school and made his debut in 1970, however, he only made a total of eleven appearances in nine seasons and in 1974, at the age of 25, Roy became reserve team coach. He became assistant manager at the end of the 1992/3 season and took over as manager in January 1994, following the departure of Graham Souness.
Played for England schools.

EVANSON, John
Oxford, Blackpool, Fulham, Bournemouth, 1966-1980

Went into catering after 19 years as a pro, becoming a partner in the Key Eating House, Southampton. Can now be found at the 'Owl & Pussycat' pub in central London.

EVANS, Tony
Blackpool, Cardiff, Birmingham, Crystal Palace, Wolves, Bolton, Exeter, Swindon, Walsall, 1973-1986
This useful striker was working as an electrician before turning pro at Blackpool and embarking on a playing career which took in no less than ten clubs. He is now a community officer at Wolves.

EVES, Mel
Wolves, Huddersfield, Sheff U, Gillingham, Mansfield, 1977-1987
Has been in the financial services industry since 1989 and is now a Director of Premier Promotions Financial Advisors - specialising in help for pro sportsmen.
Won a second Division Championship in 1977.

EYRE, Fred
Man C, Lincoln, Bradford PA, 1961-1969
Although Fred only appeared in very few league games, his football career has provided him with an abundance of memories which he now uses to very amusing effect, in his successful books and as a popular after dinner speaker. He is also a wealthy businessman running his own chain of stationery shops.

FACEY, Ken
Leyton O 1952-1960
Played over 300 games for his only club. Retired from the Post Office in 1991 and lives in Hackney.
Scored a hat trick in Orient's record 8-0 win over Palace in 1955.

FAGAN, Joe
Man C, Bradford PA, 1946-1953
Quit in tears as Liverpool boss in the wake of the Hysel riot in May 1985, less than two years after taking over from Bob Paisley. Was a former member of the famous Liverpool 'boot room' before taking over as boss. In his playing days he was a robust centre half with Manchester City and later with Bradford PA. During his relatively brief Anfield reign Liverpool continued to excel, winning the European Cup, Milk Cup and the League Championship.

FAIRBROTHER, Barrie
Orient, Millwall, 1969-1976
An Orient regular for 5 years in the early seventies before ending his career at nearby Millwall. Now lives and works in South Africa.

FAIRCLOUGH, David
Liverpool, Norwich, Oldham, Tranmere, Wigan, 1975-1990
Although he never really commanded a regular first-team place at Anfield, David did more than enough to justify his 'supersub' tag. He now lives in Formby, Liverpool and works as a freelance journalist, having successfully completed a course for the National Council for Training Journalists during his playing days.
Played in two European finals during his time at Liverpool.

FAIRFAX, Ray
WBA, Northampton, 1962-1970
Retired 1979 and worked at West Brom, first as a commercial assistant and then later as assistant secretary. In 1985 he became club secretary at Port Vale and more recently joined the ticket office at Aston Villa.

FALCO, Mark
Tottenham, Chelsea, Watford, Rangers, QPR, Millwall, 1978-1991
A striker who played most of his soccer for London clubs, interrupted by a spell at Glasgow Rangers before QPR paid £350,000 to bring him back to the capital in 1988. When his pro days were over he joined Worthing of the Isthmian League in 1994, was appointed joint manager two years later, but left in September 1996.
UEFA Cup winners medal in 1984.

FALLON, Steve
Camb U 1974-1986
Now works in the commercial department at Cambridge United, the club for whom he made over 400 appearances as a player. Also currently player/manager of neighbours Cambridge City.
Played in two Cambridge promotion sides.

FANTHAM, John
Sheff Wed, Rotherham, 1957-1969
Sturdy forward who was capped once by England and scored 147 goals in 380 games for the 'Owls'. Now a successful businessman in Sheffield.

FARM, George
Blackpool, 1948-1959
Goalie who played 462 games for Blackpool and ten games for Scotland, now living near Edinburgh and is involved in a woollen and textile business.
FA Cup winner with Blackpool in 1953.

FARMER, John
Stoke City, WBA, Leicester City, 1965-1976
A goalkeeper who lived in the shadows of Gordon Banks and then Peter Shilton. Now manages a crisp factory in Cheadle.
England under-23 international.

FARMER, Ted
Wolves 1960-1963
England under-23 international who may well have been in the 1966 World Cup Squad but for an injury sustained in 1964. Ted scored an incredible 28 goals in 27 matches in his first season. He also achieved another remarkable unique feat by scoring his 21st League Goal in his 21st League match on his 21st Birthday on the 21st of January! A serious knee injury forced Ted to retire and he became a sports outfitter. Then, after working for fifteen years in the computer industry, Ted had to retire due to an accident that left him with osteo-arthritis. Now lives in Wombourne, Wolverhampton.
Scored a remarkable 44 goals in 57 games.

FARMER, Terry
Rotherham, York, 1952-1959
Goalscoring forward of the fifties is now working as a steel erector in Rotherham.

FARRELL, Peter
Everton, Tranmere, 1946-1959
Played 421 games for Everton then moved to Tranmere where he became player/manager. Followed by spells with Hollyhead and Shamrock Rovers. Later had a job in insurance and went into broadcasting with RTE in Dublin. Now retired.
Capped 28 times by Eire.

FARRIMOND, Syd
Bolton. Tranmere, 1958-1973
Spent twelve years at Burnden Park as a reliable full back. Now owns a newsagents in Leigh.
Played 495 League games.

FASHANU, John
Norwich, Crystal Palace, Lincoln, Millwall, Wimbledon, Aston Villa, 1979-1995
Injury forced the career of 'Fash the Bash' to come to an end. H e has since had his fingers in a number of pies, including Television Presenter, Sports Marketing, International Trade Broker and African Court Commitee Member - plus being a TV Gladiator.
FA Cup winner with Wimbledon.

FASHANU, Justin
Norwich, Notts F, Southampton, Notts Co, Brighton, Man C, West Ham, Leyton O, Torquay, 1978-1991
A former ABA heavyweight boxer and elder brother of Aston Villa's John, he started his professional career with Norwich City and after shooting to fame with some spectacular goals, Brian Clough took him to Nottingham Forest in a £1m deal. However, his stay was brief and despite repeated comebacks from injury with a variety of clubs both here and abroad, he never recaptured the form that brought him to prominence. He has since had spells in Canada and Scotland and media interest in his private life means that he is probably better

known for his off the field activities which allegedly have included a rather unlikely liaison with TV actress, Julie Goodyear - Coronation Street's barmaid Bet Lynch.
Scored 'that' goal of the season for Norwich against Liverpool.

FAULKNER, John
Leeds, Luton, 1969-1977
Failed to make the grade at Leeds before moving on to Luton. Was on the coaching staff at Norwich until he resigned in February 1996 but was brought back to the club by Mike Walker.
Part of Sutton United's famous FA Cup run of 1969.

FAZACKERLEY, Derek
Blackburn, Chester, York, Bury, 1970-1988
Played seventeen season as a central defender for Blackburn Rovers. Was first team coach at Newcastle United before taking up a similar post at Ewood Park.
Played 671 games for Rovers between 1970-1986 a Club record.

FEARNLEY, Gordon
Sheffield Weds, Bristol Rovers, 1970-1977
Played nearly 100 league games for Rovers before moving to the States. Gordon has now settled in America where he qualified as a lawyer.

FEELEY, Andy
Hereford, Leicester, Brentford, Bury, 1978-1990
Psychiatric nurse at Prestwich hospital and currently playing for Bamber Bridge.
Captained Hereford at the age of 17.

FELL, Jimmy
Grimsby, Everton, Newcastle, Walsall, Lincoln, 1956-1965
Former Grimsby winger who still lives in the town and works as a recreation officer at Grimsby Leisure Centre.

FELTON, Graham
Northampton, Barnsley, 1966-1976
Now working as a painter & decorator from his home in Billing, Northants.

FENTON, Ron
Burnley, WBA, Birmingham C, Brentford, 1960-1969
Became coach at his last club, Notts County, then assistant manager at Notts Forest with Brian Clough for 16 seasons.

FENWICK, Terry
C Palace, QPR, Tottenham, Swindon, 1977-1995
A £550,000 transfer in 1987 took Terry, who won one England cap, across London to Spurs from QPR. Finished playing at Swindon to take up the vacant manager's seat at Portsmouth in February 1995.
Scored in the 1982 FA Cup final against Spurs and won a medal with them nine years later.

FERGUSON, Bobby
Kilmarnock, West Ham, Sheff Wed, Leicester C, 1967-1973
Emigrated to Australia in 1981 to take over as player/coach for Adelaide City FC. In 1982 became the owner/operator of a scuba diving business which he successfully ran for six years. However, Bobby sold his share after enduring the horror of an employee being attacked by a shark. Has been company director of a flooring business ever since.
Capped seven times by Wales.

FERGUSON, Mick
Coventry, Everton, Birmingham, Coventry, Brighton, Colchester, 1973-1987
A powerful striker whose career was blighted by injury. Now youth team coach at Sunderland.

FERGUSON, Mike
Accrington S, Blackburn, Aston V, QPR, Cambridge, Rochdale, Halifax, 1960-1976
Took over as manager of Evagoras in Cyprus in 1991 but has nowmoved back to Burnley.
Played 458 League games in a long career.

FERN, Rod
Leicester, Luton, Chesterfield, Rotherham U,

1967-1982
Was a Publican at the 'Ferriers Arms', in Lount, Leicestershire before becoming a coal merchant back in Measham.
Third Division Championship medal in 1981.

FERNS, Phil
Bournemouth, Charlton, Wimbledon, Blackpool, Aldershot, 1978-1985
Lives in Poole, is a FA coaching representative for Dorset and a FA 'fun week' director.

FERRIER, Ron
Grimsby, Man U, Oldham, Lincoln, 1933-1947
Became a schoolteacher and lived in Cleethorpes. Died in 1991.

FIDLER, Dennis
Man C, Port V, Grimsby, Halifax, Darlington, 1957-1967
A winger who started at Manchester United as an amateur. Worked as a fishmonger until selling up and retiring in 1994.

FIELDING, Wally
Everton, Southport, 1946-1959
Became player/manager at Southport before moving south as trainer/coach at Luton, then youth coach at Watford. Later scouted for Luton.
Played 381 games for Everton.

FILLERY, Mike
Chelsea, QPR, Portsmouth, Oldham, 1978-1992
Strong former Chelsea apprentice who was Assistant Manager of BHL League side Crawley Town until August 1994.

FINNEY, Richard
Rotherham 1973-1980
Now works as a regional manager for the Community Programme for Sports, in Rotherham.

FINNEY, Tom
Luton, Sunderland, Camb U, Brentford, Camb U, 1973-1985
A back injury ended his career, leading to spells in management with Jewson League clubs, Ely City, March Town, Histon and Cambridge City. Away from football, Tom now works with Securicor.
Made 15 Appearances for Northern Ireland.

FINNEY, Tom OBE
Preston NE 1946-1959

Undoubtedly one of the finest footballers ever, Tom scored 187 goals for his beloved Preston in 433 League games. In 1954 he became the first player to be chosen Footballer of the Year, an honour he received again three years later. Tom played 76 times for England, retired from the game at the age of 38 in 1960 and was awarded the OBE. the following year. He set up Tom Finney Ltd. plumbing, heating and electrical contractors in 1946, and held the role of managing director until 1992. Also worked as a part time writer for the News of the World, and was chairman of the Preston Health Authority from 1983 until 1987.
Division Two Championship medal in 1951.

FIRM, Neil
Leeds, Oldham, Peterboro, 1979-1984
A knee injury ended his career and he is now a policeman working for the Norfolk Constabulary, currently based in Thetford.

FIRMANI, Eddie

Charlton, Southend, Charlton, 1951-1967

Born in South Africa, Eddie fell in love with the south London club for whom he became an Addicks Legend. After his playing days ended, he managed Charlton until 1970. He has since spent many years coaching in North America and most recently managed New York-New Jersey Mertostars in the US Major League.

Scored a hat trick in Charlton's record League win against Middlesbrough in 1953.

FISHENDEN, Paul

Wimbledon,Fulham, Millwall, Leyton O, Crewe, 1981-1989

After leaving Crewe played for Wokingham, Crawley and, last season, Harrow Borough.

FISHER, Bobby

Leyton O, Camb U, Brentford, 1973-1984

Former Orient full back Bobby is now working as an actor in television commercials and has appeared as a baddie in Sky TV's 'Space Precinct'.

Played for Orient in the 1978 FA Cup semi final against Arsenal.

FISHER, Fred

Grimsby, Rochdale, 1938-1951

Played for two clubs either side of the second world war and after retiring from the game became a driving instructor in the Grimsby area. Died in June 1993 aged 73.

FISHER, Hugh

Blackpool, Southampton, Southport, 1963-1977

Played almost 300 games for the Saints and still lives in the area where he works as a representative for Courage brewery.

FLANAGAN, Mike

Charlton, C Palace, QPR, Charlton, Camb U, 1971-1986

After a London-based playing career Mike became manager of Gillingham – a position he held until early 1995. He then reverted back to playing, this time with Diadora League side Hornchurch.

FLETCHER, Paul

Bolton, Burnley, Blackpool, 1968-1981

Rose to the heady heights of Chief Executive at Huddersfield Town FC. He is also an accomplished after dinner speaker and left Huddersfield in August 1996 to take up a new challenge with Bolton.

FITZPATRICK, John

Man U 1964-1972

Injury forced him to quit at the young age of 26. After a year off, he joined an Aberdeen wine company before setting up on his own in the same trade. Now works as a self employed agent selling quality French and German wine. Can also be regularly heard on local radio sports programmes.

United's first ever substitute, against Spurs in October 1965.

FLINT, Kenny

Tottenham, Aldershot, Leyton O, 1947-1958

Outside left who played over 300 games for Aldershot, Kenny now works for a firm of bookmakers in Enfield, Middlesex.

FLOWERS, Ron
Wolves, Northampton, 1952-1968

Wing half who played 469 games for Wolves between 1952 and 1966 and won 49 England caps. Now lives near Stafford and runs his own sports shop in Wolverhampton.
Three League Championship medals.

FLYNN, Brian
Burnley, Leeds, Burnley, Cardiff, Doncaster, Bury, Wrexham, 1972-1991
Won 66 caps in a playing career which took him to Burnley in 1972 and then to Leeds United for five years, before returning to Turf Moor. Spells at several other clubs and a time in Ireland led him to Wrexham, where in 1989 he was appointed manager in succession to Dixie McNeill.
Lead Wrexham out of the Third Division in 1993.

FOGG, David
Wrexham, Oxford, 1970-1984
Spent fifteen years at Oxford as player,

coach and assistant manager. Then returned to his native Liverpool joining the coaching staff at Everton, before joining Chester City.

FOGGO, Ken
WBA, Norwich, Portsmouth, Southend, 1962-1975
Retired from soccer in 1982 and began working on a London market stall. Is now running a dry cleaning business in the East End.
Twice named City's player of the year.

FOGGON, Alan
Newcastle, Cardiff, Middlesboro, Man U, Sunderland, Southend, Hartlepool, 1967-1977
A winger whose 45 goals in 105 games for Middlesbrough prompted a move to Manchester United in 1976. Alan now lives in Jarrow where he currently works as a security manager for a major company.
1969 Fairs Cup winner with Newcastle.

FOLEY, Peter
Oxford, Gillingham, Aldershot, Exeter, 1974-1986
After a spell in Hong Kong Peter became Manager of Marlow FC until February 1995 when he moved to Hendon.

FOLEY, Theo
Exeter, Northampton, Charlton, 1955-1967
Was coach at Arsenal and manager of Northampton Town, before joining Southend United as assistant manager. Became part of their three-man management team in early 1995 before reverting back to the number two position.
Capped nine times by the Republic of Ireland.

FORBES, Duncan
Colchester, Norwich, Torquay, 1961-1976
Took his tally of league appearance to over 500 while at Norwich, following his move from Colchester in 1961. Works for the Canaries as their chief scout.
Won two Promotions and two Cup finals with Norwich.

F

FORD, David

Sheff Wed, Newcastle, Sheffield Utd, Halifax, 1963-1975

Inside forward David is now running a plumbing and heating business in Sheffield.
Capped twice by England at under-23 level.

FORD, Tony

Grimsby, Sunderland, Stoke, WBA, Grimsby, 1975-1992

Speedy winger who played in over 500 league games and is now a coach at Scunthorpe Utd.

FORD, Trevor

Swansea, Aston V, Sunderland, Cardiff, Newport, 1946-1960

Centre forward who played 38 internationals for Wales. Trevor now runs a garage business. He was also a capable cricketer and was playing as a substitute fielder for Glamorgan in the match that Sir Garfield Sobers set a world record by hitting six sixes in one over.
First Welsh International to score over 20 goals.

FORGAN, Tommy

Hull, York, 1953-1965

Played 388 games for Hull and also played for York in their 1955 FA Cup semi final, while in the Third Division North. Now lives in New Zealand.

FOREMAN, Dennis

Brighton 1952-1960

Played 212 games for Brighton, scoring 62 goals. Also played cricket for Sussex. Now a teacher at Shoreham Grammar school in the same county.

FORREST, Gerry

Rotherham, Southampton, Rotherham, 1977-1990

A serious knee injury suffered while at Southampton ended Gerry's career prematurely. Breifly coached at Darlington.

FORREST, James

Rangers, Preston, Aberdeen, 1960-1973

A real schoolboy whizzkid who had two good feet as well as an electrifying burst of speed. Ended his career in Hong Kong and now lives in America where he has taken out US citzenship.
Scottish League Championship in 1964.

FOSTER, Barry

Mansfield 1971-1981

Played 282 games for Mansfield in the 70s. Now runs a market stall selling footwear.

FOSTER, Colin

Mansfield, Peterborough, 1971-1980

Managed non-league sides Corby Town, Peterborough City and Stamford but now works as a painter in the Peterborough area.

FOULKES, Bill

Man Utd 1952-1969

Was sadly forced to sell his collection of medals accrued during his very successful career with Manchester United – raising £37,000 at Christies in October 1992. His last managerial post was in Japan, in charge of the Mazda Club.
European Cup Winners medal.

FOULKES, Reg

Walsall, Norwich, 1946-1955

A centre half who played over 370 games after the war. Now a retired accountant in Shrewsbury.
Former England under-15 international.

FOWLER, Tom

Northampton, Aldershot, 1946-1962

Played over 500 games for Northampton. Lives in the town working in a factory.
Holds the Northampton appearances record.

FOX, Peter

Sheff Wed, Barnsley, Stoke, 1972-1990

Took over as manager of Exeter City in June 1995 following Terry Cooper's resignation due to ill health. Peter had been voted the club's 'player of the year' the season before.
Won promotion to Division One with Stoke in 1979.

FOX, Steve
Birmingham, Wrexham, Port V, Chester, 1976-1985

A skilful winger who ended his career at Chester in 1985 and became a lorry driver. He lives in Tamworth where he is currently working as a debt collector and helping out with old peoples gardens.

FRANCIS, Gerry
QPR, C Palace, QPR, Coventry, Exeter, Cardiff, Swansea, Portsmouth, Bristol R, 1969-1987

Captained club and country and would have won more than his twelve caps but for a series of niggling injuries. Cut his managerial teeth at Bristol Rovers (1987/91) and QPR (1991-1994) before taking over at Tottenham Hotspur in November 1994. Also has a successful antiques shop in Chertsey, Surrey.
Helped QPR to the First Division in 1973.

FRANCIS, Gerry
Leeds, York, 1957-1961

A shoe repairer who became the first coloured player to wear a Leeds shirt. Although a South African by birth, he settled in England and became a postman. Played 62 games in his short career.

FRANCIS, Trevor
Birmingham, Notts F, Man C, QPR, Sheff Wed, 1970-1991

Notts Forest parted with over £1m to bring the boy-wonder from Birmingham City in February 1979. He moved into management with QPR before taking over at Sheffield Wednesday in 1991. A difficult 1994/5 season resulted in his departure from Hillsborough in May 1995. After spending a season working for Sky TV, he was appointed Birmingham boss in May 1996.
Became Britain's first million-pound footballer.

FRANKLIN, Paul
Watford, Shrewsbury, Swindon, Reading, 1981-1989

A six foot defender who has worked with Martin O'Neill at three clubs: Wycombe,

Norwich and now as coach at Leicester.
A member of Watford's 1982 FA Youth Cup winning side.

FRANKLIN, Neil
Stoke, Hull, Crewe, Stockport, 1946-1957

One of Stoke City's post war stars, Neil won 27 caps for England as a full back, managed Colchester United and had a spell in Cyprus before becoming a publican in Oswaldthistle. He died in February 1996 at his retirement home in the Potteries.
Won three caps for England during the Second World War.

FRANKS, Colin
Watford, Sheffield United, 1969-1979

After a fairly anonymous career he moved to North America and settled in Canada.

FARNWORTH, Simon
Bolton, Stockport, Tranmere, Bury, Preston, 1981-1994

A reliable goalkeeper who plied his trade at a number of clubs. Now physio at Wigan.
A former England Schools International.

FRASER, Doug
WBA, Notts F, Walsall, 1963-1973

Wing half who was a Scottish international, winning two caps in the mid sixties. He ended his playing days at Walsall where he was appointed manager in 1975. Retired from football in 1977 and became a prison warder at Nottingham.
Appeared for West Brom in three League Cup finals.

FRASER, John
Fulham, Brentford, 1971-1979
Former full back who now lives in Chertsey, Surrey and works as a London taxi driver.
Member of Fulham's 1975 FA Cup losing side.

FRIZZELL, Jimm
Oldham 1960-1969
Wing half who played over 300 games for Oldham Athletic and still lives close to Boundary Park despite having been employed by Manchester City for the past seven years.

FROGGATT, Jack
Portsmouth, Leicester, 1946-1957
Capped by England 13 times whilst at Pompey for whom he played 300 League games. Died in 1993, aged 71, having been in the licensed trade for 22 years.
Won two successive League Championship medals with Portsmouth in 1949 and 1950.

FROGGATT, John.
Notts Co, Colchester, Port V, Northampton, 1963-1978
Now a self employed painter and decorator living in Mansfield.

FROGGATT, Redfern
Sheff Weds 1946-1959
On the books at Hillsborough for seventeen years and capped four times by England, Redfern followed in his father's footsteps by playing for the Owls. Now retired from his job as a salesman for an oil fuel firm, living in Sheffield.
Won three Second Division Championships in the 1950s.

FRY, Barry
Man Utd, Bolton, Luton, Orient, 1962-1967
Known for his larger-than-life character as manager at Birmingham City, Barry was a schoolboy international with enough promise to encourage Sir Matt Busby to sign him for Manchester United. However, his league career was brief, in part due to injury. His passion for the game earned him the manager's job at non-league Dunstable and then Barnet. Although constantly in the news, more often than not due to disagreements with equally colourful Chairmen, he has proved his pedigree by gaining Barnet entry into the League; bringing life and Stan Collymore to Southend and then promotion to the Blues in his first full year in office. Sacked at the end of the 1995/6 season but bounced back by buying Peterboro United.
Took Barnet into the Football League in 1991.

FRY, Roger
Southampton, Walsall, 1970-1976
Lives near Southampton and has worked as a production planner for Aerostructures since 1990.

FRYATT, Jim
Charlton, Southend, Bradford PA, Southport, Torquay, Stockport, Blackburn, Oldham, Southport, Stockport, Torquay, 1959-1974
A traditional goal-scoring centre forward who was well travelled during his playing days. He continued this trend by moving over to America when he retired from the game, becoming a croupier in a Las Vegas Casino. Now back in the UK working for a firm of playing field contractors.
Played nearly 500 League games scoring 189 goals.

FUCCILLO, Lil
Luton, Southend, Peterboro, Camb U, 1974-1987
Now lives near Bedford and was a groundsman/coach at a local public school. He returned to the game to become a member of the coaching staff at Birmingham City, before following Barry Fry back to London Road.

FUDGE, Micky
WBA, Exeter, 1963-1967
Former Exeter inside forward who is now landlord of the 'Lord Hill' pub in Dawley, Telford.

FUNNELL, Tony
Soton, Gillingham, Brentford, Bournemouth, 1972-1982
A Sussex born forward who was an instant hit with Saints fans. Injury ended his career early and he went on to manage Wimborne Town FC in the Wessex League.
Helped Southampton to First Division Promotion in 1978.

FURNELL, Jim
Burnley, Liverpool, Arsenal, Rotherham, Plymouth, 1959-1975
Best remembered as a keeper for Arsenal in the sixties and with Plymouth Argyle in the seventies. Jim is now youth team manager at Blackburn Rovers.
Helped Liverpool to a Second Division Championship in 1962.

FURPHY, Ken
Darlington, Workington, Watford, 1953-1971
Held a number of management and coaching positions including that of England under-23 boss and managed Pele in New York. Owns a sportshop in South Devon and works for local radio.
Helped Workington to their only Football League promotion.

FUTCHER, Paul
Chester, Luton, Man C, Oldham, Derby, Barnsley, Halifax, Grimsby T, 1972-1995
Left Grimsby in January 1995 to become manager of Darlington but relinquished the role after only ten games. Now manager of non league Grestley Rovers.
Capped 11 times at under-21 level by England.

FUTCHER, Ron
Chester, Luton, Man C, Barnsley, Oxford, Bradford C, Port V, Burnley, Crewe, 1973-1993

Lives in Holmfirth a quarter of a mile away from his brother Paul. Runs a business from home selling sportswear to retail outlets throughout the north of England.

GABRIEL, Jimmy
Dundee, Everton, Southampton, Bournemouth, Swindon, Brentford, 1957-1973
One of the best strong tackling wing half's of his day. Spent ten years in America, firstly as a player then coach for Seattle Sounders, after ending his league career at Bournemouth. He returned to Bournemouth to become their assistant manager before accepting a similar post at Everton. He is now reserve team coach at Goodison Park after an unsuccessful spell as first team boss.
League Championship with Everton in 1963.

GALLAGHER, Joe
Birmingham, Wolves, West Ham, Burnley, 1973-1985
A capable defender who returned to the midlands and managed Midland Combination club Kings Heath until February 1995.

GALLEY, John
Wolves, Rotherham, Bristol C, Notts F, Peterboro, Hereford, 1961-1976
Best remembered for his goal scoring at Bristol City where he netted 82 times in 174 games. Now a rep for the Berwick Paper Group in Leicester.

GALLOGLY, Charlie
Huddersfield, Watford, Bournemouth, 1949-1954
Entered into league football at the late age of 24. Moved to America to run a bar in New York.

GALVIN, Chris
Leeds, Hull, York, Stockport, 1968-1980
Ended his career in Hong Kong but now lives in Huddersfield where he runs a sports shop.
Former England youth international.

GALVIN, Tony
Tottenham, Sheff Wed, Swindon, 1976-1989
Former Spurs and Republic of Ireland inter-
national winger (29 caps) who now works as
a college lecturer, Was manager of Royston
Town in the South Midlands League until
May 1996.
*A member of Spurs 1984 UEFA Cup winning
side.*

GARBETT, Terry
Middlesbrough, Watford, Blackburn,
Sheffield United, 1963-1976
Moved to the States where he played for
New York Cosmos and then became coach
for the University of South Carolina.
*Scored in Watford's first ever FA Cup semi
final appearance.*

GARLAND, Chris
Bristol C, Chelsea, Leicester, Bristol C, 1966-
1982
Popular blond haired forward who won one
England under-23 cap and started and
ended his career at Bristol City. Still lives in
the area but unfortunately suffers from
Parkinsons disease.
A League Cup finalist with Chelsea in 1972.

GARNER, Alan
Millwall, Luton, Watford, Portsmouth, 1969-
1981
Former Luton defender who is still a regular
at Kenilworth Road, where he has an executive box for home games.

GARRETT, Tommy
Blackpool, Millwall, 1946-1961
England international defender who played
over 300 games for Blackpool. Emigrated to
Australia.
FA Cup winner with Blackpool in 1953.

GARWOOD, Colin
Peterboro, Oldham, Huddersfield, Colchester,
Portsmouth, Aldershot, 1967-1981
Lives in Newark, Notts and works for an
engineering company in Wisbech. Holds an
FA Coaching badge and is keen to be
involved in semi-professional soccer again.

GASKELL, Dave
Man U, Wrexham, 1957-1971
A goalkeeper who was pitched into the 1956
Charity Shield when first choice Ray Wood
was injured. Lives in Wrexham and retired
from his sales managers job due to achilles
tendon trouble.
FA Cup winners medal in 1963.

GATES, Bill
Middlesboro 1961-1973
Defender who starred for the Boro for 12
years. Made his fortune from sports shops,
which he sold and subsequently moved to
live in the Cayman Islands.

GATES, Eric
Ipswich, Sunderland, Carlisle, 1973-1990
A forward who was capped twice by
England. Now lives in Barnard Castle and is
player/coach with West Auckland Town, a
team managed by his brother, Alan.
UEFA Cup winner with Ipswich in 1981.

GATTING, Steve
Arsenal, Brighton, Charlton, 1977-1993
An experienced central defender and brother
of Middlesex and England cricketer, Mike.
Now turning out for Stamco FC.
Played for Brighton in the1983 FA Cup final.

GAVIN, John
Norwich, Spurs, Norwich, Watford, Crystal
Palace, 1948-1961
A former Republic of Ireland international
who was sold back to Norwich as part of the
deal which took Maurice Norman to White
Hart Lane. Later became player manager of
Newmarket and ended up running a pub for
several years.
*Holds the Norwich record for most career
League goals (122).*

GEDDIS, David
Ipswich, Luton, Aston V, Luton, Barnsley,
Birmingham, Brentford, Shrewsbury,
Swindon, Darlington, 1976-1990
A well travelled goalscoring striker, David is
now working as youth team coach at
Middlesbrough.

GEMMELL, Tommy

Celtic, Notts Forest, Dundee, 1961-1976
Pulled on the White and Green hoops as a
Celtic player for ten glorious years, Tommy
is now a manager for Sun Life Assurance.
His career was once threatened by a lawn-
mower accident but he still managed
to score the equaliser from 25 yards in the
1967 European Cup final.

GEMMILL, Archie

St Mirren, Preston, Derby, Notts F,
Birmingham, Wigan, Derby, 1964-1984
A Scottish International who was reserve
coach at Forest until May 94. Became man-
ager of Rotherham in October 1994, linking
up again with former team-mate John
McGovern, until September 1996.
Won Three League Championship medals.

GENNOE, Terry

Bury, Halifax, Southampton, C Palace,
Blackburn, 1972-1993
Now lives in Preston and is an education
officer with the Learning Through Football
Scheme.
League Cup finalist wuth Saints in 1979.

GEORGE, Charlie

Arsenal, Derby, Southampton, Notts F,
Bournemouth, Derby, 1969-1981

One of the games most colourful characters
from the seventies and a darling of the North
Bank. After a spell in Hong Kong and running a pub in Hampshire, Charlie returned
to London to become a partner in a garage
firm. Now helps out at Highbury as a match
day host and running the club museum.
Double winner with Arsenal in 1971.

GEORGE, Ricky

Tottenham, Watford, Bournemouth, Oxford,
1963-1967
A former Spurs junior who struggled to make
the grade as a professional player and later
moved into non-league football. Now owns a
sportshop.
*Became famous overnight after scoring the
goal for non-league Hereford which knocked
Newcastle out of the FA Cup.*

GIBBINS, Roger

Tottenham, Oxford, Norwich, Cambridge,
Cardiff, Swansea, Newport, Torquay, Cardiff,
1972-1994
Stayed on as a coach at Cardiff City until
June 1994. Father Eddie was a pro at Spurs
just after the last war.

GIBSON, Dave

Hibs, Leicester, Aston Villa, Exeter C, 1956-
1972
Opened a pet food and garden shop in
Exmouth before moving back to
Leicestershire. He has been a postman for
the past twelve years and is also co-owner of
a residential rest home.
Played for Leicester in the 1963 FA Cup final.

GIBSON, Mike

Shrewsbury, Bristol C, Gillingham, 1960-
1973
Mike helps coach the Bristol City youth side
and works as a postman. He played 332
games in the Ashton Gate goal.

GIBSON, Terry

Tottenham, Coventry, Man U, Wimbledon,
Swindon, Barnet, 1979-1995
Won 11 England youth caps as a bustling
forward. Terry was Barnet caretaker manag-

er, then first team coach, leaving in October 1996.
FA Cup winner with Wimbledon in 1988.

GIDMAN, John
Aston V, Everton, Man U, Man C, Stoke, Darlington, 1972-1988
Everton broke their club record to acquire England international John from Aston Villa in 1979. Was manager of Kings Lynn until early 1995.
A League Cup and FA Cup winner.

GILBERT, Billy
Crystal Palace, Portsmouth, Colchester U, Maidstone, 1977-1990
A member of the Crystal Palace 'Team of the Eighties' and a regular England under-23 international. Now buys and sells second hand cars and manages Waterlooville in the Beazer Homes League.

GILBERT, Tim
Sunderland, Cardiff, Darlington, 1976-1983
Died suddenly in 1995 aged only 36, whilst coaching a local junior team.

GILCHRIST, Paul
Charlton, Doncaster, Southampton, Portsmouth, Swindon, Hereford, 1969-1979
Ran a health and fitness club in Swindon but now works for BMW in Sussex.
Played a part in Saints sucessful 1976 FA Cup run.

GILES, David
Cardiff, Wrexham, Swansea, Leyton O, C Palace, BirminghamC, Newport, Cardiff, 1974-1986
Became a double glazing salesman after AFC Cardiff's sponsor pulled out of support-ing the club. Now manages Ebbw Vale.
Capped 12 times by Wales between 1980-1983.

GILES, Jim
Swindon, Aldershot, Exeter, Charlton, Exeter, 1965-1980
Central defender Jim is now a builder at Ottery St Mary, Devon.

GILES, Johnny
Man U, Leeds, WBA, 1959-1976

Won trophies galore over a magnificent career of 863 League appearances. He played in 11 FA Cup semi finals and shares the record for FA Cup final appearances. He was the first Eire player to win 50 full caps for his country, ending with a total of 60, including a spell as player/manager. He moved into club management with WBA (1975/7), Philadelphia Fury NASL, Vancouver Whitecaps NASL and West Brom again (1984/5). Now writes a regular column for the Daily Express.
Twice a Fairs Cup winner with Leeds.

GILL, Eric
Charlton, Brighton, 1951-1959
A goalkeeper who played 280 games for Brighton and now runs a hotel in the Sussex seaside resort.

GILLIGAN, Jimmy
Watford, Lincoln, Grimsby, Swindon, Lincoln, Cardiff, Portsmouth, Swansea, 1981-1993
Played for seven League clubs, won FA Youth Cup winners medal in 1982 and ended his playing days with non-league Stamco. Now youth development officer at Watford.
Scored Waford's first goal in the UEFA Cup.

GILLIVER, Alan
Huddersfield, Blackburn, Rotherham,

Brighton, Lincoln, Bradford C, Stockport, Bradford C, 1962-1978
A well travelled centre forward, Alan is now working as stadium manager at Bradford City's Valley Parade.

GILZEAN, Alan
Dundee, Tottenham, 1957-1973
After his ten years at Spurs Alan had a spell in South Africa, before returning to manage Stevenage from May 1975 to August 1976. He is now a transport manager for a haulage firm in Enfield. His son Ian was also a pro with Spurs and then at Northampton.
Won the Fairs Cup with Spurs in 1972.

GLAZIER, Bill
C Palace, Coventry, Brentford, 1961-1975
Moved to Spain in 1986 having made his money through property. He once owned a hotel on Brighton seafront but now can be seen around the seafront of Benidorm in Spain, where he now lives. He earns his beer money by cleaning and maintaining swimming pools.
Second Division Championship winner with coventry in 1967.

GLOVER, Len
Charlton, Leicester, 1962-1975
A Leicester City great and speedy winger who is now a publican in Kibworth, Leicestershire and was manager of Harlow Town FC until January 1995.
Played for Leicester in the 1969 FA Cup final.

GODDARD, Paul
QPR, West Ham, Newcastle, Derby, Millwall, Ipswich, 1977-1995
Nicknamed 'Sarge' as a result of his connection with the Boys Brigade. Broke the West Ham transfer record when he moved across London to Upton Park for £800,000 in 1980. Appointed first team coach at Ipswich before taking over the youth team.
Scored in his one and only appearance for England against Iceland in 1982

GODDARD, Ray
Leyton O, Millwall, Wimbledon, 1966-1980

Kept goal in over 300 league games for his three London clubs. Ray now owns and runs a bar in Spain.

GOODFELLOW, Jimmy
Third Lanark, Leicester City, Mansfield, 1961-1971
Offically credited with being Leicester's first ever substitute. Still lives in Leicestershire and working as an electrician.
Played in the 1965 League Cup final.

GODDEN, Tony
WBA, Luton, Walsall, Chelsea, Birmingham, Bury, Peterboro, 1976-1989
Played most of his football at West Bromwich Albion. Tony was manager of Kings Lynn FC until the end of the 1994/5 season then took over as boss at Bury Town.
WBA club record of 228 consecutive appearances.

GODFREY, Brian
Everton, Scunthorpe, Preston, Aston V, Bristol R, Newport, 1959-1975
Brian appeared in 557 matches and netted 128 goals. He played for Portland Timbers, managed Gloucester City and is now in the hot seat at Stroud League Uplands. Also works as a site agent.

GODFREY, Kevin
Orient, Plymouth, Brentford, 1977-1993
Played 255 games on the wing for Orient and is now a taxi driver in West London.
Division Two Champion in 1992 with Brentford.

GODFREY, Tony
Southampton, Aldershot, Rochdale, Aldershot, 1958-1975
Now runs his own building business in Basingstoke, Hants.
Rochdale's player of the year in his second season.

GODWIN, Tommy
Leicester, Bournemouth, 1949-1961
Bournemouth's goalie for nine years, playing 350 League games. Spent 20 years as a

paint sprayer followed by 8 years as a parks patrolman before retiring. His one regret from his playing days was that he left his teeth in the dressing room during one of his 13 appearances for the Republic of Ireland: they were 2-0 up with ten minutes to go when the Danish supporters, accusing them of time-wasting, decided to pelt his penalty area with apples! Died in August 1996.

GOLAC, Ivan
Southampton, Bournemouth, Man C, Southampton, Portsmouth, 1978-1984

Succeeded Jim McLean as manager of Dundee United in 1993 and held the post until March 1995. Born in Croatia, Ivan signed for the 'Saints' in 1978 after 16 years with Partizan Belgrade. He returned home to coach Partizan and then the National team. Was also manager at Torquay before moving north of the border.

GOODFELLOW, Jim
Port V, Workington, Rotherham, Stockport, 1966-1978
Now working as club physiotherapist at Cardiff City.

GOODING, Mick
Rotherham, Chesterfield, Rotherham, Peterboro, Wolves, Reading, 1979-1996
In January 1995 was appointed joint manager of Reading with team-mate Jimmy Quinn.

Won two Division Three Champoinships as with Reading.

GOODWIN, Freddie
Wolves, Stockport, Blackburn, Southport, Port V, Stockport, 1961-1974
At 28 years old Goodwin passed his full coaching badge and after retiring as a pro embarked on a thirteen year period coaching in New Zealand. He won two championships with his first club, Stop Out, before coaching Papatoetoe, Hut Valley Utd and Columbus Waterside. He also spent two years as assistant coach to the New Zealand national team and was coaching director for the School of Excellence. Fred moved back to Stockport in November 1993 to the family home opposite the Railway End of Edgeley Park.

GOODWIN, Fred
Manchester United, Leeds U, Scunthorpe, 1953-1964
After winning a Championship Winners medal his career was ended by a triple leg fracture. Undertook a number of management appointments in England and in the USA, where he now lives.
Played in the 1958 FA Cup final.

GOODYEAR, Clive
Luton, Plymouth, Wimbledon, Brentford, 1979-1990
He was adjudged to have fouled John Aldridge which led to Dave Beasant becoming the first goalkeeper to save a penalty in an FA Cup final. Has now returned to Luton where he is club physiotherapist
Won a cup winners medal with Wimbledon in 1988.

GORDON, Colin
Swindon, Wimbledon, Gillingham, Reading, Bristol C, Fulham, Birmingham, Hereford, Walsall, Bristol R, Leicester, 1984-1993
Sacked by Stourbridge FC at the end of the 1995/6 season.

GORDON, Dennis
WBA, Brighton, 1947-1960

Now retired and living in Hove, Sussex.

GORDON, John
Portsmouth, Birmingham, Portsmouth, 1951-1966
Johnny played over 500 games in a two-club career. Now co-owner of Littles Wine Bar in Southsea. Still attends all Pompey home matches.
Division Three Championship with Portsmouth in 1962.

GORING, Peter
Arsenal 1949-1958
Played 220 games for the Gunners. Became a butcher in Cheltenham. Died in December 1994.
League Championship with Arsenal in 1953.

GORMAN, John
Celtic Carlisle, Tottenham, 1970-1978
Managed Swindon until November 1994. Then joined Bristol City as assistant manager and is currently Glenn Hoddle's assistant with the England team.

GOULD, Bobby
Coventry, Arsenal, Wolves, WBA, Bristol C, West Ham, Wolves, Bristol R, Hereford, 1963-1979
After a long career as a no-nonsense forward Gould went on to manage WBA, Coventry and Wimbledon. Presented 'Talk Back' on Sky TV and was then appointed manager of Wales.
Managed Wimbledon to a 1988 FA Cup win.

GOULD, Trevor
Coventry, Northampton, 1969-1972
Has been Director of Youth Football at Coventry City for the past three years, having previously managed Bedford and Aylesbury.

GOWLING, Alan
Man U, Huddersfield, Newcastle, Bolton, Preston, 1967-1982
A graduate of Manchester University, Alan won England under-23 honours during his four yeas at old Trafford. Is now general

Manager of a chemicals company based in Buxton, Derbyshire.
Member of Great Britain's Mexico Olympic squad.

GRAHAM, Arthur
Aberdeen, Leeds, Man U, Bradford C, 1970-1986
Coached children with the Eddie Gray coaching schools. before becoming a part time youth coach with Halifax. Still turns out for the ex-Leeds United charity side.

GRAHAM, George
Aston V, Chelsea, Arsenal, Man U, Portsmouth, C Palace, 1962-1977
Retired from playing in 1980 and joined the staff at QPR. Became manager at Millwall in December 1982, then Arsenal boss for nine years winning a whole host of trophies until early 1995. Served a years suspension for before returning to the game as Leeds boss in September 1996.
Member of The Gunners double winning side of 1971.

GRAHAM, Jackie
Brentford 1970-1979
Although born in Scotland, Jackie played 371 League games for his only League club, Brentford. He is now employed as a security guard for American Airways based at Heathrow Airport.

GRAHAM, Tommy
Barnsley, Halifax T, Doncaster R, Scunthorpe U, Scarborough, Halifax T, 1978-1992
Lives in Barnsley and works as a Chiropodist. Still plays non-league soccer.

GRANT, Jackie
Everton, Rochdale, Southport, 1946-1959
Retired in Liverpool and lives opposite Goodison Park where he played for eight years.

GRAVER, Andy
Newcastle, Lincoln, Leicester, Lincoln, Stoke, Lincoln, 1947-1960
Prolific goalscorer with Lincoln in three

spells scoring 144 times in 276 league games. Now retired and living near Lincoln after spending 15 years working for the Bank of Scotland.
Scored six times during Lincoln's record 11-1 victory in 1951.

GRAY, Andy
Dundee United, Aston V, Wolves, Everton, Aston V, Notts Co, WBA, 1973-1988

Scottish international striker Andy Gray joined Aston Villa in 1975 for £110,000. His stay at Villa Park lasted four years before Wolves broke the British transfer record fee to sign Gray for £1,469,000 in September 1989. He won 20 caps for Scotland, was voted PFA 'Player of the Year' and 'Young Player of the Year' in 1977. He returned to Villa in the summer of 1991 as assistant manger to Ron Atkinson following a period as a player for Cheltenham Town. Gray's direct attitude is now being utilised as a leading pundit on SKY Sports.
Won League, European and FA Cup medals with Everton.

GRAY, Eddie
Leeds 1965-1983
Turned professional for Leeds in 1965 and played 442 games in an accomplished career with Leeds and Scotland. Had a spell in management with Leeds, and then Rochdale. Ran soccer camps for youngsters

in Yorkshire until being appointed to the Elland Road coaching staff.
Won two League Championships; FA Cup medal; League Cup; and Fairs Cup winners medals.

GRAY, Frank
Notts F, Leeds, Sunderland, Darlington, 1972-1991
Won 32 caps for Scotland as a player and went on to manage Darlington, then scouted for Blackburn and Sheffield Wednesday. Frank resigned after a brief stay as manager of Harrogate FC in June 1994 to take up a post in Bahrain. Father of Andy who plays for Leeds.
European Cup winner with Forest in 1980.

GRAY, Stuart
Notts F, Bolton, Barnsley, Aston V, Soton, 1980-1994
When his playing career was prematurely ended by injury, Stuart joined his old boss, Graham Taylor, at Wolves in the role of reserve team manager. However, his family could not settle in the Midlands, so he returned south and played for Bognor Regis before retiring from the game.

GRAY, Terry
Huddersfield, Southend, Bradford C, Preston, 1973-1985
Now working as a financial consultant and lives in Liversedge.

GRAY, William
Leyton O, Chelsea, Burnley, Notts F, Millwall, 1947-1964
Now retired from his role as groundsman at Nottingham Forest.

GRAYDON, Ray
Bristol R, Aston V, Coventry, Oxford, 1965-1980
Scorer of the winning goal in the 1975 League Cup final for Aston Villa at Wembley. Ray had plenty of practice as a young lad, pretending to take part in a victory lap around Wembley. However, when the real moment arrived he was pulled into the

crowd and then suffered cramp for the first time in his career - and had to just watch as the rest of his team-mates enjoyed their moment of glory. Later served Coventry City and Washington Diplomats in the United States before joining Oxford United in November 1978 first as a player and thereafter as senior coach. Moved to Southampton, where he is currently youth team manager.

Played in two League Cup finals for Villa.

GREALISH, Tony

Leyton O, Luton, Brighton, WBA, Man C, Rotherham, Walsall, 1974-1991

Player/coach for Bromsgrove Rovers until Bobby Hope's resignation in January 1995, when he briefly took over the managerial reins. Now registered as a player with Sandwell Borough.

Played for Brighton in the 1983 FA Cup final.

GREAVES, Danny

Southend, Camb U, 1981-1984

Scored 14 goals in 30 games for Southend. Appointed to the coaching staff when his career ended but left in the summer of 1996. Son of Jimmy.

GREAVES, Ian

Man U, Lincoln, Oldham, 1954-1962

Manager at Mansfield Town after his playing days and now retired. Can still be seen watching matches acting as a scout for a number of clubs.

Helped Manchester United to the 1958 League Championship.

GREAVES, Jimmy

Chelsea, Tottenham, West Ham, 1957-1970

Started his career at Chelsea scoring an incredible 124 goals in 157 league games. After a spell in Italy, returned to the capital to continue rattling in the goals for Tottenham (220 goals in 330 league games) and then finally for West Ham. He was also capped 57 times by England but had to endure the agony of being left out of england's world cup final team. His witty view of life have livened up many a television sports programme.

European Cup Winners Cup winner with Spurs in 1963.

GREAVES, Roy

Bolton, Rochdale, 1965-1982

Played almost 500 games in the Bolton Wanderers midfield. Now runs the 'Monteraze' pub, close to Boundary Park.

GREEN, Billy

Hartlepool, Carlisle, West Ham, Peterborough, Chesterfield, Doncaster, 1969-1983

Central defender who played for six league clubs including a brief stint at West Ham. Resigned as manager of Buxton in the at the end of the 1995/6 season.

GREEN, Colin

Everton, Birmingham, Wrexham, 1960-1970

Full back who won 15 Welsh caps now lives in Wrexham and works as a sales representative for a veterinary company.

League Cup winner with Birmingham in 1963.

GREEN, Les

Hull, Hartlepool, Rochdale, Derby, 1961-1970

Ex-Derby County goalkeeper who was appointed manager of Bedworth in March 1995, having previously been in charge at Nuneaton Borough, Hinckley Town and Tamworth.

GREEN, Mike

Carlisle, Gillingham, Bristol Rovers, Plymouth, Torquay, 1964-1981

Spent the latter part of his career as player/manager of Torquay where he still lives and works in the town.

Won promotion to the Second Division in successive seasons.

GREEN, Tony

Albion Rovers, Blackpool, Newcastle, 1956-1972

Had to retire at the age of only 27 due to knee trouble. Now a schoolteacher in Blackpool. Also a member of Littlewoods

Pools panel.
Capped six times by Scotland.

GREENER, Ron
Newcastle, Darlington, 1953-1966
Now a car salesman in Darlington where he appeared over 400 times for Darlo in his thirteen-year playing career.

GREENHALGH, Brian
Preston, Aston V, Leicester, Huddersfield, Camb U, Bournemouth, Torquay, Watford, 1965-1975
Played for eight league clubs in ten years before finishing in 1975. Now works at Everton as their chief scout.

GREENHOFF, Brian
Man U, Leeds, Rochdale, 1973-1983
England international defender who won 18 caps. Moved from Manchester United to Leeds United for £350,000 in 1979. Now lives in Rochdale and works as a sales representative for a sports goods wholesalers, William Lindop Sports. Also helps coach Chadderton FC in the Carling North West Counties League.
FA Cup winner with Man United in 1977.

GREENHOFF, Jimmy
Leeds, Birmingham, Stoke, Man U, Crewe, Port V, Rochdale, 1963-1983

Greenhoff spent most of his career in the First Division. After making his name with Stoke City, he was sold to Man United in 1976 for £100,000. He now runs his own insurance business, Greenhoff Peutz & Co, in Audley, on the outskirts of Stoke.
FA Cup winner with Man United in 1977.

GREGG, Harry
Doncaster, Man U, Stoke, 1952-1966
Survived the Munich air crash. Harry now owns a hotel in Port Stewart, Ulster.
Reached World Cup quarter finals with Northern Ireland in 1958.

GREGORY, David
Peterborough, Stoke, Blackburn, Bury, Portsmouth. Wrexham, Peterboro, 1973-1986
Lives in Holbeach and plays for the local team in the United Counties League. Works as a self employed ceramic tiler and turns out for the ex-Peterborough XI.

GREGORY, Ernie
West Ham 1946-1959
England 'B' international who was West ham's first choice keeper for many years after the war, carrying on as part of the backroom staff until 1987. Died in Oct 1995.

GREGORY, John
Northampton, Aston V, Brighton., QPR, Derby, Portsmouth, Plymouth, Bolton, 1972-1989
Assistant manager at Leicester City until November 1994, when he followed his manager, Brian Little, to Aston Villa where he became reserve team boss.

GREGORY, Tony
Luton, Watford, 1955-1964
Former England youth international who turned out for a number of non-league sides afer dropping out of the league. Now managing director of a leading aerosol manufacturer.
Played in Luton's 1959 FA Cup final side.

GREGORY, Tony
Shrewsbury 1964-1975

Served his only club for 11 years and was pleasantly surprised to be recognised several years later by a man in the next bed to a relative that he was visiting in hospital – only to be bought back down to earth when the patient said "I used to watch you play and, by Christ, you had some bad games!" Has worked as an Executive officer for the Ministry of Defence since 1980.

GREIG, John
Rangers 1960-1978
A Scottish international who played 857 games for his club and was appointed manager weeks after retiring as a player in May 1978 – a post he held for five years. John won almost every honour the game has to offer and he was awarded the MBE in 1977. He still works at Ibrox as PR Manager and Press Officer.
Twice voted Scottish player of the year.

GREW, Mark
WBA, Wigan, Notts Co, Leicester, Oldham, Ipswich, Fulham, WBA, Derby, Port Vale, Blackburn Cardiff City, 1976-1994
A well travalled goalkeeper who in- between spending several periods on loan, spent most of his career at Vale Park. Is now youth team manager.

GRIFFIN, Colin
Derby, Shrewsbury, 1974-1988
Had a time as coach at Shrewsbury Town before leaving to play for Worcester City. Now working as a postman in the Shrewsbury area.

GRIFFITHS, Arfon
Wrexham, Arsenal, Wrexham, 1959-1978
Played almost 600 games for Wrexham and had a spell at Arsenal. Gained international recognition for Wales on 17 occasions and was awarded the MBE in 1976. Now runs his own newsagents in Gresford near Wrexham.
Holds the Wrexham appearances record.

GRIFFITHS, Harold
Swansea 1949-1963

Died in 1978 at the age of only 47 while working in the treatment room at Swansea City. He had previously served the Vetch Field Club as a player (424 appearances), coach, chief scout, assistant manager and, finally, as manager.

GRIFFITHS Neil
Chester, Port Vale, Crewe, 1970-1981
A full back who spent seven years at Vale Park where he played over 200 games. Is now community officer at Kidderminster Harriers.

GRIMES, Ashley
Man U, Coventry, Luton, Stoke, 1977-1991
A Republic of Ireland international who failed to become a first-team regular at Old Trafford. He moved to Coventry, then Luton and ended his career at Stoke, via the Spanish side Osasuna. Now coaches the reserve and youth teams under Lou Macari at Stoke.
Appeared for Luton in two League Cup finals, winning one and losing the other.

GRITT, Steve
Bournemouth, Charlton, Walsall, Charlton, 1976-1993
Until June 1995 held the post of joint-manager at Charlton, where he made over 300 league appearances as a player. Is now chief scout at Gillingham having played for a number of non-league sides.
Selected for a Football League XI in 1988.

GROVES, Alan
Southport, Chester C, Shrewsbury T, Bournemouth, Oldham, Blackpool, 1968-1977
Former Oldham Athletic wingman. Sadly died in 1978, aged only 30.

GROVES, Perry
Colchester, Arsenal, Soton, 1981-1994
Forced to retire through injury in 1994, but played in the Vauxhall Conference for Dagenham & Redbridge until February 1995. Joined Canvey Island in March 1996.
Two League Championship winners medals.

GROVES, Victor
Tottenham, Leyton O, Arsenal, 1952-1963
Retired from playing football in 1965 and became a publican in Edmonton. Later took a job as a salesman and then worked his way up to branch manager with Hambro Insurance.
Capped by England at under-23 level.

GRUMMITT, Peter
Notts F, Sheff Wed, Brighton, 1960-1976
Was first choice keeper at Nottingham Forest for almost a decade, clocking up over 500 appearances in his three-club playing career. Now the owner of a newsagents in Bourne, Lincolnshire.

GUDMUNDSSON, Albert
Arsenal 1946-1947
After a playing career which saw him play for a selection of clubs in Scotland, Italy, France and Arsenal in England, Albert returned to his native Iceland to become a successful businessman. He was President of the Icelandic FA and was later appointed French Consul in Iceland, then Finance Minister in Reykjavik. Died in May 1994, aged 70.

GUNTER, Philip
Portsmouth, Aldershot, 1951-1965
Played over 300 games for Pompey before emigrating to Australia where he now lives in retirement.

GURR, Gerry
Southampton, Aldershot, 1966-1971
Quit football in 1971 to become a musician. Now lives in Stow on the Wold, strums his guitar for a living, as well as acting as musical director for his wife, the singer Lee Ann.

GUTHRIE, Jimmy
Portsmouth, C Palace, 1937-1946
Scottish wing half who became a leading sports writer with the Sunday People. Died in a London hospital aged 68 in September 1981.
Was secretary of the PFA prior to Jimmy Hill.

GUY, Dickie
Wimbledon 1977
The Don's keeper when they joined the league and hero of their famous mid 70s FA Cup run as a Southern League side. Dickie is now a builder in Mitcham.

GWYTHER, David
Swansea, Halifax, Rotherham, Newport, 1965-1984
Welsh under-23 midfielder who is now a partner in Jones & Gwyther Painting & Decorating in Swansea.

HABBIN, Dick
Reading, Rotherham, Doncaster, 1969-1978
Dick is now running his own building business in Maltby, Rotherham.

HADDOCK, Peter
Newcastle, Burnley, Leeds, 1979-1981
A central defender whose brief three-club career was ended by a knee injury at Leeds. 'Fish' is now an insurance salesman.
Won a Second Division Championship winners medal.

HAGAN, James
Derby, Sheff U, 1935-1957
An England international who scored 116 goals in his 361 league games for Sheffield United. Now retired, living in Walsall, West Midlands.
Division Two Championship with Sheff Utd.

HAGUE, Neil
Rotherham, Plymouth, Bournemouth, Huddersfield, Darlington, 1967-1978
Now in property development in Plymouth.

HAIR, Grenville
Leeds 1950-1963
Made 443 league appearances for Leeds United in a thirteen-year career with the one club. Grenville died in March 1968, aged only 36, when as manager of Bradford City he had a heart attack while supervising a training session.
Toured three times with the FA.

HALES, Derek
Luton, Charlton, Derby, West Ham, Charlton, Gillingham, 1972-1985

Ran a pub for eight years but now lives in Sittingbourne and describes his current occupation as "constructional enterprises". *Netted 148 goals from his 312 league games.*

HALL, Brian
Liverpool, Plymouth, Burnley, 1968-1979
Now works as an Public relations executive and head of community projects at Liverpool, the club he originally joined as a player from Manchester University in 1968. *Won FA Cup, League Championship and UEFA Cup winners medals.*

HALL, Bobby
Mansfield, Colchester, 1958-1972
A left sided player who made over 300 league appearances for Colchester. He now works in the town for a heating company. *Scored four goals in Colchester's record 9-1 win over Bradford.*

HALL, Ian
Derby, Mansfield, 1959-1968
Ex-Derby County forward who also played cricket for Derbyshire has certainly made the most of life since retiring from sport. An honours degree was gained at Birmingham University, followed by a Certificate of Education at Loughborough College. He pursued a career in teaching after a spell at Coventry working as a co-ordinator of 'Enterprise Sky Blue'. Since 1990 Ian has been a freelance journalist and broadcaster for Radio Derby.

HALL, James
Northampton, Peterborough, Cambridge, 1963-1976
Now a working as a teacher in a Northampton school.

HALL, John
Bradford C 1962-1973
Spent eleven years running down the wing for Bradford. Now a postman living in Yeadon, Guiseley.

HALOM, Vic
Charlton, Leyton O, Fulham, Luton, Sunderland, Oldham, Rotherham, 1965-1980
A well travelled striker who played 439 League games scoring 131 goals. Vic managed Burton Albion after his playing days, but now works as a PR man with Oldham based firm, New Earth Plumbing. *A 1973 FA Cup winner with Sunderland.*

HAM, Bobby
Bradford PA, Grimsby, Bradford PA, Bradford C, Preston, Rotherham, Bradford, 1961-1974
Bradford born striker who had two spells with each of his home town clubs. Formed a local business called the 'Ham Group' which is made up of Ham Plant Hire, Challoner Lighting and Wall Electrical.

HAMILTON, Billy
QPR, Burnley, Oxford, 1978-1986
Northern Ireland international who won 41 caps. Combined managing Distillery in Ireland (until February 1996) with earning his living by selling sporting goods and equipment. *A member of Northern Ireland's 1982 World Cup squad.*

HAMILTON, Bryan
Ipswich, Everton, Millwall, Swindon,

Tranmere, 1971-1984
Experience gained managing Tranmere, Wigan and Leicester City made him the right man for the job when the Northern Ireland team needed a new team manager in 1994. Had previously won 50 full caps and under-23 honours as a player.
Played for Everton in 1977 League Cup final.

HAMILTON, Ian

Bristol Rovers, Exeter City, Newport County, 1958-1972
A long career was finally ended by a knee injury and he now works for Rolls Royce in Bristol.
Rovers top scorer with 21 goals in 1965.

HAMILTON, Ian 'Chico'

Chelsea, Southend, Aston V, Sheff U, 1966-1977

Ian was 18 when he joined Aston Villa from Southend for £40,000 and helped them win the Third Division Championship in 1972. In 1976 he signed for Sheffield United then spent two years in America. He now works for the Nike organisation coaching soccer and as a play-scheme organiser at Sheffield University. He also finds time to coach and organise soccer for youngsters at the local 'Ritz Super Soccer' centre.
League Cup final winner with Villa in 1975.

HAMILTON, James

Sunderland, Plymouth, Bristol Rovers, Carlisle, Hartlepool, 1972-1984
Always faced an uphill task after replacing

the popular Bruce Bannister and now runs a hotel in Dumfries.

HAMSON, Gary

Sheffield United, Leeds, Bristol City, Port Vale, 1976-1987
A former left winger who played most of his career 126 games at Elland Road. Appointed coach of non-league Stapenhill in August 1996. Works with the Stapenhill manager at Refuge Life insurance company.

HAMPTON, Peter

Leeds, Stoke, Burnley, Rochdale, Carlisle, 1971-1987
Found it hard to break into the first team at Leeds and played most of his football at Stoke. Is now physiotherapist at his last club, Carlisle.
England youth international.

HANCOCKS, Johnny

Walsall, Wolves, 1938-1955
Scorer of 158 goals from 343 appearances and winner of three England caps, this dynamic player was known as the 'Mighty Atom' because of his 5ft 4in frame and size two boots. He worked in a local iron foundry in his home town, Oakengates, before retiring in 1979. Died in 1994 aged 75.
Championship medal with Wolves in 1954.

HAND, Eoin

Swindon, Portsmouth, 1964-1978
The former Republic of Ireland player and manager clocked up 300 appearances for Portsmouth. His playing days also took him to South Africa and Limerick. Now coaching in South Africa.

HANDYSIDES, Ian

Birmingham, Walsall, Birmingham C, Wolves, 1980-1986
Former England youth international winger who died in 1990 after a two year illness, aged only 27.
Won promotion with Birmingham in 1980.

HANKIN, Ray

Burnley, Leeds, Middlesboro, Peterborough,

Wolves, 1972-1984

Ray had spells as manager of Northallerton Town and then Darlington. Now working as a football in the community officer based at Newcastle United.

HANSEN, Allan

Partick Thistle, Liverpool, 1973-1989

Joined Liverpool in 1977 as a £110,000 signing from Partick Thistle and went on to win every domestic honour possible. He played over 400 League games and was also capped 26 times by Scotland. Can now be seen working on TV as a know-all pundit, as well as writing a column for the Daily Express newspaper.
Captained the Reds to a 1986 double.

HANSON, Stanley

Bolton 1936-1955

Bolton Wanderers' first choice goalkeeper for many years, making over 350 League appearances either side of the war. Died in 1987.

HANVEY, Keith

Swansea, Rochdale, Grimsby, Huddersfield, Rochdale, 1971-1984

Now commercial executive with Huddersfield Town, where he played over 200 league games.

HARBURN, Peter

Brighton, Everton, Scunthorpe, Workington, 1954-1960

Now a pub manager in Chelmsford, Essex.

HARDWICK, George

Middlesboro, Oldham, 1937-1955

Became player/manager at Oldham, followed by managerial appointments with PSV Eindhoven, Sunderland and the Dutch national team. Lives in Stokesley near Middlesbrough and recently retired as managing director of a quality assurance company. Regularly seen at Ayresome Park, where he acts as a match-day host.
Took Oldham to Third Division North title in 1953.

HAREIDE, Aage

Manchester City, Norwich, 1981-1982

Only played a handful of games after coming over from Norway and worked for a bank whilst playing part time. Is now a manager for Volvo and keeps in touch with the game as a commentator.

HARFORD, Ray

Charlton, Exeter, Lincoln Mansfield, Port V, Colchester, 1965-1974

Ended his career at Colchester where he became coach before moving to Fulham as youth coach in 1981. Promoted to manager at Craven Cottage in May 1984 following Malcolm MacDonald's resignation. Became assistant manager at Blackburn Rovers, then team manager following Kenny Dalglish's elevation. After a disastrous start to the 1996/7 season he lost his job at Blackburn.
Managed Luton to the 1988 League Cup final.

HARLAND, Stan

Everton, Bradford C, Carlisle, Swindon, Birmingham, 1959-1972

A hard working wing half who coached at Portsmouth before taking over the delicatessen that he now runs near Yeovil.
Captained Swindon to League Cup success in 1969.

HARPER, Joe

Morton, Huddersfield, Morton, Aberdeen, Everton, Hibs, 1963-1981

A highly rated centre forward who was once transfered for a Scottish record fee of £120,000. Now works as a rep for a whiskey Company and as a radio commentator for Scot FM.
Won Scottish FA and League Cups.

HARRIS, Alan

Chelsea, Coventry, Chelsea, QPR, Plymouth, Camb U, 1960-1973

Had a lower profile career than his brother Ron. Went on to do a spell of coaching in the Middle East and has also acted as a players agent.
England youth and schoolboy international.

HARRIS, Bill
Hull, Middlesboro, Bradford C, 1949-1965
Capped six times in total and ended his
career as player/manager of Bradford City.
Died in 1989 on Tyneside aged 61.
*Voted the best wing half during the 1958
World Cup finals.*

HARRIS, Brian
Everton, Cardiff, Newport, 1955-1973
Wing half who turned out forEverton on
more than 300 occasions in the 50s and 60s.
After a period as manager of Newport, went
on to manage a pub in Chepstow, but now
runs his own promotions business in the
area.

HARRIS, Carl
Leeds, Charlton, Bury, Rochdale, Exeter C,
1974-1988
Returned to South Wales in 1989 to play for
Briton Ferry in the Welsh League. Later
appointed player/manager with the extra
duties of general manager.
Capped 23 times by Wales.

HARRIS, Peter
Portsmouth 1946-1959

An England international winger who
scored 194 goals in his 480 matches for
Portsmouth in their glory years. Now retired
and living in Hayling Island, Hampshire.
*Two Football League Championship medals
in ten years apart (1949 and 1959).*

HARRIS, Harry
Newport, Portsmouth, Newport, 1954-1970
Inside forward who clocked up over 500
league appearances for Portsmouth and
Newport County in his sixteen year career.
Now runs a double glazing business in
Leeds.
*Part of Portsmouth's back-to-back
Championship sides of 1949 and 1950.*

HARRIS, Ron
Chelsea, Brentford, 1961-1983
'Chopper' was undoubtedly one of the
sternest tests for any forward during the sixties and seventies, when he marshalled the
Chelsea defence on more than 600 occasions. After a spell as manager of Brentford,
Ron brought Bramhill golf course in Wiltshire
for £400,000 and is reputed to have sold it in
1989 for £2 million to Golf pro Roger Mace
and ex-Doncaster Rovers and Aldershot
goalkeeper Glen Johnson. Now owns a holiday chalet and fishing complex in a picturesque setting in a village near
Warminster, Wiltshire.
FA Cup winner in 1970 with Chelsea.

HARRISON, Chris
Plymouth, Swansea, 1975-1987
Played over 500 league games for his two
clubs. Now returned to his roots, running a
successful driving school back in Cornwall.
Had a spell as manager of Saltash FC in the
Great Mills Western League.

HARRISON, Mark
Soton, Port V, Stoke, 1978-1982
Manager of Stafford Rangers in the GM
Vauxhall Conference until June 1995 when
he joined the coaching staff at Oxford
United.

HARRISON, Steve
Blackpool, Watford, Charlton, 1971-1981
Resumed a successful partnership with
Graham Taylor at Wolves after a spell at
Crystal Palace. Is now coaching at Preston.

HARRISON, Wayne
Oldham, Liverpool, Crewe, 1984-1991

Became the most expensive 17 year old following a move to Liverpool in 1985. However, a succession of injuries led to his release in May 1991. Lives in Stockport in the house purchased with proceeds from the move. Now considering a career in sports management.

HART, Paul

Stockport, Blackpool, Leeds, Nottingham, Sheffield W, Birmingham, Notts C, 1970-1987
Director of youth coaching at Elland Road, where he played 191 league games between 1978 and 1983. Appointed caretaker boss for a brief spell when Howard Wilkinson left the club in September 1996.

HARTFORD, Asa

WBA, Man C, Notts F, Everton, Man C, Norwich, Bolton, Stockport, Oldham, Shrewsbury, 1967-1990
A midfield dynamo who hit the headlines when he was dramatically turned down by Leeds when it was discovered that he had a heart ailment. All this was forgotten when big money moves took him to Man City, Notts Forest and Everton. He won 50 Scottish caps and has since coached at Stockport, Oldham, Shrewsbury, Blackburn and Stoke. Asa was appointed assistant manager at Manchester City in July 1995, taking over from Alan Ball as caretaker boss 12 months later.
Twice a League Cup winner with Man City and Norwich.

HARTLE, Barry

Watford, Sheffield United, Carlisle, Stockport, Oldham, Southport, 1956-1971
A skilful winger who settled in the north when his career ended. Now works as a taxi driver in Stockport.

HARTLEY, Trevor

West Ham, Bournemouth, 1966-1970
Former Bournemouth winger who served as assistant manager to David Pleat at Luton and Tottenham, as well as being first team coach at Sunderland until June 1995.

HARVEY, Bryan

Newcastle, Blackpool, Northampton, 1958-1967
London born goalkeeper Bryan is now living in Wotton, Northants and working as a manager at a chemical company.

HARVEY, Colin

Everton, Sheff Weds, 1963-1975
Appointed assistant manager of Oldham in November 1994 after previously managing Everton, the club who for whom he made 317 League appearances.
Capped once by England against Malta in 1971.

HARVEY, David

Leeds, Bradford C, 1965-1984

After leaving the game, Harvey firstly ran a pub, then worked delivering fruit and veg to the hotels of Harrogate. Became player/manager at Whitby in 1985 and worked as a postman in Knaresborough, Yorkshire. However, he has now started a new life in the Orkney Islands, where he purchased a large old farmhouse and several animals and intends to enjoy his retirement.
Played for Leeds in the 1972 FA Cup final.

H

HARVEY, James
Arsenal, Hereford, Bristol C, Wrexham,
Tranmere, 1977-1993
Lives in Bromborough, Wirral and is current-
ly manager of Morecombe in the Northern
Premier League.

HARVEY, Martin
Sunderland 1959-1971
A great all round player, Harvey worked his
way through the junior ranks at Sunderland
and eventually took over from the great
Danny Blanchflower in the Northern Ireland
side, going on to play 33 times in all. Is now
with Jimmy Nicholl at Millwall.
Won promotion to Division One in 1970.

HARVEY, Joe
Bradford PA, Wolves, Bournemouth,
Newcastle, 1936-1952
Served Newcastle for a total of 35 years as
player, assistant manager, manager and
chief scout. Died of a heart attack at his
Tynecastle home in 1989.
*Captained Newcastle to FA Cup wins in
1951 and 1952.*

HATCH, Peter
Oxford, Exeter, 1967-1981
After fourteen years as a player at Exeter, he
remained in the area and works as a postman.

HATELEY, Tony
Notts C, Aston V, Chelsea, Liverpool,
Coventry, Birmingham, Notts C, Oldham,
1958-1973
A goal-scoring centre-forward who played
for seven clubs in twenty years. Upon retiring from the game, set up his own business
until 1978 when he became Lottery Manager
at Goodison Park. Three years later became
a drinks rep, firstly with Thwaites brewery,
and now with a soft drinks firm.
Father of Mark, the England international.

HATTON, Bob
Wolves, Bolton W, Northampton T, Carlisle U,
Birmingham C, Blackpool, Luton T, Sheff U,
Cardiff C, 1966-1982

Scored a hatful of goals for each of his nine
league clubs. After sixteen years as a player
Bob joined the PFA where he works as direc-
tor of sales, based in the organisation's
Birmingham office.
*Won promotion to the First Division with
Birmingham in 1972.*

HATTON, Dave
Bolton, Blackpool, Bury, 1961-1978
Played over 500 league games. Dave now
works in Blackpool as an estate agent.

HAWLEY, John
Hull, Leeds, Sunderland, Arsenal, Leyton O,
Hull, Bradford C, Scunthorpe, 1972-1985
After coming through the junior ranks at
Hull City, John established himself with
spells at Leeds, Sunderland and Arsenal
before returning to Humberside with
Scunthorpe. Now owns an antiques shop on
the other side of the River Humber - at
Beverley.

HAY, David
Celtic, Chelsea 1968-1978
Retired prematurely through injury in and
became first assistant manager, then manager, at Motherwell. Managed his old club
Celtic for a spell, and is now back with them
as chief scout.
*Won five successive League titles with Celtic
between 1970-1974.*

HAYDOCK, Bill
Man C, Crewe, Grimsby, Stockport Co,
Southport, 1959-1971
Full back Bill had a spell in South Africa
after twelve years and over 400 games as a
player. Became assistant manager of Cork
City in Eire before joining Blackburn Rovers
as their physiotherapist.

HAYES, Austin
Soton, Millwall, Northampton, 1976-1984
Won one Republic of Ireland cap in a career
tragically shortened by illness. Died of lung
cancer in December 1986, aged 28.
*Played for Saints in the 1979 League Cup
final.*

HAYNES, Johnny
Fulham 1952-1969
In 1961 Johnny became Britain's first ever £100-a-week footballer when the £20-a-week maximum wage was abolished. During his career with Fulham, Haynes appeared in nearly 600 league games between 1962 and 1969, scoring 146 goals. He played 56 times for England and was also capped at 'B' and Under 23 Levels. He moved to South Africa in 1970 where for the next fifteen years he played for, then coached Durban City. He now lives in Edinburgh where he runs a dry cleaning business.
Played in Fulham's record 10-1 win over Ipswich in 1963.

HAZEL, Tony
QPR, Millwall, Crystal Palace, Charlton, 1964-1980
A former England youth international who played 362 league games for QPR before moving to Millwall where he played a further 153. Now lives in Flackwell Heath and works as an engineer for British Telecom.
Played in QPR's Division Three and League Cup double-winning side of 1967.

HEASLEGRAVE, Sammy
WBA, Northampton, 1936-1947
A hard working forward who became a solicitor in Bearwood. Died in April 1975.
All-England Bowls Champion.

HEATH, Adrian
Stoke, Everton, Aston Villa, Manchester City, Burnley, Stoke, 1979-1995
Capped by England at under-21 level, his career was ended by injury and he joined Sheffield United as assistant manager. Became manager at Turf Moor in 1996.
Won two Championship medals with Everton, in 1985 and 1987.

HEATH, Don
Middlesboro, Norwich, Swindon, Oldham, Peterborough, Hartlepool, 1962-1974
Lives in Middlesboro where he is a buyer for ICI. Does some scouting.
League Cup winner with Swindon.

HEATON, Mike
Sheff U, Blackburn, 1966-1975
Former Blackburn and Everton coach who died in a car accident in April 1995 at the age of 48.
Captained Blackburn to the Division Three Championship in 1975.

HEATON, Paul
Oldham, Rochdale, 1977-1985
Former England under-21 international who went on to play in Finland where he married a local girl and stayed.

HECTOR, Kevin
Bradford PA, Derby, 1962-1981
Smashed Bradford's scoring record with 44 goals in a season before being snapped up by Derby for £40,000. Gained two Championship medals and was capped twice by England. Now a postman in the East Midlands.
Scored five times in Derby's record Cup win over Finn Harps in 1976.

HEFFER, Paul
West Ham 1966-1971
Former West Ham defender who coached at Southend but now teaches PE at an Essex school.

HEIGHWAY, Steve
Liverpool 1970-1980

Signed for Liverpool from non-league Skelmersdale in May 1970 and spent the next ten years rampaging down the wings of the First Division providing crosses for Keegan and Toshack. In over 300 appearances he appeared in three cup finals, five championship winning sides and was capped 34 times by the Republic of Ireland. Steve is still employed at Anfield where he is a youth development officer.
European Cup winner.

HEMSLEY, Ted
Shrewsbury, Sheff U, Doncaster, 1960-1978
Probably as well known as an accomplished cricketer for Worcestershire as a solid defender who played over 500 league games in his eighteen years as a pro. Now retired, although he is only 52, after ten years as a bookmaker.

HENDERSON, Mick
Sunderland, Watford, Cardiff, Sheffield United, Chesterfield, 1974-1987
His football career ended after a brief spell as caretaker manager at Saltergate. Now a police officer in Sheffield.

HENDERSON, John
Falkirk, Third Lanark, Rotherham, Leeds,1940-1955
Now a distribution fitter for the south-west Gas Board in Wiltshire.
Played in the 1948 League Cup final for Falkirk.

HENDERSON, John 'Jackie'
Portsmouth, Wolves, Arsenal, Fulham, 1951-1963
Scottish international striker who ended his professional playing days at Fulham before joining Poole Town in 1964. More recently worked for a builders merchants in Poole, until his retirement.
Scored 109 goals in 371 games.

HENDERSON, Stewart
Chelsea, Brighton, Reading, 1964-1982
Former full back Stewart is now a youth development officer at Reading.

HENDERSON, Willie
Rangers, Sheff Wed, 1960-1973
A real crowd pleaser who briefly played for Sheffield Wednesday after a very successful career with Rangers where he won silverware galore. In addition to his collection of 29 Scottish caps, he also had the distinction of captaining the Hong Kong national side!
Won two Scottsih League Championships.

HENDRIE, Paul
Birmingham, Bristol R, Halifax, Stockport, 1972-1988
Played in America with Portland Timbers before returning to England to play for a number of non-league sides in the Midlands. Was manager at Redditch United before taking over at Tamworth in February 1995. Hit the headlines with Halifax when he scored the goal which put Manchester City out of the 1980 FA Cup.

HENNESSEY, Terry
Birmingham, Notts F, Derby, 1960-1972
Emigrated to Australia following a spell as assistant manager to Alan Hinton at Vancouver Whitecaps in Canada. Now lives near Melbourne and works as a sales manager for a firm selling cling film products.
League Championship winner with Derby in 1972.

HENRY, Ron
Tottenham 1953-1969
A member of the Spurs double-winning side who left the game to run a nursery near his home in Redbourne, Hartfordshire. Still helps out with the South East Counties side at Spurs.
Won one cap for England.

HENRY, Tony
Man C, Bolton, Oldham, Stoke, Shrewsbury, 1976-1992
Now lives in Bicton near Shrewsbury and is working as a financial advisor for the Prudential Insurance Company.

HENSON, Phil
Man C, Swansea C, Sheff Wed, Stockport,

Rotherham, 1971-1983
Phil was manager at Rotherham until
September 1995 when he took on a wider
management role.

HERD, David
Stockport, Arsenal, Man U, Stoke, 1950-1969
Started his career at Stockport County, playing alongside his father, Alex. Joined
Arsenal in August 1954 for £8,000 while he
was still doing his National Service. Became
a prolific scorer, scoring over 200 league
goals for Arsenal and Manchester United.
Spent eighteen months as manager of
Lincoln City before being replaced by a
young Graham Taylor in 1964. After Lincoln
he left football for good to concentrate on his
garage business, which he still runs today.
*Won two League Championships with
Manchester United.*

HERD, George
Clyde, Sunderland, Hartlepool, 1957-1970
A Scottish international who played 275
matches for Sunderland. Was youth team
coach at Roker Park.
Scottish Cup winners medal in 1958.

HERRIOT, Jim
Dunfirmline, Birmingham, Mansfield, 1958-
1970
Capped eight times by Scotland Jim was a
reliable goalkeeper who returned to Scotland
after his playing days to become a bricklayer
in Strathclyde.
Scottish League Cup winner in 1973.

HESLOP, George
Newcastle, Everton, Man C, Bury, 1959-1972
Was on the coaching Staff at Manchester
City then became a licensee in the town,
firstly at the Hyde Road Hotel and later took
over the 'City Gates' pub.
*Won a First Division Championship and Cup
Winners Cup medal with City.*

HEWIE, John
Charlton 1951-1965
Played 495 games for Charlton in nearly
every position, including four games in goal.

Won 19 Scottish caps, but also played
against them for South Africa in 1956. To
cap this remarkable career, John played
baseball for England! Returned from south
Africa to live in the Midlands.
*Played for Charlton in their record Cup win
against Burton in 1956.*

HIBBITT, Kenny
Bradford, Wolves, Coventry, Bristol R, 1967-
1988
Ended his playing days at Bristol Rovers,
where he then became assistant to Gerry
Francis for three years. The had a four-year
stint as manager of Walsall ended in
September 1994. Is now Director of Football
with Cardiff.
League Cup winner with Wolves in 1974.

HIBBITT, Terry
Leeds, Newcastle Birmingham, Newcastle,
1965-1980
Brother of Kenny, who scored for Leeds on
his debut with his first touch. HAd a
newsagents when his career ended. Died
from stomach cancer at the age of 46.
Fairs Cup finalist with Leeds in 1968.

HICKMAN, Mike
Brighton, Grimsby, Blackburn, Torquay,
1965-1975
Was youth development manager at Reading
before following Mark McGee to Leicester
City in December 1994, and then to Wolves

HICKS, Keith
Oldham, Hereford, Rochdale, 1971-1986
Now working as a community scheme
organiser based at Rochdale FC.

HICKS, Martin
Charlton, Reading, Birmingham, 1977-1992
Was into coaching after his playing days and
played non-league football for Stratford
Town and then Worcester City until the sum-
mer of 1996. Now a postman.
Club record of 500 appearances for Reading.

HICKSON, Dave
Everton, Aston V, Huddersfield, Everton,

Liverpool, Bury, Tranmere, 1951-1963
After three years in the reserves Hickson
eventually made his first-team debut for
Everton. He left Everton in 1955 and
although he never stayed at one club for
very long, he was always among the goals,
scoring over 170 league goals in his career.
Went to Ireland as player/manager of
Ballymena, then took a job as a bricklayer
and later worked in a pub. Now lives in
Ellesmere Port where he works for the Local
Authority.
*Won promotion to Division One with Everton
in 1954.*

HICKTON, John
Sheff Wed, Middlesboro, Hull, 1963-1977
Scored 159 league goals in 395 matches during his 11 years at Middlesbrough. Now living and working in Chesterfield.
*Won promotion to Division One with Boro in
1974.*

HILDITCH, Mark
Rochdale, Tranmere, Wigan, Rochdale, 1977-
1991
Assistant manager at Northern Premier
League Mossley. and also works for
Manchester County FA as a coach. Lives
near Rochdale and works in the prison ser-
vice.

HILAIRE, Vince
Crystal Palace, Luton, Portsmouth, Leeds,
Stoke, Exeter, 1976-1993

Exciting former England under-23 wingman.
Joint manager of Waterlooville FC with his
old Palace and Pompey colleague, Billy
Gilbert. Resigned in 1994. Has recently
worked for a cable television company in
Portsmouth.
*Division Two Championship with
Portsmouth in 1987.*

HILL, Alan
Barnsley, Rotherham, Notts F, 1960-1969
Former Notts Forest keeper is now assistant
manager and chief scout at the club.

HILL, Fred
Bolton, Halifax, Man C, Peterborough, 1957-
1974
England international inside forward Fred
lives in Peterborough, home of his last club,
where he is now running a pub.
*Division Four Champion with Peterborough
in 1974.*

HILL, Gordon
Millwall, Man U, Derby, QPR, 1972-1980
England international winger Gordon went
to North America in the early eighties to
play for Montreal, then Chicago Sting before
a brief return to England to coach
Northwich. Gordon now lives in Tampa,
Florida, where he works as a tennis and
football coach.
FA Cup winner with Man United in 1977.

HILL, Jimmy
Brentford, Fulham, 1949-1960
A professional with Brentford and then
Fulham, Jimmy was Chairman of the PFA
between 1957 and 1961 during which time
he was behind the end of the maximum
wage. In 1961 he was appointed manager of
Coventry City, staying at Highfield Road for
six years before taking over as Head of Sport
at London Weekend Television. His television career has since flourished and he has
successfully managed to combine this with
his role of Fulham chairman.
*Scored five goals against Doncaster in a 1958
league game.*

HILL, Ken
Gillingham, Lincoln, 1971-1976
Former England semi-pro defender who lives in Maidstone and works as a manager at Britelite Ltd.

HILL, Richard
Leicester, Northampton, Watford, Oxford, 1981-1988
A respected striker in the lower divisions until injury ended his career. Was community officer at Reading until the summer of 1994 when he was appointed first team coach.
The £265,000 Northampton received for him from Watford is still a club record.

HILL, Ricky
Luton, Leicester, 1975-1990
Won three England caps and played over 400 games in the League for Luton Town. Ended his playing days at Chertsey Town after spells with Tampa Bay Rowdies in America, and later with non-league Hitchin Town.
League Cup winner with Luton in 1988.

HILLARD, Doug
Bristol R 1957-1968
Played over 300 league games for Rovers and later ran a string of sports shops.

HILLEY, Dave
Newcastle, Notts F, 1962-1970
Former Scotland under-23 striker who is now a schoolteacher and also writes regularly for the Sunday Post newspaper in the north east.
Second Division Championship with Newcastle in 1965.

HINCE, Paul
Man C, Charlton, Bury, Crewe, 1966-1970
Now covers Manchester City's games as a reporter with the Manchester Evening News, having taken up journalism with the Ashton Reporter before joining City.

HINDMARSH, Rob
Sunderland, Portsmouth, Derby, Wolves,
1977-1994
Returned to his home in the Stafford area after a spell in Hong Kong. Helps out on a part time basis at his last club, Wolves, in their school of excellence.
Division Two Championship with Derby in 1987.

HINNIGAN, Joe
Wigan, Sunderland, Preston, Gillingham, Wrexham, Chester, 1978-1989
Lives in Ashton and and was formerly Chester City's physio.
Played for Wigan in their first Football League game (against Hereford in 1978).

HINSHELWOOD, Martin
Crystal P 1972-1977
A short career, all at Palace, where he is now Reserve team coach at Portsmouth.

HINSHELWOOD, Paul
Crystal P, Oxford, Millwall, Colchester, 1973-1987
Now lives in Kent and is an insurance salesman.
Capped twice at under-23 level by England.

HINTON, Alan
Wolves, Notts, Derby, 1961-1975
Goalscoring winger who won three England caps to add to his seven at under-23 level. Moved to America to coach Tulsa Roughnecks, Seattle Sounders, Tacoma Stars and in 1980 was named 'Coach of the Year'. Now lives in Seattle and works as an estate agent.
League Championship winner with Derby in 1972.

HINTON, Marvin
Charlton, Chelsea, 1957-1974
England under-23 defender who turned out for Chelsea in over 250 League games. Was running his own office removals business but has been unable to work since a head on car smash he was involved in near his home in Crawley.
Played in two FA Cup finals for Chelsea in 1967 and 1970.

HIRD, Kevin
Blackburn, Leeds, Burnley, 1973-1985
Still plays for Rovers veteran's side. Lives near Burnley and has ran a soccer school for the last five years, combined with teaching at a local school.

HIRON, Ray
Portsmouth, Reading, 1964-1977
Lanky striker who joined Portsmouth in 1964 and netted 110 goals in 324 appearances. After three seasons with Reading, returned to Fareham Town in the Southern League. Now a manager at the Mountbatten Sports Centre in Portsmouth.

HOADLEY, Phil
Crystal Palace, Leyton O, Norwich, 1967-1981
Phil now works as a self employed window fitter in the Norwich area and also helps coach the youngsters at Carrow Road.
Played for Leyton Orient in their 1978 FA Cup semi final clash with Arsenal.

HOBSON, Gordon
Lincoln, Grimsby, Southampton, Lincoln, Exeter, Walsall, 1977-1992
Played 260 games for Lincoln before setting off on his travels. Now a player and assistant manager at Salisbury City in the Beazer Homes League. Away from soccer, Gordon also runs a successful sailing business in Southampton.

HOCKEY, Trevor
Bradford C, Notts F, Newcastle, Birmingham, Sheff U, Norwich, Aston V, Bradford C, 1959-1975
Played for seven clubs in 16 years, during which time he played over 600 matches. Trevor was taking part in a 5-a-side tournament in Keighley in April 1987 when he collapsed and died, aged 43.
Division Two Championship with Newcastle in 1965.

HODDLE, Glen
Tottenham, Swindon, Chelsea, 1975-1995
Made his name with Spurs in the mid seven-ties and early eighties for his creative midfield skills and knack of scoring spectacular goals. Won 53 England caps. In 1987 moved to Monaco in France for £800,000 but was dogged by injuries, returning home in 1990 to manage Swindon. Guided them to the Premiership in 1993, via the play offs, but left for Chelsea just weeks later. Appointed England boss in 1996.
FA Cup winners medals in 1981 and 1982.

HODGES, Kevin
Plymouth Argyle, Torquay U, 1978-1995
A remarkable record of over 600 games for Plymouth in a long career which ended at Torquay United where he is now manager.

HODGETTS, Frank
WBA, Millwall, 1946-1952
Became the youngest ever West Bromwich Albion player when he made his debut in 1940 aged only 16 years and 26 days. Now lives in retirement in Kidderminster, but has been active as chairman of the Herefordshire and Worcestershire County Tennis Association.

HODGKINSON, Alan
Sheff U 1954-1970
Joined Sheffield United from Worksop Town and went on to play 576 league games in goal for the Blades, Now coaches goalkeepers for a number of League clubs.
Won five England caps between 1957 and 1961.

HODGSON, Dave
Middlesboro, Liverpool, Sunderland, Norwich, Middlesboro, Sheff Wed, Swansea, 1978-1991
Went over to Japan to play for Mazda of Hiroshima and then becme a players' agent before being appointed director of coaching at Darlington in May 1995, only to leave less then six months later.
Division One Championship with Liverpool in 1983.

HODGSON, Roy
Has made his name as a successful coach

and manager in Europe. Formerly manager of Switzerland's national side and now manager of Inter Milan.

HOLD, John
Bournemouth, Crewe, Northampton, 1965-1972
Former Bournemouth forward is now working as an area manager for Presto supermarkets.

HOLDEN, Bill
Burnley, Sunderland, Stockport, Bury, Halifax, 1950-1962
Life after football proved to be extremely varied: running a driving school; owning a coffee bar; a restaurant; a newsagency; and running the recreation centre at Lancaster University. He then rented out flats and worked for the DSS before buying the guest house he now runs in Morecombe!
England 'B' international.

HOLDER, Phil
Tottenham, C Palace, Bournemouth, 1971-1979
Phil had a spell as manager at Brentford and then as youth team coach at Reading – a post that he held until the summer of 1996 when he quit after finding travelling from his Croydon home difficult.
Took Brentford to a Third Division title in 1992.

HOLE, Barry
Cardiff, Blackburn, Aston V, Swansea, 1959-1971
After retiring in 1972 followed in his father's footsteps by becoming a shopkeeper. He has now run a newsagency in the area for the last 25 years and is a member of the same golf club as Ivor Allchurch – they were room mates while at Cardiff City over 35 years ago!
Capped 30 times by Wales between 1963 and 1971.

HOLLAND, Pat
West Ham, Bournemout, 1968-1980
Pat joined Tottenham in 1988 as youth team

Coach and took over the reserves before accepting Barry Hearn's offer to become manager at Orient at the end of the 1994/5 season. Now lives in Upminster running 'Hollands' wine bar, and the 'Red Lion' pub in Barking.
FA Cup winner in 1975 with West Ham.

HOLLETT, Ivan
Mansfield, Chesterfield, Crewe, Camb U, Hereford, 1958-1972
Now an area sales representative for a metals company in Northampton.

HOLLINS, David
Brighton, Newcastle, Mansfield, Notts F, Aldershot, 1957-1970
The goalkeeping brother of John. Now runs his own painting and decorating business in London.
Capped 11 times by Wales.

HOLLINS, John MBE
Chelsea, QPR, Arsenal, Chelsea, 1963-1983
He gained an England cap against Spain in 1967 despite his brother Dave already being a Welsh international goalie. Returned to Chelsea as player/coachand took over as manager until March 1988. After a spell as a financial adviser, returned to the game as reserve team coach at QPR in February 1995.
FA Cup winner with Chelsea in 1970.

HOLLIS, Roy
Norwich, Tottenham, Southend, 1948-1960
Despite scoring twice on his debut for Spurs, he never made the grade as a first-teamer and moved to Southend where he scored 122 goals in 240 league games. He ended his career in non-league football, later becoming a bookmaker and then a betting officer manager.

HOLLOWAY, Ian
Bristol Rovers, Wimbledon, Brentford, Torquay, Bristol Rovers, QPR, Bristol R, 1981-1996
Rejoined Rovers for a third time in May 1996 as player manager after being let go by QPR.

Division Three Championship medal with Rovers in 1990.

HOLLOWBREAD, John
Tottenham, Southampton, 1958-1965
Became a publican running pubs in Southampton, then Romsey, before taking over the bar at Bramshaw Golf Club in the New Forest. Retired to Spain.

HOLLYWOOD, Dennis
Southampton 1962-1971
Works in Southampton docks and lives outside the city where he played for nine years.
Capped by Scotland at under-23 level.

HOLMES, Jimmy
Coventry, Tottenham, Leicester, Brentford, Torquay, Peterborough, 1971-1985
After ending his League days at Peterborough Jimmy joined Nuneaton and briefly managed Hitchin Town and Bedworth before joining the West Midlands police force.
Republic of Ireland international (30 caps).

HOLMES, Nick
Southampton 1973-1986
After 18 years at Southampton Nick took on the role of a village shopkeeper in Wiltshire.
FA Cup winner in 1976 with Southampton.

HOLSGROVE, John
C Palace, Wolves, Sheff Wed, Stockport Co, 1964-1975
Played almost 300 league games, more than half of which were in the gold and black of Wolves. Now works as a financial advisor in the Midlands.
Promotion with Wolves to the First Division in 1967.

HOLTON, Cliff
Arsenal, Watford, Northampton, C Palace, Watford, Charlton, Leyton O, 1950-1967
Former Arsenal centre forward who had one of the hottest shots of any post war player. Cliff broke both Watford and Northampton Town's club goalscoring records. Ran his own Precision engineering business in

Stonebridge until 1989., then spent five years organising golf tournaments prior to his retirement in April 1994. Died in June 1996 during a holiday in Spain.
League Championship with Arsenal in 1953.

HOLTON, Jim
WBA, Shrewsbury, Man U, Sunderland, Coventry, Sheff Wed, 1968-1981
Manchester United's 'Player of the Year' in 1973/4. Retired in 1982, and ran the 'Old Stag' pub in Coventry until his sudden death in 1993.
Division Two Championship with Manchester United in 1975.

HOOPER, Harry
West Ham, Wolves, Birmingham, Sunderland, 1950-1962
Former England under-23 international and 'B' winger who was the son of former Hammers trainer Harry snr. Now retired and living in Kettering where he ended his playing career.

HOOPER, Peter
Bristol R, Cardiff, Bristol C, 1953-1966
Played nearly 300 league games for Rovers later to run a pub but has spent many years working as a probabation officer for the Prison Service in North Devon. Despite being born in Devon, Peter played for Kenya against Uganda in 1951.

HOOKS, Paul
Notts Co, Derby, 1976-1984
Former Notts County winger who became a miner in Ollerton, Nottinghamshire.
Promoted to Division One with Notts Co in 1981.

HOOLICKIN, Steve
Oldham, Bury, Carlisle, Hull, 1969-1981
Former Bury and Carlisle full back. Now lives in Carlisle, where he was a publican, but is now a self employed contractor.

HOPE, Bobby
WBA, Birmingham, Sheff Weds, 1959-1977
Capped by Scotland at schoolboy, under-23

and full international levels, Bobby appeared in over 400 senior games for WBA and ranks as one of their all-time greats. Now owns a sandwich bar in Birmingham, having previously run a sub post office in the city. Was also manager of Bromsgrove Rovers until September 1994.
FA Cup winner with WBA in 1968.

HOPKINS, Mel
Tottenham, Brighton, Bradford PA, 1952-1969
First choice full back for Wales for a number of years, winning 34 caps in total, including a run of 23 consecutive appearances. He then became a sports teacher and football coach and was also secretary to Sussex Coach's Association. Currently works as a sports centre manager and lives in Horsham, Sussex.
Played for Wales in the 1958 World Cup finals in Sweden.

HOPKINS, Robert
Aston V, Birmingham, Man City, WBA, Birmingham, Shrewsbury, 1979-1991
Played in Hong Kong for Instant Dict but now home and turning out for Solihull Borough.
Won promotion to Division One with Birmingham in 1985.

HOPKINSON, Edward
Oldham, Bolton, 1951-1969
Reliable goalkeeper who was Bolton's first choice for many years (519 appearances) earning 14 full England caps in the process. Still lives in the area and works as a customer relations officer for Warburton Bakeries.
FA Cup winner with Bolton in 1958.

HORE, John
Plymouth, Exeter, 1964-1979
Played almost 600 league games. Now lives in Exeter and is the owner of a fitness club and manager of Torrington in the Western League.
Took Plymouth to a FA Cup semi final in his first season as manager.

HORSTEAD, Barry
Scunthorpe 1956-1967
Worked forBritish Sugar for 22 years before taking early retirement. Lives in Brigg, Humberside.

HORSWILL, Mick
Sunderland, Man C, Plymouth, Hull, Carlisle, 1971-1983
Now manages a pub in Boldon, Tyne and Wear.
1973 FA Cup winner with Sunderland.

HORTON, Brian
Port V, Brighton, Luton, Hull, 1970-1986
After a 16 year playing career Brian became manager at Hull, achieving promotion to the Second Division in his first season in 1984. Four years later he succeeded Mark Lawrenson at Oxford and stayed until his appointment as manager of Man City in August 1993 – where he was sacked two years later. He only had to wait five weeks before being re-employed, at Huddersfield Town.

HOSKIN, Ashley
Burnley 1985-1988

A left winger who progressed through the junior ranks at Burnley, signing pro terms in 1985. Drifted into non-league soccer with Accrington and joined Barrow at the start of the 1995/6 season.

HOUCHEN, Keith

Hartlepool, Orient, York, Scunthorpe, Coventry, Hibs, Port V, Hartlepool, 1978-1995

After a gap of over 15 years, returned to his first club, Hartlepool, as player/coach and was promoted to manager in April 1995.

Scored the winning goal in Coventry's 1987 FA Cup win.

HOUGHTON, Billy

Barnsley, Watford, Ipswich, Leicester, Rotherham, 1957-1973

Played over 500 league games in his 16 year career. Now works for British Coal building departmentt in Barnsley after spending many years as joiner.

Second Division Championship medal with Ipswich.

HOUGHTON, Eric

Aston V, Notts C, 1926-1948

Life President of Aston Villa, Eric had three spells at Villa Park, the third to pioneer a new fund raising lottery for the club. Eric died in May 1996 after living for many years at his retirement home in Sutton Coldfield.

Won a Second Division Championship with Villa in 1938.

HOUGHTON, Ken

Rotherham, Hull, Scunthorpe, 1960-1973

Manager of a freight forwarding firm in Immingham, Humberside.

Played for Rotherham in the first ever League Cup final.

HOUSEMAN, Peter

Chelsea, Oxford, 1963-1976

Winger who played 252 League games for Chelsea before moving to Oxford United. Killed in a car crash in 1977 aged 32.

1970 FA Cup winner with Chelsea.

HOUSTON, Stewart

Chelsea, Brentford, Man U, Sheff U, Colchester, 1967-1985

Player/coach at Colchester United from August 1983 until April 1986. Joined the coaching staff at Arsenal in 1986 and took over as caretaker boss twice following the sackings of George Graham and Bruce Rioch but resigned in September 1996. to take over as manager of QPR.

Played for United in the 1976 FA Cup final.

HOW, Trevor

Watford 1974-1979

Played all of his 90 games at right back. Now licensee of the 'Crown', Little Missenden, Bucks. His father was a top Sppedway rider.

HOWE, Don

WBA, Arsenal, 1952-1966

Played 375 appearances for West Brom before joining Arsenal, where a leg fracture in 1966 ended his playing career. He then coached the 'Gunners' when they lifted the League and Cup double in 1971. Returned to the Hawthorns to manage West Brom in 1971 and has since made coaching and managerial stops at: Galatasaray, Leeds United , Arsenal, England 'B', Saudi Arabia, Bristol Rovers, Wimbledon, Q.PR, Wimbledon, Barnet, Coventry, Chelsea and was involved in the England set up under Terry Venables.

Made 23 consecutive appearances for England between 1958 and 1960.

HOWE, Ernie

Fulham, QPR, Portsmouth, 1973-1983

Dominant former West Ham defender who is now manager of Basingstoke Town of the ICIS League.

HOWE, George

Huddersfield, York, 1946-1960

York City stalwart with 307 appearances. Died in 1991.

HUBBARD, Terry

Swindon 1970-1975

Welsh under-23 international midfielder is now working as shift supervisor of Cwmbran Stadium.

HUCKER, Peter

QPR, Oxford, WBA, Millwall, Aldershot, 1980-1990

Former QPR keeper who won two under-23 caps with England. Peter gave up the milk round franchise that he had owned since 1994 to try and make use of his FA Coaching qualifications.
Played for QPR in the 1982 FA Cup final.

HUDSON, Alan
Chelsea, Stoke, Arsenal, Chelsea, Stoke C, 1968-1985

Started as an apprentice with his local club, Chelsea, before signing as a professional in June 1968, stayed at Stamford Bridge until January 1974. Was transferred to Stoke for £240,000, although he returned to the capital less than two years later with Arsenal and played in America before a brief return to Chelsea. Now lives in east London and writes a column in the Sporting Life as well as working in other areas of the media.
Cup Winners Cup winner with Chelsea in 1971.

HUGHES, Billy
Sunderland, Derby, Leicester, Carlisle, 1966-1979
A Scottish international and brother of John, is now clubhouse manager and steward of the Stressholme Golf Club in Darlington.
FA Cup winner with Sunderland.

HUGHES, Emlyn
Blackpool, Liverpool, Wolves, Rotherham, Hull, Swansea, 1965-1983
Son of a former Rugby League star, Emlyn started his career with Blackpool and in 1967 Liverpool paid a then club record £65,000 for his services. Captained Liverpool for a number of years lifting a host of trophies, and was named Footballer of the Year in 1976-7. He managed Rotherham for two years before becoming a 'celebrity' - regularly appearing on television in shows such as 'Sporting Triangles' and 'Question of Sport' for a number of years.
Captained England.

HUGHES, Harry
Southport, Chelsea, Bournemouth, Gillingham, 1950-1962
Ran the club shop at Spurs for eleven years, but Harry is now self-employed living in Guildford.

HUGHES, John
Celtic, Crystal Palace, Sunderland, 1960-1973
Was forced to quit the game through injury but went on to to become the Scottish FA's first junior international team boss. Nicknamed 'Yogi' after the cartoon character and runs Yogi's Bar in his home town of Coatbridge.
League Championship winner with Celtic between 1966 and 1971.

HUGHES, Ron
Chester 1951-1961
Veteran of over 400 games for Chester, now works for the education department at Clwyd County Council.

HUGHES, William
York 1951-1961
Was forced to sell his DIY business in York 15 years ago due to serious back problems. Now retired to a life of golf and bowls.

HUGHTON, Chris
Tottenham, West Ham, Brentford, 1979-1993
Played almost 300 games for Spurs and won 53 full caps with Eire. Now reserve team boss at at White Hart Lane.

Twice an FA Cup winner with Spurs.

HUMPHRIES, Gerry
Everton, C Palace, Crewe A, 1965-1976
Gerry is now believed to be working as a taxi driver in North Wales.

HUNT, David
Derby Co, Notts Co, Aston V, Mansfield T, 1977-1989
Played 300-plus games for Notts County. Now teaches at his soccer schools in the Ashby-de-la-Zouch area.

HUNT, Ernie
Swindon, Wolves, Everton, Coventry, Doncaster, Bristol C, 1959-1974
Lives in Gloucester but a hip injury prevents Ernie from working. However, since quitting as a player he has, run a pub, taught in a childrens home, worked in the commercial departments at Gloucester City and Swindon and even had a spell cleaning windows.
'That' free-kick, with Willie Carr, v Everton at Coventry.

HUNT, Roger
Liverpool, Bolton, 1959-1971
Made a name for himself as a marksman while shooting Liverpool back into the first division in 1961-2 and topping the league scoring list with 41 goals. Won 34 England caps and scored 245 goals in 401 League starts before ending his career at Bolton in 1971. Has been a member of the Pools Panel since 1974 and runs his own haulage business on Merseyside.
1966 World Cup winner.

HUNT, Steve
Aston V, Coventry City, WBA, Aston V, 1974-1987
A midfield star who had a spell with the New York Cosmos. Appointed manager of non-league VS Rugby in August 1996.
Capped twice by England whilst at WBA.

HUNTER, Allan
Oldham, Blackburn, Ipswich, Colchester,

1966-1982
After starting out at Coleraine, his first English club was Oldham Athletic and from there he moved on to nearby Blackburn. He signed for Ipswich in September 1971 where he now lives and works as a woodwork teacher at Belstead Special school. He keeps fit by playing golf and bowls.
Ipswich's most capped player after winning 47 of his 53 caps whilst at Portman Road.

HUNTER, Norman
Leeds, Bristol C, Barnsley,1962-1982

Joined Leeds United during the 1959/60 season. Played over 700 games during the Leeds glory years, winning: two league championships; FA Cup; League Cup; and two European Fairs Cups triumphs. During his managerial career he didn't reach the heights he had as a player but Norman took Barnsley from the third to the second division. He has also been manager of Rotherham and assistant manager at West Brom and Bradford City. Also won 28 caps for England. Now a popular after dinner speaker and coaches at local schools.
Voted the first ever 'Players' Player of the Year' in 1973.

HURLEY, Charlie
Millwall, Sunderland, Bolton, 1953-1970
A living legend at Roker Park and was recently voted the club's best ever player – even the training ground is named after him. Has has spent the years since retiring as a player working in his family packaging business.
Capped 40 times for Ireland between 1957 and 1969.

HURST, Geoff

West Ham, Stoke, WBA, 1959-1975

Started his career at West Ham United, signing as a professional in April 1959. Over the next thirteen years he played over 400 League games, scoring 180 goals including one in the 1964 FA Cup final. By the time he retired in 1975 he had scored 24 goals for England and won 49 caps. Briefly managed Chelsea between 1979 and 1981, but has worked for a company selling car warranties for a number of years - he is now managing director.

The only player ever to score a hat trick in a World Cup final.

HURST, Gordon

Charlton 1946-1957

Oldham born winger who notched up 369 League appearances for his only club. Died in 1980 at the age of 56.

HURST, John

Everton, Oldham, 1965-1980

Played over 500 League games before retiring in 1980. Now works as youth team coach at Everton.

Won nine England under-23 caps.

HUTCHINS, Don

Leicester, Plymouth, Blackburn, Bradford C, 1967-1980

Made 252 league appearances as a winger for Bradford. Now a sales manager with Leyland paints.

HUTCHINSON, Ian

Chelsea 1968-1975

England under-23 cap Ian scored 43 goals in his 112 league appearances and is most frequently remembered for his famous long throw-ins. Since retiring as a player, he has since helped out with the catering at Brentford and ran a pub in Windsor with his old team-mate Peter Osgood. They are still friends and sometimes appear together as an after dinner double act.

Scored the equaliser for Chelsea in the 1970 FA Cup final.

HUTCHISON, Tommy

Blackpool, Coventry, Man C, Burnley, Swansea, 1967-1990

Ended up playing at Swansea City, where he became player/manager. Now employed as a development officer with the PFA at Merthyr & Taff Ely Borough Council working with school children, special needs schools and the unemployed. Also runs fun days during the summer holidays at a residential camp in Pontypridd.

The only player to score for both sides in an FA Cup final.

HUTT, Geoff

Huddersfield, Blackburn, York, Halifax, 1968-1979

Works in the customer services dept at Tibbett and Britten's, Huddersfield.

HUXFORD, Cliff

Chelsea, Southampton, Exeter, 1958-1967

Now works as a self employed painter & decorator, living outside Southampton. Formerly manager of Brockenhurst in the Wessex League.

Played for Southampton in their Division Four Championship season of 1960.

INGHAM, Billy

Burnley, Bradford C, 1971-1981

Midfielder who played over 200 games for Burnley. Billy still lives in the area where he is a bus driver.

ICKE, David
Coventry, Hereford, 1969-1972

As a teenager he played in the same Leicester boys team as Peter Shilton, before joining Coventry City as an apprentice at the age of 15. Transferred to Hereford United in 1972 helping them to gain promotion from the Fourth to Third Division. When his career was brought to an abrupt end by rheumatoid arthritis, David became a journalist in Leicester, going on to become a household name as a BBC television sports presenter. Now lives in relative seclusion on the Isle of Wight and has become better known for his unconventional beliefs.

IMLACH, Mike
Peterboro, Tranmere, 1982-1984
Mike now works on a North Sea Oil rig.

INGHAM, Tony
Leeds, QPR, 1947-1962
Played over 500 games for QPR in a twelve stint ending in 1962. Now retired but still helps out at the Loftus Road Club in various capacities.
Holds the QPR record for most appearances.

IRVINE, Sammy
Shrewsbury, Stoke, 1972-1979
Lives near Shrewsbury working as a groundsman, having previously undertaken a variety of jobs including running a pub, selling insurance and a time as a laboratory technician.
Promoted to Division Three with Shrewsbury in 1974.

IRWIN, Colin
Liverpool, Swansea, 1979-1983
Colin only played 29 League games for Liverpool between 1979-1981, but in that time managed to win a European Cup Winners medal although he didn't play in the final. Was forced to quit through injury at the age of 27 following a £350,000 move to Swansea. Spent two years as Phil Neal's assistant at Bolton, but now lives close to the Indian Ocean in Perth, Western Australia where he supplies wines and spirits to liquor shops and hotels.
Won a League Cup winners medal in his first season.

JACKSON, Colin
Rangers Marton, Partick Thistle, 1962-1983
Despite winning 10 trophies with Rangers he was capped only eight times by Scotland.. After his playing days were over, Colin became a partner in a East Kilbridde printing firm.
Three Scottish League Championships.

JACKETT, Kenny
Watford 1979-1989
A Watford regular for ten years in the Eighties, during which time he was also capped 31 times by his country, Wales. Kenny was appointed youth coach at Vicarage Road in January 1991, then first team coach and is now team manager..
Won two promotions with The Hornets in 1979 and 1989.

JACKSON, Barry
York 1958-1969
A one club man who has worked for the Northern Electricity Board since finishing playing 25 years ago. He started as a pre-payment collector but since slot meters were done away with, has been a meter reader.
Holds the York City appearance record (541).

JACKSON, John
C Palace, Orient, Millwall, Ipswich, Hereford, 1964-1982
Played nearly 350 League games for Palace before moving on to Orient. Now installs and fits blinds in Brighton, and is also goalkeeping coach and youth development officer for the Seagulls.

JACKSON, Tommy
Everton, Notts F, Man U, 1967-1976
A Northern Ireland international who won 35 full caps. Managed several clubs in Northern Ireland after hanging up his boots but now works as a self employed upholsterer for Bannon & Co in Belfast.

JAKUB, Joe
Burnley, Bury, Chester, Burnley, 1973-1993
A Scottish born midfield man who played 265 league games with Bury before leaving for a short spell in Holland. Is now youth team manager at Stockport.

JAMES, Glyn
Blackpool 1960-1974
Played 393 games for Blackpool and qualified for his nine Welsh caps despite being born to English parents. Now runs his own laundry and dry cleaning business which can boast having the contract for cleaning the matchday shirts of his former club!
Twice won promotion to the First Division.

JAMES, Leighton
Burnley, Derby, QPR, Burnley, Swansea, Sunderland, Bury, Newport, Burnley, 1970-1988
Ran a sweet shop close to the Burnley ground and had a spell as youth coach at Bradford City. Now manages Netherfield in the Northern Premier League.
Capped 54 times for Wales.

JAMES, Robbie
Swansea, Stoke, QPR, Leicester, Swansea, Bradford, 1972-1993
With 47 Welsh caps and over 700 league games under his belt, Robbie is still playing for Weston in the Doc Martens League.

Won five Welsh Cup winners medals.

JANKOVIC, Bozo
Middlesboro 1979-1980
Played 42 games for Middlesbrough after signing in February 1979. Born at Sarajevo in Yugoslavia and was capped for that country at both under-21 and full level. Previously played for Zeljeznicar of Yugoslavia (making 500 appearances). Returned home to set up his own law firm but was killed during the Bosnian/Serb conflict.

JARDINE, Sandy
Rangers, Hearts, 1965-1982
Wrote his name in the record books as the only Scottish player to play 1,000 games. Had a spell as co-manager of Hearts in the mid 1980's and still lives in Edinburgh where he works as marketing manager of Scottish Breweries.
Three Scottish League Championships.

JARMAN, Harold
Bristol Rovers, Newport County, 1959-1974
Played over 500 games for Rovers and played county cricket for Gloucester for ten years. Now scouts for Norwich in the west country and South Wales.
Played 440 League games for Rovers.

JEFFERSON Derek
Ipswich, Wolves, Sheff Weds, Hereford, 1967-1977
A central defender who played most of his games at Ipswich. Still involved in the game coaching school kids with Christians in Sport.

JEFFREY, Billy
Oxford, Blackpool, Northampton, 1973-1983
Has worked in Northampton as a sales office manger with an office furniture company for the past five years. Played for Kettering from 1983 until 1987, managed Irthlingborough Diamonds and is currently assistant manager at Rushden & Diamonds.

JENNINGS, Nicky
Plymouth, Portsmouth, Aldershot, Exeter,

1963-1977
Now works as a probation officer in Dorset, where he also has had much experience managing non-league sides.

JENNINGS, Pat MBE, OBE

Watford, Tottenham, Arsenal, 1962-1984
Made 472 league appearances for Tottenham Hotspur and was PFA player of the year in 1976, before moving across north London to Arsenal. Won an incredible 119 caps for Northern Ireland and was awarded the MBE in 1976, followed by the OBE in 1987. Now shares his time between coaching the goalkeepers at White Hart Lane and making personal appearances.
UEFA Cup winners medal with Spurs.

JENNSEN, Viggo

Hull 1948-1956
Left-sided Danish international who played over 300 games for Hull City before returning home to become coach at his former club Esbjerg. Now retired.
Played in the 1948 Olympic Games for Denmark.

JOBLING, Keith

Grimsby 1953-1968
Played 448League games in his thirteen years at Blundells Park. Now an upholsterer in Grimsby.
Grimsby League appearances record holder.

JOHANNESON, Albert

Leeds, York, 1961-1971
A gifted winger who was recommended to Don Revie and Leeds United by an African schoolteacher. Albert steadly declined in health over the years because of a drink problem and he was found dead in his Leeds council flat in September 1995.
The first black player to appear in an FA Cup final when he played against Liverpool in 1965.

JOHNS, Nicky

Millwall, Sheff Utd, Charlton, QPR, Maidstone, 1976-1990
Experienced goalie who pulled on a Charlton jersey close to 300 times. Finished playing at Maidstone in 1990 but Nicky is now working as a community officer based at Crystal Palace.
Twice won promotion to Division Two, with Charlton and Crystal Palace.

JOHNSON, David

Everton, Ipswich, Liverpool, Everton, Barnsley, Man C, Preston, 1970-1984
England international striker who scored on four different competition debuts for Everton: Central League; Football League; FA Cup and European Cup. Now lives in Liverpool where he works for an insurance company and is a trustee of the North-West Sport Aid Foundation.
Played for Liverpool in the 1981 European Cup final.

JOHNSON, Richard

Tranmere 1971-1981
The keepers at Liverpool now benefit from the wisdom of this ex-Tranmere Rovers keeper, who played over 300 matches in his ten years at Prenton Park. As well as part time coaching, he now holds a senior post with the sport and community department of Liverpool City Council.
Promoted to Division Three in 1975.

JOHNSON, Rob

Luton, Leicester, Barnet, 1979-1991
Ran his own health club in Hitchin and was player/coach at Bedford Town. Now training to be a physio.
Played for Barnet in their first ever League game, against Crewe in 1991.

JOHNSTON, Craig

Middlesboro, Liverpool, 1977-1987
Born in South Africa and signed for Middlesbrough in February 1978. Made his name at Liverpool before returning to his native Australia after the 1988 Cup final. Now lives in Killiney, Northern Ireland and enjoys a full life as TV producer; TV star; writer; and inventor. His latest creation, the revolutionary 'Predator' football boot has been launched by Adidas.

Four League Championship medals with Liverpool.

JOHNSTON, John
Blackpool, Halifax, Bradford, Southport, Halifax, 1968-1978
Former Northern Irish under-23 international midfielder is now sales representative for a paint company.

JOHNSTONE, Bobby
Hibs, Man C, Hibs, Oldham, 1946-1965
Scottish international inside forward who won 17 caps. Worked for many years as a controller in the building industry, then edged into retirement by driving part-time for a local seafood company. Bobby is well known in the Oldham area for his ability as a very capable bowls player.
Two Scottish League champions with Hibs.

JOHNSTONE, Derek
Rangers, Chelsea, Dundee United, Rangers, 1968-1986
A legend north of the border who moved to Chelsea for £35,000 in 1983 having been Scottish 'Player of the Year' in 1978. Played only one league games for the Londoners before moving back to Scotland where he became manager of Partick Thistle in 1986. Can now be seen on Sportscene, the Scottish version of Match of The Day and can also be heard on Radio Clyde.
European Cup Winners Cup winner with Rangers in 1972.

JOHNSTONE, Jimmy
Celtic, Sheffield United, Dundee, 1961-1977
A jinky red-headed striker who started his Parkhead career as a ball boy. Has held a varity of jobs since retiring from the game including a film presenter, lorry driver for a Celtic fan and is now a representative for a tool company.
European Cup winner with Celtic in 1967.

JOHNSTON, Tom
Kilmarnock, Oldham, Darlington, Oldham, Norwich, Newport, Orient, Blackburn, Orient, Gillingham, 1949-1961

A well travelled striker who scored goals whereever he went – many of them during his two spells at Orient. Had a bookmaking business in Fylde coast before emigrating to Australia in the early seventies where he lives in New South Wales.
Holds the record for the most goals in a season and career for Leyton Orient.

JOHNSTON, Willie
Rangers, WBA, Birmingham, Rangers, Hearts, 1964-1985
Speedy winger who won 22 full Scottish caps and had seven years south of the border, notably with West Bromwich Albion. Coached at Hearts, East Fife, Raith Rovers and Falkirk before becoming a licensee in Kirkaldy.
Won a European Cup Winners Cup medal with Rangers in 1972.

JONES, Alan
Cardiff, Exeter, Norwich, Wrexham, 1958-1963
Diced with non-league football before emigrating to Australia, eventually becoming a police officer and then becoming involved in a road haulage business.

JONES, Andy
Port V, Charlton, Port V, Bristol C, Bournemouth, Leyton O, 1985-1993
Welsh international striker whose career was ended through injury and is now a financial adviser.
Twice voted Port Vale's player of the year.

JONES, Barrie
Swansea, Plymouth, Cardiff, 1959-1969
Won Welsh under-23 honours and fifteen full caps before retiring in 1969 whilst at Cardiff. Now works at Swansea leisure centre.
Moved to Plymouth for a British record fee (£45,000) for an outside right.

JONES, Cliff
Swansea, Tottenham, Fulham, 1952-1969
Goalscoring striker whose talents were recognised by Wales on 59 occasions. Cliff had a butchers shop but when it failed he

returned briefly to sheet metal working, a trade he had learnt as a 16 year-old apprentice in Swansea dry dock. He then took employment at a sports centre before becoming games master at a London school. Now retired, living in Goffs Oak, Herts, although he does help out at Spurs games in their Legends Club.
A member of Spurs double winning side.

JONES, David
Bournemouth, Notts F, Norwich, 1970-1979
Welsh international defender, now works with Bournemouth's school of excellence after moving into a printing business.
Capped eight times by Wales.

JONES, David
Everton, Coventry, Preston, 1974-1984
A central defender during his playing days who was promoted to Stockport County boss in March 1995.

JONES, George
Bury, Blackburn, Bury, Oldham, Halifax, Southport, 1961-1977
Has been employed by British Rail for the past sixteen years. His son, Alex, had been on the books of Rochdale.

JONES, Gordon
Middlesboro, Darlington, 1960-1974
Played over 450 games in defence for Middlesbrough. Now runs his own general goods shop in Stockton.
Won 9 England under-23 Caps.

JONES, Joey
Wrexham, Liverpool, Wrexham, Chelsea, Huddersfield, Wrexham, 1972-1991
Popular with the fans at all his clubs and was voted player of the year during his times at Chelsea, Huddersfield and Wrexham. Was appointed player/coach at Wrexham in November 1989 during his third spell with the club and is now Wrexham coach.
Capped 72 times by Wales.

JONES, Lyn
Cardiff, Newport, Reading, 1978-1992

Had two spells as manager of Merthyr Tydfil and also previously managed Inter Cardiff.

JONES, Mick
Sheff U, Leeds, 1962-1973
Centre forward during the Leeds United purple years of the sixties and seventies, Mick chalked up a total of over 350 league appearances and won three England caps to add to his nine at under-23 level. Retired due to a knee injury in 1973 to become a representative for a sports goods company, then ran a sports shop in Maltby for the next fourteen years. Now runs a market stall with his son, selling sportswear in Nottingham and lives nearby, in his hometown of Worksop.
Finished an FA Cup final with his arm in plaster after breaking it crossing the ball for Allan Clarke to score the winning goal.

JONES, Paul
Bolton, Huddersfield, Oldham, Blackpool, Rochdale, Stockport Co, 1970-1989
Spent twelve years with Bolton before taking in stops at five further clubs including Blackpool, for whom he now does some scouting.
Played 440 League games for Bolton between 1970 and 1982.

JONES, Stan
Walsall, WBA, Walsall, 1957-1972
Has worked as a manufacturers agent in the sports trade since retiring from the game in 1972 after over 450 league appearances.

JONES Steve
QPR, Walsall, Wimbledon, 1978-1982
A highly promising defender whose career was cut short by injury. Owns a nightclub in Windsor.
Part of the Wimbledon team who won promotion into the Football League.

JONES, Wayne
Bristol R 1966-1972
Became Huddersfield Town's physiotherapist in 1990. Now assistant manager at Notts County.

JORDAN, Joe
Morton,Leeds, Man U, Southampton, Bristol C, 1964-1989
Scottish international Joe's heyday was during spells with Leeds and Manchester United, before moving to Italy to play for AC Milan, then Verona. Progressed into management with Bristol City 1988-1990 before successfully managing Hearts in Scotland. Returned south to briefly occupy the Stoke City managers position. Resigned in September 1994 but re-joined Bristol City for a second spell in the following November.
The first Scotland player to score in three World Cup finals.

JOYCE, Joe
Barnsley, Scunthorpe, 1979-1991
Held a regular berth at full back for Barnsley for over a decade, before ending his playing days at Scunthorpe United. Joe is currently a member of the coaching staff at Carlisle.
Played 332 league games for Barnsley.

JUDD, Mike
Southampton 1967-1969
Mike is now living in the New Forest and working in the drinks industry as a sales manager.

KAMARA, Chris
Portsmouth, Swindon, Portsmouth, Brentford, Swindon, Stoke, Leeds, Luton, Sheff U, Bradford C, 1975-1995
Former dockyard apprentice who earned a crack at top flight soccer as a player with Leeds and Sheffield United. Was appointed manager at Bradford City in November 1995.
Gained Bradford promotion in his first season as boss.

KASULE, Victor
Meadowbank Thistle, Shrewsbury, Darlington, Hamilton Ac, 1983-1993
Glasgow born Victor became a local hero at Shrewsbury but wayward behaviour and a drink problem meant a promising career faded out with only two games at Darlington, a return to Scotland and ruinous spells in Finland, Malta and Ireland. He has accounting qualifications from Glasgow University and is currently working in the telephone banking industry.

KAY, Tony
Sheff Wed, Everton, 1954-1963
After being banned from soccer for alleged 'fixing' of matches whilst with Sheffield Wednesday, went abroad and lived in Spain. Now working on a film about the infamous match-fixing years.
League Championship in 1963 with Everton.

KAYE, John
Scunthorpe, WBA, Hull, 1960-1973
A goal-scoring forward who joined West Brom from Scunthorpe for a record transfer fee. After being converted into a defender he went on to make more than 360 appearances for Albion. Transferred to Hull in 1971, became coach, then manager before retiring from the game to go into the hotel business. Currently a welder, working on gas rigs both onshore and offshore and coaching at Brigg Town.

KEAN, Stephen
Celtic, Swansea, 1986
Played only three games for the Swans and is now youth team coach at Reading.

KEEBLE, Vic
Colchester, Newcastle, West Ham, 1950-1959
Injury ended Vic's career when he was only 29. He went into soccer journalism and then served Chelsmford City for many years as General manager and then club secretry.
Played for Newcastle in the 1955 Cup final.

KEETCH, Bobby
Fulham, QPR, 1959-1968
Started his career as an amatuer at West Ham but went on to play alongside Johnny Haynes, Jimmy Hill and Bobby Robson at Fulham. A co-founder of the theme restaurent 'Football Football' in London's West End, died suddenly in June 1996.
Played for Fulham in their record 10-1 win over Ipswich in 1963.

KEEGAN, Ged

Man C, Oldham, Mansfield, Rochdale, 1974-1985
Former Manchester City apprentice who won one England under-21 cap. Ged has worked as an insurance salesman since retiring in 1985 and enjoys a regular round of golf.
League Cup winner with City in 1976.

KEEGAN, Kevin

Scunthorpe, Liverpool, Southampton, Newcastle, 1968-1983
Plucked by Bill Shankly from Scunthorpe for £35,000 in May 1981, he became an immediate success, making a rapid rise to full international level. With Liverpool he won two League Titles , FA Cup and European Cup winners medals. He left Liverpool during the summer of 1977 for SV Hamburg in Germany. He retired at the end of the 1983/4 season after spells with Southampton and Newcastle to become an unofficial soccer ambassador playing in exhibition matches throughout the world from his relaxing base on the Costa del Sol in Spain. The lure of management could be resisted no more, when in February 1992 he accepted the challenge of restoring glory to Newcastle.
European Footballer of the Year two years running.

KEELAN, Kevin

Aston V, Stockport, Wrexham, Norwich, 1959-1979
It was at his fourth League club, Norwich, that Kevin made his mark, playing 571 League games before retiring in 1979. Now sells contact lenses for a living in Florida.
Twice helped Norwich to the First Division.

KEELEY, Glen

Ipswich, Newcastle, Blackburn, Everton, Oldham, Colchester, Bolton, 1972-1988
Played 365 games in defence for Blackburn Rovers. Now a publican but uses his spare time to indulge in his passion for flying.

KEEN, Mike

QPR, Luton, Watford, 1959-1974
Now lives in High Wycombe, where he has managed 'Sport & Ski' shop in the town since his own sports shop that he ran for 25 years went bust two years ago. Is manager of Flackwell Heath in the Diadora League and coaches one night a week at West Ham's school of excellence in Slough.
Played for QPR when they completed a League Cup and Division Three double in 1967.

KELLARD, Bobby

Southend, C Palace, Ipswich, Portsmouth, Bristol C, Leicester, C Palace, Portsmouth, Hereford, Torquay, 1959-1975
This midfielder played for eight clubs before taking over as manger at Chelmsford, where he hit the headlines by signing a certain Jimmy Greaves! Ran a taxi business in Southend for several years, but now trades as an antiques dealer. Recently had a stint as joint manager with Len Glover at Harlow.
Won promotion with Leicester in 1971.

KELLOCK, Billy

Cardiff, Norwich, Millwall, Peterboro, Luton, Wolves, Southend, Port V, Halifax, 1972-1985
Midfielder who turned out for nine clubs over 13 years. Lives in Kettering where he is manager of the Barndale Country Club.

KELLOW, Tony

Exeter, Blackpool, Exeter, Plymouth, Swansea, Newport, Exeter, 1976-1987
Tony held the post of assistant manager at Exeter City, but now runs the 'Centre Spot' Social Club at their St James Park ground.
Club record 129 goals for Exeter.

KELLY, Bernard

Raith, Leicester, Notts Forest, Aberdeen, Raith, 1951-1969
Made his name with Raith with 92 goals from 207 games. Returned to Scotland because of homesickness but now lives in Canada woking in a solar heating business.

KELLY, Chris

Millwall 1974
Chris shot to fame during Leatherhead's

famous cup run of the early seventies, earning him a contract with Millwall. The 'Leatherhead Lip' is now Chief Exec and Commercial Manager at Kingstonian.

KELLY, Eddie
Arsenal, QPR, Leicester, Notts Co, Bournemouth, Leicester, Torquay, 1968-1985
Now making double glazed windows in Paignton, Devon and was appointed manager of Western League side Barnstaple in June 1995.
The first sub to score in an FA Cup final.

KELLY, Hugh
Blackpool 1946-1959
Joined Blackpool from the Scottish junior side Jeanfield Swifts in 1943. Played one game for Scotland against the USA in 1952. After over 400 games in fourteen years, he now owns a cafe in Blackpool.
Unfortunate in missing the 'Matthews final', as he had played in the two losing finals of 1948 and 1951.

KELLY, Jimmy
Watford, Blackpool, 1949-1961
Played over 200 games before moving to Australia where he became a successful player and coach. Returned to Blackpool where he embarked on a business career.
Was sold by Watford for a then club record fee of £15,000.

KELLY, Mike
QPR, Birmingham, 1967-1974
Former England amateur international goalie who has worked on the FA staff with England squad keepers. Now goalkeeping coach at Middlesbrough.
Won promotion with Birmingham in 1972.

KELLY, Phil
Wolves, Norwich, 1957-1967
A Republic of Ireland international who played for a number of non-league clubs in Norfolk when his career ended. Now runs a holiday complex with a former team-mate near Fritton Lake.

KELSEY, Jack
Arsenal 1950-1961
After making his debut in 1951, he went on to become a great goalie for both club and country. The climax of his career was when Wales won through to the quarter finals of the World Cup, eventually losing to champions Brazil. Gave over 40 years service to Arsenal, before his death in 1992.
League Championship medal in 1953.

KEMBER, Steve
C Palace, Chelsea, Leicester, C Palace, 1965-1979

His fourteen year career started and finished at Crystal Palace. Owned a wine bar in Croydon and managed Diadora League side Whyteleafe until 1992. Steve is now employed back at Selhurst Park as reserve team coach.
Three England under-23 caps.

KEMP, David
C Palace, Portsmouth, Carlisle, Plymouth, Gillingham, Brentford, 1974-1981
A goal-scoring forward in his day, David is now assistant manager to Alan Smith at Wycombe Wanderers, having previously held the same post at Crystal Palace; coached at Wimbledon; and held the managers job at Plymouth Argyle.

Cost Plymouth a club record £75,000 in 1979.

KEMP, Fred
Wolves, Southampton, Blackpool, Halifax, Hereford, 1964-1974
Fred is an office equipment salesman, living in Wolverhampton.

KENDALL, Howard
Preston, Everton, Birmingham, Stoke, Blackburn, Everton, 1962-1981
Kendall became an overnight sensation when becoming the youngest player to appear in a Wembley Cup final, when Preston lost to West Ham in 1964. He later became player/manager at Blackburn Rovers, before entering full management with Everton until 1987. Managed Greek side Xanthi then returned to the managers post at Notts County, in January 1995. Unfortunately his stay at Meadow Lane was terminated rather acrimoniously, within weeks, and he moved on to manage Sheffield United.
Division One Championship medal in 1969.

KENDALL, Mark
Tottenham, Chesterfield, Newport, Wolves, Swansea, Burnley, 1976-1992
Former Tottenham Hotspur keeper and Welsh under-21 cap. Joined the police force and is stationed at Newport in Gwent.
Won Division Three and Division Four Championship medals with Wolves.

KENNEDY, Alan
Newcastle, Liverpool, Sunderland, Hartlepool, Wigan, Wrexham, 1972-1990
Joined Liverpool from Newcastle in August 1978 for £330,000 and won two England caps. Still playing part time for Barrow in the Northern League. Lives in Ormskirk and regular contributes to programmes on Radio City, Liverpool, as well as running his own soccer schools.
Scored the winning goal in the 1981 European Cup final.

KENNEDY, Joe
WBA, Chester, 1948-1961

A solid, reliable England 'B' defender who had it not been for injuries would have won full England honours. Retired in 1966 but collapsed and died at his workplace in 1986 aged 60.

KENNEDY, Keith
Newcastle, Bury, Mansfield T, 1971-1982
Made over 400 appearances for Bury as a reliable left back, before finishing his League career at Mansfield in 1982. Keith is now running a greetings card business.

KENNEDY, Ray
Arsenal, Liverpool, Swansea, Hartlepool, 1969-1983
A great striker who signed as a professional with Arsenal in November 1968, having served his apprenticeship at Port Vale. Less than three years later played a part in the Gunner's double-winning triumph. Ray joined Liverpool in 1974 for £180,000 and won a total of seventeen England caps to add to his six at under-23 level. Finished in his native north-east with Hartlepool in 1983 and became a publican in Northumberland, but now sadly suffers from Parkinson's disease which severely limits his activities.
Arsenal double-winner.

KENNEDY, Stewart
Falkirk, Aberdeen, 1971-1983
Scottish international full back who was forced to quit the game through injury. Moved back to Falkirk where he runs a pub.
Two Scottish League Championship medals.

KENNING, Mike
Aston Villa, Shrewsbury, Charlton, Norwich, Wolves, Charlton, QPR, Watford, 1959-1973
Now lives in South Africa working as a sales representative for a safety equipment company. Kept active in the 1970s by becoming player manager to a number of African clubs.

KENNON, Sandy
Huddersfield, Norwich, Colchester, 1956-1966
A South African born goalkeeper who

played for Bulawayo before coming to join Huddersfield.. After ten years and over 300 appearances for his three clubs, became a representative for a Whisky firm and then partner in a bookmakers prior his retirement. *Played twice for Rhodesia.*

KENT, Paul
Norwich, Halifax, Cambridge, 1972-1977
A dislocated knee ended his career in a League Cup tie. Now works as a hairdresser.

KENWORTHY, Tony
Sheff U, Mansfield, 1975-1989
Although born in Leeds, Tony played most of his league soccer for another Yorkshire club - Sheffield United. Now works for a youth training programme in Scotland.

KERR, Andy
Partick Thistle, Manchester City, Kilmarnock, Sunderland, Aberdeen, 1953-1965
A former Scottish international who is a true Killie legend. Still holds the club's goalscorring record 113 goals in 134 games. Spent the final 13 years of his working life in Aberdeen with the Rolls Wood Group before retiring in June 1996.
Was a runner up in no less than five Cup Finals.

KERR, Bobby
Sunderland, Blackpool, Hartlepool, 1964-1981
Played over 350 games for Sunderland. Now runs the 'Copthill' pub in Hourton-Le-Spring in Durham.
A 1973 FA Cup winner.

KERR, George
Barnsley, Bury, Oxford, Scunthorpe, 1961-1972
Experienced manager, who held posts at Lincoln, Grimsby, Rotherham, and Boston. Although he has been unemployed since the change of management at Southampton - for whom he worked as a scout, George has travelled extensively from his home near Grimsby: taking in Venezuela where he lived

for six months ; New York; and Houston, Texas.

KETTLEBOROUGH, Keith
Rotherham U, Sheff U, Newcastle, Doncaster, Chesterfield, 1955-1968
Made over 400 league starts before ending in 1958. Lives in Rotherham and has been a sports master at a local private school since 1985.

KEVAN, Derek
Bradford PA, WBA, Chelsea, Man C, C Palace, Peterboro, Luton, Stockport, 1952-1967
Kevan made a terrific reputation with West Brom where teaming up with the great Ronnie Allen, he scored over 150 league goals. After Albion he went on a merry-go-round of clubs before retiring. Now living in Castle Vale, Birmingham and has worked as a drier for a sign company in Birmingham for the past six years.

KEYWORTH, Ken
Rotherham, Leicester City, Coventry City, Swindon, 1952-1965
Injuries received in a car crash cut short his Filbert Street career and he moved to Coventry on the day City beat them 8-1 in the League Cup. Returned to his home town, Rotherham, becoming a quantity surveyor at a steelworks before taking a job as an office manager for a building company.
The scorer of Leicester's only goal in the 1963 Cup Final.

KIDD, Brian
Man U, Arsenal, Man C, Everton, Bolton, 1967-1981
Won a European Cup winners medal at the age of 19 with Man Utd; won two England caps; and was transferred four times for six figure sums before hanging up his boots in 1981. Was assistant manager at Swindon, briefly managed Barrow and Preston, before returning to Old Trafford as assistant manager.
Scored for United in their 1968 European Cup win.

KIERNAN, Joe
Sunderland, Northampton T, 1962-1971
Wing half veteran of 300 plus games for
Northampton Town. Joe still lives in the
town and works as a painter and decorator.

KINDON, Steve
Burnley, Wolves, Burnley, Huddersfield,
1968-1981
Bustling centre forward who scored over 100
goals in a career which was ended by a serious knee injury in 1982 while at
Huddersfield, where he stayed on as promotions manager. For the past few years Steve
has been the globe-trotting sales manager at
Rolyat, a firm of basketware importers.
Former England Youth International.

KING, Alan
Tranmere R 1962-1971
Wing half Alan played 342 games for
Tranmere Rovers. Now lives in Moreton on
the Wirral, and works in the family scrap
metals business.
*Promoted to Division Three with Tranmere in
1967.*

KING, Andy
Luton, Everton, QPR, WBA, Everton, Wolves,
Luton, Aldershot, 1974-1986
Everton paid a £35,000 fee to sign Andy
from Luton, where he first appeared in 1975.
Big money moves to QPR and then West
Brom followed before he re-joined Everton.
Worked in the commercial department at
Luton before stepping into the vacant man-
ager's job at Mansfield Town until August
1996.
Capped twice by England at under-21 level.

KING, Brian
Millwall, Coventry, 1967-1975
Millwall's regular goalkeeper for many years,
after joining them from non-league
Chelmsford City in 1967. Now works as a
commentator for Norwegian television.
Played 302 League games for Millwall.

KING, Jake
Shrewsbury, Wrexham, Cardiff C, 1971-1985

Played 300 matches in a nine year stint at
Shrewsbury. Stayed in the town, where he is
now a pub landlord. Jake is still involved
with soccer, as assistant manager of Newton
FC.

KING, John
Everton, Bournemouth, Tranmere, Port V,
1957-1970
Was in charge at Prenton Park for nearly ten
years (1987-1996) before being handed the
title Director of Football. He had previously
played almost 250 league games for the
club.

KING, John
Swansea 1950-1963
Welsh international goalkeeper who played
368 League games for Swansea. Died in
1982 aged 49.
Capped once against England, in 1955.

KING, Peter
Cardiff 1961-1973
Played for Cardiff for 12 years, making over
350 appearances. Now works in the prison
service.

KINNEAR, Joe
Tottenham, Brighton, 1965-1975
Dublin born Joe won 25 caps for Eire and
played at right back for Tottenham for nine
years before ending his playing days at
Brighton. Was assistant manager to Dave
Mackay at Doncaster Rovers, eventually
becoming manager. Joined Wimbledon in
the same capacity in January 1991.
Played for Spurs in the 1972 Fairs Cup final.

KINSEY, Noel
Cardiff, Norwich, Birmingham, Port V, 1944-
1960
The proud owner of 7 Scotland Caps. Now
retired from the solicitors office of Norwich
Union Insurance.
*Scored for Birmingham in the 1956 FA Cup
final against Manchester City.*

KIRKMAN, Alan
Man C, Rotherham U, Newcastle U,

Scunthorpe U, Torquay U, Workington T, 1956-1967

Former inside forward Alan is now working as a manager for a transport company in his home town of Bolton.

Played for Rotherham in the first ever League Cup final.

KIRKUP, Joe

West Ham, Chelsea, Southampton, 1958-1973

Former England under-23 international full back, moved to South Africa in 1968 to play for Durban City, becoming their player/coach in 1974. Returned to England to run a pub in Alton, then owned 'Cranleigh Sports' shop near Guildford. However, Joe is now runnning his own newsagency in Ewell, Surrey.

Played for West Ham in the European Cup Winners Cup final.

KITCHEN, Peter

Doncaster, Leyton O, Fulham, Cardiff, Leyton O, Chester, 1970-1984

Goal-scoring forward who appeared for five league clubs before having a spell in Hong Kong with Happy Valley. Peter returned to England to manage the White Oak Leisure Centre in Kent.

Played for Leyton Orient in a 1978 FA Cup semi final.

KITCHENER, Bill

West Ham, Torquay, Bournemouth, 1963-1971

Orginally joined the Devon and Cornwall Police whilst at Torquay before transfering to Bournemouth. Has now been stationed at Burley in the New Forest for many years.

FA Youth Cup winner with West Ham in 1963.

KITCHENER, Barry

Millwall 1966-1981

A long-serving Millwall defender who made over 500 appearances for the London club in a fifteen year League career. Barry now has souvenir shops in Caistor and Great Yarmouth.

Holds the Lions' record for most number of League appearances.

KNAPP, Tony

Leicester, Southampton, Coventry, Tranmere, 1955-1970

Now coaches in Norway, with second division club Ulf-Sandnes. He had previously steered Viking Stavanger to League and Cup double and was at one time, manager of Iceland's national team.

Captain of the first ever Southampton side to reach the First Division.

KNIGHT, Ian

Barnsley, Sheff Wed, Grimsby, 1984-1995

A serious leg injury seemed to have ended Ian's career whilst at Sheffield Wednesday, however he managed to recover to play for Grimsby, where he is now a community officer.

KNOWLES, Cyril

Middlesboro, Tottenham, 1962-1975

Cyril left Spurs after 400 league appearances over a 13 year stay which saw him pick up an FA Cup winners medal in 1967. In his heyday, the hit record 'Nice One Cyril' was named after him. Became manager of Torquay but died at the age of only 47 in 1991.

Played for Spurs in the 1972 Fairs Cup final.

KNOWLES, Peter

Wolves 1963-1969

Dramatically quit Wolves in 1969 to become a Jehovah's Witness. Nowadays he works three days a week as a window cleaner and the rest of the time preaching Jehovah gospel door to door. Lives a few minutes away from Molineux.
Featured in the 1991 song 'Gods Footballer' written by Billy Bragg.

KRUSZYNSKI, Detzi
FC Hamburg, Wimbledon, Brentford, Peterboro, Coventry, 1988-1994
Detzi moved to England from German club FC 08 Hamburg in 1988. Now runs his own business in Hertfordshire and plays for St Albans City.

KRZYWICKI, Dick
WBA, Huddersfield, Scunthorpe, Northampton, Lincoln, 1964-1975
Now works in the engineering industry and coaches youngsters in his spare time.

LABONE, Brian
Everton 1957-1971
Turned professional in 1957 and went on to play over 450 league games before retiring. He was also capped 26 times by England. Forced to quit in 1972, Brian went into business on Merseyside and moved into the insurance industry. He now works in the commercial office at Goodison Park.
League Championship medal in 1963 and 1970.

LACEY, Bill
Middlesboro, Aldershot, Reading, 1952-1962
Was a carpet department manager for the Co-Op in Reading, prior to his death.

LACY, John
Fulham, Tottenham, Crystal Palace, 1972-1983
John might have become a Liverpool or Everton player had he not left Merseyside to study at the London School of Economics. He was coached in the college team by England defender George Cohen and signed for Fulham in 1972. He moved to Tottenham in July 1978, then had spell at Crystal Palace. Became the Vauxhall-Opel League's first full time manager at, Albans City, until his resignation in June 1988. Now works for a double glazing company in north London.
Played for Fulham in the 1975 FA Cup final against West Ham.

LAIDLAW, Joe
Middlesboro, Carlisle, Doncaster, Portsmouth, Hereford, Mansfield, 1967-1982
Midfield dynamo initially with Middlesboro then with five more clubs. Lives in Portsmouth where he works as a roofer and manages Portfield in the Sussex County League.
Promoted to Division One with Carlisle in 1974.

LAMBERT, Roy
Rotherham, Barnsley, 1956-1965
Played over 300 games for Rotherham, now works for Garrard Industries as a machinist, but still in Rotherham.
Played for Rotherham in the first ever League Cup final in 1961.

LAMPARD, Frank
West Ham, Southend, 1967-1985
With the exception of a brief stint at Southend as player/coach in 1985, Frank has been at West Ham for close to thirty years. As a player, made the right back berth his own for over 600 games, winning two England caps along he way. Currently assistant manager to his friend and old Hammers team-mate, Harry Redknapp.
FA Cup winner with The Hammers in 1975.

LANGAN, David
Derby, Birmingham, Oxford, Leicester, Bournemouth, Peterboro, 1976-1988
Dublin born David now lives in Peterborough, but has been forced to give up work due to a back injury sustained during his playing days. Latterly had been employed in the security industry. As a player he won 25 caps for the Republic of Ireland and played over 300 league games for his six clubs.
League Cup winner with Oxford in 1986.

LANGLEY, Jimmy
Leeds, Brighton, Fulham, QPR, 1952-1966

Speedy attacking England full back who managed Hillingdon Borough and was coach at Palace after his playing days were over. Now living in West Drayton where he is Sseward of the local British Legion Club.
Part of the QPR side which completed the League Cup and Division Two championship double.

LARGE, Frank
Halifax, Q.P.R, Northampton, Swindon, Carlisle, Oldham, Leicester, Fulham, Northampton, Chesterfield, 1958-1973
In a league career with eleven clubs he scored 210 goals from 563 games. Frank is now a farmer in County Mayo, Ireland.
Won a Third Division Championship medal with Northampton.

LARKIN, Bunny
Birmingham, Doncaster, Watford, Lincoln, 1954-1966
A more than useful player who settled in Norwich selling cakes for Lyons.

LATCHFORD, Bob
Birmingham, Everton, Swansea, Coventry, Lincoln, Newport, 1968-1985
England international forward who served his apprenticeship with Birmingham City but hit the heights with Everton, Swansea and then Coventry. Bob owned a children's clothes shop in Swansea, but now has moved back to the Midlands. He lives in Redditch and worked for a firm selling nuts and bolts, was a marketing manager by Ladbrokes and is now youth development officer at Birmingham.
League Cup finalist with Everton in 1977.

LATCHFORD, Dave
Birmingham, Bury, 1968-1978
Former Birmingham City goalkeeper. and the oldest of the three Latchford brothers. Now lives in Solihull and runs the Widney Manor Cemetery in Bentley Heath, Birmingham.
Won a Division Two promotion with Birmingham in 1972.

LATCHFORD, Peter
WBA, Celtic, Clyde, 1972-1987
An England under-23 goalkeeper who joined Celtic from West Brom in 1975. Was the Glasgow club's 'Player of the Year' in 1977/8. Retired in 1988, and now lives on a farm in Mauchline.
Won three Scottish Cups with Celtic.

LAVERICK, Mick
Mansfield, Southend, Huddersfield, York, Huddersfield, 1972-1982
Now a prison officer in Nottinghamshire.

LAW, Denis
Huddersfield, Man C, Man U, Man C, 1956-1973
Law was signed by the great Bill Shankly as a skinny bespectacled youngster for Huddersfield. He developed into one of the most dangerous forwards in the game. In a cup game against Luton in 1966, Denis had already scored six goals when the game was abandoned. Amazingly enough, they lost the replay! He moved to Torino in Italy for a season before joining Man Utd. He returned to Maine Road to end his illustrious career as undoubtedly one of soccer's great personalities. Since retiring as a player, he has worked as a commentator on both television and radio and is a popular after dinner speaker. Lives in Bowden, Cheshire.
Two League Championship medals with Manchester United.

LAWRENCE, Lennie

Plymouth, Charlton

Lennie managed Plymouth, worked wonders at Charlton, and then had a short-lived term of office at Middlesborough before accepting the post offered by Bradford City in 1994, then later took over at Luton Town.

Took Charlton into the First Division in 1986.

LAWRENCE, Tommy

Liverpool, Tranmere, 1962-1973

Affectionately nicknamed 'The Flying Pig' by the Kop due to his rather portly stature. Tommy kept goal for Liverpool in 300 league games over almost a decade. He won three full caps for his native Scotland and retired in 1973, having played a further 80 games for neighbours Tranmere Rovers. Now works night shift at a wire factory in Warrington, Cheshire.

Won League Championship medals in 1964 and 1966 and an FA Cup Winners Medal in 1965.

LAWRENSON, Mark

Preston, Brighton., Liverpool, 1974-1987

The son of a former Preston forward, started his career like his father at Deepdale. The £100,000 that Brighton paid for his services in 1977 was rewarded by starring performances and then by a very healthy profit when Liverpool parted with £900,000 to take him to Anfield. A Republic of Ireland International (38 caps) he moved into management with Oxford and Peterborough later to involve himself in the media as a pundit with BBC and Sky Television. Now a specialist defence coach at Newcastle.

Won a European Cup winners medal in 1984.

LAWRIE, Sam

Middlesborough, Charlton Ath, Bradford PA, 1951-1965

Goal-scoring winger during a 14 year career. Died in 1979.

LAWS, Brian

Burnley, Huddersfield, Middlesboro, Notts F, Grimsby 1979-1995 . England "B" international, who after fifteen years as a player was offered his first managerial opportunity by Grimsby Town in November 1994. Played for a Football League Xi and was Capped by England at B level.

LAWSON, Alan

Oldham 1964-1969

Alan was a central defender whose claim to fame is being the first ever substitute to score a goal (1965). He is now back in Scotland, living near Motherwell, and currently works as a maintenance engineer.

LAWTON, Bill

Oldham, Chester, 1946-1949

Oldham wing half of the late 40s and husband of actress, Dora Bryan. Became a Brighton hotelier.

LAWTON, Nobby

Manchester United, Preston, Brighton, Lincoln, 1958-1972

Was forced to quit by a knee injury and has worked as a sales director for an export packaging company.

Captain of Preston for the 1964 Cup Final.

LAWTON, Tommy

Burnley, Everton, Chelsea, Notts Co, Brentford, Arsenal, 1935-1955

One of the greatest ever centre forwards who made his mark at the age of 17, becoming the youngest player to score a hat-trick. Won 23 full caps and scored goals galore for all of his six league clubs. After spells as manager at Kettering and Notts County, Tommy became a publican in Lowdham and retired to Nottingham. died in november 1996.
League Championship medal with Everton in 1939.

LAYNE, David
Rotherham, Swindon, Bradford C, Sheff Wed, Hereford, 1957-1972
Retired in 1972 not long after an eight year suspension imposed by the FA ended. David is now a publican in Chesterfield.
Netted 128 times in 194 league games.

LAYTON, John
Hereford, Newport, 1974-1983
Central defender who originally signed for Hereford from non-league Gloucester in 1974. Is now back at Edgar Street as Manager.

LEA, Cyril
Leyton O, Ipswich, 1957-1968
Wrexham born wing half who had an eleven year playing career in England. Is now youth team coach at West Brom.
Won two Welsh caps in 1965.

LEACH, Mick
QPR, Cambridge, 1964-1978
Died in 1992 after a long illness. Spent 13 years at Loftus Road, playing 313 League games.
Promoted from Division Three with QPR in 1967.

LEADBETTER, James
Chelsea, Brighton, Ipswich, 1951-1966
Played 344 League games for Ipswich Town as an outside left. Worked as a newsagent, then as a salesman with Cadburys in Suffolk. Returned to Scotland in 1971 to work for the Scotsman publications - retiring in 1993.

Played in Ipswich's record 7-0 League win against Portsmouth in 1964.

LEARY, Stuart
Charlton, QPR, 1951-1965
Former England under-23 centre forward Stuart committed suicide in 1988 by jumping out of a cable car near the top of Table Mountain in his native South Africa. He was also an accomplished cricketer who played for Kent.

LEE, Bob
Leicester, Doncaster, Sunderland, Bristol R, Carlisle, Southampton, Darlington, 1972-1983
Ended his career in non-league football with Boston United, scoring twice to earn them a Wembley appearance in the FA Trophy. Now runs a pub in Loughborough.

LEE, Colin
Bristol C, Hereford, Torquay, Tottenham, Chelsea, Brentford, 1974-1988
Was youth coach at Brentford, then took the same post at Watford, where he later became manager. Joined Reading as assistant to Mark McGee, following him firstly to Leicester in December 1994 and then to Wolves.
Scored four goals on his debut for Spurs against Bristol Rovers.

LEE, Francis
Bolton, Man C, Derby, 1960-1975
Man City signed Frannie from Bolton for £60,000 in 1967. He finished with Derby County, retiring in May 1976, going into business full time. He made a fortune with diverse business interests which included owning/training racehorses and building up a recycled paper business. Returned to Maine Road in 1993 and heralded as a saviour when he headed a consortium that took control of the Manchester Club.
League Championship, FA Cup and European Cup Winners Cup winner.

LEE, Jeff
Halifax, Peterboro, 1964-1977

Having enjoyed thirteen years as a player, Jeff is currently assistant manager of Hull City. Played over 400 League games.

LEE, Sammy
Liverpool, QPR, Southampton, Bolton, 1977-1990

Developed through Liverpool's junior ranks to become a first team regular and an England international before moving on to Queens Park Rangers and then abroad for a spell in Spain with Osasuna. Returned to play for Bolton but is now back at Anfield working as reserve team manager.
Won two European Cup winners medals.

LEE, Terry
Tottenham, Cardiff, Gillingham, Torquay, Newport C, 1970-1979

Found life at White Hart Lane difficult with Pat Jennings and Barry Daines around but kept a clean sheet in his only first team game. Stayed in the West Country when his career ended but sadly died in June 1996 after collapsing with a heart attack whilst batting in a local league cricket match in Exeter.

LEEK, Ken
Northampton, Leicester, Newcastle, Birmingham, Northampton, Bradford C, 1955-1967

Lives in Northampton and works for the Ford Motor Company in Daventry. In 1963 Ken scored twice in the last three minutes for Wales against Scotland to win the game 3-2.
Scored twice for Birmingham in the 1963 League Cup final.

LEES, Walter
Celtic, Watford, 1964-1976

A cental defender who played for the Hornets in an FA Cup semi final and now works in Watford as a glazer.

LEGGAT, Graham
Aberdeen, Fulham, Birmingham, Rotherham, 1953-1968

Scottish international winger (18 caps) and scored one of the fastest hat-tricks on record (4 mins 33 secs). Graham left the UK in 1971 to set up home in Canada, where he now hosts his own soccer show for a Toronto based television station.
Scored four goals in Fulham's 10-1 record League win in 1963.

LEIGH, Dennis
Doncaster, Rotherham, Lincoln, 1966-1978

Battling left back who stayed in Lincoln after a six years with the 'Imps'. Now advertising manager at the Lincolnshire Echo.

LEIVERS, W E
Chesterfield, Man C, Doncaster, 1951-1965

Played 250 matches for Manchester City before going into management. Was in charge at Cambridge United when they won admission to the League in 1971. Now general manager of neighbours Cambridge City.
Won a FA Cup winners medal with Man City in 1956.

LELLO, Cyril
Lincoln, Everton, Rochdale, 1944-1956

Played over 200 games for Everton after the War, before becoming player/manager of Runcorn, then coach to New Brighton. Worked for a contract electricians, but is now in a Liverpool nursing home having suffered a stroke.

LENNOX, Bobby MBE
Celtic 1962-1980

Holds the post war scoring record for the Celts with 273 goals. Once his long career was over Bobby became reserve team boss and now runs 'Bobby's Bar' in Saltcoats on the Ayrshire coast.
Played for Celtic in the 1967 European Cup final.

LEONARD, Carleton
Shrewsbury, Hereford, Cardiff, 1975-1985

First choice full back for Rotherham in the 70s, has returned to his home town of Oswestry where he is now a publican.

LESLIE, John
Wimbledon, Gillingham, Millwall, 1977-1986

Finished playing for non-league Dartford, in December 1994, and now works for a central heating company in Lewisham. He has lived in the same house for many years, in fact it was Dave Bassett who sold him the insurance policy when it was first purchased! Also spent his wedding night with 'Harry' in a Huddersfield hotel after getting married the day before a game, and was then driven up to Yorkshire in Ron Noades' Rolls Royce. *Scored for Wimbledon in their first ever League game in 1978.*

LESLIE, Lawrie

Airdrie, West Ham, Stoke, Millwall, Southend, 1958-1968
After being told by doctors as a youngster he would never walk again he went on to play five times for Scotland. Now organises youth centres for Hackney School and works as head of centre at a Homerton school.
Scottish Cup runner up in 1958.

LESLIE, Steve

Colchester 1970-1983
Played over 400 matches for his only club, Colchester. Now works for Brentwood Council.
Promoted to Division Three in 1976.

LEWINGTON, Ray

Chelsea, Wimbledon, Fulham, Sheff U, Fulham, 1975-1989
Best remembered for his days at Chelsea, before returning to London for spells with Wimbledon and then became manager at Craven Cottage. Now on the coaching staff at Crystal Palace.

LEWIS, Bill

West Ham, Blackpool, Norwich, 1945-1956
Played a lot of his football during the war, turning out 129 times for the Hammers. He settled in the Norwich area after playing over 250 games in their colours and retired after working as circulation manager for Eastern Counties Newspapers.

LEWIS, Brian

C Palace, Portsmouth, Coventry, Luton,

Oxford, Colchester, Portsmouth, 1960-1974
Lewis was a member of the giant-killing Colchester team that stunned the mighty Leeds. He now works as a salesman in a furniture showroom in Bournemouth but is still involved with football running an Under-16 side.

LEWIS, Russell

Swindon, Northampton, 1976-1985
Defender who spent almost a decade in the League after joining Swindon from Bridgend in 1976. Now a bricklayer in Northampton.

LEWORTHY, Dave

Portsmouth, Tottenham, Oxford, Shrewsbury, Reading, 1981-1993
Three years after being discarded by home town club, Portsmouth, Dave was snapped up from non-league soccer by Tottenham in 1984. Went on to play for three other clubs before returning to the lower leagues where he is with currently with Dover Athletic . Was their top scorer in 1993/4 earning him England semi-pro honours.

LEY, George

Exeter, Portsmouth, Brighton, Gillingham, 1963-1975
Left back who once topped a poll for the best looking footballer, beating off the challenge of other players such as George Best! Had a spell as Luton Town youth coach before emigrating to the United States.

LEYLAND, Harry

Everton, Blackburn, Tranmere, 1951-1965
Former Blackburn and Tranmere goalkeeper, Harry is now a shop owner and market trader, living in Moels, Merseyside.
FA Cup runners up medal in 1960.

LIDDELL, Billy

Liverpool 1946-1960
Scottish international who scored 216 goals for his only club, Liverpool, despite being a winger. Worked in an accountants office throughout his career and continued once he had hung up his boots. Went on to become bursar at Liverpool University and a JP in

the city. Billy is now aged 74 and sadly suffering from altzheimers disease.
League Championship in 1947.

LILLIS, Mark
Huddersfield, Manchester City, Derby Co, Aston Villa, Scunthorpe, 1978-1992
A regular goalscorer through out his career which last nearly 15 years. Became community officer at Huddersfield, which he comined with playing for Macclesfield before being offered the chance to take over the Terriers' youth team.
Thrice promoted – twice with Huddersfield and the other with Villa.

LINDSAY, John
Rangers, Everton, Bury, 1951-1956
Full back who joined Everton from Glasgow Rangers in 1951. Stayed in Merseyside where he works in Walton hospital.

LINDSAY, Jimmy
West Ham, Watford, Colchester, Hereford, Shrewsbury, 1966-1981
Became Watford's first ever £20,000 signing. Still lives in Shrewsbury where he runs a pub.
Scottish Youth international.

LINEKER, Gary
Leicester, Everton, Tottenham, 1978-1993
The second most successful England striker with 48 goals from his 60 games. Started his career with home town club Leicester City in 1978 where he established himself as a prolific marksman, moving to Everton in 1985 for £800,000. After only a season at Goodison Park, Terry Venables took him to Spanish giants, Barcelona in a £2.75m move. Spells with Tottenham Hotspur and Japanese club Grampus followed, before he quit in 1994 to join the BBC as a presenter.
European Cup Winners Cup winner with Barcelona.

LINES, Barry
Northampton 1960-1969
Northampton winger throughout the sixties, Barry is now working as a sports equipment salesman.
Promoted to Division One with Northampton in 1965.

LISHMAN, Doug
Walsall, Arsenal, Notts F, 1946-1956
Goalscoring inside forward who hit the back of the net 125 times in 226 games for Arsenal. Won England 'B' honours before ending at Notts Forest in 1956. Returned to manage his family furniture business in Stoke-on-Trent. Died December 1994 aged 71.
League Championship winners medal with Arsenal in 1963.

LISTER, Steve
Doncaster, Scunthorpe, 1978-1987
A midfield man who played almost 350 league games in a nine-year career. Now community officer at Barnsley.

LITTLE, Alan
Aston V, Southend, Barnsley, Doncaster, Torquay, Halifax, Hartlepool, 1974-1985
Played in midfield for seven clubs. Then coached at Hartlepool until moving on to become assistant manager at York City then manager in March 1993.

LITTLE, Brian
Aston Villa 1971-1979
Played all his career at Villa until he was forced to quit through injury aged 26. Gained coaching experience at Wolves, Middlesbrough and then in 1989 was appointed manager at Darlington, leading them to the GM Vauxhall Conference title and back into the Football league in 1990. He then took them to the Fourth Division Championship in 1991, before taking the helm at Leicester City. Resigned from Filbert Street in November 1994 and caused a storm by taking over at Aston Villa after strongly denying that he would.
League Cup winner twice in 1975 and 1977.

LIVERMORE, Doug
Liverpool, Norwich, Bournemouth, Cardiff, Chester, 1967-1978

Former Liverpool junior who went on to play for four clubs. Coached at Cardiff, Norwich and Swansea and was assistant manager to Mike England for Wales. Now finally back at Anfield where he is first team coach.

LLOYD, Larry
Bristol R, Liverpool, Coventry, Notts F, Wigan, 1968-1982

Won only four England caps but was a commanding defender who enjoyed success with Liverpool and Nottingham Forest. Coached at Wigan and managed Notts County before leaving soccer. Now runs a pub in Nottingham.
Football League Championship in 1973.

LLOYD, Barry
Chelsea, Fulham, Hereford, Brentford, 1966-1977
Started at Chelsea, but had most success a little further down the Kings Road at Fulham. Manager of Brighton from 1987 until 1994 and is now back at one of his former clubs, Worthing, as a consultant.
England Youth international.

LLOYD, Brian
Stockport, Southend, Wrexham, Chester, Port V, Stockport, 1967-1982

Whilst at Stockport County he studied building design gaining an HND, which has allowed him to pursue a career in the field since retiring in 1982.

LLOYD, Cliff
Wrexham, Fulham, 1937-1946
Made only a handful of League appearances, but will always be remembered for his contribution to the PFA where he was Secretary between 1953 and 1981. Now lives in retirement near Chester.

LOCHHEAD, Andy
Burnley, Leicester, Aston V, Oldham, 1960-1974
Scottish under-23 attacker who scored on average almost every other game for Burnley in the sixties. After returning from America he coached Oldham for a number of years before scouting for several clubs including Burnley. Now, after earlier running a pub, is a steward at the Ighton Mount bowling club.
Won a Third Division title in 1972.

LOCK, Kevin
West Ham, Fulham, Southend, 1971-1985
After six years at West Ham, Kevin moved west to play over 200 games for Fulham. Won under-23 caps with England and ended at Southend United. Is now assitant manager to David Webb at Brentford.
Played for Fulham in the 1975 FA Cup final.

LOMAX, Geoff
Man City, Wolves, Carlisle, Rochdale, 1982-1987
A competent defender whose career was cut short by injury. Now community officer at Bolton.

LORD, Frank
Rochdale, Crewe, Plymouth Stockport, Blackburn, Chesterfield, Plymouth, 1953-1968
Scored goals from the centre forward position for seven clubs, averaging almost a goal every other game. In September 1991 took over as director of coaching for Western Province in South Africa.

LOFTHOUSE, Nat

Bolton W 1946-1960

One of the all time greats, earning the nickname 'the Lion of Vienna' following a game against Austria in which his style and bravery were dominant. Won 33 caps and scored 255 goals in 452 games for his only league club, Bolton. A dedicated Wanderers man, Nat has served the club as player; reserve coach; chief coach; manager; general manager; chief scout; and now club president.
Holds the Bolton goal scoring record.

LORIMER, Peter

Leeds, York, Leeds, 1963-1985
A Scottish international who played a total of 676 times for Leeds, making his debut at the age of 15 which is still a club record. Reputed to have had the hardest shot in his day, Peter had spells in Canada and Israel before finally retiring in 1985. Now landlord of the 'Commercial Inn' pub in Holbeck, Leeds and also helps to run the Leeds ex-professionals team and, in the summer of 1996, was appointed commercial manager of the Hunslet Hawks Rugby League Club.
Two League Championship winners medals.

LOVELL, Steve

C Palace, Stockport, Millwall, Swansea, Gillingham, 1980-1992
Former Crystal Palace junior who went on to play for five league clubs. Left Hastings Town in February 1995 to become player/manager of Sittingbourne Town but resigned in August 1996 to take over at Gravesend.
Won six caps for Wales between 1982 and 1986.

LOVETT, Graham

WBA, Southampton, 1964-1971
Won a FA Cup winners medal with West Brom after surviving two horrific car crashes – one prior to and one after the final. Sadly, the injuries eventually forced him to give up League soccer in 1986 at the age of 26. Is now a newspaper executive in the West Midlands.

LOWNDES, Steve

Newport, Millwall, Barnsley, Hereford, 1977-1993
Played over 400 League games for his four clubs. Now runs his own physiotherapy clinic and plays for Newport AFC.
Capped 12 times by Wales.

LUCAS, Mal

Leyton O, Norwich, Torquay, 1958-1973
Wing half who was plucked from local football by the O's in 1958. Played four times for Wales. Now an account executive/collector for Brent Leisure Services Ltd.
Helped Orient to win promotion to Division 1 in 1962.

LUMBY, Jim

Grimsby, Scunthorpe, Carlisle, Tranmere, Mansfield, 1973-1981
Licensee of the 'Hainton' pub in Grimsby, having previously worked as a pipefitter at the Conoco oil refinery.

LYALL, John

West Ham 1959-1962
Only played 31 League games but later made his name in management. Appointed assistant manager in 1971, team manager in 1974 and then manager in 1977. Has been out of the game since leaving Ipswich in December 1994.
Managed West Ham to 1980 FA Cup final success.

LYNEX, Steve
WBA, Birmingham, Leicester, Birmingham, WBA, Cardiff, 1976-1989
Winger who served his apprenticeship at his home town club but played most of his career with Leicester. Now runs the 'Red Lion' pub in West Bromwich.

LYNN, Stan
Accrington S, Aston V, Birmingham, 1946-1965
Found fame with Birmingham and Aston Villa. Retired from Soccer in 1968 and now lives in Shirley, West Midlands and works for the toolroom stores at Lucas.
Won the FA Cup once and the League Cup twice with Birmingham and Villa.

LYONS. Mick
Everton, Sheff Wed, Grimsby, 1970-1986
Gained coaching and managerial experience at Grimsby, Everton and then Huddersfield before accepting the post of coach to the Brunei national team.
Runner-up in three FA Cup finals.

McALLE, John
Wolves, Sheff U, Derby, 1967-1983
Runs his own landscape gardening business on the outskirts of Dudley, West Midlands. Made over 500 appearances for Wolves in his fourteen years at Molineux.
Second Division Championship winner with Wolves in 1977.

McANDREW, Tony
Middlesboro, Chelsea, Middlesboro, Darlington, Hartlepool, 1973-1988
Joint youth team coach at Leicester City until early 1995 and is now youth team coach at Aston Villa.

McANEARNEY, Tom
Sheff Wed, Peterboro, Aldershot, 1952-1968
Made his name with Sheff Wed in the fifties who ended his playing career at Aldershot and went on to become the Shots' boss. Has settled and retired in the area.
Won promotion to Division One with Wednesday in 1955 and 1959.

McCAFFERY, Jim
Notts F, Mansfield, Huddersfield, Portsmouth, Northampton, 1969-1979
Winger who played for five league clubs, ending his playing career at Northampton. Is now a newsagent.
Former England youth international.

McCALL, Steve
Ipswich, Sheff Wed, Carlisle, Plymouth, 1979-1995
Took over as manager of Plymouth Argyle in January 1995 but relinquished the post to concentrate on playing. Now on the coaching staff at Torquay United.
Won a UEFA Cup medal with Ipswich Town.

McCALLIOG, Jim
Chelsea, Sheff Wed, Wolves, Man U, Southampton, Lincoln, 1964-1978
Capped five times by Scotland. Played in Norway in the 1977/8 season before joining Lincoln City as player/coach in September 1978. Was manager at Halifax Town and Runcorn but is now a journalist and publican, running the 'County Hotel' in Harrogate.
Played in the 1966 and 1976 Cup Finals for Sheff Wed and Southampton.

McCANN, Albert
Luton, Coventry, Portsmouth, 1959-1973
Long serving Pompey midfielder who started his career closer to the Midlands. Now a rest home proprietor in Emsworth, Hampshire, having previously ran a newsagents in Southsea for many years.

McCARTHY, Bob
Southampton 1967-1974
Now Southampton-based area manager for Beer Seller Ltd, an independent wholesaler, having previously worked for major brewers.

McCARTNEY, Mike
WBA, Carlisle, Southampton, Plymouth, Carlisle, 1971-1986
After twice serving Carlisle, now player/manager and groundsman at Gretna in the Northern Premier Division One.

McCARTHY, Mick

Barnsley, Man C, Celtic, Millwall, 1977-1994
Appointed Millwall Manager in April 1992
following a spell as caretaker boss after
Bruce Rioch left for Bolton. He started his
career with hometown club, Barnsley, playing 272 times before a £200,000 move took
him to Manchester City. From Maine Road
he went North of the border to Celtic and
then to Lyon in France. Mick skippered the
Republic of Ireland in the 1990 World Cup
and played a total of 57 games for his country for whom he is now manager.
League Championship with Celtic in 1987.

McCLAREN, Steve

Hull, Derby, Lincoln, Bristol C, Oxford, 1979-
1981
Reserve team coach at Oxford United until
June 1995 when he returned to the Baseball
Ground to become Derby County's first team
coach.

McCLELLAND, John

Arsenal, Fulham, Lincoln, 1960-1968
Northern Ireland international goalkeeper
who died from a brain haemorrhage after a
brief illness in 1976, aged 36. His son John
now works in the accounts department at
Arsenal.
Won the Irish League Cup with Glentoran.

McCLOY, Peter

Motherwell, Rangers, 1970-1986
A Scottish international goalkeeper who
joined Rangers in exchange for two other
players. He is a Scotland amatuer golfer who
now runs a golfing complex in Ayrshire.
*European Cup winners cup winner with
Rangers in 1972.*

McCOLL, James, Miller (Ian)

Rangers 1945-1961
Appointed Scotland manager whilst still
playing and held the job for five years having
then moved onto Sunderland for another
three. Retired but still runs a guest house in
Milengarvie nr Glasgow.
*Won six league Championships, a Cup win-
ner five times and the League Cup twice.*

McCREADIE, Eddie

East Stirling, Chelsea, 1959-1975
Skipped Chelsea in the seventies and won
23 Scottish caps before he retired from playing in 1975, when he was appointed manager at Chelsea, a post he held until July 1977.
Moved to the United States in 1978 to manage Memphis Rogues and is still living
there, now working as a painter and decorator.
FA Cup winner in 1970 with Chelsea.

McCREERY, David

Man U, QPR, Newcastle, Hartlepool, 1974-
1995
Played 67 times for Northern Ireland but
spent much of his time at Old Trafford on the
bench so had move to Newcastle to play
regular football. Manager of Hartlepool from
September 1994 until April 1995.
Played in United's 1977 FA Cup success.

McCROHAN, Roy

Reading, Norwich, Colchester, Bristol R,
1949-1964
Played 426 games for Norwich in the fifties.
Living now in Tampa, Florida and coaching
youngsters.
League Cup winner with Norwich in 1962.

McCULLOCH, Andy

QPR, Cardiff, Oxford, Brentford, Sheff Wed,
C. Palace, Aldershot, 1970-1984
Career lasted 14 years and took in seven
clubs. Now owns a cleaning business based
in Hampton Court, where his wife also runs
an antiques shop.

McCULLOCH, Iain

Notts Co 1978-1983
Now lifeline co-ordinator at Notts County
and joint manager of Arnold Town in the
North East Counties League.
Scottish under-21 international.

McCULLOCH, William

Arsenal, Millwall, 1958-1966
After hanging up his boots he moved to
Ireland to manage Cork Celtic and then
Derry City. Upon retirement from soccer he

worked as an electrical engineer in his father-in-law's factory in Woodford, Essex. *Played 10 times for Northern Ireland.*

McDERMOTT, Brian
Arsenal, Fulham, Oxford, Huddersfield, Cardiff, Exeter, 1978-1990
Played for Stamco in the Sussex League and is now manager of Slough Town.

McDERMOTT, Terry
Bury, Newcastle, Liverpool, Newcastle, 1969-1983
Kevin Keegan's sidekick at Newcastle was capped by England 25 times during his time at Liverpool, where he also won every honour in the game except an FA Cup winners medal. Voted Player of the Year in 1980. *European Cup winner with Liverpool.*

McDONALD, Ian
Barrow, Workington, Liverpool, Colchester, Mansfield, York, Aldershot, 1970-1988
Played almost 500 league games during an eighteen year career and is now reserve team coach at Millwall.

McDONALD, Kevin
Leicester, Liverpool, Leicester, Rangers Coventry, Cardiff, Walsall, 1980-1993
A well polished midfield player who was appointed joint youth team coach at Leicester until early 1995 when he followed Brian Little to Aston Villa. *FA Cup winner with Liverpool 1986.*

MacDONALD, Malcolm
Fulham, Luton, Newcastle, Arsenal, 1968-1978
Malcolm was originally a full back playing for Tonbridge, until Fulham snapped him up and converted him to a centre forward. They allowed him to join Luton in 1969, where he scored 49 goals in 88 games in two sensational seasons. However, finances forced Luton to sell him to Newcastle for a club record fee of £185,000. In 14 England appearances he only scored on one occasion, but netted five times against Cyprus in that match. Arsenal signed this still dynam-

ic sharpshooter in August 1976, but within three years, injuries forced him to quit. He later returned to his first club, Fulham, as manager and then on to Huddersfield in the same capacity. Moved to Italy in 1991, lived in Milan and worked for Audiotel, setting up the equivalent of our 0891 service, until the Italian Government made such lines illegal.

McDONOUGH, Jim
Rotherham, Bolton, Everton, Bolton, Notts Co, Birmingham, Gillingham, Sunderland, Scarborough, Huddersfield, Charlton, 1970-1988
Managed Derry City until May 1989 and became reserve team coach at Telford in 1991. Now in the insurance business and playing for Arnold Town and Ilkeston Town Vets in the Umbro Vets Competition. *Second Division Champion with Bolton in 1978.*

McDONOUGH, Roy
Birmingham, Walsall, Chelsea, Colchester, Southend, Exeter, Cambridge, Southend, 1976-1989
Manager of Colchester until May 1994. He is son-in-law of Gordon Parker, the Colchester Chairman, who had to sack him! Played for Dagenham & Redbridge and Braintree before taking over as Chelmsford City boss a week before the end of the 1995/6 season.

MacDOUGALL, Ted
Liverpool, York, Bournemouth, Man U, West Ham, Norwich, Southampton, Bournemouth, Blackpool, 1966-1980

Became player/coach at Blackpool between February and October 1980, then retired. Came out of retirement in August 1981 to play a few games for Salisbury, moving to Poole Town in the following December and Gosport Borough in 1982. Owned a sports shop in Bournemouth and was licensee of a pub near Romsey, Hampshire. Emigrated to Canada with his French/Canadian wife, where he has become a wealthy property developer. Based in Vancouver, he still follows the progress of Bournemouth and was behind take-over speculation in 1994.
Found fame with Bournemouth when he scored nine goals against Margate in the 1971 FA Cup.

McDOWELL, John
West Ham, Norwich, 1970-1980
Right back John won 13 England under-23 caps and played almost 250 league games for the Hammers before ending his career with Norwich. Retired in 1980 and went on to become a publican in Essex.
FA Cup winner with West Ham in 1975.

McEWAN, Billy
Blackpool, Brighton., Chesterfield, Mansfield, Peterborough, Rotherham, 1973-1983
Manager at Rotherham between April 1988 and January 1991, before becoming coach at Derby County.

MacEWAN, Jimmy
Arbroath, Raith, Aston V, Walsall, 1947-1966
Two knee replacement operations in 1991 forced Jimmy to retire from the job that he had held in the civil service for nine years. Coached in Birmingham and South Africa before returning to Ansells Brewery then subsisting on Social Security.
League Cup winner with Villa in 1961.

McEVOY, Don
Huddersfield, Sheff Wed, Lincoln, Barrow, 1949-1961
After his playing days, Don was manager at Halifax, Barrow, Grimsby, and Southport. Now runs the Crown Hotel in Brighouse.

McFARLAND, Roy
Tranmere, Derby, Bradford C, Derby, 1966-1983
A classic centre back, who had it not been for injuries would have played for England on many more occasions than his total of 28. He started out at Tranmere before Brian Clough recognised his potential and took him to Derby County. He became manager at Derby in late 1993, having had a brief spell as caretaker manager in 1984. Failure to achieve promotion despite many inherited big money signings resulted in his dismissal at the end of the 1994/5 season. However, he was installed as Bolton boss only weeks later, reuniting him with Colin Todd, a former playing colleague.
Won two League Championships with Derby.

McFARLANE, Ian
Aberdeen, Chelsea, Leicester, 1956-1958
Only played a handful of games but made his name along side Tony Book in Bath City's Southern League winning side of 1960. Returned to Leicester to become assistant manager to both Frank McLintock and Jock Wallace, and also held the number two position at Middlesbrough, Man City and Sunderland before holding full charge at Carlisle. Later to become chief scout at Leeds United.

McFAUL, Willie
Newcastle 1966-1974
After completing almost 300 appearances for Newcastle he went on to become their manager from August 1985 until December 1988. Is now living in Northern Ireland and is part of Bryan Hamilton's national set up.
Fairs Cup winner in 1969.

McGARRY, Bill
Port Vale, Huddersfield, Bournemouth, 1946-1962
A solid right half who was capped four times by England. He managed a number of clubs including Bournemouth, Watford, Ipswich, Newcastle and Wolves as well as the Saudi Arabia national side. Is now coaching Bopnutbuswanana in South Africa.

Managed Ipswich to a second Division Championship in 1968.

McGARVEY, Scott
Man U, Wolves, Portsmouth, Carlisle, Grimsby, Bristol C, Oldham, Wigan, 1980-1989
Has set up his own company, Moneystone., which sells sand to sports clubs and agricultural concerns from a base at Levenseat Quarry near Glasgow.
Scottish under-23 international striker.

McGHEE, Mark
Morton, Newcastle, Aberdeen,Celtic, Newcastle, Reading, 1975-1993
Capped four times by Scotland during a career which saw him win many honours. Took over as player/boss at Elm Park, walked out to become Leicester manager and in December 1995 left to take over at his present club, Wolves.

McGILL, James
Arsenal, Huddersfield, Hull, Halifax, 1965-1976
Managed several clubs in Denmark after retiring as a player and took a job at ICI in Huddersfield.

McGIVEN, Mick
Sunderland, West Ham, 1969-1977
Central defender who was appointed football development manager at Ipswich, having previously been team manager. Now reserve team boss at Chelsea.

McGOVERN, John
Hartlepool, Derby, Leeds, Notts F, Bolton, 1965-1983
The backbone of many a Brian Clough side, he started with Hartlepool, before following his boss to Derby County, Leeds and then Nottingham Forest. Became assistant manager to Peter Shilton at Plymouth until September 1994, when he took on the same post at Rotherham United - offered by another former Forest colleague, Archie Gemmill, but was sacked in September 1996.
Captained Notts Forest to League

Championship and European Cup success.

McGRAIN, Danny
Celtic 1967-1986
Capped 62 times by his country as well as winning many honours in a glorious career. Overcame a fractured skull, diabetes, and arthritis along the way. Now works in corporate entertainment at the Glenneagles golf course.
Won the Scottish double in 1977.

McGRATH, Chris
Tottenham, Millwall, Man U, 1973-1980
A former Northern Ireland international who now lives in Harrow and works at an armaments factory in Enfield.
Played for Spurs in the 1974 UEFA Cup final.

McGRATH, John
Bury, Newcastle, Southampton, Brighton, 1956-1972
A no-nonsense centre half who went on to manage Port Vale, Chester City, Preston and Halifax Town, but is now a popular after dinner speaker.

McGREGOR, John
Queens Park, Liverpool, Leeds, Rangers, 1979-1988
Failed to make the grade south of the border and played his only League games on loan to Leeds. Returned to Scotland but his career was cut short by a knee injury. Now reserve team coach at Ibrox.

McGUINNESS, Wilf
Man U 1955-1959
A broken leg put a stop to what could have been a wonderful career. Has coached and scouted for Everton, Man Utd, York, Hull, Bury and the England youth team. Now lives in Timperley, Cheshire and is a regular on the after-dinner speaking circuit.
Capped twice by England in 1959.

McGUIRE, Mick
Coventry, Norwich, Barnsley, Oldham, 1971-1986
Blackpool born midfielder who served four

clubs in a 350-plus game career. Now a director of the PFA working from their Manchester headquarters.
Helped Norwich reach Division One.

McGUGAN, John
St Mirren, Leeds, Tranmere, 1956-1961
A Scottish under-23 international who ended his career in non-league football with Cambridge City, where he later ran a pub.
Won Scottish Cup winners medal with St Mirren.

McHALE, Kevin
Huddersfield, Crewe, Chester, 1956-1971
Spent eleven years on the wing for Huddersfield in the fifties and sixties. Kevin now works at David Browns in Huddersfield.

McHALE, Ray
Chesterfield, Halifax, Swindon, Brighton., Barnsley, Sheff U, Bury, Swansea, Rochdale, Scarboro, 1971-1987
Returned to manage Scarborough Town in December 1994, 21 months after being sacked from the same position. Managed Guisley Town of the Northern Premier League in the interim.

McILMOYLE, Hugh
Leicester, Rotherham, Carlisle, Wolves, Bristol C, Carlisle, Middlesboro, Preston, Carlisle, 1959-1974
A regular goalscorer who had three spells with Carlisle. Now lives in Leicester, where he works for Walkers Crisps in their warehouse.
Helped Carlisle from the Fourth to the Second Division.

McILROY, Jimmy
Burnley, Stoke, Oldham, 1950-1967
Won 55 Northern Ireland caps and also played for Great Britain against 'the rest of the Europe' in 1955. Jimmy wrote his own column in the local paper whilst a player and became a journalist with the Lancashire Evening Telegraph. After nine years with the Burnley Express, he took early retirement which now allows him to play golf and

attend Art School three times a week.
Won a Championship medal with Burnley.

McILROY, Sammy
Man U, Stoke, Man C, Bury, Preston, 1971-1989
Joined Manchester United as an apprentice in 1969 and was a regular in the Northern Ireland team, winning a total of 88 caps. Was manager of Macclesfield Town when they won the Conference and is now the boss of Northwich Victoria.
Played in three FA Cup finals with Man Utd.

McINALLY, John
Kilmarnock, Motherwell, Hamilton, 1959-1975
Spotted after playing in the Scottish Amatuer Cup final for Crosshill Thistle and won a Championship medal in 1968. Now works in a paint warehouse and is the father of former Celtic star and Bayern Munich player Alan.

McJANET, Les
Mansfield, Scarborough, Darlington, 1978-1992
Returned to league football with Scarborough after a six-year spell in non-league. Now works for Centre Parcs in Nottingham.
Played for Scarborough in their first ever League game.

McKECHNIE, Ian
Arsenal, Southend, Hull, 1961-1973
Originally signed as an outside left, played over 300 league games and became a New Zealand international as a goalkeeper. Hung up his boots in 1974 and became a prison officer, but has since worked for many years at British Aerospace in Brough. Had a two week spell as manager of Nuneaton Borough and later took over at Sligo Rovers.

McKENZIE, Duncan
Notts F, Mansfield, Leeds, Everton, Chelsea, Blackburn, 1968-1980
One of the classiest players to have graced the League during the seventies. Now a

football community officer based at Everton. Lives in Newton-le-Willow, Merseyside, owns a delicatessen and has become an accomplished after dinner speaker.
Leading scorer for Leeds in 1976.

MacKENZIE, Steve
C Palace, Man C, WBA, Charlton, Sheff W, Shrewsbury, 1979-1994
Steve joined City in 1979 for £250,000, before making even one first team appearance for Crystal Palace. Currently turning out for Stafford Rangers.
Played and scored for City in the 1981 FA Cup final.

McKINLAY, Bobby
Notts F 1951-1969
Bobby is now a retired prison officer living in a village outside Nottingham.
Played 614 league games which is still a Forest record.

McLAREN, Ross
Shrewsbury, Derby, Swindon, 1980-1992
Scottish born utility player who made over 400 League appearances before taking over as reserve team coach at Swindon Town.
Division Two Championship with Swindon in 1987.

McLAREN, Thomas
Port V 1967-1976
Played over 300 League games for Port Vale. Died in 1978 aged only 29.

McLEAN, Derek
Middlesboro, Hartlepool, 1955-1963
A goal-scoring inside forward. Works for Middlesbrough Council planning department.
Played for Middlesbrough in their record League win against Brighton in 1958.

McLEAN, George
St Mirren, Rangers, Dundee, Ayr, Hamilton, 1959-1975
Once commanded a record transfer fee when he moved to Rangers for £26,000. Capped once for his country, he still lives in Glasgow

working for a double glazing company.
Scottish League Champion with Rangers in 1964.

McLEOD, John
Hibs, Arsenal, Aston V, 1957-1967
Scottish international winger who also played in Belgium for Mechelen. Moved back to Scotland after working for an insurance company in Birmingham for many years.
Capped four times by Scotland.

McLINTOCK, Frank MBE
Leicester, Arsenal, QPR, 1959-1976

Signed by Arsenal from Leicester in 1964 for £80,000, where he became captain and regular centre-half, winning the coveted double in 1970-1. He represented Scotland nine times, was 'Footballer of the year' in 1971 and awarded the MBE in 1972. Spells in management/coaching followed at Leicester, QPR and Brentford. Became a players agent and set upthe 'Cash Converter' chain of shops – one in partnership with former boxer Dave 'Boy' Green.
Double winner with Arsenal in 1971.

McMAHON, Pat
Celtic, Aston Villa, 1967-1974
Left Villa in 1976 to join NASL club Portland

Timbers, later playing for the now defunct Caribous of Colorado and also Atlanta. McMahon is still in America, working as a partner in a company supplying aluminium to industry.
Won a Division Three title with Villa in 1972.

McMAHON, Steve
Everton, Aston Villa, Liverpool, Man C, Swindon, 1979-1996
A tough tackling midfield star who lead Swindon to the Division Two Championship in his first full season in charge having been appointed manager in November 1994. Was capped 17 times by England during his time with Liverpool.
Won three League Championships and two FA Cups with Liverpool.

McMANUS, Eric
Coventry, Notts C, Stoke, Lincoln, Bradford, Middlesboro, Peterborough, Tranmere, 1969-1986
Former supervisor for the football in the community scheme at Bradford City. Now youth team coach at Walsall.

McMILLAN, Sammy
Man U, Wrexham, Southend, Chester, Stockport, 1961-1971
Played most of his football with Wrexham. Now a process worker, living and working near Wrexham.
Capped twice by Northern Ireland.

McMORDIE, Eric
Middlesboro, Sheff Wed, York, Hartlepool, 1947-1957
Capped by Northern Ireland at under-21 and under-23 levels. Now runs a chain of greengrocers on Teeside.

McNAB, Bob
Huddersfield, Arsenal, Wolves, 1963-1975
Emigrated to manage Vancouver Whitecaps and then Tacoma stars. He opened the Vancouver Racquets Club, which once established, he sold in 1988. Now lives in California, running his own executive recruitment agency. His daughter, having already appeared in films, is tipped to be a star actress.
Double winner with Arsenal in 1971.

McNAB, Neil
Tottenham, Bolton, Brighton, Leeds, Man C, Tranmere, Huddersfield, Darlington, 1974-1993
A Scotland schoolboy, youth and under-21 international who was voted City's player of the year in 1989 before his league days ended at Darlington and moving into non-league soccer with Witton Albion. Now back at Maine Road as youth team manager.
Helped Spurs (1978) and Man City (1989) into the First Division.

McNAUGHT, Ken
Everton, Aston Villa, WBA, Man C, Sheff U, 1974-1985
Forced to retire through injury in 1986 at the age of 31 having played in 438 matches for his five professional clubs. In 1987 he became coach to Dunfermline but can now he found working in the Pro Shop at the famous Gelneagles golf course.
Won Championship and European Cup winners medals with Villa.

McNEICE, Vince
Watford 1957-1964
A former Brentford junior who played over 250 games for the Hornets. A qualified engineer who has settled in Copenhagen, Denmark.

McNEILL, Alan
Middlesboro, Huddersfield, Oldham, Stockport, 1967-1976
Joined Kirklees Metropolitan Council as a sports centre supervisor in 1977 and has now progressed to become operations manager - responsible for six sports centres in the area.

McNEILL Billy
Celtic 1957-1975
A rugged centre half who played 831 games for his beloved Celtic. Scottish player of the year in 1965 who was awarded an MBE nine

years later. Integral part of the Celtic side which achieved a record nine consecutive League Championships. Had spells in management with Celtic twice, Aberdeen, Man City and Aston Villa. Still lives in Glasgow where he combines running McNeills Bar. with media work.
Captained the 'Lisbon Lions' to European cup success in 1967.

McNEILL, Dixie
Leicester, Exeter, Northampton, Lincoln, Hereford, Wrexham, Hereford, 1964-1982
A much travelled bustling centre-forward. Best known for his scoring exploits with Hereford United, where he also later became manager. Now at the helm of Flint Town United in the Konica Welsh League.

McNEILL, Ian
Aberdeen, Leicester, Brighton, Southend, 1950-1963
Twice the manager of Wigan, including when they won promotion into the Football League. Has also been assistant manager at Chelsea and Millwall and is now chief scout at Bolton Wanderers.
Won a Second Division Championship with Leicester.

McNICHOL, Jim
Luton, Brentford, Exeter, Torquay, Exeter, Torquay, 1976-1991
Jim was once bitten by a police dog which caused a Torquay game to be held up and during the time added on they scored a goal which secured their football league status. Now landlord of the London Inn at Ashburton in Devon.

McNIVEN, David
Leeds, Bradford, Halifax Town, 1975-1985
A former Scottish under-21 international who played over 200 league games for Bradford. Had two spells in America before returning to play for Halifax. Now lives in Morcombe where he is a milkman.

McPARLAND, Peter
Aston Villa, Wolves, Plymouth, 1952-1963

One of Aston Villa's greatest post-war goalscorers, who earned the first of his 34 Northern Ireland caps before he was 20, scoring twice on his debut against Wales in 1954. Managed Glentoran 1970-1 then moved to Bournemouth in 1972 and during the past 15 years has coached in Cyprus, Kuwait and Hong Kong from his home base in Bournemouth.
Scored two goals in the 1957 FA Cup final.

McPHEE, John
Blackpool, Barnsley, Southport, 1962-1972
Now owns the Hotel Sheraton in Blackpool.

McQUEEN, Gordon
St Mirren, Leeds, Man U, 1970-1984
After a season with Seiko in Hong Kong, was bedridden and on the danger list with a combination of typhoid and septicaemia. Now fully recovered and managed Airdrie as well as working for STV, before taking up the post of reserve team coach at Middlesbrough.
League Championship winner in 1974.

McSHANE, Harry
Blackburn, Huddersfield, Bolton, Man U, Oldham, 1937-1954
Footballing father of actor Ian, star of the BBC series 'Lovejoy'. Harry still does some scouting for Manchester United and can list Andy Ritchie and Nicky Butt among his notable discoveries. Lives in Urmston and had previously spent sixteen years working for Massey Fergusons until his retirement.
Won a League Championship with United in 1952.

MCVAY, Dave
Notts Co, Torquay, Peterboro, Lincoln, 1973-1981
Former Notts Co defender Dave has now returned to the City after spells with Torquay and Peterborough to become a journalist with the Nottingham Evening Post.

McVITIE, George
Carlisle, WBA, Oldham, Carlisle, 1965-1980
Became a milkman when he hung up his

boots in 1980, but now runs a sub post office outside Carlisle.

MABBUTT, Kevin
Bristol C, C Palace, 1977-1984

Although injured, Kevin continued to play after leaving Crystal Palace, firstly for Vancouver in Canada, then Beveren in Belgium and finally in Cyprus. Is now living in California where he runs his family restaurant called 'Delicias'.
England Youth and Schoolboy international.

MABBUTT, Ray
Bristol R, Newport Co, 1957-1970
Father of Kevin and Gary at Spurs. Played almost 500 games for Bristol Rovers and once wrote a book entitled 'You can be a Soccer Star'. Now runs his own Financial Advice Business in the Bristol area.
Played alongside Albert Quixall and Tom Finney in the army.

MACARI, Lou
Celtic, Man U, Swindon, 1966-1985 .
Scottish international striker who joined Manchester United in 1973 for £200,000 from Celtic. Went on to play over 300 League games for the Reds before accepting the post of player/manager at Swindon Town in 1984. Spells at West Ham, Stoke City and Celtic followed before returning to the Potteries in October 1993 to re-join Stoke, whom he has managed to date.
Won three League Champions with Celtic and the FA Cup twice.

MACEY, John
Bristol C, Grimsby, Newport, 1965-1975
Started his career with his home town club before moving on to Grimsby and then Newport. Owner of John Macey Sports shops in Newport and Chepstow.

MACHIN, Mel
Port Vale, Gillingham, Bournemouth, Norwich, 1962-1977
Ended his playing career at Norwich in and became reserve team boss, assistant manager and coach before moving on. Managed Manchester City and then Barnsley before he was appointed manager of Bournemouth in September 1994.
Played in the 1975 League Cup final.

MACKAY, Dave
Tottenham, Derby, Swindon, 1958-1971
Dave started with Hearts, where he won the first of his 22 Scottish caps. Transferred to Tottenham Hotspur for a give-away fee and went on to become one of the finest hard tackling wing halves in Britain. He joined Derby County when Brian Clough signed him to lead them back into the First Division, which he did in 1974/5. His leadership qualities also led to management posts at Swindon, Nottingham Forest, Walsall, Arabic Sporting Club Kuwait, Doncaster, Birmingham, and currently in Qatar.
Spurs double winner.

MACKLEWORTH, Colin
West Ham, Leicester, 1964-1970
Quit the game after failing to make an impact after acting as understudy to Peter Shilton. Joined the police force, is stationed at Bow in East London and his duties include matchdays at Upton Park.

MADDEN, Craig
Bury, WBA, Blackpool, Wrexham, York, 1977-1989
A forward who scored over 150 goals from his 350-plus appearances. Now works for the football in the community scheme at Blackpool and plays for Blackpool Rovers in the Carling North West Counties League.

MADDREN, Willie
Middlesboro 1968-1977
Played almost 300 league games for his only club and went on to run a sports shop on Teeside, but now works for an insurance firm in the area.
Division Two Championship in 1973.

MADELEY, Paul
Leeds 1963-1980

Capped by England, Paul had an illustrious career, appearing over 500 times in a Leeds shirt and won almost every honour, both domestic and in Europe. He and his brothers sold their chain of 26 DIY stores for £27 million in 1987. In 1992 he successfully underwent an operation to remove a brain tumour. Now acts as a property consultant, still based in Yorkshire.
Twice a Fairs Cup winner.

MAHONEY, John
Crewe, Stoke, Middlesboro, Swansea, 1965-1982
Played well over 400 League games as a bustling midfielder. Now manager of Bangor City.
Played 51 games for Wales.

MALCOLM, Andy
West Ham, Chelsea, QPR, 1950-1964 ,
A locally born player who was one of the best wing halfs of his day. Ran three pubs in Essex but now resides in Port Elizabeth in South Africa.
The first West Ham younster to be capped at youth level by England.

MANCINI, Terry
Watford, Leyton O, QPR, Arsenal, Aldershot, 1961-1976
Since finishing in 1976, Terry has had a stint at Luton Town as assistant manager, owned a sports shop in Harrow and ran a pub in Hammersmith. He is currently living in New Malden where he is involved with the running of a car hire business in the area.
Won a Third Division Championship medal with Orient in 1970.

MANN, Arthur
Hearts,ManC, Blackpool, Notts Co, Shrewsbury, Mansfield, 1968-1981
Played 243 games for Notts County between 1972 and 1978. Was youth and reserve team coach at Grimsby Town before moving to West Bromwich Albion with Alan Buckley as his assistant manager.

MANNING, John
Tranmere, Shrewsbury, Norwich, Bolton, Walsall, Tranmere, Crewe, Barnsley, Crewe, 1962-1976
Lives in West Derby, Liverpool and works as a sales manager for a chemical company. When he retired from playing in 1976, became national coach in Saudi Arabia for three and a half years. Upon his return to Englandhe coached Brighton under Jimmy Melia reaching the FA Cup final in 1983.

MANNION, Gerry
Wolves, Norwich, Chester, 1957-1969
An England under-23 international who has held a number of jobs outside the game: a Civil Servant in the Department of Employment, manager of a TV rental shop and a worker in a paint warehouse.

MANNION, Wilf
Middlesboro, Hull, 1936-1954
Mannion was an inside forward who spent

most of his career at Middlesbrough, where his sparkling play earned him 26 England caps. Although retired and living in Redcar, he can still be seen at Ayresome Park where he acts as an ambassador for the club.
Is still Middlesbrough's most capped player.

MAPSON, Johnny

Reading, Sunderland, 1935-1952
Retired and living in Swindon, having been a self employed manufacturers agent, then 20 years as a general manager.

MARCH, Zillwood

Portsmouth, Brighton
'Zac' was the oldest surviving ex-pro until his death in September 1994, a month short of his 102nd birthday! Played for Portsmouth and Brighton, he once turned down the opportunity to join Manchester United, preferring to stay on the south coast.

MARGERRISON, John

Tottenham, Fulham, Leyton O, 1972-1981
John lives in Boreham Wood, Herts and is working as a telephone engineer. He also managed Dunstable until 1994.

MARINELLO, Peter

Hibs Arsenal, Portsmouth,Motherwell,

Fulham, Hibs, 1966-1982
Moved to Arsenal from Hibernian in 1969 amid a blaze of publicity before moving on to Portsmouth for £100,000. Later played for Motherwell, Fulham and in America. In 1983 he swapped running at defenders to running a pub, 'Marinello's', in Edinburgh. However, Peter is now living in Bournemouth, unemployed, and was officially declared bankrupt by the local County Court in March 1995.
Scottish League Cup winner with Hibs in 1969.

MARINER, Paul

Plymouth, Ipswich, Arsenal, Portsmouth, 1973-1987
In May 1993 he signed a two year deal to teach youngsters in Japan, as part of a world-wide coaching organisation masterminded by Charlie Cooke. Can also be heard on BBC Radio Suffolk sports programmes on a Saturday afternoon. In November 1996 he was appointed to the University of Arizona as football coach.
UEFA Cup winners medal with Ipswich in 1981.

MARSH, John

Stoke 1967-1978
John was Stoke's first choice right back for almost a decade. He still lives near Stoke and works as a sales representative.
Played in Stoke's 1972 League Cup success.

MARSH, Rodney

Fulham, QPR, Man C, Fulham, 1962-1976
One of the most entertaining players ever but like many of his era, only managed to win nine England caps. Became general manager of Tampa Bay Rowdies in Florida for eleven years and later took a year's sabbatical in 1994, which enabled him to tour the country with a soccer roadshow in conjunction with George Best.
Played in QPR's 1967 League Cup and Division Three double-winning side.

MARSHALL, Frank

Rotherham, Scunthorpe, Doncaster, 1951-1961

A wing half in the fifties who became coach for La Holm FC in the Swedish Football League.

MARTIN, Eric
St Johnstone, Cowdenbeath, Dunfirmline, Southampton, 1966-1974
Played 288 games for Saints. Went over to the United States to coach in Washington and worked for a television network. He still lives there and works for an American mailing company.
Former Scottish under-23 international.

MARTIN, Mick
Man U, WBA, Newcastle, Cardiff, Peterborough, Rotherham, Preston, 1972-1985
Retired after well over 500 games as a professional footballer. He made 52 appearances for the Republic of Ireland, became coach at Newcastle United in 1987 and then coach to Celtic.

MARUSTIK, Chris
Swansea, Cardiff, 1978-1986
A Swansea midfield man who played for his home town club for seven years. Joined Barry Town in 1987 but now runs a wine bar with his brother.
Capped six times by Wales.

MARWOOD, Brian
Hull, Sheff Wed, Arsenal, Sheff U, Middlesboro, Barnet, 1979- 1994
Winger who caught the eye playing for Hull City. Played for both Sheffield clubs before arriving in the capital where he won one England cap. Is now an executive with the PFA.
League Championship winner with Arsenal.

MASON, Bobby
Wolves, Leyton O, 1955-1963
Was forced to quit the game when aged only 27. Now lives in Bournemouth where he is employed by a local holiday village, having formerly worked as an HGV driver.
Won two League Championships with Wolves.

MASON, Stuart
Wrexham, Liverpool, Chester, Rochdale, Crewe, 1965-1977
A full back who played over 300 league games and now owns a sports shop in Wrexham.

MASSEY, Steve
Stockport, Bournemth, Peterboro, Northpton, Hull, Camb U, Wrexham, 1974-1987
Played for seven league clubs and now runs two holiday camps in Cornwall, the St Martin's Holiday park near Looe and the Mullion Holiday Park near Helston.

MASSIE, Les
Huddersfield, Darlington, Halifax, Bradford PA, Workington 1956-1970
A Huddersfield regular for ten years. Went into the haulage business upon leaving the game. Later took a job at Hoslets in Huddersfield.

MASSON, Don
Middlesboro, Notts Co, QPR, Derby, Notts Co, 1964-1981
Played over 600 league games and was capped by Scotland. Ended his league playing days at Notts County, where he later managed the sports complex. Now owns the Gallery Hotel in Nottingham.
Division Four Championship with County in 1971.

MATHIAS, Ray
Tranmere 1967-1984
Ray served Tranmere as a player for 17 years before becoming manager of Wigan Athletic. Now assistant manager at Tranmere.
His 626 appearances for the club is a Tranmere Rovers record.

MATTHEWS, Reginald
Coventry, Chelsea, Derby, 1950-1967
Won five England caps as a Third Division player and later worked for Massey Ferguson for twenty years before having to retire through ill health.
Played twice for the Football League.

MATTHEWS, Sir Stanley
Stoke, Blackpool, Stoke, 1931-1964

One of footballs greatest living legends, achieving world wide acclaim during a professional career that spanned 33 years. Son of a boxer, he started at his home town club, Stoke City, as a brilliant youngster. He sensationally transferred to Blackpool in 1947 for £11,500. After getting two Cup final runners-up medals, he achieved a lifetime ambition by helping them beat Bolton in the 1952-3 final, now known as the 'Matthews Final'. He returned to Stoke, assisting them back to the First Division and was still playing in that league past the age of 50. He was Footballer of the Year twice, in 1953 and 1963, and voted European Footballer of the Year in 1957, one year after being named King of Soccer in Ghana!
Twice a second division champion with Stoke either side of the war.

MAUCHLEN, Ally
Kilmarnock, Motherwell, Leicester, Leeds, Hearts, 1978-1993
A Scottish born midfield star who moved south to join Leicester and ended his career with Hearts.
Won a Scottish First Division Championship with Motherwell.

MAY, Larry
Leicester, Barnsley, Sheff Wed, Brighton, 1976-1988
A knee injury ended Larry career in 1989 and he was appointed youth team coach at Portsmouth in February 1995, having previously held the same post at Brighton.

MAYO, Joe
Walsall, WBA, Leyton O, Cambridge U, Blackpool, 1972-1982
Played over 275 league games in ten years for his five league clubs. Now a hotelier in Crriccieth, Wales – he runs the 'Plas Isa'.
Played for Orient in their 1978 FA Cup semi final.

MEAGAN, Mick
Everton, Huddersfield, Halifax, 1957-1968
After one season with Halifax, Mick returned to his native Ireland. He was involved in management and coaching with Drogheda, Shamrock Rovers and Bray, as well as working in a Dublin Hospital.

MEDHURST, Harry
West Ham, Chelsea, Brighton, 1938-1952
A steady goalkeeper who played 143 games for Chelsea. Died in 1984.

MEDLEY, Les
Tottenham 1946-1952
Scored 45 goals from his 150 league games for Tottenham immediately after the war, earning himself six England caps. Having played all of his football in the capital, Les is now retired in another London – Ontario, Canada. He had originally emigrated in 1946, but returned to England to pursue his career, leaving for Canada again in 1953.
League Championship winner in 1951.

MEDWIN, Terry
Swansea, Tottenham, 1951-1962
Swansea born winger who was capped 30 times by Wales as well as playing nearly 200 games. Back home in Swansea, but has been unable to work since 1983 due to a nervous disorder.
Double winner with Spurs.

MEE, Bertie

Played as a winger. and in 1960 joined Arsenal as trainer and physiotherapist, becoming manager in 1966-7. Retired ten years later and after a break from the game joined Watford as general manager.. Upon his final retirement in 1986, he remained a director of the Vicarage Road club.
Managed Arsenal to the 1970/1 double.

MEEK, George

Hamilton, Leeds, Walsall, Leicester, Walsall, 1952-1964
Now a postman living in Walsall whose family are following his sporting footsteps: his son has a golf handicap of two and his daughter is a Midland County rugby player.
Won promotion to the First Division with Leeds in 1956.

MEGSON, Don

Sheff Wed, Bristol R, 1959-1970
Sheffield Wednesday's first choice right back for over a decade, during which time he played 386 League games and represented the Football League. Although now technically retired, he still does some scouting for Norwich City and is the father of Blackpool boss Gary.
The Owls skipper for the 1966 FA Cup final.

MEGSON, Gary

Plymouth, Everton, Sheff Wed, Notts F, Newcastle, Sheff Wed, Man C, Norwich, 1977-1995
A well travelled midfielder who played for seven league clubs. Became assistant manager at Norwich City until moving to Bradford. A brief returned to Norwich ended in the sack and he is now in charge of Blackpool.

MELIA, Jimmy

Liverpool, Wolves, Southampton, Aldershot, Crewe, 1955-1971
Played 269 games for Liverpool and won two England caps, but is probably better known as the manager who took Brighton to the FA Cup final in 1983. Since then he has managed Belenenses Portugal, Stockport and coached in Kuwait. His most recent travels have taken him to Dallas to assist with training in their indoor soccer league.
League Championship medal with Liverpool in 1964.

MELLOR, Ian

Man C, Norwich, Brighton., Chester, Sheff Wed, Bradford C, 1970-1983
Has been an executive with the PFA for almost three years, handling commercial deals, having previously worked for sports manufacturers Puma and Gola.

MELLOR, Peter

Burnley, Chesterfield, Fulham, Hereford, Portsmouth, 1969-1980
Moved over to America in 1980 where he has prospered selling and fitting fireplaces, as well as maintaining gardens and swimming pools. He is Florida state goalkeeping coach and coaches goalkeepers throughout the States.
Kept goal for Fulham in the 1975 FA Cup final.

MELLOWS, Micky

Reading, Portsmouth, 1970-1977
Ex-amateur international who won 16 caps and a place in the 1972 Olympic team. Made almost 200 appearances for Portsmouth in five years after persuading manger John Mortimore to give him a trial. Now lives in Portsmouth where he runs an annual international tournament for kids.

MENDHAM, Peter

Norwich 1978-1987
Born in Kings Lynn and played all of his league football with Norwich. Is now community officer at the club. Still turns out for Wroxham.
League Cup and Second Division winners medals.

MEOLA, Tony

Brighton, Watford, 1990
Came over to this country in a bid to kick start his career. He also tried his luck as an American Football kicker but now plays for

the New York Metrostars in the US Major League.

MERCER, Joe OBE
Everton, Arsenal, 1932-1953
Joe suffered a double leg fracture in 1954 after a playing career with Everton and Arsenal. Moved into management with Sheffield Wednesday and then Aston Villa. He briefly retired due to ill health before returning to soccer with Manchester City, striking up a very successful partnership with Malcolm Allison and bringing a decade of glory to Maine Road. He left in 1972 to become general manager at Coventry and in 1977 took temporary control of the England team. He resigned as a Coventry director in 1981 after nine years on the board and died in 1990 aged 76.
Won three League Championships as a player and managed Man City to the title in 1966.

MEREDITH, Trevor
Burnley, Shrewsbury, 1959-1971
A winger who spent seven years with Shrewsbury before retiring in 1971. Now a school teacher in Preston.

MERRICK, Alan
WBA, Peterboro, 1968-1975
A former full back who quit the game aged only 25. Alan then went over to America to coach in Minnesota.

MERRICK, Gil
Birmingham 1946-1959
Probably the best goalkeeper in the country around the early fifties and played over 700 games for the Blues in all. Capped by England 23 times as well he later managed Birmingham between 1960 and 1964. Continued to live and work in the City but has now retired.
Division Two Championship twice, in 1948 and 1955.

MERRINGTON, Dave
Burnley, Bristol C, 1964-1971
A centre half who coached at Burnley and

Bristol City, was assistant manager at Leeds, then at Sunderland. Stepped up from youth team coach to become first team boss at Southampton on Alan Ball's departure but only lasted one season, losing his job in the 1996 close season.

METCALF, Micky
Wrexham, Chester, 1957-1968
An inside forward who played in the fifties and sixties. Now area manager with a Manchester based scientific company.

METGOD, Johnny
Notts F, Tottenham, 1984-1987
Dutch international midfielder who joined Forest from Real Madrid in 1984. He returned to Holland and is youth development officer at Feyenoord.
Helped AZ 67 Alkmaar win the Dutch Double in 1981.

METHLEY, Irvin
Wolves, Walsall, 1946-1950
Former Walsall full back who now runs a fish and chip shop in the town.

MIDDLEMASS, Clive
Leeds, Workington 1962-1969
186 appearances for Workington in the sixties and now assistant manager at Burnley.

MIELCZAREK, Ray
Wrexham, Huddersfield, Rotherham, 1964-1973
Had nine years in the professional game and now lives near Wrexham and works as a security officer.
Capped once by Wales against Finland in 1971.

MILBURN, Jackie
Newcastle 1946-1956
'Wor Jackie' died at his Northumberland home in 1988 just months after learning that he had cancer. He played in three Newcastle cup victories in the fifties and scored the fastest Cup final goal ever – after only 45 seconds in 1953. Capped by England, Jackie became coach at Linfield in Ireland before

succeeeding Alf Ramsey as Ipswich boss in 1963. Returned home to the north east to become a football writer with the News of the World for 24 years until his retirement shortly before his death.
Three times an FA cup winner with Newcastle.

MILKINS, John
Portsmouth, Oxford, 1960-1978

Milkins made 344 league appearances for Portsmouth before moving to Oxford. He was player/manager at Waterlooville, but is now general manager of a company that owns four snooker clubs along the south coast.

MILLAR, Alistair
Barnsley, York, 1970-1980
Scottish born midfielder who played almost 300 games during his nine years with Barnsley. Now works as a machine operator for PMC Redfern glass, lives in Barnsley and scouts for Carlisle United.

MILLARD, Len
WBA 1946-1957
Played 400 games in over a decade with the Baggies. Now retired and living in an old peoples home in Coseley, West Midlands. *Captained WBA to the 1954 FA Cup final.*

MILLER, Brian
Burnley 1955-1966
Played almost 400 games for his only club, Burnley. Capped once by England against Austria in 1961. Had two spells at Turf Moor as manager but is now their chief scout.
League Championship winner in 1960.

MILLER, James
Dunfirmline, Rangers, Dundee Utd, 1953-1969
A naturally gifted ball player who went on to become a Scottish international but drifted out of the game after a 12 month spell in charge of Raith Rovers. He retired in mid 1996 after spending many years as an Edinburgh publican.
Won back-to-back doubles with Rangers in the 1960s.

MILLER, Ian
Bury, Notts F, Doncaster, Swindon, Blackburn, Port V, Scunthorpe, 1973-1990
Was coach at Port Vale until November 1994, when he accepted the post of reserve team manager at Wolves who he has now left.

MILLER, Keith
West Ham, Bournemouth, 1968-1979
Former Hammers junior who went on to play 381 games for the Cherries. Manager of Poole Town and works as a sales manager for a computer typesetting company.

MILLER, Paul
Tottenham, Charlton, Watford, Bournemouth, Brentford, Swansea, 1978-1990
Spent nine years at White Hart Lane before moving on to five other clubs in quick succession. Lives in Hampstead and works as a business development manager for an employment consultancy.
Played for Spurs in their UEFA Cup success.

MILLINGTON, Anthony
WBA, C.Palace, Peterborough, Swansea, 1961-1973
Welsh international goalkeeper, now helps

run the Wrexham disabled supporters club with his brother, Grenville.
Capped 21 times between 1963 and 1972.

MILLINGTON, Grenville
Chester, Wrexham, 1968-1983
Takes weekly coaching sessions at the Racecourse Ground, helping Wrexham's up and coming goalkeepers. Employed by the Cheshire probation service and works in Chester as a community services officer.

MILLINGTON, Ralph
Tranmere 1950-1960
Wing half who made 357 appearances for Tranmere. Now living in Hesweall, Wirral, and is a self employed building and joinery contractor.

MILLS, David
Middlesboro, WBA, Newcastle, Sheff Wed, Newcastle, Middlesboro, Darlington, 1968-1986
Mills was Britain's costliest player (£516,000) when he joined Ron Atkinson at West Bromwich Albion in 1979. He retired in 1986 after a series of niggling injuries and became player/commercial manager at Whitby Town. Works as a freelance journalist for local press, TV and radio and has been a print consultant since 1986. Cost £516,000 when he moved to WBA

MILLS, Don
QPR, Torquay, QPR, Cardiff, Leeds U, Torquay, 1946-1961
Clocked up over 400 appearances after the War, most of them for Torquay. Had a few years on the Gulls coaching staff and later became a traffic warden in the town. Died in February 1994.

MILLS, Mick
Ipswich, Southampton, Stoke, 1965-1987
Mick settled down in the Ipswich defence, having originally played in midfield, after being released by Portsmouth when Pompey abandoned their youth policy. Mick went on to captain both Ipswich and England. Became manager of Stoke City before a pro-

posed move to Kuwait was thwarted by the Iraqi invasion. Now lives in Staffordshire and after a spell as chief scout for Sheffield Wednesday moved to Birmingham as assistant manager.
Captained Ipswich to UEFA Cup success and the 1978 FA Cup final win.

MILLS, Roly
Northampton 1954-1963
A Northampton regular for nearly ten years and is now involved in a promotions business and lives in Harpole, Northants.

MILLS, Steve
Southampton 1972-1976
Steve was an outstanding prospect with the Saints and an England under-23 international. His promising career was cruelly cut short by injury and he took over his parents newsagents business but sadly died in 1988 of Leukaemia. A charity was formed in his memory to raise funds for Leukaemia research.

MILNE, Gordon
Preston, Liverpool, Blackpool, 1956-1969
Manager of Grampus in Japan, the club that Gary Lineker played for, until September 1994. Took over as chief executive of the Managers & Secretarys Association in June 1995 but now works in Turkey.
League Championship with Liverpool twice.

MILNE, Ralph
Dundee United, Charlton, Bristol C, Man Utd, West Ham, 1977-1989
Scottish under-21 international who appeared to have a big future ahead of him when his £170,000 transfer from Bristol City made him one of Alex Fergusons first signings as Manchester United manager. However, he was quickly released following a press interview in which made various claims about the personal lives of his teammates. A brief spell at Bury was followed by a time in Hong Kong, but he has now been unemployed for several years, living in the Nailsea area of Bristol.
Won a Scottish Championship in 1983.

MITCHELL, Arnold
Notts Co, Exeter, 1948-1965
Wing half who made 495 league appearances for Exeter City, now retired and still living in the city.

MITCHELL, Bobby
Sunderland, Blackburn, Grimsby, Carlisle, Rotherham, Lincoln, 1973-1986
Now working with the football in the community programme at Grimsby..

MITCHELL, John
Fulham, Millwall, 1972-1980
Runs a marketing and promotions company in London's West End. Lives in Harpenden and in 1994 made a take-over bid for Luton. Played for Fulham in the 1975 FA Cup final.

MOBLEY, Vic
Sheffield Wed, QPR, 1963-1970
Now living in New Zealand.
Capped 13 times by England at under-23 level.

MOLBY, Jan
Liverpool, Barnsley, Norwich, Swansea, 1984-1996
Danish international who joined Liverpool from Ajax and played over 200 games before taking over at Swansea as player boss.
A Liverpool double-winner in 1986.

MONCUR, Bobby
Newcastle, Sunderland, Carlisle, 1962-1976

Became player/manager at Carlisle in November 1976 and player only from September 1977; Heart of Midlothian manager February 1980; Plymouth Argyle manager June 1981 until September 1983. Returned to work on Tyneside and had a brief spell coaching Whitley Bay. Now runs his own yacht charter business in Newcastle. His interest in sailing started while managing Hearts and he has since sailed in the Round Britain Race; Transatlantic Race; and the Fastnet race of 1987.
Fairs Cup winner with Newcastle in 1969.

MONEY, Richard
Scunthorpe U, Fulham, Liverpool, Derby Co, Luton, Portsmouth, Scunthorpe U, 1973-1989
A highly rated and well travelled central defender. Was manager at Scunthorpe until March 1994. Now reserve team coach at Nottingham Forest.
Won a Division Two Championship in 1982.

MONTGOMERY, Jim
Sunderland, Southampton, Birmingham C, Nottingham F, Sunderland, 1961-1980
Montgomery was one of the top class young goalkeepers of the sixties who were kept out of the England team only by the brilliance of Gordon Banks. After spells at Birmingham and Notts Forest, he returned to the Sunderland area, and was formerly director of youth football at Roker Park.
Sunderland hero in the 1973 FA Cup final.

MOORE, Bobby
West Ham U, Fulham, 1958-1976
A majestic defender who went on to captain club and country, winning 108 full caps. He collected an FA Cup winners medal in 1964, but in the twighlight of his career when playing for Fulham, was on the losing side at Wembley in 1975 against his old. Was Footballer of the Year in 1964 and when he retired after more than 650 league appearances he had achieved a world-wide reputation as one of the most accomplished players of all time. Sadly did not manage to repeat his on-field success off the field and after

brief associations with Oxford City and Southend, decided to concentrate on journalism and broadcasting. Died of cancer on February 24th 1993 aged only 51.
Lead England to 1966 World Cup glory.

MOORE, Dave
Grimsby, Carlisle U, Blackpool, Grimsby, Darlington, 1978-1988
Grimsby born defender and the brother of Kevin. Was the youngest manager in the league when appointed to the position at Scunthorpe United in June 1994, staying for nearly two years.

MOORE, Eric
Everton, Chesterfield, Tranmere, 1949-1957
First choice full back at Everton for several years in the fifties. Now a publican in Atherton.

MOORE, Graham
Cardiff, Chelsea, Man U, Northampton, Charlton, Doncaster, 1958-1973
Welsh international midfielder with 21 full caps to his name. Now running a sub post office in Scarborough after running a pub at Easingwold.
Welsh Cup winner with Cardiff in 1959.

MOORE, Jon
Millwall, Bournemouth, 1974-1980
Full back who spent four years with Millwall before ending with Bournemouth at the age of 25. Now works in the City of London for Tullett & Tokyo.

MOORE, Kevin
Grimsby, Oldham, Southampton, Bristol R, Fulham, 1976-1996
Retired at the end of the 1995-96 season at the grand age of 38 to become Fulham's ground safety officer.

MOORE, Ronnie
Tranmer, Cardiff, Rotherham, Charlton, Rochdale, Tranmere, 1971-1988
Coach at Tranmere Rovers, where he started his career at the start of a 17 year period as a player.

MORAN, Eddie
Leicester City, Stockport, Rochdale, Crewe, 1947-1959
Snatched by Leicester from under the noses of Man Utd but made his name at Stockport scoring 47 goals in 117 games. Still lives in the town where he has worked for British Aerospace, Shell and a games machine company.

MORAN, Kevin
Man U, Blackburn, 1978-1994
Republic of Ireland central defender who moved to Manchester United in 1978 from Gaelic soccer side Pegasus. After a spell in Spain became a regular at Blackburn. Retired in 1994 for concentrate on the sports promotion business he runs with former United team mate Jesper Olsen.
The only player to be sent off in a FA Cup final.

MORAN, Ronnie
Liverpool 1952-1964
Made 342 appearances in his twelve playing years at Liverpool and has given his working life to the Reds – currently first team coach. League Championship winner 1964.

MORELAND, Vic
Derby Co 1978-1979
Northern Ireland international midfielder who spent a brief time in the League. Now Manager of Tulsa, Expo Pavilion in America.

MORGAN, Roger
QPR, Tottenham, 1964-1971
Played over 250 games for his two clubs before qutting the game aged 25. Lives in Chingford and worked as a recreation officer for Haringey Council before becoming a community officer at West Ham.
England under-23 international.

MORGAN, Stuart
West Ham, Torquay, Reading, Colchester, Bournemouth, 1967-1976 Managed Dorchester FC having previously held posts at Weymouth, AFC Bournemouth and Brentford. Now with Clift Rovers in the

Western League.

MORGAN, Trevor
Bournemouth, Mansfield, Bristol C, Exeter, Bristol R, Bolton, Colchester, Exeter, 1980-1990
Ten years in the league took Trevor to several clubs. Is now assistant manager at Exeter.

MORGAN, Willie
Burnley, Manchester U, Burnley, Bolton, Blackpool, 1962-1981
Played over 600 games and was capped 21 times by Scotland before hanging up his boots. Retired from the game having invested his money in a chain of laundrettes. Briefly opened a sports shop in Altrincham, but now concentrates on the marketing and promotions firm in which he is a partner.
Won two Division Two Championships, with United and Bolton.

MORLEY, Tony
Preston, Burnley, Aston Villa, WBA, Birmingham, WBA, Burnley, 1972-1988
England 'B' International who ended his playing days in America with Tampa Bay Rowdies in 1989, then with Hamran Spartans in Malta in 1990. Following a very brief stop at Bromsgrove Rovers in January 1995, as player/coach, moved to play for Stratford Town FC.
A European Cup winner with Villa.

MORRELL, Paul
Bournemouth 1983-1993
A Cherries first team regular for ten years. Returned in late 1994 from a spell in Hong Kong to join Salisbury City in the BHL Southern Division.

MORRIS, Peter
Mansfield, Ipswich, Norwich, Mansfield, Peterborough, 1960-1979
A long career before going into coaching. Manager at Boston United until the summer of 1994 and then assistant manager at Northampton Town until February 1995.
Won three promotions, with Norwich, Ipswich and Mansfield.

MORRITT, Gordon
Rotherham, Doncaster, Northampton, York, Rochdale, Darlington, 1961-1973
Enjoyed a seven year career as a goalkeeper with six league clubs. Now a security manager in York.

MORRISSEY, John
Liverpool, Everton, Oldham, 1957-1972
Played for both Liverpool clubs, then after only six months with Oldham, his career was ended by injury. Retained his base on Merseyside and is now a successful businessman.

MORTENSEN, Henrik
Norwich C 1989-1990
Made only 18 appearances for Norwich in the late eighties and returned to play for Aarhus in his home country.

MORTENSEN, Stan
Blackpool, Hull C, Southport, 1946-1957
Played either as a centre forward or inside forward. Stan recovered from an air crash in a Wellington bomber and then proceeded to score four goals on his England debut. He will forever be associated with great comebacks and although the 1953 Cup final is remembered as the 'Matthews final', Morty scored a hat-trick. Apart from that he played in two other finals, but ended up on the losing side, however he did score 24 goals in 25 internationals. Died in 1991.

MORTIMER, Dennis
Coventry, Aston Villa, Sheffield U, Brighton, Birmingham, 1969-1984
When he retired from competitive football, he had played over 700 competitive matches for a total of five league clubs. Was player/manager at Redditch before becoming football in the community officer at West Brom in 1990, then assistant manager at the Hawthorns until October 1994.
European Cup winner in 1982.

MORTIMORE, Charlie
Aldershot, Portsmouth, Aldershot, 1949-1955
Retired deputy head of Cove Comprehensive

school. Lives in Farnborough where he is director of youth football.
England amatuer international.

MORTIMORE, John

Chelsea, QPR, 1955-1965
Was dismissed by Benfica in 1987 after steering them to a Portuguese league and cup double. Previously spent two years at Southampton as assistant to Ted Bates, then Lawrie McMenemy, and quickly earned another place in the sun with Real Betis before another spell at the Dell, this time as chief scout.

MOSS, David

Swindon, Luton, Swindon, 1971-1985
Played over 400 games with Luton before being appointed assistant manager of Swindon. Moved to Manchester City with Brian Horton and is now with him as coach at Huddersfield.
Scored 148 League goals in his career as a winger.

MOSS, Ernie

Chesterfield, Peterborough, Mansfield, Chesterfield, Port Vale, Lincoln C, Doncaster R, Chesterfield, Stockport Co, Scarborough, Rochdale, 1968-1987
Ernie played 271 games for Chesterfield in seven years before moving on to a host of other clubs before retiring in 1987. He is now a sports outfitter in Chesterfield and was appointed manager of Gainsborough Trinity of the Unibond League in May 1995.

MOSS, Frank

Sheffield Wed, Aston Villa, 1936-1954
He coached the youngsters at Aston Villa in 1955-6 but then left the club to concentrate on his newsagents business at Kingstanding, then retiring to the Cornish resort of Looe.
Played 313 League games for Villa.

MUDIE, Jackie

Blackpool, Stoke C, Port Vale, 1949-1966
Scottish international striker who scored 143 goals for Blackpool during the 1950s. Jackie

went on to run his own successful painting and decorating business in the Potteries area before his death in 1992.
FA cup winner with Blackpool in 1953.

MUHREN, Arnold

Ipswich, Man U, 1978-1984
A stylish Dutch international who spent a successful six years in England. Now lives back in Holland in Volendam and is employed by a Dutch football magazine to train youngsters. Still plays for the ex-Ajax and ex-Holland teams.
UEFA Cup winner in 1981 with Ipswich.

MULHEARN, Ken

Everton, Stockport Co, Man C, Shrewsbury, Crewe A, 1963-1981
After fininshing his playing career at 37 years of age with Crewe, he bought a pub in the Shrewsbury area.

MULLEN, Jimmy

Sheffield Wed, Rotherham U, Preston, Cardiff, Newport Co, 1970-1986
After a playing career mainly as a centre back, Mullen moved into management as player/manager of Newport County in 1986. He was assistant manager to Ian Porterfield at Aberdeen and assistant to Sam Ellis at Blackpool before joining Burnley as assistant to Frank Casper. Taking over as boss in 1991, he subsequently celebrated a second promotion since becoming manager when in 1994, Burnley were promoted into the Endsleigh First Division. He later resigned after a poor run.

MULLEN, Jimmy

Wolves 1938-1958
Mullen joined Wolves straight from school in 1937 after winning England schoolboy honours and made his debut in 1939, when only 16. He played in two World Cups for England and was capped 12 times in all .He formed one of the great wing partnerships with Johnny Hancocks. Retired from soccer in the fifties and died aged 64 in 1987.
Won Two League Championships with Wolves.

MULLERY, Alan
Fulham, Tottenham, Fulham, 1958-1975
Two spells at Fulham were seperated by eight years with Tottenham Hotspur where he established himself as one of the best wing-halves of his day. Alan won 35 caps, was Player of the Year in 1975 and was awarded the MBE the following year upon his retirement from the game. He then tried his hand at management with spells at Brighton twice, Charlton and QPR. Appointed director of football at Barnet in 1996 he also acts as a football presenter on Capital Gold Radio in London.
Fairs Cup winner with Spurs in 1972.

MULLETT, Joe
Birmingham, Norwich, 1955-1968
A solid left back who played nearly 250 games for Norwich, returned to his native Midlands where he ran a pub, but has run a shop for the the last few years.

MULLIGAN, Paddy
Chelsea, Crystal P, West Brom, 1969-1977
An attacking right back who won 51 full caps for the Republic of Ireland. After a spell as assistant manager to Panathinaikos in Greece he retired in 1982 to become an insurance agent in west London.
A member of Chelsea's League Cup final team of 1972.

MUNDY, Albert
Portsmouth, Brighton, Aldershot, 1950-1960
Played as an inside forward during his ten year career and is now working for Charringtons in Portsmouth.

MUNKS, David
Sheff U, Portsmouth, Swindon, Exeter, 1965-1975
Sheffield born defender now lives in Bedhampton near Portsmouth and took a management job in a Southampton sports centre after hanging up his boots.

MUNRO, Francis
Dundee U, Aberdeen, Wolves, Celtic, 1963-1976
Coached and managed teams in Australia between 1981 and 1989 then worked as a salesman for a garden furniture company. In January 1993, Francis suffered a severe stroke which has left him unable to work and he can only walk with the aid of a stick.
Fairs Cup runner up with Wolves in 1972.

MUNRO, Malcolm
Leicester 1970-1974
After waiting three years for his chance Malcolm scored an own goal on his league debut but after losing his place in the side 12 months later walked out on the club and emigrated to Canada. City held his registration for six years until 1980 when it was evident he wasn't going to return.

MURDOCH, Bobby
Celtic, Middlesboro, 1959-1976
A tough midfielder who made 12 appearances for Scotland while with Celtic. When transferred to Middlesborough he was an immediate success and played a big part in the club's Second Division Championship success and return to the top flight. Went on to become youth team coach and then manager at Ayresome Park before returning to Glasgow where he ran a pub until bad ankles made it difficult to get around.
European Cup winner with Celtic in 1967.

MURPHY, Barry
Barnsley 1962-1978
After clocking up 514 league appearances for Barnsley Barry became their youth team coach, then coach to the first team. After spending four years in the same post at Leeds United, he left the game to work for Barnsley Borough Council firstly as a sports development officer and currently as manager of Penistone Leisure Centre.
Holds the Barnsley record for number of appearances.

MURRAY, Alan
Middlesboro, York, Brentford, Doncaster, 1969-1976
Managed Darlington between 1993 and 1995 and prior to that was in charge at Hartlepool

for two years from 1991 and is now youth team manager at Southampton.

MURRAY, Bob
Stockport Co 1952-1963
In an eleven year stay he was to set an appearance record of 465 games that would stand for 29 years. Worked at British Aerospace as an aircraft interior finisher until retiring in 1993.

MURRAY, Jimmy
Wolves, Manchester C, Walsall, 1955-1968
A centre forward who netted over 200 goals from his 400 games in the league. Now a greengrocer in Tamworth, Staffordshire.
Won two Championship medals with Wolves in their glory years.

MUSGROVE, Malcolm
West Ham U, Leyton Orient, 1953-1965
Former West Ham wingman who played over 350 league games in the fifties and sixties. Very experienced coach now in his 43rd year in the game, currently employed as the physio at Shrewsbury Town.

MUZINIC, Drazen
Norwich 1980-1982
A Yugoslavia international who never settled on the Norfolk coast. Was last heard of running his own wine bar and restaurant in Brac.

NATTRASS, Irving
Newcastle, Middlesboro, 1970-1985

Former England under-23 international right back who went on to run his own clothes shop in Chester Le Street. Irving is now a horse breeder.
League Cup finalist with Newcastle in 1976.

NAYLOR, Terry
Tottenham, Charlton, 1969-1983
Former Spurs defender Terry went on to run the 'Pickwick' pub in south-east London and also worked as a football reporter for the Sunday Sport.
Played in the 1974 UEFA Cup final..

NEAL, John
Hull, Swindon, Aston V, Southend, 1949-1965
When he finally hung up his boots after 416 league appearances, Neal managed Wrexham, Middlesborough, then Chelsea. He is now retired but still doing some scouting for Charlton and Shrewsbury from his home in Edinburgh.
Second Division Championship winner in 1960.

NEAL, Phil
Northampton, Liverpool, Bolton, 1968-1988
Played 455 League games for Liverpool and was a regular in the England team before becoming player-manager, then manager at Bolton. Managed Coventry City until February 1995 and was Graham Taylor's assistant in the England set up. Managed Cardiff before joining Man City.
Won seven League Championships and four European Cups with Liverpool.

NEALE, Phil
Lincoln, 1974-1984
A Russian-speaking left back who combined his role at Lincoln City with his career as a county cricketer for Worcestershire. Now team manager at Warwickshire CCC.
Promoted to Division Three in 1976.

NEATE, Gordon
Reading 1958-1965
Groundsman at Elm Park, the home of the only club he served as a player.

NEEDHAM, Dave
Notts C, QPR, Notts F, 1965-1981
Central defender who played over 400
games for Notts County before ending his
career across the River Trent at Forest. Now
a successful businessman in Leicester. His
son Ben is currently on the books at Notts
County. Won
European Cup winners medal with Forest.

NEIGHBOUR, Jimmy
Tottenham, Norwich, West Ham,
Bournemouth, 1970-1982
Jimmy ran a sports shop in Chingford as
well as coaching at Wimbledon and then at
Doncaster Rovers until December 1994. Now
returned to live in Woodford, Essex.
*Scored the winner for the Hammers in the
1981 League Cup final.*

NEIL, Pat
Portsmouth, Wolves Portsmouth, 1955-1962
Now living in Purbrook, Hampshire and is a
teacher at Midhurst Intermediate school.

NEILL, Terry
Arsenal, Hull, 1960-1972
Captain of both club and country, Neill won
59 Irish caps before moving into club management with Hull City. Took over at Arsenal
in July 1976 and during his seven years in
office led them to three successive FA Cup
finals. Now runs his own bar in London –
the Terry Neill Sports Bar & Brasserie.
League Cup finalist in 1968.

NELSON, Andy
West Ham, Ipswich, Orient, Plymouth, 1957-
1967
Better known as a manager having taken
the helm at many clubs, including Plymouth
and Charlton. Now retired to Alicante, Spain
and reached the semi finals of the Spanish
National Bowling Championship in 1995.
*Won first and second division championship
medals with Ipswich.*

NELSON, Sammy
Arsenal, Brighton, 1969-1982
Belfast born full back capped 51 times by

Northern Ireland. Now works for Save &
Prosper in the insurance industry and lives
in Brighton.
FA Cup winner in 1979.

NETHERCOTT, Ken
Norwich 1947-1958
Now retired and living in Norwich after
spending 25 years with Rowntree
Mackintosh as a plant operator. Played over
400 games for Norwich and won one
England 'B' cap.

NEWMAN, John
Birmingham, Leicester, Plymouth, Exeter,
1951-1971
Wing half who made almost 300 league
appearances for Plymouth Argyle and Exeter
City. Was assistant manager at Mansfield
and is now assistant manager at Burton
Albion.
*Division Two Champion in 1955 and played
in an FA Cup final twelve months later.*

NEWMAN, Ron
Portsmouth, Leyton O, C Palace, Gillingham,
1954-1965
Ron has been coaching in America for some
years, with Dallas Tornado, Fort Lauderdale,
and latterly with San Diego Sockers, where
he is general manager and coach.

NEWTON, Henry
Notts F, Everton, Derby, Walsall, 1963-1977

Henry established himself as a regular with three of his four clubs and was capped four times by England at under-23 level. Now combines his love of playing golf with his duties as a postmaster in Derby.
Division One Championship with Derby in 1975.

NEWTON, Keith
Blackburn, Everton, Burnley, 1960-1977

An England full back who joined Everton from Blackburn Rovers mid-way through the 1969/70 season. Had a second crack at the First Division after winning promotion with Burnley, then went on to play non-league soccer with Morecambe and Clitheroe where he was player/manager. Later set up a sports trophy business and a newsagents in Blackburn and is now working with a local garage group in the town.
Division Two Championship with Burnley in 1973.

NICHOLAS, Peter
C Palace, Arsenal, C Palace, Luton, Chelsea, Watford, 1977-1993
Welsh international who was capped 73 times by his country. Peter is now first team coach at Crystal Palace.

NICHOLL, Chris
Burnley, Halifax, Luton, Aston V, Southampton, Grimsby, 1965-1984
Centre half who had a splendid career in first class football before being appointed manager at Southampton in July 1985. In seventeen years he had amassed 754 League and Cup appearances and 51 caps for Northern Ireland. Appointed manager at Walsall in September 1994, having had a few years break after leaving the same post at Southampton in 1991.
Won Division Three Championship in 1973 and League Cup in 1975.

NICHOLL, Jimmy
Man U, Sunderland, WBA, 1974-1985
A former Northern Ireland international who managed Raith Rovers in Scotland before moving south to Millwall.
Capped 73 times between 1975-1984.

NICHOLLS, Johnny
WBA, Cardiff, Exeter, 1951-1958
One of the great goal 'poachers' of his day and one half of the deadly striking duo he formed with Ronnie Allen. Died in April 1995, aged 64.
FA Cup winner with West Brom in 1954.

NICHOLSON, Bill
Tottenham 1938-1954
A war-time signing who made 306 appearances at wing half between 1946-1954, won one England cap and three at 'B' level. Was appointed Spurs manager in 1958 and led them to their double success in 1961 and to two other FA Cup victories. Left the job in 1974 was appointed Club President.
Won Division Two and Division One winners medals with Spurs in successive years.

NICHOLSON, Jimmy
Man U, Huddersfield, Bury, 1960-1975
A Northern Ireland international who spent nine years with Huddersfield playing 300 League games. Now manager of Sale sports centre.
Won 31 of his 41 Irish caps with Huddersfield – a club record.

NICHOLSON, Peter

Blackpool, Bolton, Rochdale, Carlisle, 1970-1983

Works part time for Bolton Wanderers helping with the coaching and commercial activities. As a player he had been at Bolton for ten years in the seventies and played in more then 300 league games.

NIEDZWIEKI, Eddie

Wrexham, Chelsea, 1977-1987

Forced to retire after six opersations on his knee and became youth team coach at Chelsea. In 1990 Eddie went to coach Reading and later became assistant manager to Ian Porterfield at Elm Park. When the Berkshire club decided that they could not afford an assistant manager, he returned to Chelsea where he was reserve team manager until May 1995.

NIGHTINGALE, Albert

Sheff U, Huddersfield, Blackburn, Leeds, 1946-1956

An inside forward who had a ten year career until his playing days were ended by a knee injury. Now a retired greenkeeper.

NILLSON, Roland

Sheff Wed 1989-1993

Swedish international defender who joined Wednesday from IFK Gotenburg in November 1989 but returned to Sweden to play for Helsingborg in 1994 for family reasons.

Played for Wednesday in the 1993 FA Cup and League Cup finals.

NISBET, Gordon

WBA, Hull, Plymouth, Exeter, 1969-1987

England under-23 international who normally played at right back, however he did make one appearance in goal while at West Brom. Played for Ottery St Mary and then coached Plymouth Argyle. Became a director of the Bealon Group in charge of property but is now with the Devon & Cornwall Police and playing for a police team in the local league.

Appeared in an FA Cup semi final with Plymouth in 1984.

NISH, David

Leicester, Derby, 1966-1978

Former England international full back created history when he skippered Leicester in the 1969 FA Cup final at only 21 years of age. Ran a post office in Derby but was appointed youth team coach at Middlesborough in June 1988 and currently holds the same post at Leicester City.

Football League championship winners medal with Derby in 1975.

NIXON, Jon

Derby, Notts Co, Peterboro, Shrewsbury, Barnsley, Halifax, 1965-1978

Former winger who is working for his old team-mate, Dave Needham, in a company specialising in personalised number plates.

NOBLE, Bobby

Manchester United 1962-1969

A former youth team mate of George Best who was forced to quit two years after a road crash. Now lives in Sale and works for a Manchester printing company.

FA Youth Cup winner in 1964.

NOBLE, Norman

Rotherham 1948-1957

Played over 300 league games for Rotherham United, his only club. Died in 1973 aged 50.

NOBLE, Peter

Newcastle, Swindon, Burnley, Blackpool, 1965-1982

Played over 500 games in a seventeen year career. Has had his own sports stall in Burnley market since.

League Cup winner with Swindon in 1969.

NORMAN, Maurice

Norwich, Tottenham, 1954-1965

Played over 350 games for Tottenham and was capped 23 times by England before having to retire through injury in 1967. Became assistant manager of a London garage and then opened a wool shop with his wife in Frinton-on-Sea. worked as a landscape gardener in Suffolk before retiring.

A Spurs double-winner.

NORMAN, Richie
Leicester, Peterboro, 1959-1968
Played over 300 games for Leicester in the
left back slot and now runs his own physio-
therapy clinic in Leicester and is physio to
Numeaton Borough.
On the losing side in two FA Cup finals.

NORTHCOTT, Tom
Torquay, Cardiff, Lincoln, Torquay, 1948-1965
Spent eight years at Plainmoor scoring 125
League goals and still lives in Torquay
where he is employed as a builder.
*Scored in Torquay's record League and Cup
wins.*

NURSE, Mel
Swansea, Middlesboro, Swindon, Swansea,
1955-1970
Started his career at the Vetch Field and
ended it there 15 years later. Now a businessman and property owner running a
boarding house in Wales. As a director of
Swansea, was involved in their fight for sur-
vival in 1985/6.
Capped 12 times by Wales.

NUTT, Gordon
Coventry, Cardiff, Arsenal, Southend, 1951-
1960
Winger who played for four clubs in the
fifties which included four years at Arsenal.
Went over to Australia to play for
Corinthians of Sydney, and stayed.

O' BRIEN, George
Leeds, Southampton, Leyton O, Aldershot,
1956-1967
Netted an impressive 178 goals in his 277
games for Southampton following a move
from Leeds. Now a publican in Southampton
running the 'Star & Garter', Freemantle.
*Third Division championship with Saints in
1960.*

O' BRIEN, Gerry
Clydebank, Southampton, Bristol R,
Swindon, Clydebank, 1968-1977

Returned to the Clydebank area of Scotland
to resume work as a bricklayer - his trade
prior to becoming a professional.

O'BRIEN, Ray
Man U, Notts Co, Derby, 1973-1983
Now a reprographics manager with
Nottinghamshire County Council and living
in Nottingham. Joint manager of Arnold
Town in the NE Counties League.

O'CALLAGHAN, Brendan
Doncaster, Stoke, Oldham, 1973-1985
Was a manager with the PFA but then
decided to study for a degree in business
administration at the University of Dublin.
Also helps out with sports programmes on
local radio in the Stoke area.

O'DONNELL, Neil
Norwich, Gillingham, Sheffield Wed, 1966-
1976
A Scottish born inside right who quit the
game after breaking a bone in his back. Still
lives in Sheffield where he works for a
finance company.

O'DRISCOLL, Jack
Swansea 1947-1951
Northern Ireland international who joined
Swansea from Cork City in 1947. Jack
became a bookmaker prior to his death.

O'DRISCOLL, Sean
Fulham, Bournemouth, 1979-1994
Played over 500 games in a long career and
is now a coach at Dean Court.
*Capped three times by the Republic of
Ireland.*

O'FARRELL, Frank
West Ham, Preston, 1950-1960
Now retired, living in Torquay. He remem-
bers with amusement an incident that
occured whilst managing non-League
Weymouth. They had reached the fourth
round of the FA Cup, but urgently needed a
goalkeeper for their forthcoming tie at
Preston. Through his contacts, Frank managed to acquire the services of 42 year old

Billy Bly, who had recently retired from Hull City. The weather on the day of the match was appalling with thick fog and very poor visability and eventually the referee was forced to order the players off the pitch. It was sometime later in the dressing room that it becamre apparent that Billy was missing – a subsequent search found him dutifully guarding his goal blissfully unaware of the abandonment. When asked about the incident afterwards, he said that he thought they were putting Preston under a lot of pressure at the other end!
Capped nine times for Ireland.

O'FLANAGAN, Dr Kevin
Arsenal, Brentford, 1945-1949
An all-round sportsman who represented the Republic of Ireland at football and rugby, as well as winning sprint and long jump championships in Ireland. After his playing days with Arsenal he resumed a career in medicine, firstly at a hospital in Ruislip, then back in his native Ireland, where he was doctor for the Ireland Olympic team on several occasions.

O'GRADY, Mike
Huddersfield, Leeds, Wolves, Birmingham, Rotherham, 1959-1973
Another astute Don Revie buy who was capped once during his time at Elland Road. Worked as a grip forYorkshire Television for eighteen years until being made redundant two years ago. Now works behind the bar of the Royal Oak pub in Aberford, Wetherby, and still plays for the ex-Leeds side.
Won a League Championship with Leeds.

O'HARE, John
Sunderland, Derby, Leeds, Notts F, 1964-1979
Left the first class game in 1981 and spent the following season with Belper Town. After giving up playing he managed a local Derby side, Ockbrook FC and was a licensee in Derby before taking up an appointment with a combustion firm in 1981. Now works as a stock controller with a Derby car dealer.
Won League Championship and European Cup winners medals.

O'KANE, Liam
Notts F 1968-1975
Capped 20 times by Ireland, Liam crossed the water in 1968 and has been employed at the City Ground ever since where he is now first team coach at Forest.

O'KEEFE, Vince
Birmingham, Walsall, Exeter, Torquay, Blackburn, Bury, Blackpool, Wrexham, 1975-1993
Having failed to make a first team appearance for his first two clubs, Vince finally proved himself by playing over 300 games. Now a financial advisor for the PFA based in Birmingham.

O'LEARY, David
Arsenal, Leeds, 1975-1995
Moved to Leeds after being handed a free transfer by Arsenal after 18 years at Highbury, but injury restricted his appearances at Elland Road. Capped 67 times by Ireland he worked for the BBC when his career ended before being appointed assistant manager of Leeds by George Graham.
Won two League championships, two FA Cups and two League Cups.

O'NEILL Brian
Burnley, Southampton, Huddersfield, 1962-1975
Speedy winger who won England under-23 honours and League representative honours. Brain was a Civil Engineer until a serious accident left Brian unable to work. Lives in Hedge End just outside Southampton.
Joined Saints for a then club record fee of £75,000.

O'NEILL, John
Leicester, QPR, Norwich, 1978-1987
His career was cut short at the age of 29 as a result of a clash with John Fashanu which resulted in a much publicised court case in 1994. He has now returned home to Derry where he is in charge of a wines and spirits business.
Played in two World Cups with Northern Ireland.

O

O'NEILL, Martin
Notts F, Norwich, Man C, Norwich, Notts Co, 1971-1984

A former Northern Ireland international captain who joined Notts Forest from Derry City. During his ten years at the City Ground he won a host of medals and at the end of his playing days moved into management with Grantham and Shepshed Charterhouse before business commitments forced him to quit. Wycombe Wanderers lured him back in February 1990 and he lead them into the League in 1993. Despite resisting offers from larger clubs, Martin finally returned to one of his former clubs, Norwich, as manager in June 1995 but left six months later to take over at Leicester City.

A European Cup winner with Notts Forest.

O'REILLY, Gary
Tottenham, Brighton, Crystal Palace, Birmingham, Brighton, 1979-1993

Capped for Ireland at youth level and was the natinal schools javelin champion in 1978. Scored for the Eagles in the 1990 FA Cup final and is now a television presenter with SKY TV.

Helped Palace win promotion to the First Division in 1989.

O'ROURKE, John
Chelsea, Luton, Middlesboro, Ipswich, Coventry, QPR, Bournemouth, 1962-1974

England under-23 international who scored 64 goals in 84 games at Luton. Now lives in Bournemouth where he runs a newsagents.

O'SHEA, Danny
Arsenal, Charlton, Exeter, Southend, Camb U, Northampton, 1982-1995

Now player/coach at Northampton Town and is former manager of Arsenal Women's reserve team.

O'SULLIVAN, Peter
Man U, Brighton, Fulham, Charlton, Reading, Aldershot, 1968-1983

Peter played over 400 games for Brighton in a ten year spell on the south coast and is now an insurance salesman in Sussex.

OAKES, Alan
Man C, Chester, Port V, 1959-1983

Alan made his debut for Manchester City in 1959 and was still going strong 22 years later at Chester City. He was one of the cornerstones in the great side of Mercer and Allison. He joined Chester in July 1976 in a player/manager role and returned to the club as a coach.

League Championship, FA Cup, European Cup Winners Cup and League Cup winner.

OGLEY, Alan
Barnsley, Man City, Stockport, Darlington, 1962-1976

Stockport County's first choice keeper for many years now lives in Barnsley, working for a haulage contractor.

OLSEN, Jesper
Man U 1984-1988

A Danish international winger who became a popluar import with the Manchester United fans when he joined United from Ajax. Retired because of injury and now lives in Alderley Edge, Cheshire, and runs a sports management company with Kevin Moran.

Played in the 1985 FA Cup final against Everton.

ORMSBY, Brendan
Aston V, Leeds, Shrewsbury, Doncaster, 1978-1993

Former Villa and Leeds defender is currently playing for Garforth Town, having previously been assistant manager at Farsley Celtic and manager of Waterford in Ireland.

OSBORNE, John
Chesterfield, WBA, Walsall, 1960-1972

A product of Chesterfield's great goalkeeping 'academy', Osborne kept goal for West Bromwich Albion for almost ten years. Once ran a sports wear business with Jim Cumbes and in later years worked in the promotions department of the Sandwell & Birmingham Evening Mail.

Now commercial manager at Worcestershire Cricket Club.

OSBORNE, Roger

Ipswich, Colchester, 1973-1985

Now drives a fruit and veg lorry for one of his brothers and is still playing back at his very first club, Westerfield United. Helps out at Portman Road's school of excellence a few hours each week.

Scored the winner in the 1978 FA Cup final for Ipswich.

OSGOOD, Peter

Chelsea, Southampton, Norwich, Chelsea, 1964-1979

Windsor born Ossie achieved god-like status at Stamford Bridge but was only capped four times by England. After retiring he ran a pub and later became youth team coach at Portsmouth until the end of the 1987/8 season. Now lives near Southampton and is a very popular after dinner speaker, acts as match day host at Chelsea, arranges celebrity golfing breaks, as well as being able to find time to give expert analysis for Sky TV.

OTTO, Heine

Middlesboro 1981-1984

Was an executive with Den Haag FC back home in Holland. Now involved with the youth team at Ajax.

OWEN, Brian

Watford, Colchester, Wolves, 1962-1972

Former Watford winger who was reserve team manager at Ipswich and is now physio at Colchester United.

Third Division Championship with Watford in 1969.

OWEN, Gary

Man C, WBA, Sheff Wed, 1975-1987

A skilful midfield player whose career was marred by a series of injuries. During his time with Manchester City he won England recognition at youth, 'B' and under-21 levels and holds the record for most under-21 caps (22). Had a spell in Cyprus after being released by Sheffield Wednesday, then retired in 1989 to become an art dealer running 'Gary Owen Fine Art' from his Manchester base.

PADDON, Graham

Coventry, Norwich, West Ham, Norwich, Millwall, 1968-1981

Classy England under-23 international midfielder. His second spell as assistant manager at Pompey lasted until February 1995.

FA Cup winner with West Ham in 1975.

PAGE, Malcolm

Birmingham, Oxford, 1964-1982

Long serving Birmingham defender who won 28 Welsh caps during his eighteen year career. Melcolm retired in March 1982 to work as an insurance representative.

PAINE, Terry

Southampton, Hereford, 1956-1976

Played a massive 713 League games for Southampton between 1956 and 1973 during which time he was capped 19 times by England. He signed as player/coach at Hereford in August 1974, but has now been a football coach in South Africa for several years, interupted by a brief return to Coventry City.

His number of League appearances is second only to Peter Shilton.

PAISLEY, Bob

Liverpool 1946-1953

Bob is a one club man who gave Liverpool sterling service. It was as long ago as 1939 that he joined the Merseysiders as a player from Bishop Auckland. A left half, he had

played in Bishop's FA Amateur Cup winning team in April of that year. After his war service Bob returned to Anfield and remained as a player with the club until 1954, when he was appointed to Liverpool's training staff. He succeeded the late Bill Shankly as Liverpool's manager in 1974 and enjoyed spectacular success until his retirement in 1983. Died in February in a Liverpool nursing home following a long illness.
Won the League Championship as a player with Liverpool.

PALIN, Leigh
Shrewsbury, Notts F, Bradford C, Stoke, Hull, Rochdale, 1983-1992
Promotions officer and player for Immingham Town in South Humberside.

PALIOS, Mark
Tranmere, Crewe, Tranmere R, 1973-1984
Former midfielder. Now a Chartered Accountant working for a firm of liquidators, and living in Lode, near Cambridge.

PALMER, Geoff
Wolves, Burnley, Wolves, 1973-1986
Geoff played over 400 games for Wolves and won 12 England under-23 caps. Now a police constable stationed at Darlaston, having joined the West Midlands force in 1986.
Played in two League Cup winning sides.

PARDOE, Glyn
Man C 1961-1974
Former England under-23 international who was working on the coaching staff until he was sacked by Peter Reid in May 1992 and now works for a security company.
Scored the winner in the 1970 League Cup final.

PARK, Terry
Stockport, Man C, Bury, 1974-1983
Bought and ran a post office for seven years, but in 1990 joined a Liverpool haulage firm.

PARKER, Albert
Crewe, Wrexham, 1948-1958
Wrexham defender of the fifties and was the clubs groundsman and a Town Councillor. Now retired but still living in Wrexham.

PARKER, Alex
Falkirk, Everton, Southport, 1952-1967
Former Scottish Player of the Year prior to his move south. Managed Southport and also had a brief spell in management in Northern Ireland, before taking a pub called 'The Swinging Sporron'. Then returned to his native Scotland to run a pub in Gretna Green.
Won FA Cups on both sides of the border.

PARKER, Bobby
Coventry, Carlisle, 1969-1983
Played over 400 League games before becoming a health & safety officer for a foods firm in Carlisle.

PARKER, Derrick
Burnley, Southend, Barnsley, Oldham, Doncaster, Burnley, Rochdale, 1974-1987
Lives in Barnsley and works as a salesman for a brick manufacturing company. Has been in sales since 1989 and in his current job since 1991 - previously with Doncaster Rovers as Community Officer.

PARKER, John Willie
Everton, Bury, 1950-1958
After five years at Everton went to Bury in 1956, but eventually returned to Merseyside where he worked in a pub. Died 1988.

PARKER, Tommy
Ipswich 1946-1956

Long serving player and captain for Ipswich Town, for whom he notched up 493 appearances. Became a publican and worked in a timber merchants before returning to Portman Road as commercial manager, a post that he held for 19 years until his retirement. Died in early 1996.

PARKES, Harry
Aston V 1946-1954
Played 320 games for Villa before retiring in 1955 to concentrate on his flourishing sports-outfitters business, which he still runs today in Corporation Street, Birmingham. He was appointed to the Aston Villa board and later elected to the board of Birmingham City.

PARKES, Phil
Walsall, QPR, West Ham, Ipswich, 1968-1990
The Hammers smashed the transfer record for a goalkeeper to take Phil across London to Upton Park in 1979 when they paid £560,000. Returned to Queens Park Rangers in September 1991 as goalkeeping coach.
Played for West Ham in the 1980 FA Cup final.

PARKES, Tony
Blackburn, 1970-1980
A former Rovers favourite who played nearly 350 times for the club before a broken leg ended his career. Was caretaker boss for a short spell before becoming assistant manager to Don Mackay at Ewood Park and is now chief coach.
Won promotions in 1975 and 1980.

PARKIN, Derek
Huddersfield, Wolves, Stoke, 1964-1982
Wolves' long serving left-back who was signed from Huddersfield for £80,000 to set a record for a full back. Lives in Wheaton Aston, near Bridgenorth, and works as a professional gardener.
Holds the Wolves record for most number of career and League appearances.

PARKIN, Tim
Blackburn, Bristol R, Swindon, Port V,

Shrewsbury, 1976-1992
A well travelled central defender who became football in the community officer at Middlesborough until he left to join the police force.

PARKINSON, Noel
Ipswich, Bristol Rovers, Brentford, Mansfield, Scunthorpe, Colchester, 1976-1986
After being forced to retire through injury, Noel now commentates on football for local radio in the Scunthorpe area.

PARLANE, Derek
Rangers, Leeds U, Man C, Swansea, Rochdale, 1970-1987
A full Scottish international before he joined Leeds and ended his career after two spells in Kong Kong. Now a sportswear agent in the north-west of England, living in Wilmslow, Cheshire.
Won two Scottish League Championships.

PARSONS, Lindsay
Bristol R, Torquay, 1963-1978
Played 353 league games for Bristol Rovers and was manager of Cheltenham Town for four years. Is now assistant to Tony Pulis at Gillingham.

PARTRIDGE, Malcolm
Mansfield, Leicester, Charlton, Grimsby, Scunthorpe, 1967-1981
A tall striker who had a long career with five clubs. Now runs the Millfields Hotel in Grimsby.

PASHLEY, Terry
Burnley, Blackpool, Bury, 1973-1988
A left back who played over 400 career games and is now youth team coach at Burnley.
A former England schoolboy international.

PATE, Alex 'Sandy'
Watford, Mansfield, 1964-1977
Played over 400 games for Mansfield. Now a publican at 'the Travellers Rest' in Ashfield, Notts.

PATES, Colin
Chelsea, Charlton, Arsenal, Brighton, 1979-1994

A commanding central defender who was forced to quit in December 1994 due to a knee injury. Colin joined Crawley and was appointed as their manager in May 1995 but left less than six months later. Also helped out at the Arsenal school of excellence.
Division Two Championship medal in 1984 with Chelsea.

PAUL, Roy
Swansea, Man C, 1944-1956

Joined Swansea City during the War and played 160 League games before making the unusual move to South America to join Bogota. Returned to the UK to play for ManchesterCity and was capped 33 times by Wales. Roy is now retired from his job as a lorry driver and lives in Mid Glamorgan.
Helped Man City to FA Cup success in 1956.

PAYNE, Clive
Norwich, Bournemouth, 1965-1976

A right back who played over 100 games for each of his two clubs. Ran a sports shop, but has now been in the window trade for a number of years.

PAYNE, George
Tranmere 1946-1960

Goalkeeper who played over 400 League games for his only club. No longer alive.

PEACH, David
Gillingham, Southampton, Swindon, Leyton O, 1969-1982

Former England under-23 international full back who enjoyed a long League career is now working in the building trade and living in Milford on Sea, near Lymington, Hampshire.
FA Cup final winner in 1976 with the Saints.

PEACOCK, Alan
Middlesboro, Leeds, Plymouth, 1955-1967

Won full England caps after scoring 153 league goals in 284 league games for Boro in the fifties and sixties. Now co-owner of a cleaning products business after opening a newsagents upon retirement.
Helped Leeds into Division One in 1964.

PEACOCK, Keith
Charlton 1962-1978

Appeared in over 500 league games for the Addicks during a sixteen year career. A former Gillingham manager who is now reserve team coach at Charlton Athletic. Father of Gavin, who plays for Chelsea.

PEAKE, Andy
Leicester, Grimsby, Charlton, Middlesboro, 1978-1992

A former England youth international who never lived up to his early promise. After a stint as manager of Ayssriska in Sweden, is now back in the UK having joined the police force.
Second Division Championship with Leicester.

PEARCE, Jimmy
Tottenham 1968-1972

England youth international who was a very skillful winger on his da. Finished playing at the age of only 25 after suffering from a rare bone complaint. Is now working in the fashion industry, running a clothes shop in Essex.
Won a League Cup final with Spurs in 1973.

PEARSON, Jim
St Johnstone, Everton, Newcastle, 1974-1979

Scottish under-23 international who moved south to join Everton from St Johnstone in 1974. Now works for Nike.

PEARSON, John
Sheffield Weds, Charlton, Leeds, Rotherham, Barnsley, Hull City, Carlisle, Mansfield, Cardiff, 1981-1995

A former England youth international who was forced to quit the game with a neck injury. Now plays non-league football and works as an insurance salesman.
Leading scorer for Charlton when they won promotion to the First Division in 1985.

PEARSON, Lawrie
Hull, Bristol C, Port Vale, 1984-1987
Former Hull City full back is now a football
in the community officer at Middlesbrough
and plays for Whitby Town in the Northern
League.

PEARSON, Stan
Man U, Bury, Chester, 1937-1958
A key figure in Busby's first side who played
eight times for England after the war.
Became a newsagent and is now retired, liv-
ing in Prestbury, Lancashire.
Division One Champion in 1952.

PEARSON, Stuart
Hull C, Man U, West Ham, 1969-1981

Began his pro career at Hull City and moved
to Manchester United in 1974 for £200,000,
scoring 55 goals in 139 league games and
winning 15 England caps. Since ending his
career at West Ham, Stuart has held coaching and managerial posts at Stockport,
Northwich Victoria, West Brom, and more
recently was assistant manager at Bradford
City. Lives in Sale, Cheshire.
FA Cup winner with West Ham in 1980.

PEJIC, Mel
Stoke City, Hereford, Wrexham, 1977-1994
Commanding central defender and brother
of Mike is now physio at Wrexham.

*Played a record 412 league games for
Hereford between 1980 and 1992.*

PEJIC, Mike
Stoke, Everton, Aston Villa, 1968-1979
A former England international who had
spells as assistant manager of Port Vale and
coaching in Kuwait before becoming manager of Chester City in 1994. However, Mike
was sacked in January 1995.
*Played for Stoke in the 1972 League Cup
Final.*

PENDRY, Gary
Birmingham, WBA, Torquay, Bristol R,
Walsall, 1966-1982
Managed former club, Birmingham City,
where he has played over 300 games, then
worked at Wolves as a coach until the arrival
of Graham Taylor. After scouting for Derby
County is now coaching at Coventry City.

PENK, Harry
Portsmouth, Plymouth, Soton, 1955-1963
Lives in Southampton and works as a
painter and decorator.

PENMAN, Willie
Glasgow Rangers, Newcastle, Swindon,
Walsall, 1962-1972
Scottish born midfielder who settled in the
West Midlands and is a sales representative
for sports goods firm.
*Substitute for Swindon in the 1969 League
Cup final.*

PERRIN, Steve
C Palace, Plymouth, Portsmouth,
Northampton, 1976-1982
Midfielder who moved into League football
at a late age and is now deputy headmaster
at a primary school in Bushey, Herts. Is also
physical training instructor with Hillingdon
FC.

PERRY, Bill
Blackpool, Southport, 1949-1962
A South African who was capped by
England and scorer of the winning goal in
the 1953 Cup final. Now in business as a

promotional match-book manufacturer near Preston, but still lives in Blackpool.
Capped three times by England in 1956.

PERRYMAN, Steve
Tottenham, Oxford, Brentford, 1969-1989
Won only one England cap but holds the Spurs record for the most number of League games played, (655). Was manager of Brentford and Watford before returning to Tottenham Hotspur as assistant manager then briefly caretaker manager prior to Gerry Francis arriving at White Hart Lane. Since January 1995 has been assistant to Ardiles at Shimizu S-Pulse of Japan's J-League.
Fairs Cup and UEFA Cup winner with Spurs.

PETERS, Gary
Reading, Fulham, Wimbledon, Aldershot, Reading, Fulham, 1975-1989
Played nearly 300 games for Reading then went into management with Cambridge. Took his present club, Preston, to the Third Division title in 1996.

PETCHEY, George
West Ham, QPR, Crystal Palace, 1952-1963
Played over 400 games at wing half for his three clubs and also managed Leyton Orient. After a long spell out of the game was appointed coach at Brighton.

PETERS, Martin
West Ham, Tottenham, Norwich, Sheff U, 1961-1980

Peters was one of the great talents of the modern game and was once described by the England tam manager, Alf Ramsey, as "ten years ahead of his time". He was a member of the 1966 World Cup winning side before signing for Spurs in March 1970 to become Britain's first £200,000 player. Later he played for Norwich and in 1980 made a step towards management when he became player/manager to Sheffield United. After deciding to pursue a business career outside the game, he works for the same motor insurance company as his former West Ham and England striking partner, Geoff Hurst.
Won UEFA Cup and Fairs Cup winners medals.

PEYTON, Gerry
Burnley, Fulham, Southend, Bournemouth, Everton, Bolton, Brentford, West Ham, 1975-1994
Played in over 600 league games before moving to Japan in a player coach capacity, but is now in Hong Kong.

PHILLIPS, Ernie
Man C, Hull, York, 1948-1957
Skipper of the famous York City team that reached the FA Cup semi-finals in 1954-5 as a Third Division North club. Now retired but can be found playing indoor bowls in York.

PHILLIPS, John
Shrewsbury, Aston V, Chelsea, Crewe, Brighton, Charlton, C Palace, 1968-1983
Welsh international goakeeper who played 125 games for Chelsea in the seventies. Now runs the motor factors company that he set up in Mitcham, while still playing for Crystal Palace.
Both his father and grandfather played League football.

PHILLIPS, Len
Portsmouth 1946-1954
Inside forward who won eight post war England caps. Worked for an engineering firm in the city from 1959 but is now retired, living in Hilsea, Portsmouth.
Twice a League Champion with Pompey.

PHILLIPS, Leighton

Cardiff, Aston V, Swansea, Charlton, Exeter, 1967-1982

Welsh international who won over 58 full caps for his countr and played over 500 games in a long career. Lives in Neath and has worked for Confederation Life insurance company since retiring from professional football. He is now a senior life underwriter for the company.
League Cup winner with Villa.

PHILLIPS, Steve

Birmingham, Torquay, Northampton, Brentford, Northampton, Southend, Torquay, Peterboro, 1971-1987
Played over 700 games scoring 250 goals in his career. Took to selling double glazing in the Peterborough area.

PHILPOTTS, Dave

Coventry, Southport, Tranmere, 1971-1984
Now on the scouting staff at Tranmere Rovers after spells as Wigan boss and then youth team coach at Stockport County.

PICKERING, Fred

Blackburn, Everton, Birmingham, Blackpool, Blackburn, 1959-1970
Won three England caps before retiring from soccer in 1971. Lives in his home town of Blackburn and is a fork lift truck driver at a local factory.

PICKERING, John

Newcastle, Halifax, Barnsley, 1963-1974
First team coach at Middlesborough, having previously coached at Blackburn, Bolton, Carlisle, Lincoln and Newcastle.

PICKWICK, Don

Norwich 1947-1956
Played nearly 250 League games during his career and hung up his boots after a spell in non-league football. Now lives in Melbourne, Australia.
Broke his leg in Norwich's record 8-1 away win at Shrewsbury.

PIERCE, Gary

Huddersfield, Wolves, Barnsley, Blackpool, 1971-1983
Returned to play non-league football for his first club, Mosseley. Now living near Bolton, Gary is currently unemployed and having to rely on invalidity benefit as a result of back trouble.
Division Two title winner with Wolves in 1977.

PIPER, Norman

Plymouth, Portsmouth, 1964-1977
After signing from Plymouth, this stylish England under-23 international served Portsmouth for more than 350 matches. Moved over to America to play for Fort Lauderdale Strikers and then on to become assistant coach for the Wichita Wings. Now believed to be living in Canada.

PIPER, Steve

Brighton, Portsmouth, 1972-1978
Former Seagulls and Pompey defender who is now a mortgage and insurance broker living in Southwick, Sussex.

PLATT, Jim

Middlesboro, Hartlepool, Cardiff, 1971-1982
Middlesbrough's goalkeeper for over ten years who was capped 22 times by Northern Ireland. Played 401 League games then ran a fashion business in Ballymena, Northern Ireland before being appointed manager of Darlington.

P

PLATT, John
Oldham, Bury, Bolton, Tranmere, Preston, 1975-1985
Now lives in Ashton-under-Lyme and works for the community programme attached to Oldham Athletic.

PLEAT, David
Notts F, Luton, Shrewsbury, Exeter, Peterborough, 1961-1970
Won England schoolboy and youth honours as a player but made his name in management, initially by guiding Luton Town to the First Division in 1978. Spells at Spurs, Leicester and a second stint at Luton followed, before David eventually joined Sheffield Wednesday in June 1995.

PLUMMER, Calvin
Notts F, Chesterfield, Derby, Barnsley, Plymouth, Chesterfield, 1981-1990
Since 1990 has had spells with Gainsborough Trinity, Shepshed Albion, Corby Town and Nuneaton Borough. Now plays for Leicestershire Senior League side Birstall Utd.

PLUMMER, Norman
Leicester, Mansfield, 1947-1955
Centre half, who played his first and last games at City as a centre forward. A clothing retailer until his retirement, he still lives in Leicester.
Captained Leicester's 1949 Cup final side.

PODD, Ces
Bradford, Halifax, Scarboro, 1970-1987
Ces was born on the Island of St Kitts. Now community officer at Leeds having previously managed Eccleshill in the North East Counties League.
His 502 League games is a Bradford record.

POINTER, Ray
Burnley, Bury, Coventry, Portsmouth, 1957-1972
Won three England caps during his time with Burnley and worked as commercial manager at Turf Moor and youth coach at Bury before retiring in 1990 aged only 54.
Won a League Championship medal with Burnley in 1960.

POOLE, Terry
Huddersfield, Bolton, Sheff U, 1968-1979
Former Manchester United apprentice who now lives in Wingerworth near Chesterfield and is manager of a cash & carry video wholesalers.

PORTERFIELD, Ian
Raith, Sunderland, Reading, Sheff Wed, 1967-1979
Made his name with Sunderland and went into management after his playing days. Acted as national team manager to Zambia, who lost eighteen of their players in a disastrous air crash in 1993, then moved back to the UK to take up a position with Bolton, until moving to Wothing, who he left in September 1996.
Scored the winning goal in the 1973 FA Cup final for Sunderland.

PORTEUS, Trevor
Hull, Stockport, 1951-1964
Was deputy officer at an old peoples home in Stockport. Underwent heart bypass surgery in 1990, but is now fully recovered and is a regular visitor to Stockport County, where during his 40 year love affair with the club he had been sacked three times and left on his own accord more than once.

PORTWOOD, Cliff
Preston, Port V, Grimsby, Portsmouth, 1955-1968
Reached the final of the BBC TV programme 'Rising Stars' in 1980 - as a singer! These days makes his living as a licensee, having run several pubs in the Alton area of Hampshire.

POSSEE, Derek
Tottenham, Millwall, Crystal Palace, Orient, 1963-1977
Despite being a regular scorer for the reserve side Derek failed to hold down a regular first team place in the face of stiff competition and moved to Millwall for £25,000. When his

career ended in this country he spent three summers playing in Canada for the Vancouver Whitecaps where he later settled there and worked as a coach for the Canadian FA.

POTTS, Harry
Burnley, Everton, 1946-1955
An inside forward bor Burnley and Everton who then became an outstanding manager for Burnley. Lived in the town until his death in January 1996 aged 75.
Took Burnley to a League Championship in 1960.

POUNTNEY, Ron
Walsall, Port V, Southend, 1973-1984
Playing almost 350 league games for Southend. Now a painter & decorator in the Southend area.

POWELL, Barry
Wolves, Coventry, Derby, Burnley, Swansea, Wolves, 1972-1987
England under-23 midfield star who turned out for six clubs. Now working with the football in the community scheme based at Coventry City, having previously been first team coach at Wolves between 1987 and 1991,
1974 League Cup final winner with Wolves.

POWELL, Colin
Charlton, Gillingham, 1972-1982
Paddy has two spells with the Addicks either side of a period in America for New England. Was coach and assistant manager at Bromley and is now groundsman at Charlton Athletic's ground, The Valley.

POWELL, David
Wrexham, Sheff U, Cardiff, 1962-1974
Capped eleven times for Wales in the sixties. Joined the police force at Bridgend in 1974.

POWELL, Steve
Derby 1971-1984
England under-23 international who played over 350 games for Derby. Manages a sports centre in the Derby area. His son is following the family tradition and is now on the books at the Baseball Ground.
League Championship with Derby in 1975.

POWELL, Thomas
Derby 1948-1961
Father of Steve. Still lives in Derby having played 380 league games and is a keen Rams follower.

POWELL, Tony
Norwich 1974-1981
Played 272 games for Norwich before having a couple of spells in the NASL. Thought to be living in San Francisco.
League Cup runner up in 1975.

POWER, Paul
Man C, Everton, 1975-1987
Paul joined City from Leeds Polytechnic before going on to make 350 appearances for the Maine Road club. Coached at Everton, then joined the PFA as a community officer, but is now working for them as a coaching secretary.
League Championship winner with Everton.

PRATT, John
Tottenham 1968-1979
When dismissed from his post as assistant manager at Spurs in 1986, he left League soccer and landed a coaching job in Nigeria, eventually returning to Chigwell to set up his own window cleaning business. Joined the backroom staff at Stevenage Borough FC for a short spell and was joint manager of Worthing until September 1996.

PRESLAND, Eddie
West Ham, C Palace, Colchester, 1964-1969
Former defender who now lives in Chelmsford and is a games instructor at Stepney Green School. Has also scouted for Ipswich Town.

PRICE, David
Arsenal, Peterboro, C Palace, Leyton O, 1972-1982
David played over 100 games for the Gunners. Joined Palace in 1981 but was

forced to quit through injury less than two years later. Now a mini cab driver and plays for West Wickham in the southern amateur league.
FA Cup winner with Arsenal in 1979.

PRICE, Johnny
Burnley, Stockport, Blackburn, Stockport, 1960-1975
Licensee of the 'Grey Horse' pub in Heaton Norris, near Stockport, until committing suicide in Stockport in 1994.

PRICE, Paul
Luton, Tottenham, Swansea, Peterboro, 1971-1987
A solid central defender who played 25 matches for Wales. After making his name at Luton, Price joined Tottenham Hotspur in a £200,000 deal in 1981, then had spells at Swansea and Peterborough before moving into non-league soccer. Was player boss at Hitchin Town with Micky Hazard until they were both sacked in September 1996.

PRING, Keith
Newport, Rotherham, Notts Co, Southport, 1961-1970
Now a sales representative for Bass Charrington in West Lancashire.

PRITCHARD, Roy
Wolves, Aston Villa, Notts Co, Port V, 1946-1959
Tough tackling full eback who made his name with Wolves before moving to Villa but broke his jaw on on league debut for them. Continued to play in charity matches until 1990, three years before his death at Willenhall in March 1993.
League Championship winner with Wolves.

PRITCHETT, Keith
Wolves, Doncaster, QPR, Brentford, Watford, Blackpool, 1972-1984
A well travelled Scotsman who was three times handed a free transfer. Emigrated to New Zealand where he became a successful manager and later a football journalist.

PROBERT, Eric
Burnley, Notts Co, Darlington 1968-1979
Retired to become landlord of a pub in North Yorkshire.

PROVAN, David
Rangers, C. Palace, Plymouth, St Mirren, 1958-1975
Scottish international defender who moved south spending four years with Plymouth Argyle. Now based at Morton where he works as Scottish youth development officer.
A Double double-winner with Rangers.

PROVAN, Davie
Kilmarnock, Celtic, 1974-1986
David was once transferred for a Scottish record £120,000. He now has a successful media career with SKY and BBC Radio.
Four times Scottish League champion with Celtic.

PUCKETT, Dave
Southampton, Bournemouth, Stoke, Swansea, Aldershot, Bournemouth, 1980-1992
Played for Woking in their FA Vase victory but is now a player with Newport IOW in the BHL.

PUGH Graham
Sheff Wed, Huddersfield, Chester, Barnsley, Scunthorpe, 1965-1980
Graham won England under-23 international caps and enjoyed a fifteen year career. He is now a publican in Sheffield close to Hillsborough.
Played for Wednesday in the 1966 FA Cup final.

PULIS, Tony
Bristol R, Newport, Bournemouth, Gillingham, Bournemouth, 1975-1994
Manager of AFC Bournemouth until August 1994. Returned to Priestfield eleven months later taking them to promotion in his first season.
Won a Division Three Championship with Newport County in 1987.

PURDIE, Bernard
Wrexham, Chester, Crewe, Huddersfield, Crewe, 1968-1982
Played over 200 games for Crewe Alex and now works as a postman in Wrexham.

QUAIRNEY, John
Rotherham 1948-1959
Goalkeeper who played over 260 games for Rotherham. Now working for Charlton Bros. in Scotland.

QUINN, Jimmy
Swindon, Blackburn, Swindon, Leicester, Bradford C, West Ham, Bournemouth, Reading, 1981-1996
Appointed joint player/manager at Reading in January 1995.
Capped over 50 times by Northern Ireland.

QUINN, Johnny
Sheff Wed, Rotherham, Halifax, 1959-1974
One of Wednesday's stars of the sixties. Now has a sports outfitting business in Hillsborough, Sheffield.
Played in the 1966 FA Cup final.

QUINN, Mick
Derby, Wigan, Stockport, Oldham, Portsmouth, Newcastle, Coventry, Plymouth, Watford, 1978-1995
A top class goal poacher who had a spell in prison as well. Finished his career in Greece and now works as a trainee racehorse trainer.
Played a part in Newcastle's 1993 Division One Championship winning side.

QUIXALL, Albert
Sheff Wed, Man U, Oldham, Stockport, 1950-1966
A full England international who was also capped at three other levels. Joined United post Munich for a then British record fee of £45,000. Now a scrap dealer in the Manchester area.
Division Two Champion with Wednesday in 1952 and 1956.

RADFORD, John
Arsenal, West Ham, Blackburn, 1963-1978
A true Gunners legend to rank along side Bastin and James. Became a publican in Essex and is now general manager of Bishops Stortford FC of the ICIS League.
An Arsenal double winner.

RADFORD, Ron
Leeds, Newport, Hereford, 1961-1973

Scorer of a famous FA Cup goal for Hereford against Newcastle United, Ronnie now lives in Wakefield and runs his own joinery business. He also manages Ossett Albion.
Played for Hereford in their first ever league game, against Colchester in 1972.

RAFFERTY, Billy
Coventry, Blackpool, Plymouth, Carlisle, Wolves, Newcastle, Portsmouth, Bournemouth, 1969-1984
Played in Portugal for several years and at the age of 37 scored 20 goals in the 1987-8 season to spark Loultanos's bid for promotion to the Portuguese first division. Now runs a health and fitness club in Carlisle.

RAFFERTY, Ron
Portsmouth, Grimsby, Hull, Aldershot, 1954-1968
Ron scored 145 goals in his 264 games for Grimsby between 1956-1962. Medically retired through arthritis, he is now living in Aldershot, Hampshire.

RAMSEY, Sir Alf
Southampton, Tottenham, 1946-1954
Started his career at Southampton but
moved to Spurs in 1949, where he helped
them to Second and First Division titles in
successive years. Was appointed England
manager in 1963, and three years later led
them to World Cup glory earning a knight-
hood the following year. Remained manager
until 1974 then retired to Suffolk.
World Cup winner in 1966.

RANDALL, Kevin
Bury, Chesterfield, Notts Co, Mansfield, York,
1965-1980
Currently assistant manager at Chesterfield.

RANDALL, Paul
Bristol R, Stoke, Bristol R, 1977-1985
Scored just under 100 goals in two spells at
Rovers . Was groundsman at the Tor Leisure
Centre and is now in the building industry,
living in Glastonbury, Somerset.
Promoted to Division One with Stoke in 1979.

RANKIN, Andy
Everton, Watford, Huddersfield, 1963-1981
An England under-23 international goalkeeper who was an understudy at Everton
before moving to Watford. Is now a warehouseman for a Huddersfield firm.

RANKMORE, Frank
Cardiff, Peterboro, Northampton, 1961-1970
Centre half who played over 200 games for
Peterboro. Now a publican in Cardiff.
Won one Welsh cap.

RANSON, Ray
Man C, Birmingham, Newcastle, 1978-1994
Ray won ten England under-23 caps during
his time with Man City. Appointed
player/manager at Witton Albion in 1995.
Played for City in the 1981 FA Cup final.

RATCLIFFE, Kevin
Everton, Cardiff, Derby, Chester, 1979-1995
Won 56 caps for Wales in.a long career
which saw him rated among the best
defenders in the world. Was appointed

Chester boss in April 1995.
*Won two League Championships, a Cup
Winners Cup and FA Cup winners medal.*

RATTRAY, Peter
Dundee, Plymouth, Norwich, Stirling Albion,
St Johnstone, 1946-1954
A Scottish war time international who was a
big success on both sides of the border.
Lives in retirement in Alloa.
Played in the 1946 Scottish Cup Final.

REAGAN, Martin
York, Hull, Middlesboro, Shrewsbury,
Portsmouth, Norwich, 1946-1955
Winger who appeared for six league clubs
during the fifties. Was manager of the
England Womens team.

REANEY, Paul
Leeds, Bradford C, 1962-1979
Stylish defender who played over 745 games
for Leeds United and was capped three
times by England before moving to Bradford
City in 1978. Was voted Australia's player of
the year in 1980 but now lives near
Knaresborough and runs coaching courses
for the World in Sport organisation as well as
being a partner in the Classic Portrait
Company.
Won two Football League Championships.

REDKNAPP, Harry
West Ham, Bournemouth, Brentford,
Bournemouth, 1965-1982
East End born Redknapp played on the West
Ham wing for six years prior to moving to
Bournemouth. Became manager of The
Cherries until accepting the role of assistant
manager at West Ham in 1992, where he
became manager in 1994.
*Lead Bournemouth to a Third Division title in
1987.*

REECE, Gil
Cardiff, Newport, Sheff U, Cardiff Swansea,
1961-1976
Best remembered for his time at Sheffield
United, Gil ended his days back in Wales, for
whom he won 29 caps, before setting up a

successful plumbing and heating business with his brother. Now runs a hotel in Cardiff.

REES, Ronnie
Coventry, WBA, Notts F, Swansea, 1962-1974
Retired in 1975 and worked behind the scenes at Cardiff City before taking a job with a large car manufacturer in Bridgend.

REEVES, Derek
Southampton, Bournemouth, 1954-1964
Derek topped Saints goal charts in four consecutive seasons. Moved to Bournemouth in 1962, where he continued to live and work as a representative for a building firm then as an ambulance driver for Dorset Social Services. Died of cancer in 1995 aged 60.
Scored 39 goals in 1960 – a Soton record.

REEVES, Kevin
Bournemouth, Norwich, Man C, Burnley, 1974-1983
An England international who began with Bournemouth and moved to Norwich for £50,000 in February 1977. Joined the 'Million Pound Club' when sold by John Bond, then manager of Norwich City, to Manchester City in 1980 for £1,250,000. Now assistant manager at Wrexham.
Scored a penalty for City in the 1991 FA Cup final replay.

REID, Duggie
Stockport, Portsmouth, 1936-1955
Former Pompey inside forward Duggie is now retired in Portsmouth, having been groundsman at Fratton Park for 20 years.

REID, John
Hamilton, Bradford C, Northampton, Luton, Torquay, Rochdale, 1957-1967
Played over 400 league games in a decade south of the border and is now a newsagent in Bradford.

REID, Peter
Bolton, Everton, QPR, Man C, Bury, Soton, Bolton, Sunderland, 1971-1995
England international midfield star who started his management career at Man City

and put his boots back on at Bury, Southampton, Sunderland and Bolton after leaving Maine Road. Appointed player/manager at Sunderland in March 1995.
Played in three successive Cup finals with Everton but ended up on losing side twice.

REILLY, George
Northampton, Camb U, Watford, Newcastle, WBA, Camb U, 1976-1988
A powerful striker who shot to fame after scoring the winner in the 1984 FA Cup semi final whilst at Watford. Forced to quit through injury and now runs his own building firm in Ely, Cambs.
FA Cup runner-up in 1984.

RELISH, John
Chester, Newport, 1972-1986
Managed Newport County, the club he played for over twelve years. Now a training officer for football in the community, based in Newport, which he combines with being assistant manager of Weston-Super-Mare.

REYNOLDS, Ritchie
Plymouth, Portsmouth, 1964-1975

Former Argyle and Pompey defender who owned a fish and chip shop in Portsmouth and also had a spell as manager of Fareham Town. Now runs a sandwich bar in Fratton.

REYNOLDS, Ron
Aldershot, Tottenham, Soton, 1945-1963
Understudy to Ted Ditchburn and then John
Hollowbread, became a deadline day trans-
fer to the Saints for £10,000. After three sea-
sons, a shoulder injury forced him to quit.
Later scouted for Saints and Crystal Palace
before setting up his own insurance agency.
Now retired living in Haslemere.
Third Division Championship with Soton.

REVIE, Don
Leicester, Hull, Man C, Sunderland, Leeds,
1946-1961
Died in May 1989 after a courageous fight
against motor neurone disease. In an
extremely successful management career he
won two League titles, League Cup, FA Cup
and the European Fairs Cup with Leeds
United. Despite being banned from English
Football for ten years after giving up the
England manager's job to take a lucrative
post in the United Arab Emirates, he will
always be remembered as one of the great
motivators. Shortly before his death he asked
that his ashes be strewn over the Leeds
pitch and in 1994 his wife Elsie opened the
new Don Revie North Stand at Elland Road.

RHODES-BROWN, Peter
Chelsea, Oxford, 1979-1988
Works in the commercial office at Oxford
United. Was also player/manager at Marlow
FC and was a member of their side which
knocked his employers out of the 1994/5 FA
Cup! Now plays for Abingdon Town.

RICE, Pat
Arsenal, Watford, 1967-1983
Belfast born, Rice came through the
Highbury junior ranks to turn professional in
1966. Went on to play nearly 400 league
games for the Gunners, also gaining 49 caps
for his country. Pat then joined Watford in
1980 where he gained promotion to the First
Division in 1981/2 and then next season finishing runners up to Liverpool. Returned to
Arsenal as youth team coach but is now
assistant manager.
Won the double with the Gunners in 1971.

RICHARDS, John
Wolves, Derby, 1969-1982

Joined Wolves straight from school. Now
Head of Leisure for Staffordshire Council.
Still a hero at Molineux, John was made a
Director of the Club in early 1995.
*Scored the winning goal when they defeated
Man City in the 1974 League Cup final.*

RICHARDS, John
Swindon, Norwich, Aldershot, 1956-1962
Retired as a director of Thorn EMI, and is
now a self employed consultant specialising
in industrial relations.

RICHARDS, Pedro
Notts Co 1974-1985
Played almost 400 league games for County.
Pedro is now a builder in Nottingham.

RICHARDS, Tony
Birmingham, Walsall, Port V, 1951-1965
Went on to net more goals for Walsall than
anyone had done before, including the leg-
endary Gilbert Alsop. Now working for a tyre
company in Walsall.

RICHARDSON, Damien
Gillingham 1972-1980
Republic of Ireland international, who after
playing over 300 games for Gillingham has
returned to Ireland to manage Cork City.

RICKABY, Stan
Middlesboro, WBA, 1947-1954
Capped once by England, Rickaby was a strong right back who retired in 1964. He went into insurance before emigrating to Australia in 1969. Now living in Perth, Australia and works in accountancy.

RICKARD, Derek
Plymouth, Bournemouth, 1969-1975
Now a newsagent in Plymouth and chairman of Oak Villa FC in the local League.

RIDDICK, Gordon
Luton, Gillingham, Charlton, Leyton O, Northampton, Brentford, 1962-1976
Lives in Watford where he used to run his own building company, then managed a builders merchants and kitchen company. Now employed as a sales executive and has worked freelance for BBC Match of the day since he finished playing.

RIDLEY, John
Port V, Leicester, Chesterfield, Port V, 1973-1984
Joined Port Vale from Sheffield University and made 400 league appearances before returned to education to become a Maths teacher in the Stoke area.
Promoted to the Third Division with Port Vale in 1983.

RIMMER, Jimmy
Man U, Swansea, Arsenal, Aston V, Swansea, 1967-1985
Found his chances limited at United by Alex Stepney. Moved to Arsenal and Villa, and won one England cap in 1976. Returned to Swansea where he was youth team coach.
European Cup winner with Villa in 1982.

RIMMER, Warwick
Bolton, Crewe A, 1960-1978
Former schoolboy international who is now youth development officer at Tranmere.
Played 462 League games for Bolton.

RIOCH, Bruce
Luton, Aston V, Derby, Everton, Derby,
Birmingham, Sheff U, Torquay, 1964-1983
Bruce first came to prominence when cracking in 24 goals in 44 games to collect a Fourth Division medal with Luton Town. He signed for Aston Villa in 1969 then moved on to Derby County in 1974. A £300,000 move took him to Everton, but after less than a year he was back at the Baseball Ground. Later he played for Seattle Sounders in the States before coming home to play for, then manage, Torquay. He took over as coach at Middlesborough in January 1986 and caretaker manager the following month. He then managed Millwall until taking over at Bolton who he took to the Premiership. He accepted the offer of the managers job at Arsenal only to be sacked in August 1996. He is now number two to Stuart Houston at QPR.
League Championship winner with Derby.

RIOCH, Neil
Luton, Aston Villa, York, Northampton, Plymouth Argyle 1968-1975
A former England youth international and younger brother of Bruce. Works as a players agent with his other brother Ian.

RITCHIE, John
Stoke, Sheff Wed, Stoke, 1962-1974
John scored an average of more than a goal every two games during his twelve years at the Victoria Ground. Now lives in Stoke and runs his own business selling crockery to hotels and restaurants.
League Cup winner with Stoke in 1972.

RITCHIE, Tom
Bristol C, Sunderland, Carlisle, Bristol C, 1972-1984
Edinburgh born striker who made Bristol is adopted his home after playing 400 league games in his two stints. Lives in Clevedon, Avon and is a postman.

RITSON, John
Bolton, Bury, 1967-1979
Bolton's first chice right back for almost a decade now owns a newsagents in the Potteries.

RIX, Graham
Arsenal, Brentford, 1976-1987
Won seven England caps during many successful years at Highbury. Ended his career in France with Caen. Returned to be youth team manager at Chelsea where he is now first team coach.
FA cup winner with Arsenal in 1979.

ROBB, Dave
Aberdeen, Norwich, 1965-1979
Enjoyed a long career with two clubs before spending the latter part of his career in North America. Still has a house in Banchory, near Aberdeen, but lives in Denmark where he is employed by an Oil company.
Came off the bench to net the winner in the 1977 League Cup final.

ROBB, George
Tottenham 1951-1958
England international both as an amateur and professional, George was a teacher and only turned pro at the age of 25. After seven years with his only club he returned to teaching, firstly in Edgware, but now in Ardingly, Sussex.

ROBERTS, Bobby
Motherwell, Leicester, Mansfield, Colchester, 1958-1973
A one-time Leicester record signing and Scottish under-23 international who missed the 1964 League Cup final after scoring in both legs of the semi. Was forced to come out of retirement as Wrexham boss, to play in goal, and has recently been coaching in Kuwait.
Played for Leicester in the 1969 FA Cup final.

ROBERTS, Brian
Coventry, Hereford, Birmingham, Wolves, 1975-1990
Manchester born full back who clocked up nearly 400 games for three Midlands clubs. Is now reserve team coach at Coventry.

ROBERTS, Dave
Aston V, Shrewsbury, Swansea, 1965-1974
Played over 200 games on the wing for Shrewsbury from 1967 - 1973. Now working as commercial manager with Redditch and living in Solihull.

ROBERTS, Dave
Fulham, Oxford, Hull, Cardiff, 1968-1980
Central defender who is now working as an advertising sales representative for a newspaper in South Wales.
Capped seventeen times by Wales.

ROBERTS, Dudley
Coventry, Mansfield, Doncaster, Scunthorpe, 1965-1975
Forward who played the majority of his League soccer with Mansfield. Now a self employed painter & decorator in the town.

ROBERTS, Gary
Brentford 1980-1985
A Welsh under-21 international who played the whole of his career with The Bees and is now a policeman based at Welwyn Garden City after working an insurance consultant.

ROBERTS, Garreth
Hull, 1978-1990
Welsh under 21-international who played over 400 games for his only club. Works for Humberside Leisure Services.
Helped the Tigers to two promotions from the Fourth Division.

ROBERTS, Graham
Portsmouth, Tottenham, Rangers, Chelsea, WBA, 1977-1993
Capped six times by England after being signed by Spurs from non-league Weymouth. A highly rated defender who went on to star for Rangers and Chelsea. Joined Slough Town in the Summer of 1994 after a stint as player/manager at Enfield. Appointed manager of Yeovil Town in January 1995.
Won Scottish League titles with Rangers.

ROBERTS, John
Swansea, Northampton, Arsenal, Birmingham, Wrexham, Hull, 1965-1980
After retiring through injury in 1981 he

became a salesman for a stationery company but is now a driving instructor in Chester. *Division One champion with Arsenal in 1971.*

ROBERTS, Phil
Bristol R, Portsmouth, Hereford, Exeter, 1969-1981
Became a self-employed builder in Whimple, near Exeter, but is now living in Bangkok after setting up a bicycle export business. *Capped four times by Wales.*

ROBERTS, Trevor
Liverpool, Southend, Cambridge U, 1963-1971
Welsh amatuer international keeper who died in 1972 aged only 30.
Played in goal for Cambridge in their first ever League game, against Lincoln in 1970.

ROBERTSON, Alistair
WBA, Wolves, 1969-1989
After 18 years and over 700 first team games, Ally Robertson left West Brom in 1986. Became player/manager at Worcester City and then was made manager at Cheltenham Town in 1991/2. Now runs the Throstles Club at West Brom.
Won Third and Fourth Division Championship medals with Wolves.

ROBERTSON, George
Plymouth 1950-1963
Argyle's first choice full back for thirteen years. Now a milkman in Plymouth, having previously been landlord of the 'Golden Hind' public house near Home Park.

ROBERTSON, Jimmy
St Mirren, Tottenham, Arsenal, Ipswich, Stoke, Walsall, Crewe, 1962-1978
Capped once by Scotland durig his time at White Hart Lane. Now lives in the Potteries area and is a director of The Task Force Group, a computer insurance company.
Scored for Spurs in their 1967 FA Cup final win.

ROBERTSON, John
Notts F, Derby, Notts F, 1970-1985

Robertson began with Forest as a 17 year old in 1970. In 1976/7 he helped the club into third place in the Second Division, and the following year gained a Championship medal plus a League Cup winners medal. Became a licensee, then a sales associate with Save & Prosper Group. Now works for his old mate Martin O'Neill at Wycombe Wanderers as chief scout.
Won his second European Cup winners medal scoring the only goal of the game against SV Hamburg.

ROBERTSON, Stuart
Newcastle, Aldershot, 1977-1982
Played over 200 games for each of his two League clubs and ended his career with Northampton in 1978. Stuart is now a sports complex manager in the town.

ROBERTSON, William
Chelsea, Leyton O, 1950-1962
Chelsea's first choice goalkeeper during the fifties played 199 League games for the Blues and died in 1973 aged only 45.

ROBINS, Ian
Oldham, Bury, Huddersfield, 1969-1981
A vetrean stiker with over 400 games to his name.Now works for Port Petroleum as well as being the landlord of 'Clowns Bar' in Wigan.

ROBINSON, Mike
Preston. Man C, Brighton., Liverpool, QPR, 1975-1986
Capped 23 times by the Republic of Ireland before quitting in 1986. Now a television pundit and commentator in Spain. His fluent Spanish can also be heard on the country's most popular football radio programme.
League Championship winner with Liverpool in 1984.

ROBSON, Bobby
Fulham, WBA, Fulham, 1950-1966
After leaving Fulham for West Bromwich Albion in 1956, he was converted from a goalscoring inside-right to an international right-half, going on to win 20 England caps

before retiring to Fulham where he ended his League career in 1967 after 585 appearances. He coached Oxford University, Vancouver Royals, and was a scout for Chelsea before achieving real managerial success at Ipswich. An eight-year reign as England manager followed, where he was in charge for 90 matches before handing over to Graham Taylor in 1990. Despite many offers in this country, Bobby then accepted the challenge of managing PSV Eindhoven who he guided to League and Cup success before moving to Portugal to become manager of Porto. Now manager of Barcelona.
Scored in Fulham's record 10-1 win over Ipswich on Boxing Day 1963.

ROBSON, Bryan 'Pop'

Newcastle, West Ham, Sunderland, West Ham, Sunderland, Carlisle, Chelsea, Carlisle, Sunderland, Carlisle, 1964-1985

A small stocky forward, Robson turned professional in 1962 for Newcastle where he gained under-23 honours before leaving for West Ham after playing over 200 games and scoring 81 goals. He became known as 'Pop' to the fans because of his shooting at the slightest chance of an opening. A prolific scorer, he had two spells at West Ham and Sunderland before, in his 35th year, he was scoring regularly for Carlisle United. Joined Chelsea as player/coach for a while before

returning to the north east where he owns a newsagents.
Won an Adidas Golden Boot in 1979 after leading the Second Division scoring charts.

ROBSON, Bryan OBE

WBA, Man U, 1974-1995
Robson became the costliest player in Britain when he moved from West Bromwich Albion to Manchester United for around £2 million. Despite breaking his leg three times, he won 90 full caps for England and was regarded by many as the best midfielder since the war. Appointed player/manager of Middlesborough in May 1994.
Lead Manchester United to their first League Championship in 25 years, in 1993.

ROBSON, Jimmy

Burnley, Blackpool, Barnsley, Bury, 1956-1972
Played over 450 League games in a long career which ended at Bury. Now works for a small printing company and is a part-time coach at Rochdale.

ROBSON, John

Derby C, Aston V 1962-1977
Capped seven times by England at under-23 level, John was a valuable member of the Aston Villa defence before being forced to quit the game with multiple sclerosis in August 1978. Lives in Sutton Coldfeld.
League Championship winner with Derby.

ROBSON, Tom

Northampton, Chelsea, Newcastle, Peterborough, 1961-1980
Joined Peterborough in 1968 and played 450 league games for them, still a regular at the age of 35. Now property manager for a local newspaper in Peterborough.
Holds the Posh record for most number of league games.

ROCHE, Paddy

Man U, Brentford, Halifax, Chester, 1974-1988
Capped seven times by the Republic of Ireland but played most of his 250 league

games for Halifax. Now football in the community officer based at The Shay.

RODAWAY, Billy
Burnley, Peterboro, 1971-1982
Liverpool born central defender who played most of his league football at Turf Moor now works as a scaffolder. He is also assistant manager of Halifax Town.

RODRIGUES, Peter
Cardiff, Leicester, Sheff Wed, Southampton, 1963-1976

A serious knee injury ended his career and he became a publican outside Southampton. He still lives in the area and works in a Conservative Club.
Captained Saints to 1976 FA Cup final win.

ROEDER, Glenn
Orient, QPR, Notts Co, Newcastle, Watford, Orient, 1974-1995
Appointed manager of Watford in 1993 after turning down the chance of travelling to Italy as Gazza's minder. Started and ended his pro playing career at Orient and had a spell at non-league Purfleet prior to becoming the Hornet's boss from which he was sacked in 1996. Now scouting for England coach Glenn Hoddle.
Played for QPR in the 1982 FA Cup final.

ROFE, Denis
Leyton O, Leicester, Chelsea, Southampton, 1967-1983
Capped once by England at under-23 level. Was reserve team coach at Southampton before joining Bristol Rovers as assistant manager. His last job was as reserve team manager at Stoke City.

ROGERS, Alan
Plymouth, Portsmouth, Southend, Cardiff, 1973-1986
Tricky winger who notched up close to 400 league appearances before returning to Plymouth to run the Swinton Hotel.

ROGERS, Andy
Peterborough, Southampton, Plymouth, Reading, Southend, 1976-1987
Now lives near Walsall and works as a consultant for a building products company.
Scored the goal which took Plymouth into the 1983 FA Cup semi finals.

ROGERS, Don
Swindon, C Palace, QPR, Swindon, 1962-1976

Played over 400 games in a long career and was capped by England at under-23 level. Has run his own sports shop in Swindon for the past 27 years.
Scored the winner in Swindon's 1969 League Cup final win.

R

ROGERS, Martyn
Bristol C, Exeter, 1973-1984
Defender who spent five years at Exeter and is currently manager of Tiverton Town.

ROLLINGS, Andy
Norwich, Brighton, Swindon, Portsmouth, Torquay, Brentford, 1973-1983
A strong centre half who played for a number of clubs. Still plays for Newhaven in the Sussex League, and runs a cafe in Hove.
Twice won promotion with Brighton.

ROPER, Don
Soton, Arsenal, Soton, 1946-1958
Played nearly 300 league games for the Gunners between 1947 and 1957. Also played county cricket for Hampshire. Now retired having worked in engineering, and lives in Southampton.
Two League championship medals with Arsenal in 1948 and 1953.

ROSENIOR, Leroy
Fulham, QPR, Fulham, West Ham, Fulham, Charlton, Bristol City, 1982-1995
A forward who did the rounds of four London clubs before becoming Bristol City's youth coach until the end of the 1994/5 season. Went on to play for Fleet Town then appointed player/manager at Gloucester City.

ROSS, Alan
Carlisle 1963-1978
Played 465 league games between the sticks for Carlisle. Alan is now a housing worker for Carlisle City Council.
Holds the Carlisle record for the most number of League games played.

ROSS, Ian
Liverpool, Aston V, Notts C, Northampton, Peterboro, Wolves, Hereford, 1966-1982
Moved into coaching, firstly with Wolves, and then Aston Villa. Posts followed in the Middle East, South Africa and Australia, before returning to assist Hereford United in 1982. Ross was appointed manager of the Icelandic Club FC Valur in 1983-4, and more recently was reserve team manager at Sunderland until June 1995.
Captain of the Villa side which won the League Cup and promotion to Division One in 1975.

ROUGVIE, Doug
Aberdeen, Chelsea, Brighton, Shrewsbury, Fulham, 1974-1988
A tough Scottish international defender who made his name with Chelsea is now back in Scotland, currently playing part-time for Huntly.
Cup Winners Cup winner with Aberdeen.

ROUSE, Victor
Millwall, C Palace, Oxford, Leyton O, 1953-1966
A reliable goalkeeper who gave sterling service to Crystal Palace and was ever present in their championship win of 1960/1. He ended up playing in America for Atlanta Chiefs, where he also became coach for several years. On his return to England, he became manager and coach to the Metropolitan Police team.
Victor became the first Fourth Division player to win full international honours.

ROWELL, Gary
Sunderland, Norwich, Middlesbrough, Brighton, Carlisle, Burnley, 1974-1988
Gary is among Sunderland's all time greats but a number of injuries forced him to retire and he is now a financial consultant in Burnley.
Second Division Championship with Sunderland.

ROWLAND, Andy
Derby, Bury, Swindon, 1972-1985
A former England youth International who played over 300 games for The Robins. Was first team coach at the County Ground until October 1996.
Scored 138 League goals in his career.

ROWLEY, Arthur
WBA, Fulham, Leicester, Shrewsbury, 1946-1964

Arthur made his reputation as the most prolific goalscorer of all time, scoring a record 433 goals in a career stretching from 1946 to 1965. He played a leading role in getting firstly Fulham, and then Leicester, into the First Division. Later became player/manager at Shrewsbury. Unfortunately he fell on hard times and the prospect of him having to sell his medals prompted media interest and resulted in a testimonial match being played in his honour. Lives in Shrewsbury after spending many years as a district manager for Vernons Pools.
Shrewsbury club record with 152 goals.

ROWLEY, Jack

Wolves, Bournemouth, Man U, Plymouth, 1935-1956
One of Manchester United's finest forwards. Scored over 200 league goals and was capped six times by England. Coached Ajax in Holland, and managed Wrexham, Bradford and Oldham. He is now retired and living in Shaw, Oldham after running a newsagents and then a post office.
League Championship in 1952 with Man U.

ROYLE, Joe

Everton, Man C, Bristol C, Norwich, 1965-1981
Joe scored over 100 goals and was capped six times by England before being forced to retire in 1982 because of a knee injury, entering management later that year with Oldham. He resigned in November 1994 to take up the vacant managers seat at his old club Everton.
League Championship with Everton in 1970.

RUDGE, Dale

Wolves, Preston, 1982-1985
Former Wolves and Preston defender who is now player/coach at Stourbridge.

RUDGE, John

Huddersfield, Carlisle, Torquay, Bristol R, Bournemouth, 1962-1976
Has been manager of Port Vale since March 1984 and is now the second longest serving manager in the game.

RUSHBURY, Dave

WBA, Sheff Wed, Swansea, Carlisle, 1974-1984
Former Sheffield Weds defender who now lives in Doncaster and is currently physio/coach at Chesterfield.

RUTTER, John

Bournemouth, Exeter, Stockport, 1973-1985
Commercial manager at Stockport County where he played over 400 league games at full back between 1976 and 1985.

RYAN, Jim

Man U, Luton, 1965-1976
Reserve team coach at Manchester United after holding a similar post at Luton. Had a spell in America playing alongside Alex Stepney before returning to Kenilworth Road in 1990.

RYAN, John

Arsenal, Fulham, Luton, Norwich, Sheff U, Man C, Stockport, Chester, Camb U, 1964-1984
Ran a transport business in Maidstone and managed Sittingbourne but left to take over at Dover Athletic in February 1995. Now works for the FA School of Excellence.
Won promotion to Division One with Luton.

RYDEN, Hugh

Leeds, Bristol R, Stockport Co, Chester, Halifax, Stockport, 1962-1972
A former striker who now lives in Stockport and works in Bolton as a fleet sales manager for the Gordon Ford Dealership.

RYDEN, John

Alloa Athletic, Accrington Stanley, Tottenham, Watford, 1953-1962
Moved into the full-time game with Accrington developing into a tough tackling centre half. Made Spurs skipper in 1957 but was pushed into the shadows by Dave Mackay. After his career ended he moved into finance manging the Maidstone office and then the Richmond branch of a finance and insurance brokers.

SABELLA, Alex
Sheff U, Leeds, 1978-1980
Born in Buenos Aires and played for the River Plate club before signing for Sheffield United in August 1978, a month after Ossie Ardiles and Ricky Villa signed for Spurs. Now in business back in Argentina.

SADLER, David
Man U, Preston, 1963-1976
Capped four times by England, David spent ten years at Old Trafford but was forced to retire through injury. Spent many years as a branch manager for a Building Society but now runs his own corporate hospitality company in Manchester.
European Cup winner in 1968.

ST JOHN, Ian
Motherwell, Liverpool, Coventry, Tranmere, 1956-1972
Saint set a record in 1959 for the quickest hat trick scored in Scotland, (150 seconds) while playing for Motherwell. Liverpool snapped him up for £37,500 and he played for them in the next nine years and was capped 21 times by Scotland. Ended his playing days at Coventry where he became assistant manager in 1971. Became manager at Portsmouth then had a spell as coach at Sheffield Wednesday before leaving to concentrate on television work.
Headed the winning goal in the 1965 FA Cup final.

SALMAN, Danis
Brentford, Millwall, Plymouth, Peterboro 1975-1991
Played over 300 games for Brentford. Became commercial manager at Torquay, but now helps ex-Plymouth manager Dave Smith with coaching courses for youngsters.

SAMMELS, Jon
Arsenal, Leicester, 1962-1977
Former England youth international who made 212 league appearances for Arsenal and won nine England under-23 caps before moving to Leicester City. Now a driving instructor, living near Leicester

SANCHEZ, Lawrie
Reading, Wimbledon, 1977-1993
A striker who made his name with Reading before moving to The Dons. Appointed manager of Sligo Rovers in September 1994 leaving less than a year later to take over as Wimbledon reserve team boss.
Sscored the winner in the 1988 FA Cup final.

SANDERS, Jimmy
Charlton, WBA, Coventry, 1944-1958
Played in goal for West Brom for a decade after signing pro terms in 1945. Now living in retirement in Tamworth.

SANSOM, Kenny
C Palace, Arsenal, Newcastle, QPR, Coventry, Everton, Brentford, 1974-1993
Capped no less then 86 times by England and he played over 300 games for the Gunners after joining from Palace in a million pound deal. Became assistant manager at Watford in August 1994, after a brief spell with Chertsey Town, and left along with Glenn Roeder in early 1996. Plays in the ICIS League for Croydon.
League Cup winner with Arsenal in 1987.

SARTORI, Carlos
Man U 1968-1971
After leaving Manchester United in 1971, he played in Italian football for eleven years. Now runs a successful knife sharpening business, which has brought him three homes in Italy and a comfortable house on the outskirts of Rochdale.
Italian Cup winner with Bologna in 1974.

SAUL, Frank
Tottenham, Southampton, QPR, Millwall, 1960-1975
Lives in Canvey Island and worked in building and decorating, but now runs a fashion business in the East End of London.
Scored the winning goal for Spurs in the 1967 FA Cup final.

SAUNDERS, Derek
Chelsea 1953-1958
Chelsea wing half of the fifties who was

groundsman and chief soccer coach at Westminster School. Derek is now groundsman at Hampstead Cricket Club.
League Championship with Chelsea in 1955.

SAUNDERS, John
Mansfield, Huddersfield, Barnsley, Lincoln, Doncaster, 1969-1980
Was chairman of Worksop Town FC, and owner of their 'Tigers Club'. When the football club moved to a new ground John retained ownership of the old social club which he now runs as the 'Riverside Club'.

SAUNDERS, Ron
Everton, Gillingham, Portsmouth, Watford, Charlton, 1954-1966
Ron was in charge of Yeovil, Oxford Utd, Norwich City, Manchester City, Aston Villa and West Brom. When he left West Brom he had completed 36 years connected with professional football in a career which had encompassed 11 League clubs. Officially retired, but still acts as an advisor and scout.
Scored 140 goals in 234 games for Pompey.

SAVINO, Ray
Norwich, Bristol City, 1957-1967
After failing to make the grade at Norwich moved on to Bristol City helping them to a Second Division title. Moved back to Norfolk where he still lives today working as a bricklayer.

SAWARD, Pat
Millwall, Aston V, Huddersfield, 1951-1962
Skippered Aston Villa and Huddersfield Town in the fifties and sixties and won 18 caps for the Republic of Ireland. He was appointed player/coach by Coventry City in October 1963, then took the managers job at Brighton in 1970 guiding them into the Second Division . He was coach to the Saudi Arabian side, AL-NASR, and now he runs a holiday business in Minorca.
FA Cup winners medal with Villa in 1957.

SAXTON, Bobby
Derby, Plymouth, Exeter, 1964-1977
Managed Blackburn Rovers and York

Citythen linked up with Peter Reid for the second time by accepting a coaching post at Sunderland in June 1995. They were previously together during Reid's short reign at Manchester City.

SAYER, Peter
Cardiff, Brighton., Preston, Cardiff, Chester, 1973-1984
Cardiff born winger who was capped by Wales seven times but was forced to retire in 1984 aged 27. Peter is now works commercial & community assistant at Preston.

SBRAGIA, Ricky
Birmingham, Walsall, Blackpool, York, Darlington, 1974-1985
Youth coach at York City prior to moving to Sunderland when offered a similiar position.
Promoted to Division Three in 1988 with York.

SCHOFIELD, Johnny
Birmingham, Wrexham, 1952-1967
Goalkeeper who was on the books of Birmingham for fifteen years, during which time he notched up over 200 appearances. Now runshis own off-licence in Atherstone.
Division Two Championship in 1955.

SCOTSON, Reg
Sunderland, Grimsby, 1946-1954
Former Grimsby Town wing half who is now an arcade manager in Cleethorpes.

SCOTT, Alex
Rangers, Everton Hibs, Falkirk, 1955-1972
Scottish international striker who ventured south in a £39,000 move to Everton in 1963. However, after four years at Goodison he returned home to join Hibernian. Now a publican in his home town of Falkirk.
League Championship winner on both sides of the border.

SCOTT, Laurie
Bradford C, Arsenal, C Palace, 1935-1952
Full back who won fifteen caps for England while with Arsenal. Spent three years as manager of Crystal Palace, before working

for the Club's chairman. Retired at the age of 64 and now lives in South Yorkshire.
League Championship winner with Arsenal in 1948.

SCOTT, Richard
Norwich, Cardiff, Scunthorpe, Lincoln 1961-1967
A well travelled right half who managed non-league Thetford for 13 years. Now looks after the Caldecott Hall complex with former team mate Phil Kelly.
League Cup winner with Norwich.

SCOULER, Jimmy
Portsmouth, Newcastle, Bradford PA, 1946-1963
Won nine England caps during his time at Portsmouth, before ending his playing days at Bradford. Was their player/manager from 1961 until February 1964 when he retired as a player but continued as manager until May 1964. Took over at Cardiff in June 1964, a post he held for over nine years. Later scouted for Aston Villa , Wolves, and managed Newport County. After spells in the jewellery trade and chemical industry, retired to his home near Cardiff.
Won two Championship winners medals with Pompey.

SEACOLE, Jason
Oxford 1976-1981
Former Oxford United forward whose promising career ended at the age of only 21 and is now a wood machinist at a furniture factory in Witney.

SEALEY, Alan
Leyton O, West Ham, Plymouth, 1960-1967
Died suddenly at his home in Collier Row near Romford in February 1996 after a heart attack. Worked in a betting shop for many years then returned to the Hammers in a Scouting Capacity. Cousin of Les Sealey, now at Leyton Orient.
Scored two goals in the 1965 Cup Winners Cup final.

SEALY, Tony
Southampton, C Palace, Port V, QPR, Port V, Fulham, Leicester, Bournemouth, Brentford, Bristol R, Brentford, 1977-1993
Went over to Hong Kong, but is now employed on the Island by the Hong Kong Football Club as Sporting Manager.

SEAR, Cliff
Manchester C, Chester C, 1956-1969
Full back who won his only Welsh Cap during his nine years at Manchester City. Ended his playing days at Chester City, where he became coach, assistant manager, then manager. Now with Wrexham as youth development officer.

SELKIRK, Jack
Rotherham 1946-1956
Played over 400 league matches in his ten years at Millmoor. No longer alive.

SELLERS, John
Stoke City 1946-1957
A Stoke City regular who played 384 games in the wing half position from 1946 until 1957. No longer alive.

SENIOR, Steve
York C, Darlington, Northampton T, Wigan Ath, Preston, 1980-1993
Defender with over 300 games to his name. Now works with his father in law's building business.

SENIOR, Trevor
Portsmouth, Aldershot, Reading, Watford, Middlesboro, Reading, 1981-1991
Goalscoring centre forward who moved to Weymouth FC in May 1994 to become player/coach and then had a brief spell as manager before re-joining Farnborough Town as a player in May 1995. Now commercial manager at Dorchester Town.
Division Three Championship with Reading in 1986.

SETTERS, Maurice
Exeter, WBA, Man U, Stoke, Coventry, Charlton, 1953-1969
A robust player who after a career which

took in six league clubs, went into management with Doncaster Rovers, then had stops at Sheffield Wednesday (coach), Rotherham (assistant manager) and Newcastle United (chief scout). Although English, with 16 under-23 caps to his name, Setters was assistant manager of the Republic of Ireland team for ten years. Lives in Tichill, Doncaster.
Won an FA Cup winners medal with Manchester United in 1963.

SEWELL, Jack

Notts Co, Sheff Wed, Aston V, Hull, 1946-1960

Was once Britain's most expensive player, after Sheffield Wednesday had paid Notts County £34,500 in March 1951. In 1960 went over to Rhodesia for three months but stayed for thirteen years! Later working as a coach-manager in Zambia and the Belgian Congo. Since 1973 had been working as a car sales-man for Bristol Street Motors in Nottingham. Now retired but still living in the City.
England International who won an FA Cup winners medal in 1957.

SEWELL, John

Charlton, C Palace, Leyton O, 1956-1971

Full back who played over 400 games for his three clubs - all London based. However, he has now ventured substantially further away, to run a teashop in America.

SEXTON, Dave

Luton, West Ham, Leyton O, Brighton, C Palace, 1951-1959

An inside forward who started his playing career at Chelmsford City and made his first appearance in League football with Luton Town. Service with West Ham, Orient, Brighton and Crystal Palace followed, and when his playing days were over, he spent four years as coach at Chelsea. Dave next took over as manager of Orient, and after spells as coach to Fulham and Arsenal, he returned to Chelsea as manager. Also managed QPR and Manchester United before taking over responsibility for the England Under 21's.

Won a Division Three South Championship with Brighton.

SHACKLETON, Len

Bradford PA, Newcastle, Sunderland, 1946-1957

The 'clown prince' of soccer started his career as an amateur with Arsenal. However it was in the north-east that he made his name – moves to Newcastle and then Sunderland both broke the exsisting transfer records. Capped five times by England, Len became a journalist following his retirement through injury in 1957. Now lives in Grange-over-Sands, Cumbria.

SHANKLY, Bill

Carlisle, Preston, 1932-1948

Died on 25th September 1981, just days after his 68th birthday. Capped five times by Scotland, Bill was appointed manager of Liverpool in 1959 after a spell with Huddersfield, leading them to promotion in his second full season after finishing third twice. Went on to become one of the greatest managers of all time before his surprising resignation in 1974 following their FA Cup victory. Awarded the OBE in 1974, Bill will always be rememberd as part of Liverpool folklore and the 'Shankly Gates' erected at Anfield will serve as a permanent memorial.
FA Cup winner in 1958.

SHANNON, Les

Liverpool, Burnley, 1947-1958

Wing half who achieved international recognition with the England 'B' team. Retired in 1958, but was briefly manager at Blackpool. Acted as football advisor to the Channel 4 series 'The Manageress' and now works as a scout for Luton Town.

SHARP, Graeme

Dumbarton, Everton, Oldham, 1980-1996

Appointed manager of Oldham in November 1994 but made his name at Goodison where he won his 12 Scottish caps. Scored 111 goals in 306 League games.
Won two Championships, an FA Cup and a

Cup Winners Cup medal with Everton.

SHARPE, Fred

Tottenham, Norwich, Reading, 1956-1971
Coached at two schools in Berkshire before
becoming a salesman for a food business
and now runs a car valetting buiness. Keeps
in touch with Maurice Norman who is his
daughter's godfather.

SHAW, David

Huddersfield, Oldham, WBA, Oldham, 1966-
1977
Scored a host of goals in his two spells with
Oldham. Now works for an engineering company in Yorkshire.

SHAW, Gary

Aston V, Blackpool, Walsall, Shrewsbury,
1978-1990
Has the distinction of being the only
Birmingham born player in Aston Villa's
League Championship and European Cup
winning sides of 1981 and 1982. An England
under-23 international, he was voted 'Young
Player of the Year' in 1981. Went over to
Hong Kong where he worked as a sales
executive and was head coach at the international school. Now works as a representative for Carlsberg Tetley and helps coach the
youngsters at Villa Park once a week
European Cup winner with Villa.

SHAW, Graham

Sheff U, Doncaster, 1951-1967
A former ABA Boxing Champion, Graham
later proved to be an equally good footballer
who was capped five times by England.
Now works in business in the Sheffield mar-
kets.
*Division Two Championship with Sheffield
Utd in 1962.*

SHAW, Joseph

Sheff U 1948-1965
Played 629 matches for Sheffield United
between 1948 and 1965. Now retired in the
Sheffield area.
*Holds the Blades record for most number of
appearances.*

SHAW, Peter

Charlton, Exeter, Gillingham, 1977-1985
Former Charlton and Gillingham defender
who is now coaching at Tooting & Mitcham.

SHEARER, Robert

Hamilton, Rangers, Queen of the South,
1956-1966
Won the double with Rangers in 1963 and
then a treble 12 months later. Was the manager of Third Lanark when they folded and is
now semi retired after building a number of
successful businesses which included a
coach hire and building firm.
Double 'double' winner with Rangers.

SHEFFIELD, Lawrie

Bristol R, Newport Co, Doncaster,
Rotherham, Oldham, Luton, Doncaster,
Peterborough, 1956-1972
Appointed Doncaster's youth team coach
when his career ended because of a broken
ankle. Became a car dealer later on for many
years. Still lives in Doncaster working as an
independent financial adviser.

SHEPHARD, Jamie

Norwich, Southend, Peterborough, 1979-
1987
Never really fulfilled his potential and was
forced to quit the game with a knee injury.
Became a publican for five years before joining the police force.
Helped Norwich to promotion in 1981.

SHEPHERDSON, Harold

Middlesboro 1936-1946
Will always be remembered as a member of
the England coaching staff which took the
national side to victory in the 1966 World
Cup. Lived in Middlesborough and helped
out as an ambassador at Ayresome Park
until his death in September 1995.

SHERWOOD, Alf

Cardiff, Newport, 1946-1960
Made over 500 League appearances for his
two clubs and achieved international recognition on 41 occasions for Wales. Died in
March 1989 at his home in Cardiff aged 66.

Won 39 of his caps with Cardiff which is a club record.

SHERWOOD, Steve
Chelsea, Millwall, Brentford, Watford, Grimsby 1971-1994
Blond haired goalkeeper of the Elton John/Graham Taylor Watford side of the eighties. Played for Immingham Town and Gateshead and is youth development officer at Grimsby.
Played for Watford in the 1984 FA Cup final.

SHILTON, Peter
Leicester, Stoke, Notts F, Southampton, Derby, Plymouth, Wimbledon, Bolton, Coventry, West Ham, 1966-1996
The Peter Shilton playing career seems likely to carry on for some time, with his services still in demand since his very public and well documented departure from the manager's post at Plymouth Argyle. The tabloid press's fascination with his private life should not take way from the fact that he ranks among the all time great goalkeepers, respected by players and fans alike.
European Cup winner with Notts Forest.

SHIMWELL, Eddie
Sheff U, Blackpool, Oldham, 1946-1957
England international who played in three FA Cup finals, scoring from the penalty spot in the losing final of 1948. Lived in retirement in Thornton Clevelys on the outskirts of Blackpool until his death in October 1988 aged 68.

SHINER, Roy
Huddersfield, Sheff Wed, Hull, 1951-1959
Former Sheffield Wednesday centre half of the fifties who scored 93 goals in 153 League games prior to his death on the Isle of Wight in 1958.

SHINTON, Bobby
Walsall, Camb U, Wrexham, Man C, Millwall, Newcastle, Millwall, 1971-1982
Played close on 400 League games in his eleven year career. Now a glazier in Cambridgeshire, and playing for Willingham

in the local league.

SHIPLEY, George
Southampton, Reading, Lincoln, Charlton, Gillingham, 1979-1988
Made a number of appearances for Saints before establishing himself as a Lincoln regular for five years. Assistant manager at Bradford City until 1995, when he took on the role of first team coach.

SHIRTLIFF, Paul
Sheff Wed, Northampton, 1980-1984
Now a bank clerk living in Barnsley.
An England semi-pro international.

SHORTHOUSE, W H
Wolves 1947-1956
Now retired after successful playing and coaching careers. Played 379 games for Wolves, then coached Wolves and Birmingham before becoming manager of the England Youth team which won the European Youth Cup in 1971.
Won FA Cup and Championship medals.

SHOTTON, Malcolm
Leicester, Oxford, Portsmouth, Huddersfield, Barnsley, Hull, Barnsley, 1975-1995
Familair figure in the Oxford United back four throughout the 1980s. He then went on to give service to four more clubs before becoming reserve team coach at Oakwell.
Captained Oxford to Second Division Championship and League Cup wins.

SHOULDER, Alan
Newcastle, Carlisle, Hartlepool, 1978-1987
Scored almost 100 league goals for his three north east based clubs. Now poultry farming in Bishop Auckland and manages Crook Town in the Northern League.

SHOWELL, George
Wolves, Bristol C, Wrexham, 1954-1967
After playing almost 200 games in Wolves colours, George had a sepll as assistant manager at his last club, Wrexham.
FA Cup winners medal in 1960.

SHOWERS, Derek
Cardiff, Bournemouth, Portsmouth, Hereford, 1970-1982
Former Cardiff junior who won six under-23 caps with Wales and appeared in almost 300 League games between 1970 and 1982. Now works for the Royal Mail in South Wales.
Capped twice by Wales.

SHREEVES, Peter
Reading 1958-1965
Peter was an inside forward with Reading playing over 100 games. Then coached at QPR until July 1989 and moved on to Spurs where he had two spells as manager. Is now first team coach at Sheffield Wednesday.

SHUKER, John
Oxford 1962-1976
A one club man who was a permanent fixture ar left back. Went on to run the 'Eagle Inn' in Bampton, where he still lives, from 1978 until 1984. Since then has been a self employed haulier.
The 478 games he played is a club record.

SIBBALD, Bobby
Leeds, York, Southport, 1965-1976
Played 240 games for Southport after joining on a short trial period. Moved to California and played in the same Aztecs side as Johan Cruyff and George Best, becoming one of NASL's all time greats. Still lives in the States after a massive lottery win!

SIBLEY, Frank
QPR 1963-1970
Played over 150 games before becoming chief scout then assistant manager at QPR. Resigned from Rangers in September 1996 after Stewart Houston took over as manager.
Played for Rangers in their Division Three and League Cup double winning side.

SIDDALL, Barry
Bolton, Sunderland, Port V, Stoke, Blackpool, Stockport, Hartlepool, Carlisle, Chester, 1972-1991
Now using the considerable experience gained from his nomadic playing career to help coach goalkeepers at a number of clubs, including Burnley.

SILKMAN, Barry
Hereford, C Palace, Plymouth, Luton, Man C, Brentford, QPR, Leyton O, Southend, Crewe, 1974-1986
Barry now acts as a players agent; turns out for the Showbiz XI; and trains greyhounds at Canterbury stadium in Kent. Plays for Wingate & Finchley in the ICIS League.

SILLETT, John
Chelsea, Coventry, Plymouth, 1956-1967
Jovial John was manager of Coventry between 1987 and 1990, and guided them to a famous FA Cup victory in 1987. Most recently worked as chief scout at Portsmouth, until the shake up at Fratton Park in early 1995 following Jim Smith's departure. Now works for Central Television.

SILLETT, Peter
Southampton, Chelsea, 1951-1961
Former England international capped three times. Now lives is Ashford, Kent, but arthritis of the knee prevents him from working.
Football League Champion with Chelsea in 1955.

SIMMONS, David
Arsenal, Bournemouth, Aston V, Walsall, Colchester, Camb U, Brentford, Camb U, 1965-1975
A member of the Colchester side which shocked Leeds in the FA Cup. Now an insurance agent for the Prudential in Cambridge.

SIMONSEN, Allan
Charlton 1982
A big money signing who failed to last the pace with Charlton when he joined from Barcelona. Now manager of the Faroes Islands national team.

SIMPSON, Owen
Rotherham, Leyton Orient, Colchester, Southend, Darlington, Grimsby, 1964-1971
Now a representative for an upholstery firm in Grimsby.

SIMPSON, Peter
Arsenal 1963-1977
A commanding central defender who during his fifteen years at Arsenal played in 353 League games. Now working as a fork lift truck driver for a roofing materials firm in Hertfordshire.
A member of the Gunners double winning side of 1971.

SIMPSON, Ronnie
Queen's Park, Third Lanark, Newcastle, Hibs, Celtic, 1945-1970
Won his first Scottish cap aged 36 and played in the Olympic games. Coached and scouted for Celtic before drifting out of the game. Ran a pub near Easter Road before retiring but is still active in the game as a member of the Littlewoods Pools Panel.
European Cup winner with Celtic in 1967.

SIMS, Steve
Leicester, Watford, Notts Co, Watford, Aston V, Lincoln, 1975-1990
A midfield star who spent two years managing an indoor football and cricket stadium prior to joining the youth development team at Coventry City.
Won promotion to the First Division with both Watford and Aston Villa.

SINCLAIR, Colin
Raith Rovers, Darlington, Hereford, Newport Co, 1968-1978
A midfielder who played over 200 league games scoring 59 goals for Darlington. Moved back to Scotland where he is a hotelier.

SINCLAIR, Roy
Tranmere, Watford, Chester, Tranmere, 1963-1974
Scored the goal which secured The Hornets promotion to the Second Divison for the first time. Now lives in Seattle where he has qualified as a referee and works as an insurance manager.

SIRRELL, Jimmy
Bradford PA, Brighton, Aldershot, 1949-1956
Chief Scout at Notts County where he became a legend during three spells as manager which totalled thirteen years.

SISSONS, John
West Ham, Sheff Wed, Norwich, Chelsea, 1962-1974
Won ten under caps for England as an exciting winger in the sixties. Played over 300 games for West Ham and Sheff Wed before retiring in 1974 while with Chelsea. Now works for a motor products firm in Cape Town, South Africa.
European Cup Winners Cup winner with the Hammers.

SITTON, John
Chelsea, Millwall, Gillingham, Leyton O, 1978-1990
Became part of the management team at his last club, Leyton Orient, but left in April 1995 following the club's takeover by Snooker impresario, Barry Hearn. Is now coaching abroad.

SJOBERG, John
Liecester City, Rotherham, 1958-1973
Played 412 games for Leicester over the years. John is the only City player to have ever scored two own goals in one game. Started a printing business during his playing days with the club and returned to this when his playing days ended.
Played for Leicester in the 1963 FA Cup final.

SKEEN, Ken
Swindon, Oxford, 1964-1973
Former Oxford midfielder is now secretary at a golf course in Cheltenham.

SKIRTON, Alan
Arsenal, Blackpool, Bristol C, Torquay, 1960-1971
Winger who played 145 games for Arsenal in the 1960s. Alan now works as commercial manager at Yeovil Town.

SLATER, Bill OBE
Blackpool, Brentford, Wolves, Brentford, 1949-1963

An accomplished amateur centre half who played in the 1952 Olympic Games before turning pro with Wolves at the age of 27. Voted 'Player of the Year' in 1959/60 and capped 12 times by England, he retired in 1963 having made over 300 appearances for Wolves. After holding posts at Liverpool and Birmingham Universities, Bill is now president of the Amateur Gymnastics Association.
Three League Championships with Wolves.

SLATTER, Neil
Bristol R, Oxford, Bournemouth, 1980-1989
Although forced to retire at the age of 25, Slatter had made 22 international appearances for Wales. Now works in administration for a large supermarket chain.

SLEEUWENHOEK, John
Aston V, Birmingham, Torquay, Oldham, 1961-1971
Finished his career in 1972 to work as a joiner at an Aldridge firm with his former Villa colleague, Alan Deakin. John sadly died in Birmingham in 1989 aged only 45.

SLOUGH, Alan
Luton, Fulham, Peterboro, Millwall, 1965-1981
Alan is now a window cleaner living in Devon and is player/manager of Torquay Christians in the South Devon League.
Played for Fulham in the 1975 FA Cup final.

SMALL, Mike
Luton, Peterboro, Brighton, West Ham, Wolves, Charlton, 1981-1993
Made his name with Brighton and won an England call up whilst at West Ham. Is now playing for Baldock Town in the Doc Martens League.
Helped Brighton reach a play-off final at Wembley.

SMALLMAN, David
Wrexham, Everton, 1972-1976
Welsh international forward who was forced to quit the game in 1976 aged 23, shortly after joining Everton. Emigrated to Australia in 1982, but returned to Wales in 1988 and took a job with the local council.

SMART, Roger
Swindon, Charlton, 1961-1973
A first choice defender with Swindon for eleven years, appearing in 346 league games. He now runs the 'Plough' pub in the town.
Scored for the Robins in their 1969 League Cup final win over Arsenal.

SMEE, Roger
Chelsea, Reading, 1966-1973
Went on to to become chairman of the Royals and is now a successful businessman in the town.

SMETHURST, Derek
Chelsea, Millwall, 1970-1974
South African born forward signed by Chelsea from Durban United is now involved with youth soccer in Florida. Is a born again Christian after experiencing a vision whilst watching television in San Diego in 1978. Even has a daughter called Chelsea!
A sub for the 1971 Cup Winners Cup side.

SMILLIE, Andy
West Ham, Crystal Palace, Scunthorpe,

Southend, Gillingham, 1958-1970
An inside forward who was a former England youth international. Had the longest spell of his career at Southend where he still lives running a seafront restaurant.

SMILLIE, Neil C.
Palace, Brighton, Watford, Reading, Brentford, Gilligham, 1976-1995
Son of a former professional who enjoyed a long successful career. Had a brief spell as caretaker boss of Gillingham and is now youth coach at Wycombe Wanderers.

SMITH, Alan
Never played a league game but has been a successful coach mainly with Crystal Palace. Quit his job as stockbroker to manage the Eagles youth team after a spell as Dulwich Hamlet boss. Appointed Palace boss for two seasons and had been in charge of Wycombe until September 1995 when he was fired.
Took Palace to the First Division title in 1994.

SMITH Alan
Leicester City, Arsenal, 1982-1995
A former England semi pro international striker who went on to play for the professional national side whilst at Arsenal. Served the Gunners well until a knee injury forced him to quit. Has become a journalist after the help of a PFA grant allowed him to study at the London School of Journalism.
Scored the only goal of the 1994 Cup Winners Cup final.

SMITH, Bobby
Hibs, Leicester, Peterborough, Hibs, Dunfirmline, Partick Thistle, Berwick Rangers, 1970-1993
Shared a league debut in England with Gary Lineker. Career games on both sides of the border totalled over 500. Bobby is now a pub landlord in Dalkeith.

SMITH, Bobby
Chelsea, Tottenham, Brighton, 1950-1964
A truly great striker who scored 251 goals for Spurs in 358 games. Became a painter & decorator and has needed a double hip replacement operation, relying on crutches to get around.
A double winner with Spurs.

SMITH, Dave
Burnley, Brighton, Bristol City, 1950-1962
A highly successful manager with Southend, Plymouth, Dundee and Torquay. Now organises coaching courses for youngsters in Devon. In March 1995 turned down the chance to return to League management by declining an offer from Argyle.

SMITH, Denis
Stoke, York, 1968-1982
Played 406 League games for Stoke and is the current manager of Oxford United having been appointed in September 1993. Previously managed York City, Bristol City and Sunderland.
League Cup winner with Stoke in 1972.

SMITH, Fred
Burnley, Portsmouth, Halifax, 1963-1974
Employed as a community worker by the borough council in Burnley, having previously had a milkround, a restaurant and then a newsagents.

SMITH, George
Newcastle, Barrow, Portsmouth, Middlesboro, Birmingham, Cardiff, Swansea, Hartlepool, 1963-1979
Assistant manager at Doncaster Rovers until September 1994.

SMITH, Gordon
Brighton, Man C, Oldham, 1980-1985
Might have won the FA Cup for Brighton when Gary Bailey saved his shot during the closing stages of the 1983 final. Gordon played in the first division of four countries, including Switzerland and Austria. Now leads a busy life working as a financial consultant. Also writes two weekly newspaper columns as well as appearing on radio and TV in Scotland.
Immortalised by the words ". . . and Smith must score".

SMITH, Granville
Bristol R, Newport, 1958-1967
Former Newport County winger, Granville is now a boiler attendant in the town.

SMITH, Jim
Sheff U, Aldershot, Halifax, Lincoln, Colchester, 1959-1972
Jim spent his playing days as a half-back with Sheffield Utd, Aldershot, Halifax Town and Lincoln City. He acquired the rudiments of management at Boston United, where he spent four years before taking up his first appointment in the football league with Colchester. Manager of Portsmouth until February 1995 and is now at Derby County.
Won five promotions as a manager.

SMITH, Jimmy
Aberdeen, Newcastle, Celtic, 1965-1976
Nicknamed 'Jinky' because of his tricky ball skills, he joined Newcastle from Aberdeen in 1969, but was forced to retire through injury in 1976. Unfortunately his love of gambling has cost him a fortune and he currently drives a taxi for a living on Tyneside.
A Scottish Cup finalist in 1967.

SMITH, John
West Ham, Tottenham, Coventry, Leyton O, Torquay, Swindon, Walsall, 1956-1971
A former Walsall boss who died aged 49 in February 1988 of a heart attack after working as a manager of a social club in north west London.
A member of Swindon's 1969 League Cup winning side.

SMITH, Leslie
Brentford, Aston V, Brentford, 1936-1952
A winger who was capped once by England in 1939 and played a further ten times during the war. Owned a radio and television shop in Aston and was living in retirement in Lichfield, Staffs until his death in 1995.

SMITH, Malcolm
Middlesboro, Bury, Blackpool, Burnley, York, 1971-1981
Malcolm's ten year League career ended in 1981 at York City and he is now working as a vehicle hire manager.

SMITH, Steve
Huddersfield, Bolton, Halifax T, 1964-1978
Steve spent twelve years at Huddersfield where he made over 330 league appearances. Now youth coach at Bradford City.

SMITH, Tommy
Liverpool, Swansea, 1962-1978

Tommy is remembered for his no-nonsense style of defending, which was the foundation stone of the great Liverpool sides of the sixties and seventies. In his fifteen years at Anfield, Smith collected winners medals for: European Cup, European Cup Winners Cup, UEFA Cup, the FA Cup (twice), and the League Championship(four times). He joined Swansea City in 1978, becoming their player/coach the following year. When a knee injury eventually ended his career he briefly returned to Liverpool to coach the youth team. He is still involved with the 'Reds', in a public relations capacity.
Capped once by England in 1971.

SMITH, Trevor
Birmingham, Walsall, 1953-1966
Played in the same school side as Duncan Edwards and went on to become a regular in the heart of the Blues defence. Managed

a pub for a while before becoming a manager for a Thresher's wine shop.
Part of the Blues 1963 League Cup winning side.

SMITH, Wilf
Sheff W, Coventry, Brighton, Millwall, Bristol R, Chesterfield, 1964-1976
An England youth internationa skipper who became a skillful left back. Now in the insurance business in Coventry.
Played for Wednesday in the 1966 FA Cup final.

SNEDDEN, John
Arsenal, Charlton, Orient, Halifax, 1959-1967
Scottish schoolboy international centre half who finished playing at the age of only 25. Married a German girl and moved to Germany, where they still live.

SOUNESS, Graeme
Tottenham, Middlesboro, Liverpool, 1970-1983
Souness was initially an apprentice at Tottenham, but made his name at Middlesbrough, as a 'take-no-prisoners' midfielder. Consistent performances encouraged Liverpool to sign him for £352,000 in 1978. A £650,000 deal then took him to Sampdoria in Italy six years later before becoming player/manager of Rangers in 1986. The almost inevitable return to Anfield as manager was completed in March 1991. However, despite winning the FA Cup, his stay was relatively brief. Spent a season in Turkey with Galatasaray but was sacked after winning the Championship. In July 1996 was appointed manager of Southampton.
Won five League Championships and three European Cups with Liverpool.

SPACKMAN, Nigel
Bournemouth, Chelsea, Liverpool, QPR, Glasgow Rangers, Chelsea, Sheffield United, 1980-1996
Took up the challenge offered by Howard Kendall at Sheffield United to become assistant manager after a long playing career.
Won a Division Two winners medal in 1984 with Chelsea and a Division One medal with Liverpool four years later.

SPARROW, Brian
Arsenal, Wimbledon, Millwall, Gillingham, C. Palace, 1983-1986
Reserve team coach at Wimbledon in 1992 after a successful spell in charge of non-league Crawley. Moved to Crystal Palace in the summer of 1995 as youth team coach but lost his job in a re-schuffle of coaching staff less than a year later.

SPAVIN, Alan
Preston 1960-1978
Played over 400 games for Preston between 1960 and 1973, then after a four year gap, put his boots back on to add a few more to his tally. Moved to America to play for Washington and now lives in Florida, running his own travel company.

SPENCE, Derek
Oldham, Bury, Blackpool, Southend, Bury, 1971-1983
Irish international forward who had spells in Greece and Hong Kong. Ran an off-licence but now concentrates on coaching youngsters.

SPENCER, Tommy
Southampton, York City, Workington, Lincoln, Rotherham, 1965-1977
Now area coach/community worker in Worksop and manager of Worksop Town in the Unibond League.

SPOONER, Steve
Derby, Halifax, Chesterfield, Hereford, York, Rotherham, Mansfield, Chesterfield, 1978-1994
Played for Rushden & Diamonds in the Beazer Homes League but joined Burton Albion in the summer of 1996.

SPRAGGON, Frank
Middlesborough, Hartlepool 1963-1976
Frank works as a part time coach at Middlesbrough's School of Excellence.

SPRAKE, Gary
Leeds, Birmingham, 1961-1974
Played for Leeds during their glory days and won 37 full Welsh caps. Gary ended his playing days at Birmingham City and still lives in Solihull. Briefly worked as a rep for a sports goods firm but now works for the local council as a training officer, responsible for placing business trainees and monitoring their progress.
Twice a Fairs Cup winner with Leeds.

SPRINGETT, Peter
QPR, Sheff Wed, Barnsley, 1962-1979
The younger of two goalkeeping brothers, he joined the South Yorkshire police and for the past eleven years has been Community Constable at Sheffield United. Travels to United's away games as a spotter.
A member of the Rangers League Cup and Division Three double winning side.

SPRINGETT, Ron
QPR, Sheff Wed, QPR, 1955-1968
In between two spells with QPR, Ron played 345 League games for Sheffield Wednesday and was capped 33 times by England. He is now retired, having been involved in a gardening business.
Division Two Championship with Wednesday in 1959.

SPROSON, Roy
Port V 1950-1971
Now running a post office in Stoke-on-Trent. Played 756 league games for Port Vale in a career which included their famous FA Cup run of 1953/4 when Vale reached the semis.
Holds the Vale record for the most number of league appearances.

SPROSTON, Bert
Leeds, Tottenham, Man C, 1933-1949
Capped eleven times as a full back by England and played for three of the top sides in the country. Has now retired after 30 years as trainer & physio at Bolton Wanderers. Lives in Bolton and still scouts.
Division Two Champion with Man City in 1947.

STAINROD, Simon
Sheff U, Oldham, QPR, Sheff Wed, Aston V, Stoke, 1975-1988
After a thirteen year career, Simon moved to Strasbourg before heading north of the border where he is manager of Ayr United.
Helped QPR to a Second Division title in 1983.

STANCLIFFE, Paul
Rotherham, Sheffield United, Rotherham, Wolves, York, 1975-1994
A strong central defender who gave great service in particular to Sheffield United. Is now assistant manager at his last club, York.

STANDEN, Jim
Arsenal, Luton, West Ham, Millwall, Portsmouth, 1957-1971
Had success with Worcestershire in County Cricket and now lives in California and works for a Honda car leasing company. He still plays cricket and coaches young goalkeepers. His car now bears the instantly recognisable registration, FA CUP 64, a reminder of cup winning success achieved as a West Ham goalkeeper.
Played for the Hammers in their Cup Winners Cup success.

STANIFORTH, Ron
Stockport, Huddersfield, Sheff Wed, Barrow, 1946-1960
England international full back with eight caps to his credit. Played over 450 games before coaching at Barrow and Wednesday.
Twice a Division Two Champion with Wednesday.

STANLEY, Garry
Chelsea, Everton, Swansea, Portsmouth, Bristol, 1975-1988
A former defender who now lives in the Portsmouth area, where he works for Nynex Communications.
Helped Swansea to Division One.

STAPLETON, Frank
Arsenal, Man U, Derby, Blackburn, Aldershot, Huddersfield, Bradford C,

Brighton, 1974-1994
Republic of Ireland international striker.
Managed Bradford City until May 1994, followed by brief spells at Brighton as player and at QPR as reserve team coach. Appointed manager of New England in the US Major League until September 1996.
Won FA Cup winners medals with Arsenal and Man Utd.

STARLING, Ron
Hull, Newcastle, Sheff Wed, Aston V, 1927-1946

Played in FA Cup semi finals with four different clubs. In June 1950 Starling left football to open a newsagents opposite the Sheffield Wednesday ground. He died in Sheffield December 1991.
Skippered Wednesday to FA Cup final success in 1935.

STATHAM, Derek
WBA, Southampton, Stoke, Walsall, 1976-1991
Derek Statham was one of the finest left backs of the early 1980s who won three full England caps. Finished his playing days at Kings Lynn.

STEAD, Mickey
Tottenham, Swansea, Southend, Doncaster, 1975-1987
A former Southend full back who is now co-manager at Fisher 93.

STEBBING, Gary
C Palace, Southend, Maidstone, 1983-1992
Midfielder who appeared in Belgium with KV Ostend. Gary played for Dagenham & Redbridge FC then joined Dover Athletic in the summer of 1996.

STEEL, Jim
Oldham, Port Vale, Wrexham, Tranmere, 1977-1992
After fifteen years as a player he retired at the end of the 1991/2 season and joined the Merseyside Police. Jim is staitioned on the Wirral not far away from Tranmere's Prenton Park and still turns out for the police side.

STEELE, Eric
Peterboro, Brighton, Watford, Cardiff, Derby, Southend, Mansfield, 1972-1987
Full time goalkeeping coach at Leeds United, Manchester City, Derby County, Barnsley, and Grimsby Town, having previously spent four and a half years at Wolves. While he coaches, his wife runs a freehouse restaurant that they bought in Derby in 1988.

STEELE, Jim
Southampton, Rangers, 1971-1976
Able to play at either full back or in central d defence, Jim played nearly 200 games for the Saints. Became a bar owner in Washington, USA, and then foreman of an electrical plant. Has now returned home to the UK.
Man-of-the-match in the 1976 FA Cup final.

STEIN, Brian
Luton 1977-1993
Scored 125 league goals and was capped once by England in 1984. The brother of Chelsea striker Mark, Brian is now manager of non-league Baldock Town.
Won a League Cup winners medal in 1988.

STEIN, Colin
Hibs, Rangers, Coventry, Rangers, Kilmarnock, 1965-1978
Joined Rangers from Hibernian in October

1968 for £100,000, which was the first six figure fee between Scottish clubs. Had a spell south of the Border with Coventry from 1972 until 1974. Now back in his home town of Linlithgow working as a joiner. He and his wife are both local bowls champions.
Cup Winners Cup winner with Rangers.

STEPHENS, Kirk
Luton, Coventry, 1978-1985
Works as a director /owner of a building and civil engineering business.

STEPNEY, Alex
Millwall, Chelsea, Manchester U, 1963-1977
First choice goalkeeper at Old Trafford for over ten years, he is now goalkeeping coach at Manchester City. Capped once by England in his career. He ran a van hire business in Rochdale, having previously held a variety of jobs, including running a pub, working in a car body repair shop and had a spell as commercial manager at Rochdale.

STEVENS, Dennis
Bolton, Everton, Oldham, Tranmere, 1953-1967
After finishing his career at Tranmere, where he played his last game against his old club, Everton, he opened a menswear shop in Bolton. Now retired but still living in the town.

STEVENS, Gary
Brighton, Tottenham, Portsmouth, 1979-1993
Joined Tottenham from Brighton for £350,000 and became an England international. Gary was forced to quit in 1990 while with Portsmouth. He has since had a brief spell as manager of Petersfield, but is now Sales Director for a firm specialising in icepacks and heatpacks. He is also matchday PA announcer and video presenter at White Hart Lane.
Reached an FA Cup final with Brighton.

STEVENS, Paul
Bristol C 1977-1984
Former Robins full back who played 146 league games and is now a sales representa-tive living in Bristol.

STEVENSON, Alan
Chesterfield, Burnley, Rotherham, Hartlepool, 1969-1984
Best remembered from his time with Burnley and is still commercial manager at Hartlepool.

STEVENSON, Byron
Leeds, Birmingham, Bristol R, 1974-1985
A former Welsh international midfield man who now runs the 'Golden Lion' in Pudsey, West Yorkhire.

STEWART, David
Ayr, Leeds, WBA, Swansea, 1967-1980
Joined Leeds from Ayr United in 1973 as understudy to David Harvey. Won full Scottish caps before ending his career with two seasons in Hong Kong. Now lives on the Gower Coast and works as a goldsmith in Swansea.
Played in the 1974 European Cup final.

STEWART, Jim
Kilmarnock, Middlesboro, Rangers, Dumbarton, St Mirren, 1970-1984
A Scottish international goalkeeper who was unlucky to stay as number two to Jim Platt at Middlesbrough and is now a Ministry of Defence Policeman.
Scottish FA Cup winner with Rangers in 1981.

STEWART, Ray
Dundee United, West Ham, 1975-1990
A full back who was deadly from the penalty spot, capped seven times by Scotland and was Scotland's 'Young Player of the Year' in 1979. Moved south to play for West Ham and is now assistant manager at Stirling Albion.
FA Cup winner in 1980.

STILES, Nobby
Man U, Middlesboro, Preston, 1960-1974
Stiles became a national hero due to his heroic play in the 1966 World Cup and his never-say-die-spirit which characterisedhis playing days. Was a co-director of

Manchester United's School of Excellence from 1989 until 1995.
1968 European Cup winner.

STITFALL, Ron
Cardiff 1947-1963
Won two caps for Wales during his sixteen years at Cardiff City, for whom he made over 400 League appearances. Now works with the FA of Wales.

STOBART, Barry
Wolves, Man C, Aston V, Shrewsbury, 1959-1968
Able to play at either inside or centre forward. Is now a window cleaner in Sedgley, near Wolverhampton, after running a grocery shop.
An FA Cup winner with Wolves in only his sixth first team game.

STOKES, Alf
Tottenham, Fulham, Watford, 1953-1961
An England under-23 and 'B' international. Spent some time as a driver before emigrating to Australia where he still lives.

STOKES, Bobby
Southampton, Portsmouth, 1968-1977
A former England youth international who spent eight years at the Dell before making the short trip to Portsmouth in 1977. Worked at the Harbour View cafe, Southsea until his shock death at his Portsmouth home in May 1995 aged only 44.
Shot to fame after scoring the winner in the 1976 FA Cup final.

STOKOE, Bob
Newcastle, Bury, 1950-1963
Centre half with Newcastle, for whom he played over 250 league games before moving to Bury as player/manager. It will be as a manager that Bob will probably be best remembered, having led Sunderland to a famous FA Cup victory over Leeds in 1973. Now lives back in the North East after many years in Bury.
Won an FA Cup winners medal in 1955.

STONE, John
Middlesboro, York, Darlington, Grimsby, Rotherham, 1971-1983
Former full back who now owns a sports shop in Grimsby.

STORE, Peter
Arsenal, Fulham, 1965-1977
Joined Arsenal in October 1962 and played 387 games for the Gunners. Now lives in Woodford, Essex and ran a market stall in the West End of London after spells as a publican.
Arsenal double-winner in 1971.

STONEYHOUSE, Steve
Blackburn, Huddesfield, Blackpool, 1979-1994
Returned to his native north-east to play for Bishop Auckland, South Bank and Northallerton Town. Currently player/coach and physio at Willington.

STOREY, Sydney
York, Barnsley, Accrington St, Bradford PA, 1947-1959
Played over 300 league games for York City, but was recently recognised at a cabaret concert by the star, Charlie Williams, an old Barnsley team-mate! Worked as a bus driver for many years, before his retirement.

STOREY-MOORE, Ian
Notts F, Man U, 1963-1973
Forest's top scorer for four years running from 1969-1972, but was forced to retire the following year due to an ankle injury. Capped once by England and he has since become a successful businessman in Nottingham where he is a publican and owns a bookmakers. Also employed by Nottingham Forest as a fully qualified FA coach.

STORTON, Stan
Bradford C, Darlington, Hartlepool, Tranmere, 1959-1969
After many years in management, Stan lives in Ellesmere port and runs a window cleaning business.

STRACHAN, Gordon
Dundee, Aberdeen, Man U, Leeds, Coventry, 1971-1996
Accepted the role of Ron Atkinson's assistant and manager-designate at Coventry City in early 1995 after spending a successful spell with Leeds with whom he rediscovered the kind of form which saw Manchester United bring him south of the border. A regular for Scotland between 1980 and 1992.
League Championship with Leeds United.

STRATFORD, Paul
Northampton 1972-1977
Works for a publishing company in Duston, Northants.

STRINGER, Dave
Norwich, Camb U, 1964-1980
Lives in Great Yarmouth and is still working for Norwich City for whom he made over 400 League appearances, in an advisory capacity having previously held the posts of youth and then first team manager.
Division Two Championship medal in 1972.

STRINGFELLOW, Mike
Mansfield, Leicester City, 1960-1975
Played 344 games for Leicester scoring 97 goals. Since retiring has run pubs in Narborough and Littlethorpe before buying a newsagents in Enderby.
A scorer in the 1964 League Cup final for Leicester.

STRONG, Geoff
Arsenal, Liverpool, Coventry, 1960-1971
Played 150 games for Liverpool following his move from Arsenal. Now lives in Birkdale and is a successful businessman on Merseyside where he owns a thriving hotel furnishing company. Also co-owns a pub with his old Liverpool team-mate, Ian Callaghan.
League Championship in 1966 with Liverpool.

STRONG, Les
Fulham, Brentford, C Palace, Rochdale, 1972-1984

The profits from selling a successful pub allow him to travel the world. To add to the colour of his life, he had a spell as manager of the Antiguan national side.

STUBBS, Brian
Notts Co 1968-1979
While Brian is out at work as a decorator in Nottingham, his wife is employed by Notts County, his one and only former club, for whom he appeared more than 400 times.

STUBBS, Robin
Birmingham, Torquay, Bristol R, Torquay, 1958-1972
Former Torquay forward and one time husband to Anthea Redfern is now a sales representative based in Paignton, Devon.

STUCKEY, Bruce
Exeter, Sunderland, Torquay, Reading, Torquay, Bournemouth, 1965-1976
Bruce is a child care officer in Dawlish and lives in nearby Torquay.

SUDDICK, Alan
Newcastle, Blackpool, Stoke, Southport, Bury, 1961-1977
Former England under-23 international who after playing over 300 games for the town's side now lives in Blackpool and is self-employed.

SUGGETT, Colin
Sunderland, WBA, Norwich, Newcastle, 1966-1978

Retired in 1979. Was youth coach at Newcastle United until February 1994 when he was sacked after a row over policy. Is now director of coaching at Ipswich. *Played in two League Cup finals.*

SULLIVAN, Colin
Plymouth, Norwich, Cardiff, Hereford, Portsmouth, Swansea, 1968-1985
A former England youth international. Worked as a postman until 1992 when he bcame a landscape gardener, based in Titchfield, Hants.

SUMMERBEE, Mike
Swindon, Man C, Burnley, Blackpool, Stockport, 1959-1979
An exciting winger, notably with Manchester City, who also played eight times for England before finishing his career as player/manager at Stockport County. He is chairman of his own bespoke shirt making business and his client list boasts names such as, David Bowie, Michael Caine and Sylvester Stallone. He also helps the commercial department at Maine Road.
League Champion with Man City in 1968.

SUNDERLAND, Alan
Wolves, Arsenal, Ipswich, 1971-1985
A striker who was capped by England. Ran a property rental company and sold insurance before becoming licencee of the 'Halberd Inn' near Ipswich.
Scored the winner in the 1979 FA Cup final against Man Utd.

SUTTON, Dave
Plymouth, Reading, Huddersfield, Bolton, Rochdale, 1973-1994
Resigned as manager of Rochdale in November 1994 and was appointed manager of Chorley in March 1995.

SUTTON, Mike
Norwich, Chester, Carlisle, 1962-1972
Better known as the father of Blackburn striker Chris who also played for City. Has coached the under-14s and -15s at Carrow Road and works as a sports master.

SVARC, Bobby
Leicester, Lincoln, Barrow, Colchester, Blackburn, Watford, 1964-1977
Of Czech decent, claimed 59 strikes in 116 games. A Jehovah's Witness as well, he is now proprietor of a burglar alarm company in Blackburn.

SWAIN, Ken
Chelsea, Aston V, Notts F, Portsmouth, WBA, Crewe, 1973-1994
He played the best football of his career after joining Aston Villa from Chelsea in December 1978. In 1988 he had a spell on loan to West Brom before joining Crewe Alexandra as player/coach and helping them win promotion from Division Four in his first season at Gresty Road. A poor start to the 1994/5 season led to his dismissal in September 1994. However, he was appointed assistant manager at Grimsby less than two months later.
League Championship, European Cup and European Super Cup triumphs with Villa.

SWAN, Peter
Sheff Wed, Bury, 1955-1973
An England international centre forward who was banned from playing by the FA for seven years after being jailed for match fixing. Is now a publican in the Chesterfield .
Division Two Championship in 1959.

SWAN, Ron
Oldham, Luton, 1964-1966
Has been in the police force since 1971 and his duties include policing the Oldham Athletic home games, but he has plans to move to Spain upon retirement.

SWEENEY, Gerry
Bristol C, York, 1971-1981
Played over 400 games at Ashton Gate before ending his career with York in 1981. After moving to Walsall as assistant manager, is now back at Bristol City in the same capacity.
Played in the Robins Division One promotion side of 1979.

SWEENIE, Tom
Leicester, York, 1963-1969
Tom's top class career was cut short by injury after being offered trials by Arsenal and Huddersfield when attempting a come-back. Now lives in Yorkshire and owns a car-pet fitting business.
Played in two League Cup finals.

SWIFT, Frank
Man City 1932-1949
Capped 19 times by his country after the war, goalkeeper Frank was killed in the Munich Air disaster of 1958, when accompa-nying the Manchester United team as a newspaper reporter.
Division One Champion with City in 1937.

SWINBOURNE, Roy
Wolves 1949-1955
A great centre forward who scored an aver-age of more than a goal every other game in his six post war years at Molineux. Worked for Goodyear tyres before setting up his own successful tyre distribution business. Now retired, living in Stourbridge.
Helped Wolves to their first ever League Championship, in 1954.

SWINDLEHURST, Dave
C Palace, Derby, West Ham, Sunderland, Wimbledon, Colchester, Peterboro, 1973-1988
Lives in Kent and installs computer systems. Also helps at Palace's school of excellence.

SWORD, Tommy
Stockport, Hartlepool, Halifax, Stockport, 1979-1987
Popular goalscoring defender, now runs the 'Powder Monkey' public house in Wallsend, Tyne & Wear.

SYDENHAM, John
Southampton, Aldershot, 1956-1971
Made 341 appearances for Southampton. Emigrated to Australia where he runs an insurance consultancy.

SYRETT, Dave
Swindon, Mansfield, Walsall, Peterboro,
Northampton, 1973-1983
Now a milkman living in Towcester, Northants.

TALBOT, Brian
Ipswich, Arsenal, Watford, Stoke, WBA, Fulham, Aldershot, 1973-1990
After a successful playing career during which time he won six full England caps, Brian became player/manager at West Bromwich Albion for two years in 1988. He then had a spell as manager of Aldershot before moving overseas to become manager of Hibernians inMalta.
Played in three successive FA Cup finals.

TALBUT, John
Burnley, WBA, 1958-1970
Former Burnley centre half, John was an England under-23 international. His playing days ended finally in 1974 and he moved to Belgium where he became the owner of the 'Kup Winna' bar in Mechelen.

TAMBLING, Bobby
Chelsea, C Palace, 1958-1973
bobby scored 164 league goals for Chelsea between 1958 and 1970. For many years he ran a sports shop in Havant, Hampshire, but then worked locally as a hod carrier and in 1994 was declared bankrupt in the County Court at Portsmouth. Later that year he moved to live in Ireland.
Holds the career goals scored aggregate record for Chelsea.

TANNER, Nicky
Bristol R, Liverpool, Norwich, Swindon, 1985 -1994
The former Liverpool centre half joined non-league Bath City in 1994, having had to retire early from the professional game due to injury. He was able to turn an interest into a business and he now owns and breeds racehorses.

TARRANT, Ted
Hull, Walsall, 1950-1957
After a non-eventful career Ted eventually retired to live in Marbella.

TAYLOR, Alan

Rochdale, West Ham, Norwich, Camb U,
Hull, Burnley, Bury, Norwich, 1973-1988
A well travelled striker who is now a milk-
man in Norfolk.
*Scored both goals in West Ham's FA Cup
victory of 1975.*

TAYLOR, Brian

Walsall, Birmingham, Rotherham,
Shrewsbury, Port V, Barnsley, 1954-1967
Played over 400 matches for Walsall in two
spells. Now a painter and decorator living
near Stourbridge.

TAYLOR, Dick

Grimsby, Scunthorpe, 1938-1953
Retired in 1954 to become chief coach at the
Old Show Ground. In 1956 he linked up with
Joe Mercer at Sheffield and moved to Villa
Park as Mercer's assistant in 1958, taking
over as manager in 1964. Became a success-
ful businessman after leaving Villa and ran a
sports shop 600 yards from Villa Park.

TAYLOR, Gerry

Wolves, Swindon, 1966-1975
With the exception of a brief spell as a publican, this former full back has been a policeman since 1976.
Played for Wolves in a Fairs Cup final.

TAYLOR, Gordon

Bolton, Birmingham, Blackburn, Bury, 1962-
1979
Joined Bolton in 1962 from non-league
Curzon Ashton and went on to play over 500
League games before ending at Bury fifteen
years later. Took over from Cliff Lloyd as sec-
retary of the PFA in 1981 and is now the
chairman of the players' union.
*Won a promotion from Division Two with
Birmingham in 1972.*

TAYLOR, Graham

Grimsby, Lincoln, 1963-1972
A full back, he joined Grimsby Town straight
from school and turned professional in 1962.
He remained with Grimsby until 1968 when
he was transferred to Lincoln City. In the
summer of 1972 he was appointed player-
coach at Sincil Bank and later that year took
over as manager. He quickly established
himself as a leading manager and was
snapped up by Watford in June 1977. They
progressed from the Fourth to the First
Division between 1978 and 1982 and in 1983
they were runners up in the First Division,
and in 1984 reached the FA Cup final.He
accepted the challenge of taking over at
Aston Villa but left in 1990 to take over from
Bobby Robson as England manager – resign-
ing in 1994. After a brief spell at wolves he
is general manager back at Watford.

TAYLOR, Les

Oxford, Watford, Reading, Colchester 1974-
1989
Now works as a hospital porter in Oxford.
*Helped Reading win the Full Members Cup
at Wembley.*

TAYLOR, Peter

Southend, C Palace, Tottenham, Leyton O,
Oldham, Exeter, 1970-1983
Capped four times by England in 1974
whilst at Crystal Palace. Manager at
Southend United until March 1995. Had previously managed Dartford FC and worked in
the insurance industry. Moved into non-
league again with Dover before being apppointed England under-21 boss in July 1996.

TAYLOR, Steve

Bolton, Port V, Oldham, Luton, Mansfield,
Burnley, Wigan, Stockport, Rochdale,
Preston, Burnley, Rochdale, 1974-1988
Lives in Shaw, Oldham and does part time
coaching with Oldham Athletic.

TAYLOR, Stuart

Bristol Rovers 1965-1980
Played nearly 550 league games for Rovers
and had a spell as commercial manager. Has
since been a publican and night club owner.
*Holder of Rovers record for most number of
appearances.*

TAYLOR, Tommy

Leyton O, West Ham, Leyton O, Charlton,

1967-1983
Coached at Maidstone and managed
Margate before joining Cambridge United –
initially as youth coach, then as manager
from April 1995.
FA Cup winner with West Ham in 1975.

TAYLOR, Tony
Kilmarnock, Celtic Morton,C Palace,
Southend, Swindon, Bristol R, Portsmouth,
Northampton, 1962-1979
Spent five weeks as Celtic's assistant man-
ager then moved to Canada to coach the
national youth team. Is now back scouting
in England.

TEES, Matt
Grimsby, Charlton, Luton, Grimsby, 1963-
1972
Matt is now working at the Volvo import car
terminal in Grimsby.

TEMPLE, Derek
Everton, Preston, 1956-1969
He started at Everton before he went to
Preston for £35,000 and had three years at
Deepdale, winning one England cap in the
process. Now lives in Ormskirk and is in
charge of the Merseyside branch of anl
industrial cleaning company. Had previously
worked in the glass industry for fifteen
years.
*Scored the winning goal for Everton in the
1966 FA Cup final.*

TEMPLEMAN, John
Brighton, Exeter, Swindon, 1966-1980
Former Brighton and Exeter full back who is
now a district agent with the Prudential and
lives in Pagham near Bognor.

TERNENT, Stan
Burnley, Carlisle, 1966-1973
Coached at Crystal Palace, followed by a
spell as manager of Hull City. Assistant
manager at Bury until Mike Walsh's departure in September 1995 when he was
appointed manager.
Took Bury to the Second Division in 1996.

TERRY, Steve
Watford, Hull, Northampton, 1979-1993
A popular centre half with Watford for eight
years and now player/assistant manager for
Enfield.
*Played for Watford in their FA Cup final
defeat against Everton.*

THIJSSEN, Frans
Ipswich, Notts F 1978-1983
Since leaving Nottingham Forest in 1983,
this Dutch International has played for
Fortuna Sittard, FC Groningen and Vitesse
Arnhem - who now employ him as full time
coach.
A UEFA Cup winner with Ipswich.

THOMAS, Andy
Oxford, Fulham, Derby, Newcastle, Bradford,
Plymouth 1980-1991
A forward who found the net on a regular
basis until a back injury forced his career to
come to an early end but has carved as
sucessful career in non league football taking Oxford City into the ICIS Premier
Division.
*A League Cup final winner with Oxford in
1986.*

THOMAS, Danny
Coventry, Tottenham, 1979-1987
Former England Under-21 international
signed as a pro in 1979 with Coventry,. earning two full England Caps. He earned a
£650,000 transfer to Spurs before injury
ended his career. Was the club physio at
West Brom until the summer of 1996. Now in
private practice in London.
A UEFA Cup winner with Spurs in 1984.

THOMAS, Dave
Burnley, QPR, Everton, Wolves, Middlesboro,
Portsmouth, 1967-1984
Former England winger who now lives in
Sussex and has set him self up as a
Landscape gardener. Was Portsmouth's
Youth Coach and then helped out at Bognor
Regis FC before accepting David Webb's
invitation to help out at Brentford FC.

THOMAS, Geoff
Swansea 1966-1975
Played almost 350 games for the Swans and earned three Welsh under-23 caps. Is now manager of Pontypool sports centre.

THOMAS, Mike
Wrexham, Man U, Everton, Brighton, Stoke, Chelsea, W.B.A., Derby, Shrewsbury, Leeds, Stoke, Wrexham, 1971-1991
A cheuered career which was never short of excitement. Having spent a short stretch at Her Majesty's pleasure, Mickey had a spell in Wales managing Portmadog in the Konica League but is now out of the game.
Capped 51 times by Wales.

THOMAS, Rod
Swindon, Derby, Cardiff, Newport, 1965-1981
Welsh international right back and a first choice for Swindon for over eighteen years. After retiring in 1981 he worked for Francis Lee's paper company for a while but now runs a pub near Stroud in Gloucestershire.
League Cup winner with Swindon in 1969.

THOMPSON, Ian
Bournemouth 1983-1985
A striker who is now teaching mathematics at a school near his home in Swansea.

THOMPSON, Peter
Preston, Liverpool, Bolton, 1960-1977
Spent eight years at Anfield supplying crosses for some of the era's greatest strikers. Capped six times by England. After seven years running two caravan parks, Peter moved to the Lake District where he has run a country pub for the past fourteen years.
Two League Championships with Liverpool.

THOMPSON, Phil
Liverpool, Sheff U, 1971-1985
Played 337 League games during his eleven years at Liverpool and was capped 42 times by England, winning almost every honour in the game before moving off to Sheffield United. Since retiring   has been involved in a number of businesses including a fireplace showroom, a pine shop and two firms mak-

ing conservatories. Spent six years coaching at Liverpool, but now writes for a local newspaper and works for Sky Sports.
Five League Championships.

THOMPSON, Steve
Lincoln, Charlton, 1980-87
Joined Southend United as director of football in early 1995 and appointed manager in April of the same year. However, less than three months later, Steve accepted the post of team manager at Notts County.

THOMSON, Bobby
Wolves, Birmingham, Walsall, Luton, Port V 1961-1976
Bobby won eight England caps during his stay with Wolves in the sixties. Spent several years in America and now runs a sports shop in Sedgeley, near Dudley.
League Cup winner with Wolves in 1961.

THOMSON, George
Hearts, Everton, Brentford, 1960-1967
Spent five years with Brentford before returning to live in the Chester area. Now has a thriving salvage business.

THOMSON, Jim
Chelsea, Burnley, 1965-1980
Played almost 300 games for Burnley where he became commercial manager. Now a sales executive with Ben Shaw's Soft Drinks Co. in Huddersfield, but still lives in Burnley.

THORNE, Adrian
Brighton, Plymouth, Exeter, Leyton O, 1957-1965
Former goalscoring winger Adrian is now teaching PE in Ealing, West London.

THURLOW, Bryan
Norwich, Bristol City, 1954-1964
Quit after never playing a game for City after an achilles tendon injury. Continued to play non-league and works as a coach builder.

TILER, Brian
Rotherham, Aston V, Carlisle, 1962-1973
Spent fours years in the heart of the Villa

defence following his move from Rotherham. Became managing director at Bournemouth before dying in a tragic car accident in Spain during the World Cup Finals.
Third Division title with Villa in 1973.

TINDALL, Ron
Chelsea, West Ham, Reading, Portsmouth, 1953-1969
An all rounder who also played cricket for Surrey – once missed the start of the soccer season becase Surrey were chasing the County Championship. Emigrated to Australia and now lives in Perth where he is state director of sport.

TODD, Colin
Sunderland, Derby, Everton, Birmingham, Notts F, Oxford, Luton, 1966-1984
Awarded the first of his 27 England caps after Derby County splashed out £170,000 to take the 22 year-old to the Baseball Ground. A key member of Brian Clough's side, he formed a partnership with Roy McFarland, at international as well as club level. He became assistant manager at Middlesboro and held the same post at Bolton until promoted to manager in January 1996.
League Championship winner in his first season with Derby and collected another in 1974-5.

TOPPING, Chris
York, Huddersfield, 1968-1980
Played over 400 League games for York City, including an amazing run of 378 consecutive appearances. Now runs his family market garden in Selby.

TOSHACK, John MBE
Cardiff, Liverpool, Swansea, 1965-1983
A natural goalscorer who formed a deadly partnership with Kevin Keegan at Liverpool. Had moved to Anfield in a £110,000 deal from Cardiff City in 1970, and in his seven year stay scored 74 goals in 174 appearances. As a manager, he inspired Swansea's dramatic rise from the Fourth to First Division. His departure opened the door to a new challenges abroad, notably in Spain,

where he managed Real Sociedad, then the mighty Real Madrid, winning the championship in his first season. Despite this, the club sacked him shortly afterwards, and in 1991 he returned to Real Sociedad as General Manager. In March 1994, a spell as Welsh national team boss lasted a mere 44 days and one game, before John returned to Spain to take over at Deportivo La Coruna.
Won a UEFA Cup winners medal in 1973.

TOWNER, Tony
Brighton, Millwall, Rotherham, Wolves, Charlton, Rochdale, Camb U, 1972-1986
Drives a van for furniture giants 'Courts', but is still involved in football as player/coach of Saltdean in the Unijet Sussex County League.
The most expensive player in Rotherham's history.

TRAIN, Ray
Walsall, Carlisle, Sunderland, Bolton, Watford, Oxford, Bournemouth, Northampton, Tranmere, Walsall, 1968-1986
Well travelled tiny midfield man who notched up 500 games. Became Port Vale community officer in 1990 and less than a year later chief scout at Middlesboro.
Helped Watford win promotion to the First Division.

TRAUTMANN, Bert
Man C 1949-1963

Best known for a heroic display in the 1956 Cup final, when the blond goalie sustained a broken neck but insisted on completing the match. This German ex-paratrooper went on to represent the Football league and to play over 500 games for Man City. Now owns a house in his native Germany, but lives in retirement in Valencia, Spain.

A crowd of 48,000 turned out for his testimonial in 1963.

TRAYNOR, Tommy

Southampton 1952-1965

Played 480 games for the Saints and eight times for his country, Ireland. Still lives in Southampton and works in the docks.

TREACY, Ray

WBA, Charlton, Swindon, Preston, Oldham, WBA, 1964-1976

Managed the Northern Ireland side Crusaders. Now a travel agent in Dublin.

TREBILCOCK, Mike

Plymouth, Everton, Portsmouth, Torquay, 1962-1972

Helped Everton pull off one of the most dramatic comebacks in FA Cup final history in 1966. The merseysiders were trailing 2-0 to Sheffield Wednesday, but won 3-2 thanks to two goals by Trebilcock and a Derek Temple winner. Now lives in Australia at Lake Maquarie, sixty miles north of Sydney. Mike works as a storeman and coaches a local semi-pro side at weekends.

TREWICK, John

WBA, Newcastle, Oxford, Birmingham, Hartlepool, 1974-1989

Reserve team coach at West Brom after taking over as caretaker manager in October 1994 following Keith Burkenshaw's dismissal.

League Cup winner with Oxford in 1986.

TROLLOPE, John

Swindon 1960-1980

A long serving single club man, Trollope made his debut in 1960 before going on to play 770 league games for Swindon. The highlight of his career came in 1968-9 when, as a Third Division club, Swindon beat the mighty Arsenal to win the League Cup. Ran the Youth team at the County Ground, until mid 1996.

Holds the Robins' record for most number of League appearances.

TUDOR, John

Coventry, Sheff U, Newcastle, Stoke, 1966-1976

Scored over 100 goals during his time with four League clubs. Ended his career with Stoke in 1976 andnow runs a pub.

Played in Newcastle's 1974 FA Cup losing side.

TUEART, Dennis

Sunderland, Man C, Stoke, Burnley, 1968-1983

Dennis started his career at Sunderland before a £250,000 transfer took him to Maine Road in 1974. Now runs his own corporate promotions company in Manchester and can regularly be seen at Maine Road, where he leases an executive box.

FA Cup winner with Sunderland in 1973.

TUNKS, Roy

Rotherham, York, Preston, Wigan, Hartlepool, Preston, 1967-1989

Played over 700 games in goal during a career which lasted for well over twenty years. Now works as a coach for the Lancashire FA.

T

TURNBULL, Fred
Aston V, Halifax, 1967-1973
He had to retire at the age of 28 due to injury. Now lives in Northumberland and runs his own business in Blyth.
Division Three Championship winner with Villa in 1972.

TURNER, Chris
Sheffield Weds, Lincoln, Sunderland, Man U, Sheffield Weds, Leyton O, 1976-1994
A former England youth international who gave good service before moving into management with Leyton Oreint for an ill-fated partnership with John Sitton. Moved to Leicester as youth team coach, a position he new holds with Wolves.
Won a League Cups winners medal for Sheffield Wednesday against his former team, Manchester United.

TURNER, Gordon
Luton 1950-1963
Prolific goalscorer who netted 243 times from 406 appearances with his one and only club. Died in 1976.
Holds the Hatters record for most goals in a League career.

TURNER, Graham
Wrexham, Chester, Shrewsbury, 1964-1983
Turner was a midfielder with Wrexham and Chester before reverting to a defensive role for Shrewsbury, where he made over 700 appearances.. Became manager at Shrewsbury and took them from the Fourth Division to the Second. A two year stint at Aston Villa preceded a move to Wolves where he repeated the feat of climbing from the Fourth to the Second Division. Despite this, pressure mounted and he was replaced by Graham Taylor in 1994. Appointed director of football with Hereford in 1995.

TURNER, Ian
Huddersfield, Grimsby, Walsall, Southampton, Newport, Lincoln, Walsall, Halifax, 1970-1980
A goalkeeper who played just under 100 games with Saints, where he is best remembered. Now a mechanical supervisor, living in Southampton.
FA Cup winner with Saints in 1976.

TURNER, John
Derby, Doncaster, Huddersfield, Reading, Torquay, Chesterfield, Torquay, Burnley, Peterboro, 1972-1985
Landlord of the 'Fortune of War' public house in Torquay.

TWENTYMAN, Geoff
Carlisle, Liverpool, Carlisle, 1946-1963
Chief scout at Liverpool for many years, but is now retired and still living in the City.
Captained Liverpool in 1957-58.

TWENTYMAN, Geoff
Preston, Bristol Rovers, 1983-1993
Son of Geoff, appointed assistant manger to Ian Holloway at Rovers in May 1996 after working as a producer with BBC Radio.

TYDEMAN, Dick
Gillingham, Charlton, Gillingham, Peterboro, 1969-1983
Long servicing Chatham born midfield man who played over 500 games with his four clubs. Dick is now working for the Prudential assurance company.

TYNAN, Bobby
Tranmere, Blackpool, 1972-1978
Quit the game at the age of 22 having already played 200 games for Tranmere. Now lives in Birkenhead and runs a shop/post office.

TYNAN, Tommy
Liverpool, Swansea, Sheff Wed, Lincoln, Newport, Plymouth, Rotherham, Plymouth, 1972-1992
Won a trial with home town club Liverpool after winning a competition organised by a local newspaper. Went on to become a striker with a superb scoring record. Lives in Stocksbridge, near Sheffield, and until the summer of 1996 worked as a pub landlord.
Scored nine goals in nine games to take Plymouth to the Third Division in 1986.

UGOLINI, Rolando

Hearts, Celtic, Middlesboro, Wrexham, Dundee Utd, Berwick, 1943-1962

Italian born Rolando played over 300 games in goal for Middlesbrough. Established his own chain of betting shops which he sold in 1984 before retiring back to Scotland.

UPRICHARD, Norman

Swindon, Portsmouth, Southend, 1949-1959

Irish international keeper who moved to Ireland to run the bar at Queens University after his playing days. Returned to England after twelve years to retire to Hastings.

URE, Ian

Dundee, Arsenal, Man U, St Mirren, 1953-1973

Retired through injury during the 1973/4 season. Managed East Stirling for a year, then coached in Iceland before returning in 1977 to take up social work in a Glasgow Prison.

Scottish Cup winner with Dundee.

VAESSEN, Paul

Arsenal 1978-1981

Scored the goal which took Arsenal into the 1980 Cup Winners Cup final. Since injury ended his career has had numerous jobs, including building work and as a postman.

VAN BREUKELEN, Hans

Notts F 1982-1983

Returned to Holland and joined PSV.

VAN DER ELST, Frankie

West Ham 1981-1982

A Belgian international who had a short spell at Upton Park in the early '80s. Now runs a chain of cafes and coaches for the Belgium FA. Returned to the club in 1996 whilst making a film of his career.

VAN WIJK, Dennis

Norwich 1982-1986

His career ended when he broke his leg whilst playing in Belgium. Now runs the Los Amigos Bar in Bruges.

VASPER, Peter

Leyton O, Norwich, Camb U, 1963-1973

Former Bank of England clerk who played nearly all of his football with Cambridge. Now works an insurance agent for the Prudential and lives in Birmingham.

VAUGHAN, Nigel

Newport, Cardiff, Reading, Wolves, Hereford, 1976-1992

Former Welsh international who lives in Telford and works as a production controller for Bundy UK. Still playing, in non-league soccer, for Newport where he is player/boss.

VEALL, Ray

Doncaster, Everton, Preston, Huddersfield, 1960-1966

Played for four league clubs before the age of 24 and is now living in New Zealand.

VENABLES, Terry

Chelsea, Spurs, QPR, C Palace, 1959-1974

Former England midfield man who played for four London clubs in his long career. Moved into coaching at Palace, becoming manager in 1976, and moved to QPR four years later when he was appointed a director with the second biggest shareholding. Took up the challenge of Barcelona and after helping them to their first Championship for eleven years again was sacked after fan pressure following a lean spell. Appointed manager of Spurs and later chief executive but was sacked during a well-publicised conflict with Alan Sugar. Managed England for two years and bowed out after Euro 96. Now director of football with Portsmouth.

FA Cup winner with Spurs in 1967.

VERNON, Roy

Blackburn, Everton, Stoke, Halifax, 1955-1969

Welsh international with 32 full appearances, Vernon was an inside forward with a great knack of scoring goals, netting 172 times from 395 League appearances. Ran an antiques business in Blackburn before his death in December 1993 aged 56.

Won a League Championship with Everton.

V/W

VILJOEN, Colin
Ipswich, Man C, Chelsea, 1966-1981

A South African born midfielder who was capped twice by England after becoming a British subject in 1971. Made his name at Ipswich where he played over 350 games during his eleven years of service. Became the licensee of a pub near Heathrow Airport when his career ended.

Division Two Champion with Ipswich in 1968.

VILLA, Ricardo
Tottenham 1978-1982

Joined Tottenham in 1978 for £375,000 from Racing Club of Buenos Aires, having been a member of the Argentinian World Cup winning squad. After leaving Spurs, he spent a year in America, then Columbia, before finishing his playing days in the Argentine second division at the age of 37. Now owns a 740 acre ranch in Argentina, south of Buenos Aires.

An FA Cup winner with Spurs in 1981 when he scored twice in the replay against Man City.

VINEY, Keith
Portsmouth, Exeter, Bristol C, 1975-1988

Now an insurance agent for the Britannic Assurance Company in Exeter. His sister is married to current Portsmouth keeper, Alan Knight.

VINTER, Mick
Notts Co, Wrexham, Oxford, Mansfield, Newport, 1972-1986

A striker who is now a salesman in Nottingham.

VIOLLET, Dennis
Man U, Stoke, 1952-1966

Spent thirteen successful years at Manchester United, before ending his career at Stoke City. In 1967 moved to the United States as one of the pioneers of soccer in America. He is still over there now directing the Dennis Viollet Dolphin Soccer Camps in addition to his duties as head coach of Jacksonville University.

Two League Championships with Man Utd.

VOWDEN, Geoff
Notts F, Birmingham, Aston V, 1959-1973

After a wonderful career as a goalscorer for four clubs, Vowden left competitive football in December 1974 and concentrated on coaching youngsters in the Kettering area after service with Kettering Town and in Saudi Arabia - still plays local Sunday league soccer.

Division Two promotion in 1972.

WADE, Joe
Arsenal 1946-1954

Upon leaving Arsenal in 1956, Joe ended his playing career at Hereford United, as player and manager for six years. Remaining in the area, he then opened two sports shops, in Hereford and Leominster, a business which was to last thirty years. Now retired, Joe still lives in Hereford in a house named 'Highbury'.

League Championship in 1953 with The Gunners.

WADSWORTH, Mick
Scunthorpe U 1976

Former Scunthrope winger who was director of coaching of Carlisle and Norwich City assistant manager. Is now in charge of Scarborough.

WAGSTAFF, Ken
Mansfield, Hull, 1960-1975

One of Hull City's greatest scorers, Ken struck up a partnership with Chris Chilton. Returned to the UK after a spell in Australia, where he was player/coach for George Cross of Melbourne. Now owns 'Waggy's' club in Hessle, Humberside, and as well as writing a column for the local newspaper Ken helps out as an after lunch speaker in the sponsors lounge at Hull City home games.
Leading scorer in Division Three in 1963 with 34 goals.

WAGSTAFFE, Dave
Man C, Wolves, Blackburn, Blackpool, Blackburn, 1960-1978
Played in over 550 league games, most of them in his ten years at Wolves. The connection with the club continues to date, as he now runs 'Waggy's Bar' inside Molineux.
League Cup winner with Wolves in 1974.

WAINMAN, Harry
Grimsby, Rochdale 1964-1972
Harry now owns the Saxon House Hotel in Cleethorpes.

WAINWRIGHT, Eddie
Everton, Rochdale, 1946-1958
Former Everton and Rochdale foward who became landlord of 'The Acorn' in Bebington.

WAITERS, Tony
Blackpool, Burnley, 1959-1971
Capped five times with England whilst at Blackpool. Retired in 1967 to become FA regional coach. Held coaching posts at Liverpool, Burnley, Coventry and Plymouth. Tony then moved over to Canada to assist the Vancouver Whitecaps and was named 'Coach of the Year' in 1978. Nows runs his own soccer school and in 1984 was coach to the Canadian Olympic Games team.
Played five times for the Football League.

WALDEN, Richard
Aldershot, Sheff Wed, Newport C, 1964-1981
Played over 400 games for Aldershot. Now manages a sports wholesale business, Midas Leisure Ltd. in Hampshire.

WALDRON, Colin
Bury, Chelsea, Burnley, Man U, Sunderland, Rochdale, 1966-1979
Former Burnley central defender (308 appearances) who now runs a bookmakers in Nelson, Lancs as well as having business interests with Colin Bell in Bury.
Second Division Champion in 1973.

WALDRON, Malcolm
Southampton, Burnley, Portsmouth, 1974-1984
A former England under-23 international who became an advertising representative in Portsmouth, but now believed to be selling Double Glazing.
Saints player of the year in 1979.

WALFORD, Steve
Tottenham, Arsenal, Norwich, West Ham, Huddersfield, Gillingham, WBA, 1975-1988
A former England youth international who won a Championship winners medal in Hong Kong. Returned after a spell in Turkey and was appointed youth development manager at Wycombe Wanderers but has since followed Martin O'Neill to both Norwich and Leicester City.
Came on as a sub for Arsenal in the 1979 FA Cup final.

WALKER, Clive
Chelsea, Sunderland, QPR, Fulham, Brighton, 1976-1991
Chelsea enjoyed Clive's skills on the wing for seven years before he moved on to play for four more League clubs, ending at Brighton. Now works for an auction house in Surrey and plays for Woking.

WALKER, Clive
Leicester, Northampton, Mansfield, 1963-1974
Clive played over 225 games for the Stags as a left back. Now lives in Gillingham and was assistant manager at Kettering Town until February 1995.

WALKER, David
Burnley, Southampton, 1960-1973

Played almost 200 games for Southampton. Defender David finished his career in South Africa, playing for Cape Town. When he returned to England he set up a successful antiques business.

WALKER, James
Derby, Hartlepool, Brighton, Peterboro, Chester, 1967-1980
Has been physio at Aston Villa since 1987.

WALKER, Len
Newcastle, Aldershot, Darlington, 1963-1977
Len became manager of Aldershot and is now with Fulham as assistant manager.
Played 440 league games for Aldershot between 1964 and 1975.

WALKER, Mike
Reading, Shrewsbury, York, Watford, Charlton, Colchester U, 1963-1982
A reliable keeper who made over 700 league appearances since starting out with Reading in January 1963. He signed for Colchester in 1973, becoming a mainstay in the club, moved to Norwich as reserve team boss in 1987 before steping up to the first team five years later. He walked out to take over at Everton but was sacked in November 1994. Started his own skip hire company in Norwich until being re appointed at Carrow Road in June 1996.
Twice won promotion with Colchester from Division Four.

WALKER, Nigel
Newcastle, Crewe, Sunderland, Blackpool, Chester, Hartlepool, 1977-1986
Nigel played for six league clubs in his career and is now teaching at St Bedes School in Chester.

WALKER, Tommy
Newcastle, Oldham, Chesterfield, Oldham, 1946-1958
An outside right who plied his trade on the wing for Newcastle and Oldham Athletic in the late forties and fifties. Now living in retirement in Edinburgh.
Won back-to-back FA Cups with Newcastle.

WALLACE, Willie
Stenhousemuir, Raith, Hearts, Celtic, Crystal Palace, Dumbarton 1958-1972
Moved to Australia after his playing days were over and coached two local sides in Sydney. Still lives in Sydney and works for a Sportsware company in Mount Druitt.
European Cup winner with Celtic in 1967.

WALLEY, Tom
Arsenal, Watford, Leyton O, Watford, 1965-1976
For a long time was youth coach at Watford and responsible for developing many youngsters, including John Barnes. Coached the youth teams at Watford, Millwall and his present club Arsenal.
Managed Watford's 1991 FA Youth Cup winning side.

WALLINGTON, Mark
Walsall, Leicester, Derby, Lincoln, 1971-1990
England under-23 international goalkeeper who played 400 games between the sticks for Leicester City. Mark is now a PE teacher at a Grantham school and is assitant manager of Grantham.
Won a Second Division Championship with Leicester.

WALSH, Dave
W.B.A., Aston V, Walsall, 1946-1955
He won 29 caps for Northern Ireland and the Republic of Ireland, played twice for the Irish League and was named reserve for the Great Britain side. Walsh continued running a sports shop and newsagents in Droitwich before retiring to Kingsbridge near Plymouth in 1984.
Won promotion to Division One with WBA in 1959.

WALSH, Ian
C Palace, Swansea, Barnsley, Grimsby, Cardiff, 1976-1988
Lives and works in Cardiff, where he sells insurance and can often be heard on BBC Radio Wales. In his playing days, won eighteen full Welsh caps during his successful five year stay at Crystal Palace.

Division Two Championship with Palace in 1979.

WALSH, Jimmy
Celtic, Leicester, 1949-1962
Now runs a newsagency in the centre of Leicester where he played as a centre forward for the local side.
Scored the first ever hat trick in the League Cup.

WALSH, Mike
Bolton, Everton, Norwich, Burnley, Man C, Blackpool, Bury, 1974-1989
A Republic of Ireland international who made a name for himself as a quality central defender. Spent almost five years as manager of Bury until losing his job in 1995. After a short spell at non-league Barrow, became Swindon first team coach in October 1996.
Won a Second Division Championship with Bolton.

WALSH, Micky
Blackpool, Everton, QPR, 1971-1979
Former Republic of Ireland forward who attracted the bigger clubs whilst at Blackpool but was forced to quit the game at 26. Latterly managed Chertsey Town in the ICIS League.

WALTERS, George
Shrewsbury, Newport , 1956-1965
Ex-Shrews right back is now a maintenance supervisor in Newport, Gwent.

WALTON, Ronnie
Northampton, Crewe, Carlisle, Aldershot, Camb U, Aldershot, 1964-1976
Now a chain store owner in his home town of Newcastle. Played over 300 League games for Aldershot in two spells during the sixties and seventies.

WANT, Tony
Tottenham, Birmingham, 1967-1977
Failed to make a breakthrough at White Hart Lane and ended his career at Birmingham, where he works as warehouse manager for a frozen food company.

WARBOYS, Alan
Doncaster, Sheff Wed, Cardiff, Sheff U, Bristol R, Fulham, Hull, Doncaster, 1966-1981
Scored goals for fun during his career. Now Landlord of 'The Ring O' Bells' in Swinton which he took over when he retired from the game with a back injury.

WARD, David (Dai)
Bristol Rovers, Cardiff, Watford, Brentford, 1954-1964
A Welsh international inside forward who made his name with Bristol Rovers, playing 175 league games and scoring 90 goals. Retired to Cambridge where he died in early 1996.
Once scored a hat-trick for Rovers in a four-minute spell.

WARD, Gerry
Arsenal, Leyton O, 1953-1964
Former Arsenal and Orient wing half, Gerry died January 1994 aged 57.

WARD, John
Lincoln, Workington, Watford, Grimsby, Lincoln, 1970-1981
Scored nearly 100 League goals for Lincoln, Workington, and Watford before moving into coaching and then management with York City. Moved to Bristol Rovers, losing his job at the end of the 1995/6 season and is now assistant manager with Burnley.
Leading scorer when Lincoln won the Fourth Division in 1976.

WARK, John
Ipswich, Liverpool, Ipswich, Middlesboro, Ipswich 1974-1996
P.F.A. 'Player of the Year' in 1991, John was still enjoying his football 22 years after signing as a pro. Won 29 Scotland caps before he joined Liverpool in 1984 for £450,000, returning to Portman Road four years later. Now works as community officer.
UEFA Cup Winners Cup winner with Ipswich.

WARNOCK, Neil
Chesterfield, Rotherham, Hartlepool,

Scunthorpe, Aldershot, Barnsley, York, Crewe, 1967-1978
Manager of Huddersfield Town until he resigned shortly after guiding the club to victory in the play-offs. Took Plymouth into the Second Division, again via the play-offs at Wembley. Previously took Notts County to two promotions.
Guided Scarborough into the Football League in 1987.

WATERHOUSE, Ken
Preston, Rotherham, Bristol C, Darlington, 1953-1964
Wing half who played for Rotherham who is now an enforcement officer for the North West Water Authority.

WATSON, Dave
Notts Co, Rotherham, Sunderland, Man C, Southampton, Stoke, Derby, Notts Co, 1966-1984
Began with Notts County, then moved to Rotherham, Sunderland and Manchester City. Transferred to West German club Werder Bremen for £200,000 in June 1979, but he did not settle and within four months was back in England with Southampton before he left to play in quick succession for Stoke City, Vancouver Whitecaps and Derby County. Now back in the Midlands, living in West Bridgeford and runs a marketing business, Dave Watson International.
FA Cup winner in 1973 with Sunderland.

WATSON, Graham
Doncaster, Rotherham, Doncaster, Camb U, Lincoln, Camb U, 1966-1979
Graham's 400-plus game career took in two stops each at Cambridge and Doncaster. He is now Landlord at 'The Three Horseshoes' pub in Comberton, Cambridgeshire.

WAYMAN, Charlie
Newcastle, Southampton, Preston., Middlesboro, Darlington, 1946-1957
Centre forward who was a prolific goalscorer for all his clubs, scoring 254 goals in 382 League games, Now a sales representative for a brewery in Bishop Auckland.

Helped Preston to promotion in 1951.

WATSON, Willie
Huddersfield, Sunderland, Halifax T, 1937-1955
One of a rare bunch of players who played both cricket and football for England. Now retired and living in South Africa.
Won three League Champoinships with Huddersfield.

WEALANDS, Jeff
Wolves, Darlington, Hull, Birmingham, Man U, Oldham, Preston, 1968-1984
A property developer living in Wilmslow, Cheshire and helps coach the goalkeepers at Bury. Also a director of Altrincham FC for whom he kept goal after playing for several League clubs.
Helped Birmingham win promotion from Division Two.

WEARE, Len
Newport, 1955-1969
Was the talented custodian of the Newport goal for over fifteen seasons, playing a total of 524 games.

WEBB, David
Leyton O, Southampton, Chelsea, QPR, Leicester, QPR, Leicester, Derby, Bournemouth, Torquay, 1964-1984
Started with Orient and Southampton before hitting the big time with Chelsea. Left to serve three more clubs before going into management with Torquay, Bournemouth, Southend and Chelsea. Manager of Brentford since 1993.
Scored the winner in the 1970 FA Cup final replay.

WEBSTER, Colin
Cardiff, Manchester United, Swansea, Newport Co,1950-1964
Worked as a fitter, playing part-time, when United offered him a trial. Has since worked as a scaffolder and then a park ranger in Swansea.
Played for United in the 1958 FA Cup final.

WEBSTER, Malcolm

Arsenal, Fulham, Southend, Camb U, 1969-1983

Recently started up his own goalkeeping schools to add to his duties coaching keepers at various League Clubs, including Peterborough and Cambridge.

WEBSTER, Ron

Derby 1961-1977

Long serving right back who played over 450 League games for the Rams over sixteen years. Is now minding cattle on a 100-acre beef farm north of Nottingham.
Won a League Championship medal with Derby.

WEBB, Dougie

Reading 1956-1966

An inside forward with Reading for a decade before becoming a decorator, living in the Reading area. Father of Neil.

WEBSTER, Barry

Rotherham, Bradford, 1956-1963

Former Rotherham winger who now works for an engineering company in Sheffield.

WELBOURNE, Duncan

Grimsby, Watford, Southport, 1957-1975

Started as a defender at Grimsby but played 400 games for Watford having joined them in 1963. Delivers potatoes for a living and has had a variety of jobs since finishing playing, including digging a tunnel under London's Albert Dock!
Won a Third Division title with The Hornets.

WELLER, Keith

Tottenham, Millwall, Chelsea, Leicester C, 1964-1978

A skillful striker who had success with Millwall and then Chelsea. However, it was during his time with Leicester that he was finally rewarded with four England caps. A £40,000 transfer to the New England Team took him to the States where Keith still lives today, in Seattle. He is a driver for an outside broadcastunit for an American TV company.

WENT, Paul

Leyton O, Charlton, Fulham, Portsmouth, Cardiff, Leyton O, 1965-1979

Started and ended his career at Orient where he also had a disastrous 20 day spell as manager. Retired in 1979 after almost 500 League appearances. Most of his playing days were based in London and he is now a representative for Courage Brewery.

WEST, Alan

Burnley, Luton, Millwall, 1969-1982

Former England under-23 international midfielder who played close on 300 League games for Luton. He is a pastor living in Luton and is involved with the Christians in Sport organisation.

WEST, Gordon

Blackpool, Everton, Tranmere, 1960-1978

A goalkeeper who won three England caps with Everton and later played for Tranmere Rovers, where he went on to work on the ground staff at Prenton Park. Currently works in security on Merseyside.
Two League Championshipships with Everton.

WESTON, Don

Wrexham, Birmingham, Rotherham, Leeds, Huddersfield, Wrexham, Chester, 1958-1968

Don played 275 league games scoring 95 goals and is now a senior salesman in a Vauxhall dealership in Wrexham.
Division Two Championship with Leeds in 1964.

WHATMORE, Neil

Bolton , Birmingham, Bolton, Oxford, Bolton, Burnley, Mansfield, Bolton, Mansfield, 1972-1987

Played consistently for Bolton in the seventies before leaving for Birmingham in 1981. Had three more spells at Boundary Park before quitting in 1987 and now works as a milkman in the Mansfield area and manages Rainworth MW in the local Notts Alliance League.
Division Two Champion with Bolton in 1978.

WHELAN, David
Blackburn, Crewe, 1956-1965
Bradford born defender who signed for
Blackburn in 1953 and played 78 league
games before moving to Crewe where his
playing days ended in 1965. Set up his own
sports shop business, JJB sports, which
blossomed to become a chain of 115 stores.
The company was floated on the stock market in 1994, making the ex-Blackburn Rovers
defender an estimated £13.5 million.
*Broke his leg in the 1960 FA Cup final whilst
playing for Blackburn.*

WHELAN, Ronnie
Liverpool, Southend, 1979-1996
Signed by The Reds on a free transfer from
Home Farm, Ronnie went on to to play over
350 league games for Liverpool. Moved to
the Essex coast on a free transfer and was
apppointed manager of Southend in July
1995. Capped 45 times by his native
Republic of Ireland.
*Won Six league Championships, Two FA
Cup's, three League Cups and a European
Cup with Liverpool.*

WHITAKER, Colin
Sheff Wed, Bradford PA, Shrewsbury, QPR.,
Rochdale, Oldham, Barrow, 1951-1964
After managing Stalybridge and then
Buxton, Colin purchased a 46-acre farm and
built a golf course. Now retired and man-
ages to escape from the British weather by
living part of the year in Spain.

WHITE, Dick
Scunthorpe, Liverpool, Doncaster, 1950-1963
Scunthorpe born central defender who
joined Liverpool from his home town club in
1955. Dick is now a garage proprietor in
Nottingham and a keen golfer who is a past
Captain and President of Scunthorpe Golf
Club - but can often now be found on the
links of the Chilwell Manor Club in Beeston.
*Division Two Championship with Liverpool
in 1962.*

WHITE, Ian
Celtic, Leicester, Southampton, 1956-1966
Never made the grade at Celtic and moved
south to play for Leicester and then to
Southampton. Now runs a sports shop in
Totton, Hampshire.

WHITE, John
Alloa, Falkirk, Tottenham, 1956-1963
Scottish international nicknamed 'The
Ghost' who made 183 appearances for
Tottenham. in his four years at White Hart
Lane. Was tipped to go on and become one
of Spurs all time greats until he died 1964
aged only 27 after being struck by lightning
on an Enfield golf course.
Spurs double-winner..

WHITE, Len
Rotherham, Newcastle, Huddersfield,
Stockport, 1950-1965
A centre forward who played 244 league
games for Newcastle, scoring 142 goals in
his nine year stay. He died in the June 1994
after a long fight against cancer, aged 64.
A 1955 FA Cup final winner with Newcastle.

WHITE, Winston
Leicester, Hereford, Chesterfield, Port V,
Stockport, Bury, Rochdale, Colchester,
Burnley, WBA, 1976-1991
Purchased a restaurant in Padiham after
hanging up his well travelled boots.

WHITEFOOT, Jeff
Man U, Grimsby, Notts F, 1949-1967
Former under-23 international wing half who
became licensee of a pub after a career
which took in three clubs and over 350
appearances.
FA Cup winners medal with Forest in 1959.

WHITEHEAD, Clive
Bristol C, WBA, Wolves, Portsmouth, Exeter,
1973-1990
Played 256 games for Bristol City prior to
joining West Brom for £100,000. Ended his
League playing days at Exeter before
becoming manager of Yeovil Town. More
recently was with Bristol City as
reserve/youth coach but was sacked as a
cost cutting measure in May 1995.

Helped City win promotion to the First Division in 1976 by scoring the promotion winning goal against Portsmouth.

WHITEHOUSE, Brian
WBA, Norwich, Wrexham, C.Palace, Charlton, Leyton O, 1955-1967
Played most of his football in the lower divisions, but since ending his playing caree he's made a name for himself as a top class coach working with Arsenal, West Brom, Manchester United and Aston Villa. Was chief scout at Aston Villa until Ron Atkinson's surprise departure.
Scored Norwich's first ever League Cup goal.

WHITEHURST, Billy
Hull, Newcastle, Oxford, Reading, Sunderland, Hull, Sheffield U, Stoke, Doncaster, Crewe A, 1980-1993
Powerful striker who led the Hull line in the early eighties. Nine stops later, Billy went abroad to play in Hong Kong but returned home to manage Frickley Athletic where he was sacked in the 1995/6 season. Has recently taken over 'The Cricketers Arms' pub in Hull.

WHITESIDE, Norman
Manchester U, Everton, 1981-1990
Although forced to retire in 1990 at the age of 25, Norman had already proved himself to be one of the most exciting players of his day and had won 38 caps for Northern Ireland. Was a full time student at Salford University where he qualified as a chiropodist. Also plays in occasional charity matches and undertakes after dinner speaking.
Scored the winner in the 1985 FA Cup final against Everton.

WHITTLE, Alan
Everton, C Palace, Leyton O, Bournemouth, 1967-1980
The blond bombshell who took Everton by storm when he scored eleven goals in fifteen games in 1969-70. He was only 20 at the time, but the early success petered out and he was sold to Crystal Palace for £100,000 in

1972. He played for Orient and Bournemouth before going to Australia. Now lives on the Wirral and works for football in the community, based at Everton.
Won a Division One Championship in 1970.

WHITTLE, Maurice
Blackburn, Oldham, Wigan, 1966-1980
Played over 300 games for Oldham then spent three years in the States with Fort Lauderdale Strikers, followed by a spell in Finland. Now lives in Wigan and is manager of the JJB Sports shop in Chorley.

WHITTON, Steve
Coventry, West Ham, Birmingham, Sheff Wed, Ipswich, Colchester, 1979-1996
Former Coventry City junior who played professionally for six clubs and is now assistant manager at Colchester United.
Leading scorer in 1983 for Coventry with 12 goals.

WHYMARK, Trevor
Ipswich, Derby, Grimsby, Southend, Peterboro, Colchester, 1969-1985
Trevor won one England cap whilst playing for Ipswich Town in the late seventies. Grmsby later broke their transfer record to sign him from Derby. Coached youngsters and ran courses at holiday camps for four years, but now works as a van salesman.

WHYTE, David
Leeds, Hibs, Bradford, Barnsley, 1977-1980
Failed to make the grade as a professional and now works as a fireman and plays local league football for Harrogate Railway Athletic.

WICKS, Steve
Chelsea, Derby, QPR, C.Palace, QPR, Chelsea, 1974-1987
Won England under-23 honours as a Chelsea player in the seventies. He started and ended his career at Stamford Bridge before becoming assistant manager at Portsmouth until August 1989. He then linked up with Paul Mariner to run an agency handling players affairs. Returned to League manage-

ment at Scarborough for less than a season, and has since had a spells with Lincoln and Newcastle as chief scout.

WIGG, Ron
Ipswich, Watford, Rotherham, Grimsby, Bransley, Scunthorpe, 1967-1979
Grimsby paid a record fee for Ron who now lives in America where he is Ohio South coaching director and is also on the National Staff Coaching Board.

WIGGINGTON, Clive
Grimsby, Scunthorpe, Lincoln, Grimsby, Doncaster, Torquay, Doncaster, 1968-1982
Experienced defender who spent nine years at Grimsby in two spells and is now a manager for a Grimsby pipework company.

WIGLEY, Steve
Notts F, Sheff U, Birmingham, Portsmouth, Exeter, 1982-1993
Former Notts Forest winger who was appointed manager of Aldershot Town in January 1995 after a spell with Bognor.

WIGNALL, Frank
Everton, Notts F, Wolves, Derby, Mansfield, 1959-1972
Winner of two England caps in 1965, the former Notts Forest forward had a stint as the national coach to Qatar in the Persian Gulf. Now owns a garage and car showroom in Nottingham.

WIGNALL, Steve
Doncaster, Colchester, Brentford, Aldershot, 1972-1990
Manager of Aldershot Town until January 1995, when he returned to his former club, Colchster United, as manager.

WILE, John
Sunderland, Peterboro, WBA, Peterboro, 1966-1985
Played 500 games for West Brom before leaving to take over as player/manager of Peterborough United in 1983. Later involved in indoor cricket at Walsall and Solihull. Lives in Lichfield.

WILKINS, Ray
Chelsea, Man U, QPR, C. Palace, QPR, Wycombe, Hibs, 1973-1996
A glorious career began at Chelsea, with a debut in 1973 at the age of 17, 'Butch' played in Italy before returning home and was appointed QPR manager in November 1994 but was fired in September 1996. Returned to play for Wycombe the same week and then Hibs a week later.
Capped 84 times by England and scored in the 1983 FA Cup final.

WILKINSON, Howard
Sheff Wed, Brighton, 1964-1980
Manager at Sheffield Wednesday until October 1988 when he left to take the helm at Leeds United. Achieved promotion in 1990, winning the Championship title two years later. He took Leeds to a losing Coca Cola Cup final apperance at Wembley in 1996 but was sacked less than six months later. Can now be heard on Radio Five.
Played for England at youth and semi professional levels.

WILKINSON, Norman
Hull, York, 1952-1965
Played his entire career as a part timer and was given time off from his job as a shoe repairer to play. He worked in a Newcastle shoe factory for eleven years before retiring.
The 125 goals he scored for York is a club record.

WILLIAMS, Alex
Man City, Port V, 1980-87
A former England youth international goalkeeper who played over 100 games for City. Is now back at Maine Road as a football in the community officer.

WILLIAMS, Bert
Walsall, Wolves, 1937-1956
Played 381 matches for Wolves and won 24 England caps. Retired in 1957 and worked in a sports clothing business in Bilston. However, Bert now lives in Saifrial, Salop and works in an engineering firm.
League Championship in 1954.

WILLIAMS, Bobby

Bristol C, Rotherham, Bristol R, Reading, 1958-1970

Now working as a courier, but since 1972 has worked with the youth team at Reading, which has produced the likes of Neil Webb and Lawrie Sanchez.

WILLIAMS, Charlie

Doncaster 1949-1958

"Hello, me old flower!" The catch phrase of Charlie Williams, one of Britain's best loved comedians. Charlie never intended to become a comedian – he had his sights firmly set on a career in professional football. He played for Doncaster for twelve years. and, encouraged by his team mates, he started entertaining in the Working Men's Clubs in Yorkshire on Saturday evenings - and the rest as they say -is history! In spite of his fame and fortune, Charlie still lives a simple life in a little village near Barnsley. His main hobby is golf when he can get away from work and he also gives much of his time to charity shows.

WILLIAMS, Danny

Rotherham 1946-1959

The manager who guided Swindon to League Cup and promotion in the same season. He made 459 league appearances for Rotherham where he also managed. Retired and living in Bournemouth.

WILLIAMS, David

Bristol Rovers, Norwich, 1975-1988

Played over 350 league games for Rovers. Moved to Norwich City, won a Division Two Championship medal and held the assistant manager's job at Norwich, Bournemouth and Everton. Is now first team coach at Leeds United.

Appointed caretaker boss of Wales for one match in 1988.

WILLIAMS, Graham

WBA 1955-1970

Made 308 appearances for West Brom and earned 26 Welsh Caps. Retired as a professional player in 1972 and became player/manager at Weymouth. He then served at a host of clubs; Sports Club Kuwait, OFI Greece, Poole Town, Cardiff City, Newport, Leopards FC, Nigeria and FC Rovaniemen, Finland. He is now based in Oswestry but currently coaching in Kuwait.

Played in the 1968 FA Cup winning side.

WILLIAMS, Graham

Bradford C, Everton, Swansea, Wrexham, Tranmere, Port V, 1955-1968

Former Welsh outside left, Graham now works as a carpenter in the Wrexham area.

WILLIAMS, Herbie

Swansea 1958-1974

Became player/coach to Woollongong in Australia in 1975 after sixteen years with Swansea City. However he and his family could not settle, so he returned home to Port Talbot, where he now works as a postman.

WILLIAMS, John

Watford, Colchester, 1964-1977

Held the left back position at Watford for ten years before ending at Colchester in 1977. John now lives in Great Horksley near Colchester and works for a local electrical firm.

Played for Watford in the their rise to Division Three.

WILLIAMS, Oshor

Man U, Southampton, Exeter, Stockport, Port

V, Preston, 1976-1987
As well as being assistant manager at Hyde United, Osher has been a full time student at Salford Universtity studying History and Politics. Also lectures in sports studies on a part-time basis at Trafford College.

WILLIAMS, Stuart
Wrexham, WBA, Southampton, 1947-1965
After a League career which included over 350 appearances, Williams became trainer at West Bromwich Albion in 1967, then was employed as Aston Villa trainer, Payhaam Holland manager, Morton trainer/coach, Southampton coach and assistant manager , Carlisle United scout and Stavanger, Norway, manager. Now works as a financial controller with a transport company, having spent the previous twelve years as a commercial tyre salesman.
Played for Wales in the 1958 World Cup finals.

WILLIAMS, Tommy
Leicester, Birmingham, Grimsby, 1975-1990
A utility player whose career was dogged by two broken legs. With his senior career over, Tommy joined Leicestershire Police.
Division Two Championship with Leicester in 1980.

WILLS, Len
Arsenal 1953-1960
Former Arsenal full back who now lives in Chigwell, Essex, and worked in the DIY retail trade before retiring.
Chairty Shield winners medal in 1953.

WILSHAW, Dennis
Wolves, Walsall, Stoke, 1948-1960
Fearsome Wolves striker of the fifties who won twelve England caps before retring in 1961. Is now a teacher, living in Newcastle-under-Lyme.
League Championship with Wolves in 1954.

WILSON, Billy
Blackburn, Portsmouth, 1964-1978
A defender who played over 200 times for Portsmouth after signing from Blackburn

Rovers. Has been a publican for many years, currently licensee of the 'Horse & Jockey' in Curbridge, Hampshire.

WILSON, Bob
Aston V, Cardiff, Bristol, Exeter, 1963-1975
Played in goal for Cardiff in the sixties and with Exeter through to his retirement in 1975. Bob now works for the post office and lives in Exeter, Devon.

WILSON, Bob
Arsenal 1963-1973
Scottish international goalkeeper who retired in 1973 to concentrate on his television work. He also runs a successful goalkeeping school. In 1994, a lucrative offer and the opportunity of a new challenge persuaded Bob to switch from the BBC after over twenty years.
Double winner with Arsenal.

WILSON, Danny
Bury, Chesterfield, Notts F, Scunthorpe, Brighton, Luton, Sheff Wed, Barnsley, 1977-1995
A Northern Ireland international (winning 25 caps) who took over as manger of Barnsley in July 1994 when Viv Anderson joined up with Bryan Robson at Middlesbrough.
Appeared in Two League Cup finals, winning one with Sheffield Wednesday and losing once with Luton.

WILSON, David
Rangers, Dundee United, Dumbarton, 1966-1972
Made a one-off appearance as a 44 year old for Kilmarnock and was Dumbarton's manager for a year. He been employed in the whiskey industry and catering trade but now works as a financial adviser for a Glasgow based company.

WILSON, Glen
Brighton, Exeter, 1949-1961
Played over 400 games for Brighton and ended his career at Exeter before returning to Brighton where he lives and works.

WILSON, Kevin
Derby, Ipswich, Chelsea, Notts C, Walsall, 1979-1995
Northern Ireland striker who is now a coach at his last club as a player.

WILSON, Ray
Huddersfield, Everton, Oldham, Bradford C, 1955-1970
Played over 400 league games and won 63 England caps, including one for the victorious 1966 World Cup final. Now one of the most famous undertakers in Britain, running the family business from its base near Oldham.
FA Cup winner with Everton in 1966.

WILSON, Tom
Millwall, Hull, 1961-1969
After running his own shops for five years, decided to pursue a career in the legal profession, joining a fim of solicitors in 1972. In 1986 Tom re-joined one of his former clubs, Hull City, where he worked as coach, assistant manager and caretaker manager no less than four times! Following two years as company secretary, he returned to the legal profession in October 1993.

WINFIELD, John
Notts F, Peterboro, 1961-1974
Now runs a newsagency in Woollaton, Notts having played over 350 games as a left back for Notts Forest from 1971 to 1973.

WINSTANLEY, Eric
Barnsley, Chesterfield, 1961-1976
A former England youth international who became first team coach at Barnsley, where he had made over 400 appearances as a player. Now a football in the community officer at Barnsley.
Won promotion to the Third Division with Barsnley in 1968.

WITHE, Peter
Southport, Barrow, Wolves, Birmingham, Notts F, Newcastle, Aston V, Sheff U, Birmingham, Huddersfield, 1970-1989
A full England international and a much-travelled player. In his early years played for Southport and Barrow, both then in the Football League. Then came a spell in South African football followed by a return to this country to sign for Wolves. Next came service with Portland Timbers in the USA, and then Birmingham, before he won Championship medals with Nottingham Forest and then again at Aston Villa. Was appointed player/coach of Huddersfield Town and then had a brief spell as assistant manager to Josef Venglos at Aston Villa before taking over as manager of First Division Wimbledon, losing his job there in 1991. In February 1992 he signed as a player for Evesham United, but now works at Aston Villa as youth development director.
Netted the winner for Villa in the European Cup final.

WITHERS, Colin
Birmingham, Aston V, Lincoln, 1957-1969
A goalkeeper who let in six goals on his league debut. Became a hotelier in Blackpool and later ran a pub in Bridgenorth.

WOMBLE, Trevor
Rotherham, Crewe, Halifax, 1968-1972
Trevor works in the catering trade in Rotherham.

WOOD, Alf
Man C, Shrewsbury, Millwall, Hull, Middlesboro, Walsall, 1963-1977
Runs his own promotions company in the Midlands which he set up after three years as promotions manager at Birmingham City. The firm used to supply the trophies for the Barclays League and the Autoglass Trophy.

WOOD, George
Blackpool, Everton, Arsenal, C Palace, Cardiff, Blackpool, Hereford U, 1971-1990
Former Arsenal and Everton goalkeeper who was capped four times by Scotland. He is an ornithologist with Glamorgan Wildlife Trust and currently manages Inter Cardiff.

WOOD, Ian
Oldham, Burnley, 1965-1980

Full back who made 517 league appearances for Oldham Athletic. Is now a butcher.
League appearances record for the Latics.

WOOD, Ray
Darlington, Man U, Huddersfield, Bradford C, Barnsley 1949-1967
Goalkeeper who won three England caps and was a survivor of the Munich air disaster. He qualified as an FA Coach, and has had jobs in Greece, Kuwait, Canada, United Arab Emirates and Cyprus. In Kenya he won the League title three times and the Cup once. Also won the Eastern Central National Championship of Africa with Kenya in 1975. Based in Bexhill, Sussex.

WOODCOCK, Tony
Notts F, Lincoln, Doncaster, Arsenal, 1973-1985
Won 42 England caps, but has now made Germany his adopted home. Lives in Cologne, where he had previously spent two spells with the local club as a player – his intial £650,000 move in 1982 breaking the German transfer record. Now a qualified coach, Tony's most recent appointment was with VFB Leipzig.
European Cup winner with Forest in 1979.

WOODHEAD, Dennis
Sheff Wed, Chesterfield, Derby, Southport, 1948-1954
Former Wednesday outside left who scored 73 goals in 213 League games and retired to Sheffield. Died July 1996.

WOODS, Charlie
Newcastle, Bournemouth, C Palace, Ipswich, Watford, Colchester, 1960-1971
Career ended in 1971 and he became youth manager of Blackburn. Returned to Ipswich two years later and has since been reserve team manager, first team coach, assistant manager and has been chief scout since January 1995. Has also represented Suffolk at golf.

WOODS, Clive
Ipswich, Norwich, 1969-1981

Played over 200 games for Ipswich but finished with Norwich in 1981. Now lives near Norwich and still turns out for Newton Flotman in the Anglian Combination League.
Played for Ipswich in the 1978 FA Cup final.

WOODS, Matt
Everton, Blackburn, Luton, Stockport, 1952-1967
Long serving cntre half who played in excess of 380 League appearances, the majority in the colours of Blackburn Rovers. Matt left football after an 18 month spell as manager of Stockport County to run his own haulage company, and was still behind the wheel well into his sixties.

WOODWARD, Alan
Sheff U 1963-1978
A long serving wingman, Woodward played 550 games for his only club. Now lives in Oklahoma and has worked for American Airways in their maintenance department for the past seven years.
Broke the Sheffield United goalscoring record with 158.

WOOLLETT, Alan
Leicester, Northampton T, 1966-1978
Spent 15 years at Leicester. Alan is now a Prison Officer.

WOOSNAM, Phil
Man C, Leyton O, West Ham, Aston V, 1952-1965
In 1969/70, Woosnam, who is a cousin to golfer Ian Woosnam, coached the USA World Cup side. In English football, he appeared in a total of 358 games and scored 68 goals. In 1965 he was widely tipped to become player/manager at Aston Villa, but chose instead to move to America, where he was given the task of developing soccer. He was US Soccer league Commissioner until 1982, when he became managing director of Kick Enterprises - the marketing group of the US Soccer Federation.
Helped Orient to a Third Divison South title in 1956.

WORTHINGTON, Bob
Halifax, Middlesboro, Notts Co, Southend, Hartlepool, 1964-1974
Notts County first team left back of the late sixties and seventies and now runs a sports promotion firm in Halifax.

WORTHINGTON, Frank
Huddersfield, Leicester, Bolton, Birmingham, Leeds, Sunderland, Southampton, Brighton, Tranmere, Preston, Stockport, 1966-1987

A colourful forward who has been through more clubs than Nick Faldo. Brought a smile and plenty of goals to all of them during a career that spanned more than twenty years. Now lives in Shelf, near Halifax and utilises his larger-than-life character to entertainas an after dinner speaker.
Two Second Division Championships.

WRAGG, Peter
Rotherham, Sheff U, York, Bradford C, 1948-1964
Managed Macclesfield until the summer of 1994 then spent two years as manager of Stalybridge Celtic.

WRIGHT, Billy
Wolves 1946-1958
One of football's all-time greats, Billy Wright began with Wolves straight from school. He became an inspiring captain for both club and country, making his international debut for England in 1946 and going on to make a then record 105 appearances, including a run of 46 consecutive matches. Holder of three League Championship medals, he also captained Wolves in winning the 1949 Cup Final against Leicester City. He was Player of the Year in 1951-2, awarded the OBE and was married to Joy of the Beverley sisters. Died September 1994.
Three times a Football League champion.

WRIGHT, Charlie
Workington, Grimsby, Charlton, Bolton, 1958-1972

A goalkeeper best known from his time with Charlton. Now runs a cafe called 'Charlies Place' in Charlton.

WRIGHT, Mick
Aston V 1963-1972
Full back who played 280 games for Aston Villa in ten seasons before having to retire through injury in May 1973. He now works for an engineering firm.
Won a Third Division Championship medal with Villa.

WRIGHT, Pat
Birmingham, Shrewsbury, Derby, Southend, Rotherham, 1959-1970
Now back in his home town of Birmingham

where he is managing director of P & E Sports Enterprises Ltd. His coaching talents have been in great demand all over the world and he has at various times been National Coach for Zambia, United Arab Emirates, Saudi Arabia and Malaysia.

WRIGHT, Peter
Colchester 1951-1963
Long serving winger who appeared for Colchester United more than 400 times. Now works as a steward at a leisure club in the town.

WRIGHT, Tommy
Everton 1964-1972
With Ball, Labone and Newton, gave Everton a four-man involvement in the Mexico World Cup. Made 308 appearances and played eleven times for England before retiring at the age of 29. Still a regular attendee at Goodison park and works in the docks at Garston.
League Championship winner with Everton.

WYLDE, Rodger
Sheff Wed, Oldham, Sunderland, Barnsley, Rotherham, Stockport, 1972-1988
Had a stint in Portugal with Sporting Lisbon before returning to Barnsley. Is now physio at Stockport County.
Scored over 100 League goals in his career.

WYLIE, Ron
Notts Co, Aston V, Birmingham, 1951-1969
He finished with Birmingham City at the age of 36, after playing nearly 550 League games. In June 1970 he returned to one of his old clubs, Aston Villa as Coach, then moved on to Coventry City, initially as coach, and later as assistant manager. He went to Cyprus as coach/advisor and was appointed manager of Bulova in Hong Kong before returning to England, as team manager of West Brom in July 1982. Wylie left the Hawthorns in February 1984 to join Villa for a third time but lost his job in 1987 when Graham Taylor took over, only tyo re-emerge at Villa Park again in 1990 as a football in the community officer.

YEATS, Ron
Dundee United, Liverpool, Tranmere, 1957-1973

Made his name in his ten years with Liverpool after joining them from Dundee United in 1961 for £22,000. Moved on to nearby Tranmere Rovers as player./assistant manager in 1971 and then manager until April 1975. Spells then followed at Stalybridge Celtic and Barrow before going into the haulage business, then the catering trade. Still lives in Liverpool and is chief scout for 'The Reds'.
Twice a Football League champion with Liverpool.

YORATH, Terry
Leeds, Coventry, Tottenham, Bradford C, Swansea, 1967-1986
A midfielder allocated defensive duties under Don Revie at Leeds. Although never sure of a first team place in his ten years at Elland Road, Terry was capped over 50 times by Wales. He then played for Coventry City and Spurs before a lengthy spell in the USA with Vancouver Whitecaps. Returned to Yorkshire in 1982 to become player/coach at Bradford City. Terry was general manager at Cardiff City until a takeover he put together failed. He is now managing the Lebanon National side.

YOUNG, Alex

Hearts, Everton, Stockport, 1955-1968

Left Everton in 1968 to become player/manager of Glentoran, but soon returned to England with Stockport County. He retired in 1969 through injury and went back to Scotland where he runs a wholesale business in Edinburgh.

Won League Championship medals on both sides of the border.

YOUNG, Gerry

Sheffield Wed 1956-1970

Played over 300 games for Sheffield Wednesday and was capped once by England, before running a sports shop with John Quinn in Sheffield.

Runner-up in the 1966 FA Cup final.

YOUNG, Kevin

Burnley, Torquay U, Port Vale, Bury, 1978-1986

Kevin was a left winger with Burnley for a number of years and is now a prison officer.

YOUNG, Neil

Manchester C, Preston, Rochdale, 1961-1974

A fixture on the Manchester City teamsheet for ten years. Runs his own soccer school in Wilmslow and helps coach youngsters in Cheshire schools.

Scored the winner in the 1969 FA Cup final.

YOUNG, Tommy

Tranmere R, Rotherham U, 1972-1978

Lives in Maltby, and from 1979 until 1993 worked in the local colliery before being made redundant. Now employed as a platelayer.

YOUNG, Willie

Aberdeen, Tottenham, Arsenal, Notts F, Norwich, Brighton, Darlington, 1969-1984

Started his playing days in Scotland and was capped by Scotland at under-23 level before being signed by Terry Neill for Spurs. He followed his manager to north London rivals Arsenal in 1977 for £80,000. He now runs a country pub, 'Bramcote Manor' on the outskirts of Nottingham.

Where Are They Now?

Keeping track of hundreds of ex-professional footballers is no easy task!

If one of your old favourites has slipped our net, or you have some up-to-date information on a player listed in this book, please drop us a line at the address below.

WATN
FREEPOST
LON 6708
LONDON
N19 3BR